LINDA

Pathways to Self-Discovery and Change
A Guide for Responsible Living

Second Edition

Pathways to Self-Discovery and Change

A Guide for Responsible Living

Second Edition

The Participant's Workbook

Harvey B. Milkman
Metropolitan State University of Denver

Kenneth W. Wanberg
Center for Addictions Research and Evaluation - CARE, Arvada, Colorado

SAGE

Los Angeles | London | New Delhi
Singapore | Washington DC

SAGE

Los Angeles | London | New Delhi
Singapore | Washington DC

FOR INFORMATION:

SAGE Publications, Inc.
2455 Teller Road
Thousand Oaks, California 91320
E-mail: order@sagepub.com

SAGE Publications Ltd.
1 Oliver's Yard
55 City Road
London EC1Y 1SP
United Kingdom

SAGE Publications India Pvt. Ltd.
B 1/I 1 Mohan Cooperative Industrial Area
Mathura Road, New Delhi 110 044
India

SAGE Publications Asia-Pacific Pte. Ltd.
3 Church Street
#10-04 Samsung Hub
Singapore 049483

Acquisitions Editor: Kassie Graves
Editorial Assistant: Elizabeth Luizzi
Production Editor: Laureen Gleason
Copy Editor: Megan Markanich
Typesetter: C&M Digitals (P) Ltd.
Proofreader: Rae-Ann Goodwin
Cover Designer: Candice Harman
Marketing Manager: Lisa Brown
Permissions Editor: Adele Hutchinson
Lesson Adaptations and
Narratives for Females: Joelle Johnson and Carrie Lutkehus
Project Coordination: Vickie Blinn
Illustration: Erica Jacobs and Derek Lawrey (2nd ed.)

Preparation and development of this 2nd edition of *Pathways to Self-Discovery and Change: A Guide to Responsible Living* was supported by the time, efforts, and resources of the authors.

Geoffrey Canada's poem "The Runaway Train" is used in Chapter 14 with permission.

Printed in the United States of America

Correspondence should be sent to:

Harvey Milkman, PhD
Department of Psychology
Metropolitan State University of Denver
Campus Box 54
PO Box 173362
Denver, Colorado 80204

or

Kenneth Wanberg
Center for Addictions and Evaluation (CARE)
PO Box 1975
Arvada, CO 80001-1975

Library of Congress Cataloging-in-Publication Data

Milkman, Harvey B.
Pathways to self-discovery and change: a guide for responsible living. The participant's workbook/ Harvey B. Milkman, Kenneth W. Wanberg.—2nd ed.

p. cm.
Companion vol. to the authors' Criminal conduct and substance abuse treatment for adolescents: the provider's guide.

ISBN 978-1-4522-1789-5 (pbk.)

1. Problem youth—Substance use—Problems, exercises, etc. 2. Problem youth–Behavior modification—Problems, exercises, etc. 3. Cognitive therapy for teenagers—Problems, exercises, etc. 4. Substance abuse—Treatment—Problems, exercises, etc. 5. Social work with juvenile delinquents—Problems, exercises, etc. I. Wanberg, Kenneth W. II. Milkman, Harvey B. Criminal conduct and substance abuse treatment for adolescents. III. Title.

HV4999.Y68M575 2012
364.36—dc23 2012008887

This book is printed on acid-free paper.

15 16 17 10 9 8 7 6 5 4 3

Harvey B. Milkman, PhD is professor of psychology at Metropolitan State University of Denver.

Kenneth W. Wanberg, ThD, PhD, is a private practice psychologist and director of the Center for Addictions Research and Evaluation (CARE) in Arvada, Colorado.

SAGE and the authors gratefully acknowledge the contributions of the following reviewers: Rose Barcellano, Morrison Child and Family Services; Phyllis Giambrone, Texas Youth Commission; Jennifer Pealer, Kansas Juvenile Justice Authority; Lilas Rajaee-Moore, Denver Juvenile TASC; and Tom Snyder, The Staff of Larned Juvenile Correctional Facility.

CONTENTS

LIST OF WORKSHEETS

LIST OF FIGURES

LIST OF TABLES

PROGRAM GUIDES

WELCOME!

Welcome to *Pathways to Self-Discovery and Change.* You have been selected because you have expressed concern about your past experiences with crime and substance abuse and a willingness to explore the possibility of change. As many as 90% of people in the criminal justice system have substance abuse problems. There are programs that work with people with criminal problems and there are programs that work with substance use problems, but this program is different in that we are *combining* criminal activity with substance use problems. We understand that there is a part of you that may not want to be here, which views treatment as a form of punishment. Yet there is another part that has a genuine concern about your future, the people you care about, and a desire to change the direction of your life. That is the part we want to support and help grow.

Thinking, Freedom, and Change

The *Pathways to Self-Discovery and Change* program helps us to gain *freedom and strength* by learning how to control the most important part of our mind: *our own thoughts.* Thoughts about ourselves, the world around us, and the feelings that come from those thoughts decide our behavior and actions. This program is designed to provide you with the knowledge and skills to become clear about how people and situations affect us and to *gain control over our own thoughts and feelings.* Then it is possible to *change and adjust our actions.*

To some extent, things that happen outside of us are not in our control because we are not of age, and we have lost some freedom because of our actions. But the actions that got us here in the program are *completely in our control,* and by *changing our thoughts,* we can avoid having our freedom and choice taken away. The idea is *not to tell* you *who and what to be* but to help you to gain a better understanding of the *events in your life and the workings of your own mind.* Then you can begin to feel the *power of self-improvement,* doing positive things for yourself and others.

What Does This Program Have To Do With Me?

Crime and drugs can be *very exciting,* and in the short run, they can bring a lot of things we want. They get the adrenaline moving, prop up our courage, and allow us to do things that set us apart from the crowd. Sometimes they seem to help us to get things that we think we deserve for our friends or even our families. But there are a lot of *bad things that come* from participating in those actions, as most of you in this program already know.

So what this program is really designed to do is to show you that you can be different, have personal strength, feel good, and gain respect from those around you, *without* using substances or committing crimes. There are a lot of things in the world that are just as, if not more, exciting—without the bad outcomes—as drugs and crime. Our goals are to see you increase your personal power, gain the freedom of making your own choices, become all that you can be, and to feel self-respect while earning trust from those around you.

HOW THE PROGRAM WORKS: PHASES I, II, AND III

This program is different from most others in that it is made for people who are in situations like yours. Notice that there are comics as well as stories of youth who have struggled with problems concerning substance abuse and crime. Although they are artistically interesting, the main purpose of the comic strip drawings is to help you understand the ideas within each session. The illustrations are *artistic ways to explain* the stories, and they contain details that help the stories come to life. They contain very serious content in picture format—not to be confused with a lighthearted comic strip in the Sunday newspaper. Within each session is a *section of the full story,* which can be applied to the *specific ideas* from that session. In most cases, the stories are told from both male and female perspectives. Program participants have found it very useful to understand gender differences in the causes, patterns, and consequences of substance abuse and crime and means to resolve problems in these areas.

You do not have to read the full-page stories, although your counselor may find them helpful depending on the subject matter. We do suggest reading them, however, in order to help you develop a better understanding of the program and how it can be applied to your life.

Each session is set up for an interesting and meaningful learning experience. Your counselor will use role-playing, modeling, performing action skits, and small group discussions designed to help you to *put into action and practice* life skills that will be of great help to you in real situations. The activities and worksheet exercises will allow you to get a better look at what you are thinking and feeling in different situations and help you to decide on *your own programs for change.*

We will take one step at a time in the process of change. There are *three phases* to the program, with each phase separated into several *chapters.* At the end of each phase, we will take a moment to *look at how you are doing* and whether or not you should continue on to the next phase. For the most part, you are required to be here. If that is the case, then we will take a break between each phase to *give you feedback* as to how you are doing in the program. During the feedback, you will be given a chance to explain what you think and feel about the program, and we will talk with you about how you can better make the program work for you. Now let's take a look at the phases.

PHASE I: WHAT? CHALLENGE TO CHANGE

Deciding What to Change

There are *10 sessions* in this phase and *five* important things that we want you to do.

First, we want you to *build trust:* trust in the counselor or counselors who will be running the program and trust in those who are in the program with you. Most importantly, we want you to build a *trust in the program itself.* The reason we want you to trust your counselor and peers in the program is because we want you to open up and share with us your feelings and thoughts—essentially your story. Being open to *sharing your story* and considering your options by *hearing what others have to say* is the *essential pathway to self-discovery and change.* It is important, though, that you start talking about your *alcohol and other drug* (AOD) use, your criminal activities in the past, your worries and fears, and your problems and troubles in your life. Some of you may be more open than others, and some of you may have a lot of distrust, but we just ask that you give it a try.

Second, we want you to learn the facts about AOD and about criminal behavior. We will teach you some important ideas, some of which you will already know. But we want you to learn about how you have come to rely on drugs and criminal activities as you attempt to satisfy some of your needs and resolve some of the problems in your surroundings.

Third, we want you to become more aware of yourself; your relationship with AOD use and criminal behavior; and your thoughts, feelings, and actions about both. We want you to make a commitment to a long-term change in your thinking, believing, and acting.

Fourth, we will spend time helping you to understand the triggers that could lead you to *a relapse* (return to substance use) and/or *recidivism* (return to criminal behavior). We will teach you how to *avoid and prevent returning* to negative behavior, and this will be a very important part of this phase of the program.

Finally, we want to help you in developing a Self-Portrait (SP), or view of yourself that is a mirror of your many strengths and the problems that you have had to face in your life. You will be working together with your counselor and peers to help get an in-depth look into who you are and what you do. In this phase, you will decide on specific targets of thinking, feeling, and acting that you want to change. We will work together to develop your own Plan for Change (PFC)—the things that you decide on and can really do to gain your freedom, respect from others, and most importantly, your self-respect and optimism about your future.

PHASE II: HOW? COMMITMENT TO CHANGE

Using the Tools for Change

The idea of Phase II is to *discover the tools* and *learn the skills* to achieve the changes that you decided on in Phase I: What? Challenge to Change: Deciding What to Change. This phase will allow you to get stronger in your desire and ability to remain drug and crime free and to improve the quality of your life. The sessions in Phase II are designed to improve communication, deal with cravings and urges, develop a sense of responsibility to others, overcome prejudice, zero in on negative thinking, and manage uncomfortable feelings—particularly anger, guilt, and depression. Within the group setting, you will test out and practice these skills, which will allow you to live a comfortable, responsible, and fulfilling life.

PHASE III: NOW! OWNERSHIP OF CHANGE
Calling the Shots

Phases I and II of *Pathways to Self-Discovery and Change* are preparation for Phase III. In this final phase of the program, you will be *putting the knowledge* that you gained in the previous phases *into use* within your own life situation. That means looking at how to *avoid relapse and recidivism* (RR) (avoiding AOD use and crime) by mastering the skills of problem solving, decision making, and negotiating, as well as learning how to develop alternative lifestyles and activities that will help you maintain the changes you have made.

As a means to help you in real life, we will be taking some time to look at family, school, and job issues. An important part of *calling the shots* is to develop a sense of personal identity and to understand the importance of forming healthy and close relationships. Together, we will take an honest look at the connections between sexuality and affection and how to make responsible choices in this important area of our lives.

At this time, you will put together what you have learned and in the end make those things work for you. The power of ideas, skill, thoughts, and action that you have learned will become yours, as well as the freedom of choice over your thoughts and actions. At this point, the change becomes you, and you *begin calling the shots* over your actions instead of letting your actions control you.

Program Guidelines

These rules are to help you have a safe environment in order for everyone to be comfortable sharing and thus making the program mean something to everyone.

Abstinence: To Be Alcohol, Drug, and Crime Free

While in this program, we expect your goal to be AOD free and crime free. You might experience relapse in your thinking. Some people even backslide into using substances or committing crimes. If you are taking this program in a community setting, you may have cravings or slip into AOD use outside of the group, which might cause you to face increased criminal penalties. We want you to talk about these cravings and urges. You are expected to stop at this very dangerous and illegal lapse point and discuss your drug use with your counselor and judicial supervisor. We are not saying that we want you to quit the program if you have a relapse; however, you are not allowed to come to a session if you have been using drugs or alcohol. We may ask you to take a urine or breath sample, and if you are positive, you will be asked to leave. You are expected to set up an appointment with your counselor to discuss your relapse and how you can return to being AOD free and remain in treatment. You will probably have mixed feelings about all of this, but you will begin to feel the power of self-control if this is accomplished.

Be on Time and Attend All Groups

We ask that you are on time to the sessions, and if you must be late or absent, you are asked to let your counselor know ahead of time. You will be expected to attend all sessions, and if you are having some problems in attending, you will be asked to talk with your counselor and the group.

Taking an Active Part in the Program

You are expected to be an active member of the group, as this program is about your efforts to change. This means you take part in the discussions, activities, and your own learning process. By doing this, you show you want to change.

Confidentiality: Keeping What Is Said in the Group, in the Group

This is one of the most important guidelines for the program. In Phase I, we spend a great deal of time trying to build and develop trust between the members of the group and with the counseling staff as well. What is said and heard in the group is to stay in the group at all times. The counselors of this program will be held to the same confidentiality as the group. The only time the counselor can break the promise of confidentiality is if the counselor is concerned about your safety or the safety of others—if you are in danger of hurting yourself or another person or if there are people who need to be held accountable for child abuse.

Smoking and Eating in the Sessions

Smoking is not allowed in the group, and it will be left up to the group and counselor whether or not snacks and beverages will be allowed and what kind of breaks you will have.

It is now time to start the program. Good luck!

PHASE 1

WHAT?

CHALLENGE TO CHANGE:
Deciding What To Change

Chapter One:
Building Trust and Motivation to Change

GOALS OF THIS CHAPTER

- To discuss the program.
- To get to know each other.
- To learn how thoughts affect feelings and actions.
- To recognize the importance of change.
- To unfold program guides and tools for change.

JEB'S STORY

I never thought I would end up here. I started smoking weed when I was 12 years old. By the age of 15, I was a full time pusher.
By 16, I was bringing in steady cash, which spent itself as quickly as I made it. I gave my mom money for food and bills. I also spent alot on my little sister. The rest I spent on me.
I was a satellite dealer, I got paged and delivered. There didn't seem to be any risk involved.
4209
$$
Slowly, I began to lose my clients. I came home one night to my mom yelling. My little sister had been caught using weed. Mom was blaming me.
I sat at a corner, wondering if it was my fault, when a car rolled up and asked if I had anything. Falling into old habit, I asked what they were looking for. Before I could even blink, I was manhandled and slapped with handcuffs. So here I sit......
... not knowing what's going to happen tomorrow.
I wonder...
where did I go wrong?

Janay's Story

SESSION 1: GETTING STARTED

Objectives

- Discuss the purpose of the program and why you are here.
- Cover program guidelines and rules.
- Discuss program outline and the goals of Phase I.
- Learn the purpose of change.
- Get to know each other.
- Build trust in each other.

Jeb: *I started smoking weed when I was 12. I didn't really listen to my mom when she gave me her antidrug lecture. After all, what did she know? People wanted drugs, but they couldn't get them on a regular basis. That is when I became a drug pusher. Things were going good until some other dealers moved in to the neighborhood. I had to struggle to keep up with my old customers. I started pushing on the streets. I ended up trying to sell to an undercover, and now I'm here in jail, waiting to be tried as an adult.*

Janay: *I was just trying to have some fun. I didn't want to be Daddy's Little Girl anymore. He made me sick. Just about the time I discovered how really miserable I was at home, I met Matt. When I was drinking with him I felt different, free in some way. One night, things got a little out of hand, though. The plan was easy: I parked in the back alley behind the store . . . I was waiting with the car doors wide open when I heard the shot. I should be graduating, but instead a judge and a jury will be deciding the course of my life.*

What Is This Program About?

Alcohol and drug use—and doing things we're not supposed to—can make us *feel good* and are *exciting* when we first do them. Why else would we do them? The excitement goes away, however, and leaves us with feelings that are *not good,* such as worry, guilt, anger, or isolation from people we like. For some reason, almost all of us go back to the drugs or trouble even though we had the bad feelings. It probably has something to do with the *excitement* or the feeling of *being different* that we like.

Most of us don't even want to be here. After all, this may seem like a punishment, and no one likes to be told what he or she can or cannot do. This program is not meant as punishment; rather, this is about seeing our own special **talents** and **strengths** so that we can make good decisions on our own, without someone telling us what to do.

Why Are We Here?

- To **learn** how to recognize thoughts that can cause us to do harmful things
- To **build** skills that will help us to change or manage our thoughts so we can do things that are positive

SESSION 1: GETTING STARTED

This program has **three phases**; each of which is meant to help us gain power and control over our thoughts. You are expected to take part in some exercises as well as be a part of the group. At first this may seem like a waste of time, but the purpose is to help you be a great person to know. We would like you to be a part of the group and give it a try.

Basic Ideas About This Program

- Our thoughts, beliefs, and feelings can cause us to do things that have negative outcomes or are bad for us.
- We have the ability to control our thoughts, beliefs, feelings, and actions.
- By sharing our experiences, thoughts, and feelings with people we trust, changes become easier.

Activity: The Power of Thought

A volunteer participates in a skit in which the group leader thinks that he or she is being **disrespected** by the youth. Your counselor **becomes overrun** by feelings, and the situation turns out negatively. The situation is **redone,** but this time the counselor talks about their thoughts as the skit is acted out, emphasizing that **we can change or manage our thoughts and feelings** and ultimately our actions.

What This Program Has to Offer

- Getting **control** of our thoughts and beliefs can help us change.
- Putting **changes** into action can help us stay out of trouble.
- Staying out of trouble means **freedom** and getting things we want, which gives us an even better reason to stay out of trouble.

We can change or manage our thoughts and feelings!

Activity: Jeb's and Janay's Negative Thinking

Break into groups of three or four. Take a look at Jeb's story. What were his **thoughts** about selling drugs? He only smoked marijuana and sold drugs. How did doing this **bring problems** into his life? How could Jeb have stayed out of trouble? Use **specific examples** from the story to support your opinions. Then get back together with the larger group for a discussion. How did Janay's thinking cause problems in her life? What role did her friends play? How was alcohol involved?

SESSION 1: GETTING STARTED

Activity: Beginning to Share

Now it is time for us to get to know each other. Tell us one thing about yourself for each piece of candy (bead, piece of paper, or whatever item your counselor makes available) you take. Here are some suggestions for things we would like to know about you:

- How old are you?
- What is your favorite music or sport?
- What do you want out of the program?

Building Trust

Let's talk a moment about trust. How do you *begin to trust* someone? How does trust work with getting into trouble, or does trust have nothing to do with trouble? How can trusting the people around you help you to change?

Activity: The Real Me

You are asked to tell three stories about yourself, two of which **are true** and one of which is **a lie.** Tell your stories, and then as a group we will **ask questions** to determine which ones are true. After a certain amount of time, tell the group which stories are true. Does getting to know the truth about someone help to build trust?

Activity: Whom Do We Trust?

We have probably all played a game called **telephone.** The difference, though, is that we are going to apply the idea to **trust.** Tell something **about yourself.** As the story gets passed around, the information becomes different. When you trust someone who does not deserve your trust, the information about ourselves gets **messed up, or distorted.** When you trust someone who deserves your trust, the information only gets passed once. This helps us feel comfortable with the person, and the information does not get distorted or ruined. You feel **good about the person and good about yourself.** Who did Jeb trust in his decisions? Who should have Jeb trusted? Who did Janay trust, and how did that affect important events in her life?

What we're going to talk about right now is *why we are here* and the *different programs* we might have already gone to. This may seem scary, but talking about ourselves and getting feedback leads to change.

We will talk to each other about *what we think about alcohol and drug use, getting into trouble,* and *being punished for our actions.* You may not want to tell strangers about personal things. But we want you to get know each other, and we have to start somewhere.

Thinking About Change

Let us each take a second to think about how we got here, sitting in this room. Then ask yourself, what is my goal of change? Use the following list to help decide what you want:

- I really haven't thought about changing anything in my life.
- I've thought about change a little bit.
- I think I want to change, but I'm not sure.
- I want to change.
- If you have some ideas, say what you would like to change at this time.

We talked earlier about how thoughts can lead us to feelings and actions. Can you give the group an example of when your thoughts led you to feel and then do something? Something negative? Something positive?

Talk with your counselor or the group about how thinking about drug use and criminal acts might have gotten you in trouble.

Putting It Together

- Jeb sold drugs to make money and because he saw a job opportunity. How did Jeb's lack of trust play in to that? What could Jeb have done to stay out of trouble?
- Janay met Matt, whom she thought was an escape from boredom, and she lived for the moment. How did her thinking cause trouble in her life?
- Why is it important to stay out of trouble, and why is it that drugs and alcohol are not good for you (even though they seem like fun)?
- Discuss how taking control of your thoughts instead of letting your thoughts control you can make you happier.
- What is expected of you, and what do you expect of yourself, to complete Phase I?

Program Guides and Tools for Change

Your counselor explains the Program Guides and Tools for Change, which will be used throughout the three phases of *Pathways to Self-Discovery and Change (PSDC).*

- **Tools:** (1) Pathways of Learning and Change (CB Map) and (2) Pathways Change Scale (PCS)
- **Guides:** (1) Telling My Story (TS), (2) Master Skills List (MSL), (3) Self-Portrait (SP), (4) Plan for Change (PFC), (5) Thinking and Action Pattern Charting (TAP), and (6) Stages of Change Scales (SOC)

SESSION 2: THE POWER OF THOUGHT

Objectives

- Review Session 1: Getting Started.
- Discuss how attitudes, beliefs, and thinking patterns control our actions.
- Realize that we may have mixed feelings about change.
- Know that people who search out drugs and get in trouble often keep themselves from change.
- Discover that change is something exciting, and use your freedom of choice to begin the change process.
- Begin using Program Guides and Tools for Change.

Jeb: *It wasn't like I was hurting anyone or getting anyone hooked. My customers had already chosen their paths in life, and I was merely meeting a demand. If I hadn't done it, someone else would have. And my smoking weed was no big deal. Everyone knows that weed is natural and can't really hurt you. There really wasn't any risk involved. I realized how much I would have to work flipping burgers to get even one fourth of what I was making already. I was living good, so why would I want to change?*

Janay: *Matt was an escape from everything that was so boring. When I was drinking with him I felt different, free in some way. I stopped caring about what everyone else thought and was finally able to live for me and for the moment. It was all about the moment and having as much fun in that moment as possible. My parents soon began nagging me for not coming home on time, for finding an empty bottle under my bed, and getting caught skipping school. I mean, if I was an adult, I wouldn't have even been breaking the law. It really wasn't a big deal. Everyone else I knew was drinking too. Most of them were just hiding it better, I guess.*

Looking Back Before We Move On

The last time we were together we began talking and thinking about what this program is about. We told you the *rules* and *phases* and hope you began to think about your role in the program and why you are here. We also talked about how *thinking* and *feeling* get wrapped up in our actions, and how *changing our thoughts* can help us to change our actions.

We then spent a little time getting to know each other. Although this might not have been easy for you, we hope you know why it is important to build a level of trust within our group.

Now it's time to begin to take a look at how change is helpful in giving us power.

~ ***Positive Change*** = FREEDOM & POWER ~

Activity: Who Are We With?

Right now we are going to go around in a circle, and try to **remember one thing** about each person in the group. This is not a test, so you don't have to get everything right. We just would like to make sure everyone knows everyone else. If you are new to the group, tell a few things about yourself when it is your turn.

Six Building Blocks of Change

1. Our Attitudes, Beliefs, and Thinking Patterns Affect the Things We Feel and Do

We all like to think that no one and nothing controls our actions, and that is *exactly true* since how we feel and act is based on our own thoughts, attitudes, and beliefs. *We can control what we think, feel, and do.*

An **attitude** is an opinion that we hold about everything outside of us. Attitudes will cause us to act in a certain way to people or situations around us and are usually affected by *feelings.* If your parent or an adult says they don't like your attitude, it usually means they don't like how you are acting or the feelings that are causing you to be like that. An example of having an attitude is saying something like "school sucks."

A **belief** is an idea we use to judge the outside world and ourselves. A belief, or value, is a truth that we hold on to, sometimes with more strength than needed. It is these beliefs that cause us to have uncomfortable feelings or to have attitudes that might very well lead to trouble. The *belief* that adults or the system are just out to get you is probably going to make you feel *angry* and act mean when they try to talk to you. We form our beliefs from what we learn during childhood from our parents, brothers and sisters, relatives, and other role models—good or bad!

A **thinking pattern or thought habit** is an immediate reaction within our brains without us even knowing it, and the thought habit likes to hang out with attitudes and beliefs. Let's say the kid across from you is laughing. Your *immediate thought* could be that they are *dissing* or making fun of you. This causes your feeling to be *anger* and is possibly based in the *belief* that people are always trying to put you down. But the reaction doesn't have to be bad. . . . you could say to yourself, "I'm going to check it out further" and might find out that the kid next to him just said something funny and it has nothing to do with you.

What could your constructive thoughts be if the kid actually was laughing at something about you?

Our attitudes, beliefs, and thinking patterns control how we act and behave.

SESSION 2: THE POWER OF THOUGHT

Activity: Jeb's Negative Attitudes

Let's get in a group and **discuss Jeb** for a moment. What are some of Jeb's **attitudes** toward selling drugs and the people who buy the drugs from him? What is the **belief** that supports his **attitudes?**

2. Everyone Likes to Think They Are in Control

We like to think we are the only ones who have control over our actions. And for the most part that is true. Whose thoughts are those in your head? They are yours and yours only. But sometimes the thought is not something that has our best interests in mind. All three parts of our minds (attitudes, beliefs, and thought habits) get together in our brains when something happens to help us make a choice. The choice made, depending on our attitudes, beliefs, and thought habits, will either have positive or negative results for us. In this program, we learn to have control over our thoughts, feelings, and actions.

To see a picture of what we are talking about, take a look at Figure 1. This figure shows the path your mind moves along when an action takes place. After the choice of how to act has been made by your thoughts and feelings, the end result can be positive or negative.

Activity: How Thinking Leads To Feelings And Actions

Break into small groups, and discuss the chart that shows how **thinking leads to feelings and actions.** Discuss the situation that Jeb or Janay is currently in, and show how **their thoughts** can lead to more negative outcomes. What thoughts might he or she choose to have that might lead to positive outcomes? Pick an event in your life that had a negative outcome, and discuss how you could **change or manage your thought habits** to lead to more positive results. Have different people **represent parts** of the Pathways of Learning and Change (Figure 1).

3. No One Likes Changing

In fact, pretty much everyone doesn't like and is afraid of change. But when we fight against change we are really sticking up for how we see ourselves. We've been ourselves and probably have seen ourselves a certain way for a very long time. And since we see our beliefs as part of our identity, it's really hard to think about changing. But change is not a bad thing or even all that scary. It's like an adventure. And as we change, we don't become different people. Who would want to change if it meant being a completely new person? We become stronger people who have more freedom and power over our actions, because we went on the adventure that other people are afraid of.

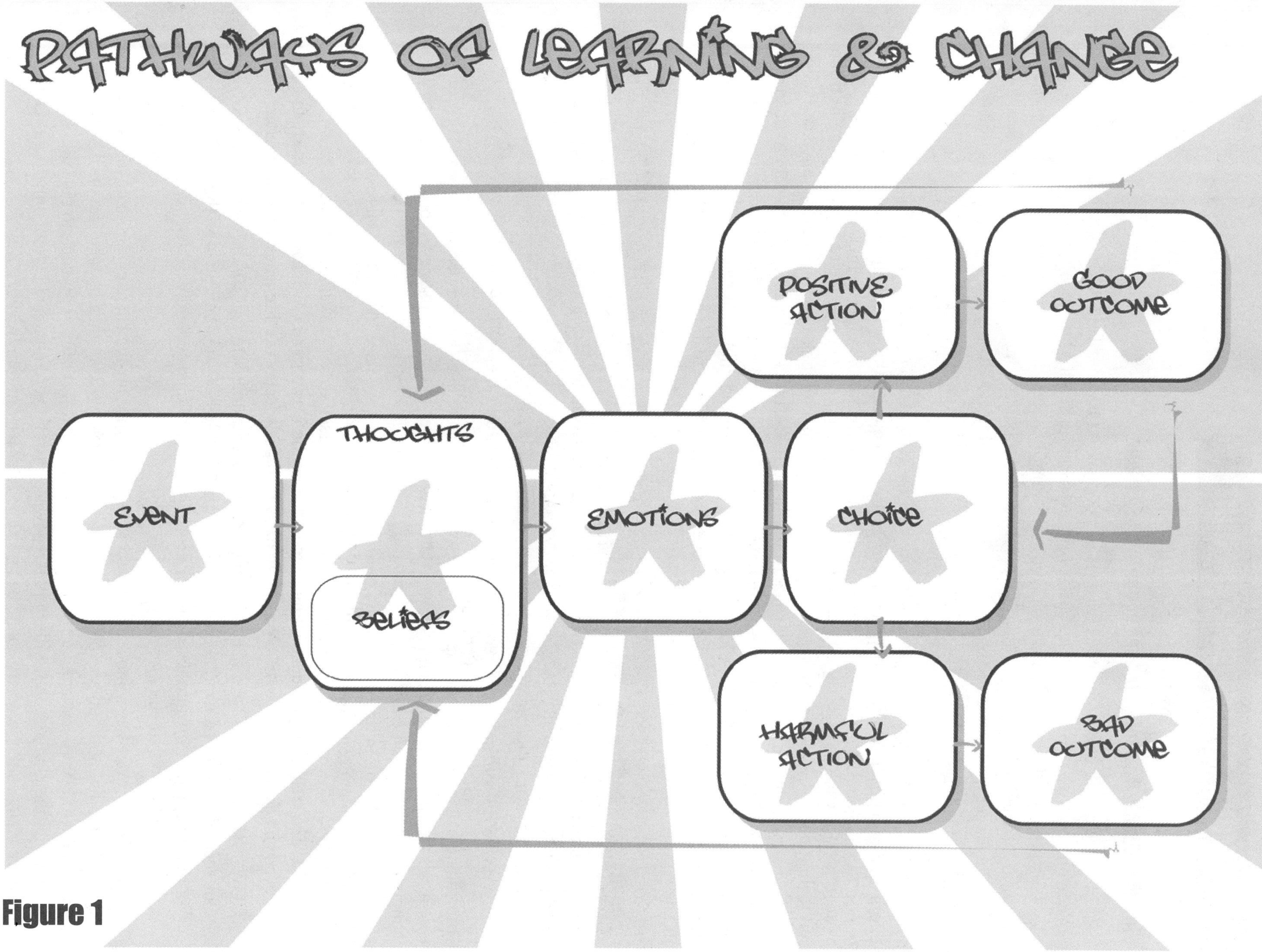
PATHWAYS OF LEARNING & CHANGE
EVENT
THOUGHTS
BELIEFS
EMOTIONS
CHOICE
POSITIVE ACTION
GOOD OUTCOME
HARMFUL ACTION
BAD OUTCOME

Figure 1

Activity: Taking Control Over Our Thoughts and Actions

Sit in a circle, and choose one of the other participants to be your leader. But don't tell that person or anyone else who your leader is. Close your eyes, and when told to open them, copy your leader's pose. Each time the leader changes positions, change in order to copy them. Now imagine that the leader is your belief. We mold ourselves to our belief. But let's say you just stop doing what the leader is doing. You are still the same person, but now you control your own actions and choices.

4. We Are Confused and Have Mixed Feelings About Change

Sometimes it's really hard to figure out why we should change. Sometimes we're tired of being in trouble and feeling down, but other times we're having so much fun and think we're not hurting anyone. Feeling confused about why we should change is part of the same scariness that makes us not want to change. Everything gets mixed up in our heads, and most of the time we like doing the things we are doing. Otherwise we wouldn't do them. But some of those thoughts and choices we make are hurting us more than we realize. And when we gain freedom over our thoughts, we really begin to see how good it feels and how good we feel with ourselves.

Activity: Jeb's and Janay's Mixed Feelings

Group Discussion: Give an example of Jeb's or Janay's mixed feelings about changing. How were their choices hurting them? How could they have changed to avoid being put in detention?

5. We Are Responsible for Bringing About Change in Our Lives

Unfortunately, change does not happen while we sleep. Change does not happen *all at once.* If there were a pill we could take or a sentence we could read in order to change, then everybody would be changing and it wouldn't be so special. Changing, however, *is special* and so are the people who are able to change. Change often happens slowly in different steps that we have to work at. Here are the *three stages of change* in our program:

- WHAT: The Challenge to Change is something that begins in our minds. We may even be ready to change or even talk about and do some changing. We target some aspect of our life that we intend to alter.
- HOW: Using the Tools for Change is our pledge or commitment to make a difference in ourselves. Our second step is that we make the choice to change. We become committed to the change process. We put time and effort into the program, learn the skills to change, and we even begin to feel freedom and power in being ourselves.
- NOW: Calling Your Own Shots means taking responsibility for the changes we made and our new thoughts and being proud and powerful in those changes. We own the change! The third step is to learn ways to keep the change going. We learn about what it means to go back to our old lives. We realize that the changes, the skills, and the power of change are ours and belong only to us. The positive changes that we have made become a regular part of our everyday life.

Activity: Setting Goals For Change

Let's take a moment to individually write down one goal for each of the previous steps. How will you keep your goals in mind while you progress through this program? How might you achieve the goals you have set for yourself?

6. Keep the Future in Mind

When we drink or do drugs—or even do something that will get us in trouble—we don't usually spend any time thinking about it. Why think about tomorrow when the party is tonight? But not thinking about tomorrow makes us weak. Before we even know it, we are being controlled by our actions and not even doing the things we like to do. It's like being in a pool, and at first the swimming is easy and fun. But as time goes on, we get tired and weight gets added to our shoulders, making the swimming not so fun and a lot more work. Before we know it, our head slips below the surface and we have lost all control. Instead, we should just get out of the pool and find something else that's fun, too.

Activity: Visualizing the Ideas

To better understand how change happens, we are going to participate in a role-play of the **different parts of your mind.** We would like five volunteers to play the parts of the following:

1. Attitude
2. Thought habit
3. Belief
4. Block to change
5. Urge to change

We will set up a negative situation for the first three, with the attitude being the feelings about the situation, the thought habit being the reaction to the situation, and the belief as the reasoning behind the situation.

The **urge to change** will then begin saying things to convince the thought habit to change, while the **block to change** will tell the beliefs things that will keep them from changing. As a group, make a suggestion to help get rid of the block to change. How are the attitude, belief, and thought habit different when they can listen to the urge to change?

Putting It Together

- What were Jeb's beliefs, thoughts, and feelings about selling and doing drugs? How did they change? What were the other choices Jeb could have made?

- What were Janay's thoughts about drinking and partying? How did they result in serious problems?

SESSION 2: THE POWER OF THOUGHT

- Think about how your beliefs or view of yourself has led to some choices that may have gotten you in trouble.
- Think about a choice you've made. What were your thoughts and beliefs? How did they help you make your choice? If you had thought something different, what would the choice have been?

Using the Program Guides and Tools for Change

- Discuss with your counselor how you will be using the Program Guides and Tools for Change.
- Complete your first self-rating on the SOC program guide (Program Guide 5).
- Use the PCS to indicate your level of understanding and willingness to participate in the PSDC program.

Measuring Your Knowledge and Skill Development: The Pathways Change Scale

At the end of most sessions you are asked to measure your level of knowledge and skill using the Pathways Change Scale (PCS). The scale is from 0 to 10. The markers are low, medium, or high levels of knowledge and skills use. Sometimes you are asked to measure your level of understanding of certain ideas. You start using the PCS by showing the degree to which you understand the PSDC program and the degree to which you think you will take part in the program. Put an X at the level that best fits you.

Understanding the *PSDC* program

0	1	2	3	4	5	6	7	8	9	10
Low					Medium					High

Degree you will take part in *PSDC*

0	1	2	3	4	5	6	7	8	9	10
Low					Medium					High

JEB'S STORY

I never thought I would end up here. After all, I was merely doing business that would have been done by someone else if I hadn't.

I had started smoking weed when I was 12 years old just to pass the time. I never even thought about my mom's drug lecture since weed's not a drug, as everyone knows. Around 14, I began to buy directly from a dealer. There was more consistency in how I got my stash this way, and there wasn't as much waiting around and wondering. Slowly, kids began asking me if I knew someone who could get them what they wanted, and without even trying I stepped into being a middle man, getting smoke for other people when they couldn't find any.

My mom, a woman with two too many kids and not enough time, was usually working at one of her jobs, so for the most part I was left to my own devices. My friends' parents made sure they had after school activities, so most afternoons I would sit on the porch or wander the park smoking a joint. Slowly I got to be known by the locals, most of whom had jobs but usually at night or part time, and we would sit and smoke as the larger world ignored us. As conversations flowed, I began to get a glimpse into a possible job scene. These people had a demand that was not being met. Namely, most of the people wanted drugs, usually pills or speed, yet their connections were not consistent enough to meet the needs of these paying customers. It was that realization that began my career in pushing. I was already running for most people I knew when their guys fell through, so I waited until I had several orders and then I would buy at the bulk rate. I pocketed the change, got my smoke for cheaper, my man was getting more money without exposing himself to more people, and the customers were getting the regular rate plus reliability. For everyone involved, it was a win.

By the age of 15, I was considered a full-time pusher. I had a steady clientele, restricted to those I knew and those who knew the game (no street pushing for me), with posted business hours that guaranteed I would get home before my mom. As I was what I call a satellite dealer, meaning I got paged and then I delivered, there didn't seem to be any risk involved. And it wasn't like these people were my friends. The dozen or so in my client base had already chosen their life courses. Although my friends and I partied once in awhile when there was nothing else to do, I made it a rule not to sell my hard merchandise to my friends. The way I figured it, I was merely meeting a demand for a product. It wasn't like I was getting kids hooked, and if I wasn't there to push the drugs and take the money, someone else would have.

By 16, I was bringing in steady cash that spent itself almost as quickly as I made it. I gave my mom a large amount each month to help with food and bills. I'm pretty sure she suspected how I got my money, yet she took the cash anyway. I also spent a lot of money on my little sister. I wanted her to have everything that I went without when I was younger. The rest was spent on me. I was living my life in the fast lane, the life of a celebrity, the life I never knew existed. It was just after my 17th birthday when things began to go wrong. Suddenly there were new pushers in the area offering a quicker and cheaper high. Slowly I began to lose my clients to crystal and crack. At first it was not big deal, as I am not greedy. I even thought of getting out of the game clean. Then I figured how many hours I would have to work at some greasy joint to make a fourth of the cash. So after school I started wandering the streets, not necessarily pushing but just getting a feel and seeing if I ran into anyone desiring some merchandise.

Things were going all right, despite the higher risk and not as much flow, when I came home one night to my mom throwing things at me and yelling. Slowly it came out that my sister had been caught smoking weed behind the gym at her school. My 10-year-old sister, the kid I took care of and adored, was the one who wasn't going to be like the rest of us and who would get out of this dump. I was in a rage. I would kill the scum that sold her that bag. I would make sure she never saw her so-called friends again. And then I realized my mom was still yelling at me, blaming me. I went cold inside, as if a stake of ice was shoved through my heart. I left right after that to wander around and clear my head. I knew I had no business being out on the streets, but I couldn't get through the cotton that had my mind numb. Pondering, I sat at a corner, wondering if it was my fault, if I shouldn't have quit while I was ahead, if clothes maybe weren't what my sister needed from me, when a car rolled up and asked if I had anything. Falling into habit, I asked what they were looking for. Before I could even blink, I was manhandled and slapped with handcuffs.

So here I sit, not knowing what's going to happen tomorrow. My mom's been in to see me once, just to let me know there was no way she was going to bail me out and that I could sit here and rot. The lawyer the state gave me said they could easily charge me as an adult since I'm so close to 18, and that could mean a sentence of years. As I stare at my twisted reflection in the stainless steel sink stare back at me, and as the frigid coldness of the cinder block walls seeps into my bones, I wonder where I went wrong.

JANAY'S STORY

I was just trying to have some fun. My parents have always been so strict, and I had always done exactly what I was told—especially by my dad. I guess I had just gotten sick of it all. I didn't want to be Daddy's Little Girl anymore—he made me sick. Just about the time I discovered how really miserable I was at home, I met Matt.

He was an escape from everything that was so boring. We started partying together, and I slowly began to come out of my little box. When I was drinking with him I felt different, free in some way. I stopped caring about what everyone else thought and was finally able to live for me and for the moment. It was all about the moment and having as much fun in that moment as possible. The pressure to be perfect suddenly wore off, and for a year or so, I was happy, but that happiness began to slip away.

There were little problems at first. You know, my parents were nagging me for not coming home on time, for finding an empty bottle under my bed, and getting caught skipping school. I mean, if I was an adult, I wouldn't have even been breaking the law. It really wasn't a big deal. Everyone else I knew was drinking too, but most of them were just hiding it better, I guess.

One night, things got a little out of hand, though. We had all been drinking and were about out of booze—and money—but we were having so much fun. The party just couldn't stop. We had to get more. Since I was the only one with a car, I drove to the 7-Eleven. The plan was easy: I parked in the back alley behind the store when Matt and his buddy ran in the store to steal more beer. What minimum wage gas station clerk is going to waste his time and energy to run down two teenagers with a few beers? They'd probably call it in, but with no vehicle description the cops couldn't do much.

I was waiting with the car doors wide open when I heard the shot. The noise and my imagination of what had just happened froze me like a statue. I couldn't think and I couldn't move. When the cops got there I was almost relieved. At least then I would know what had happened. But things didn't go as I had hoped.

I was jerked from my car, handcuffed, and thrown into the back of the cop car. I tried to ask what had happened—if my friends were all right, if the clerk was all right—but I was told they were the ones asking questions. Some hours later, I discovered Matt's buddy had brought a gun. When the clerk threatened to call the police, he shot the clerk and hurt him badly. No one told me about that part of the plan, but it doesn't seem to matter. I'm being held on the same charges as Matt—accessory to robbery and attempted homicide.

This should be my senior year. I should be graduating, but instead a judge and a jury will be deciding the course of my life.

Chapter Two:

Building a Knowledge Base

GOALS OF THIS CHAPTER

- To learn how thinking and feeling affect our actions.
- To learn basic facts about drugs and addiction.
- To understand how getting in trouble is connected with doing drugs.

JARROD'S STORY

Mary's Story

January 21: I went to that shrink again today. What a quack. He told me I'm "depressed." Wow, it took him that long to figure that one out. Whatever. I guess I'm going to start taking some pill that will help me feel better. I'm not convinced, but I guess I don't have much to lose.
February 14: Still depressed, just in case you (or anyone else) cared. I've been taking these pills for three weeks now and haven't noticed any difference.This was not part of the deal. What's the point?
March 3: Went to the quack's again today. Felt depressed when I got there and GREAT by the time I left! I met this guy in the waiting room just as we were both leaving from our appointments. March 29: I quit taking those pills from the quack. The pills I found in the waiting room work much quicker. I'm meeting with that guy tomorrow at the mall. April 8: I have found heaven,like I'm floating on a cloud.
May 16: My day floated by in endless pleasure—until I met Jarrod. He was sitting all alone, looking like an old version of myself; it made me sad for a moment. I had to share my experience with him; I couldn't let him suffer anymore. I hope it works as well for him! June 15: A party tonight—I'm taking Jarrod. He's such a doll! We will have a fantastic time, I can feel it!

SESSION 3: HOW THOUGHTS AND FEELINGS AFFECT BEHAVIOR

Objectives

- Review Chapter 1: Building Trust and Motivation to Change.
- Learn how thinking helps us to learn and change.
- Understand and learn five principles about thinking and doing.
- Know and use the concepts of how we learn behavior.
- Understand how learning behavior works with change.

Jarrod's Story: *I have always felt lonely, isolated until I met Mary. Being with her and taking pills allowed me to belong. And I wanted that feeling more than anything.*

Mary's Story: *I popped a pill again before school today. My day floated by in endless pleasure—until I met Jarrod. He was sitting all alone, looking like an old version of myself. A party tonight—I'm taking Jarrod. He's such a doll! We will have a fantastic time! I can feel it!*

Thinking Back

In Session 2, we began to learn the ins and outs of our minds and how change can help us as well as be exciting. We talked about what attitudes, beliefs, and thought habits were and how we can change how our mind thinks in order to have more freedom in our actions and choices.

Activity: Remembering as a Group

Let's take a moment as a group to remember these concepts. What is a thought habit? What is a belief? What is an attitude, and how are those affected by our beliefs? Go around the room, and give an example of each. Who is responsible for change? How do we change?

The Principles of Thinking and Acting

There are certain principles that guide our thoughts and actions:

Principle 1: Our Beliefs, Attitudes, and Thoughts Control Our Actions and Feelings

We usually think it's the other way around—that what happens outside of us is what controls our actions and thoughts. It is actually being able to control your thoughts that can help control your actions, leading to freedom of choice.

Our beliefs, attitudes, and thoughts control our actions and feelings.

SESSION 3: HOW THOUGHTS AND FEELINGS AFFECT BEHAVIOR

Activity: Fly By Design

Everyone will receive a piece of paper to make a paper airplane. Use any design for your airplane. Standing along a single line, throw the airplanes and see whose plane can fly the farthest. Go back and make another plane—preferably with a different design—and see how far the second plane can fly. Your thoughts are like the design of the plane, and the distance is the action that you take part in. The design of the plane controlled how far the plane flew, just as your thoughts control your actions. By changing your design, or thought, you are able to control the plane, or action.

Principle 2: Everyone Sees Themselves and the World From Different Points of View

How you see the world and how the person sitting next to you sees the world is different because our thoughts and beliefs are different. This also means that what we feel about the situation is different. One of us may think that a sunny day means a good thing, while another may feel upset because it's going to be hot. The idea of seeing things differently pushes us toward certain concepts:

We have certain ideas (beliefs) about what we think about the world. Our thoughts and actions are based on those ideas.

There is no right or wrong way to look at the world. But some of us do have some common ideas or beliefs. This forms a group in which the beliefs become rules of belonging to the group. If one belief is that the sky is gray, then everyone in that group has that common belief. But if one of us were to say the sky is blue, that concept would go against the group belief. It is when you go against the common rules of a larger group that your thoughts and actions can cause problems.

Activity: Rules of a Group

By now we've gotten to know each other. Without speaking to each other, get into small groups according to what you think are some common rules of the group. An example of a group would be people who listen to heavy rock or dress the same. Talk about what everyone thinks are the common rules. Now rearrange the groups, with one person from each previous group in the new groups. Try to get in a group with completely different people. Are there common rules the new group can agree on?

Principle 3: Our Ideas and Thought Habits (the Ideas That Pop Into Our Head Automatically) About Everything Around Us and Ourselves Are Filtered Through the Lens of Our Past Experiences

Imagine sitting outside without sunglasses on, and think about the different colors and images that can be seen. When sunglasses with let's say green lenses are put on, suddenly certain objects come out more than others do and yet everything has changed. This sometimes happens to our thoughts and can cause us to act out or have feelings that cause problems.

SESSION 3: HOW THOUGHTS AND FEELINGS AFFECT BEHAVIOR

Principle 4: Our Thoughts, Emotions, and Actions Are Not Separate

It's like that meeting we keep talking about. All three parts of our mind are at the gathering talking and having fun together. How we feel can lead to thoughts, actions can change how we think and feel, and our feelings about a thought can cause actions. If we take a look at Figure 2, we can see how all three are connected.

Figure 2 **Interaction of Thoughts, Feelings, and Actions**

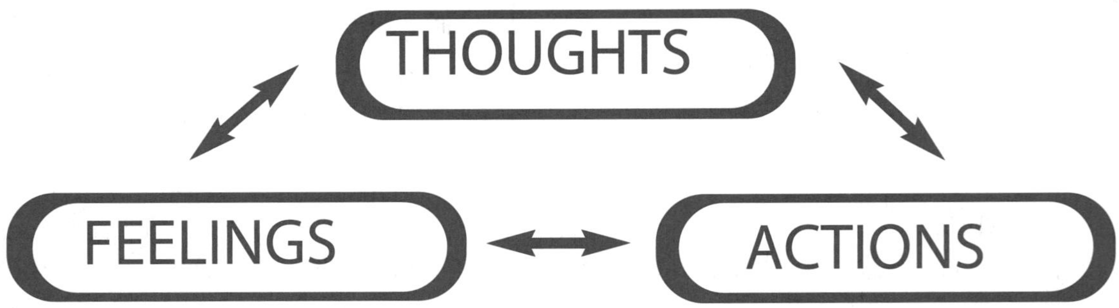

Keep in mind Principle 1. Things outside of you do not control your actions and feelings. Your beliefs, attitudes, and thoughts control your feelings and actions.

Activity: A Meeting of Difference

Divide into three groups of about the same number of people. Take a couple of minutes apart with your group to come up with a collective *sound and a motion* that you think will make the other groups laugh—for example, patting the top of your head while mooing like a cow. The sounds and motions should not be longer than a couple of seconds in length.

Once a sound and a motion have been decided upon, get back together with the other two groups and form a triangle, with each group facing the other two. Each group will then demonstrate the sound and motion they have decided on for the other two groups. After each group has presented their sound/motion, all three groups will try to re-create and practice the sound and motion they just witnessed. Have each of the three groups present, and allow time for all the sounds and motions to be practiced.

Now comes the difficult part. You have just practiced three different sound/motion combinations. Separate into your groups, and discuss which sound/motion you will do when you return to the triangle. The point is to get all three groups to do the same sound/motion combination at the same time without discussing it between the groups. Pay attention to what the other groups are doing, and keep repeating the last step until all three groups perform the same sound/motion in sync with the other groups.

You may have noticed that one or two particular groups insisted on doing their sound/motion at all times or decided not to change according to what the other groups were doing. This group represents our beliefs, which often insist on not changing despite what is going on around us. The other two groups represent our attitudes and thoughts, which may change according to what is going on around us and often influence each other in what they do. All three—our beliefs, attitudes, and thoughts—interact with each other in our mind to help us make the choices we make. But when our beliefs insist on not changing, our attitudes and thoughts change to go along with that belief.

SESSION 3: HOW THOUGHTS AND FEELINGS AFFECT BEHAVIOR

How does the following statement by a famous philosopher relate to your understanding of beliefs?

> *You have your way. I have my way. As for the right way, the correct way and the only way, it does not exist.*
>
> —*Nietzsche*

Principle 5: What Happens Outside of Us May Cause Thoughts That Are Based on Our Beliefs and Attitudes

These thoughts can make us feel a certain way, which may cause us to act or behave a certain way. Let's say a person offers you a hit of weed. In the meeting in your mind, the automatic thought may be "I'm gonna do it" because you believe that weed can't hurt you. So the thought affects your feelings, which are excitement and anticipation of pleasure. Since your feelings are good, your action is to take the drug. However, we can decide to adjust our earlier beliefs like "weed can't hurt you." That means we have a choice in whether we take the drugs or not. Take a look at Figure 3.

When you have a thought, you have the freedom to decide whether to take the hit or not. You can decide to change your earlier beliefs and the thoughts that automatically pop up in your head. Your choice of thought then decides the results you will have. The actions you choose will then affect your thoughts and emotions.

Activity: Jarrod's Principles

Break into smaller groups to discuss the Five Principles of Thinking and Acting and how they might apply to Jarrod's and Mary's stories. Here are some things to think about:

- What was Jarrod's thought about taking the pills? What were Mary's thoughts?
- How did Jarrod's and Mary's thoughts and feelings affect their actions?
- How may have Jarrod's and Mary's beliefs about themselves shaped their view of doing pills?

One Step Further

Now let's take our action one step beyond the acting out. So the choice ended with you taking a drug. What happens after that? One outcome is that it was a onetime hit and it will never happen again. Another possibility is that we smoke weed again, but it doesn't happen all the time. The third result is that we begin smoking a lot or all the time, forming what we'll call an action habit. The action habit is similar to our thought habits in that they happen automatically without much thinking on our parts.

So how do these actions become a habit? Well, we have results from the actions that we decide to take part in. Sometimes the results are positive for us, and sometimes the results are not positive. Whether the results are positive or not, there are certain concepts that help us to decide on the action again or not.

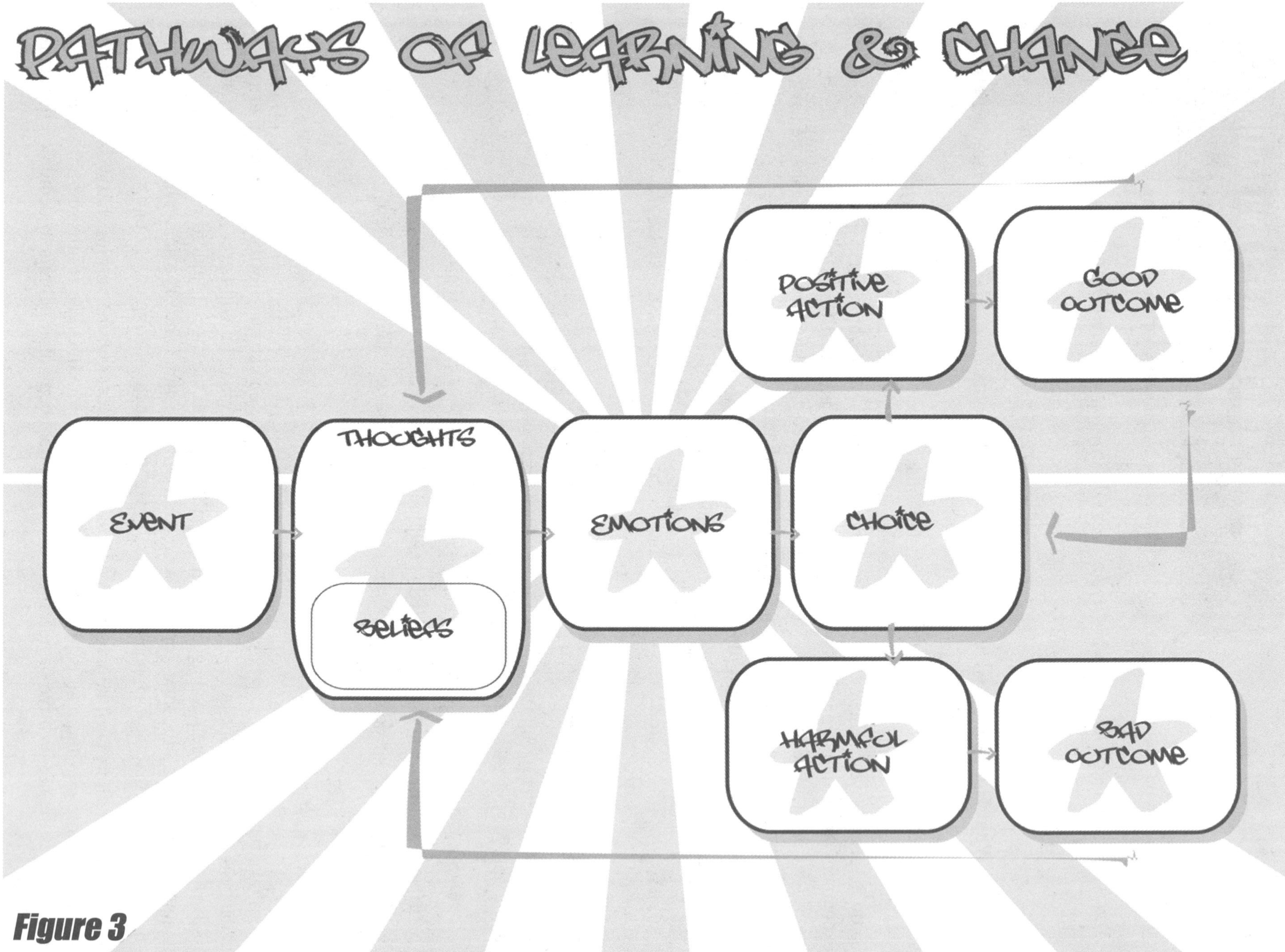
PATHWAYS OF LEARNING & CHANGE
EVENT
THOUGHTS
BELIEFS
EMOTIONS
CHOICE
POSITIVE ACTION
GOOD OUTCOME
HARMFUL ACTION
BAD OUTCOME

Figure 3

SESSION 3: HOW THOUGHTS AND FEELINGS AFFECT BEHAVIOR

Learning Concept I—Turning On Positive Feelings

If an action that we participate in gives us a good feeling, then we are likely to do that action again. We may repeat it until it becomes a habit. When something causes us to feel good, then the action gets strengthened. If smoking weed results in excitement or happiness, then the smoking is strengthened and we are likely to do it again.

Learning Concept II—Turning Off Negative Feelings

If an action stops a negative feeling, such as pain or worry, that action gets strengthened and will become a habit. This is a very strong way that learning takes place. When we feel pain, perhaps from some memory or even a problem that we are now experiencing, we may choose to deal with these uncomfortable states of mind by smoking weed (some people use other drugs for the same purpose). The pain goes away and drug use gets strengthened.

Learning Concept III—Turning On Negative Feelings

Let's say smoking marijuana causes us to be paranoid and confused. These negative feelings weaken the desire to get high, and it's unlikely we will continue to smoke. But sometimes we still do. Why do we keep smoking after we get bad feelings?

Activity: Jarrod's and Mary's Learning

- Take a moment to look at the three learning concepts that were just given.
- Which learning concept(s) can be applied to Jarrod's and Mary's use of pills?
- What are the feelings that might lead up to their use?
- Use examples from the story for details about the learning concepts and Mary's and Jarrod's use.

Learning Concept III does not always work in changing behavior. Why would we continue doing something that causes us negative feelings? Well, sometimes Learning Concepts I and II are really strong. When we smoke marijuana, for example, our immediate feelings are an increase in comfort or a decrease in pain—just like what we were talking about in Session 2, about how we don't always think beyond the night of the party. The reward for our actions, either the positive feelings or the decrease in negative feelings, is something that happens right away while the negative feelings that come from our choice don't come around for a while. The reward is stronger in our learning than the negative results from our actions. Take a look at Figure 4 to get a better idea of how this might work.

Figure 4

THREE RULES OF LEARNING BEHAVIOR

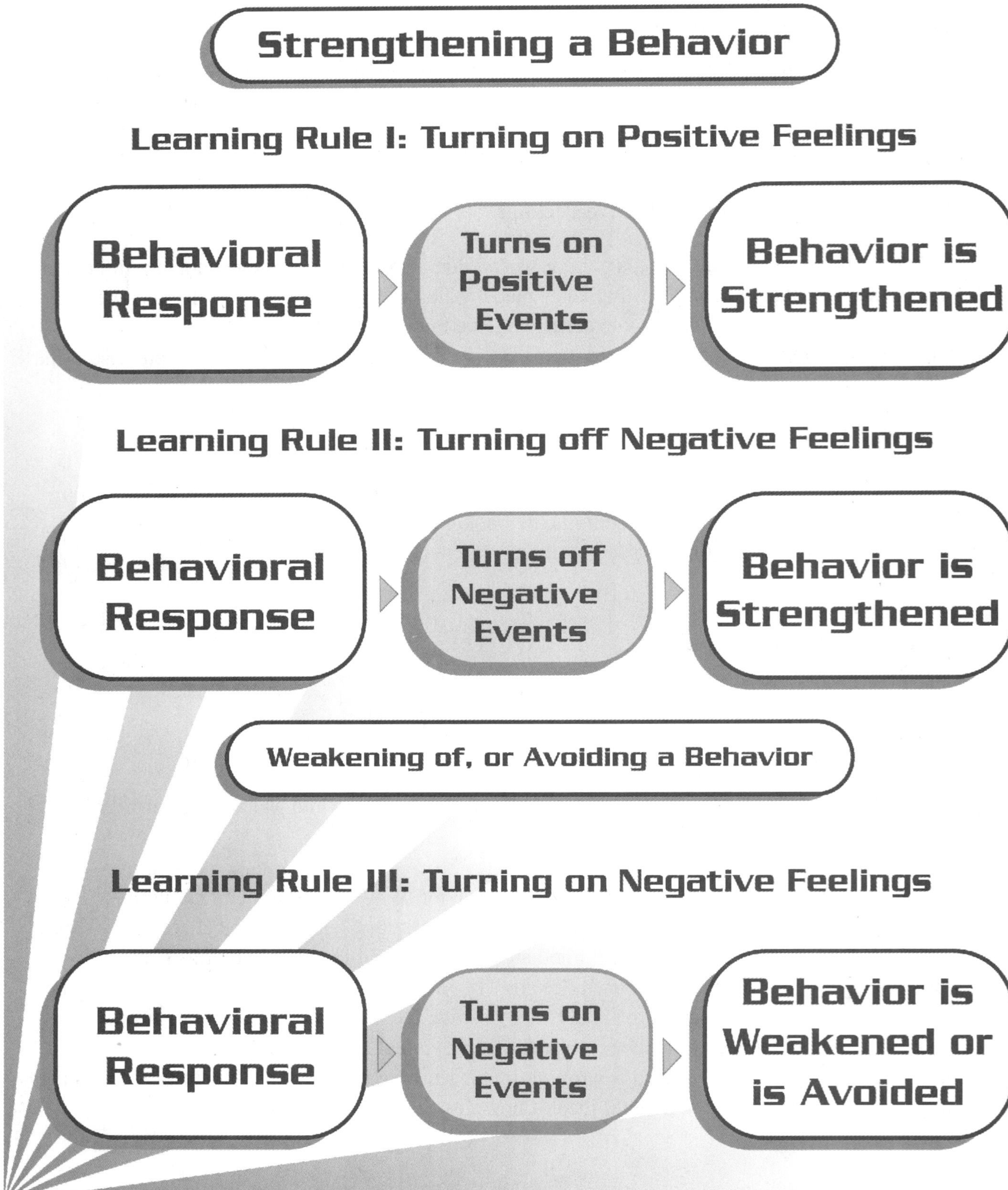

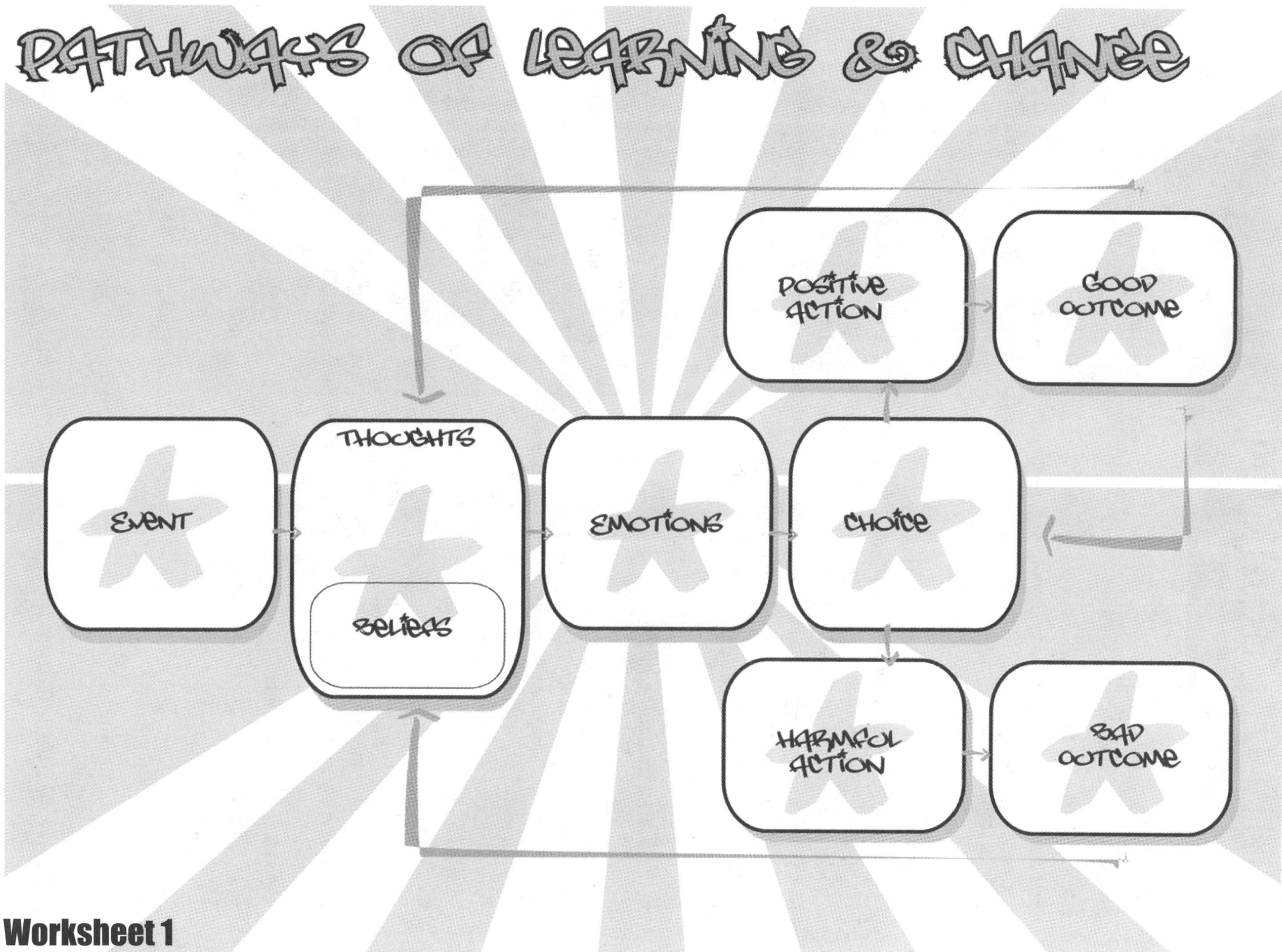
PATHWAYS OF LEARNING & CHANGE
EVENT
THOUGHTS
BELIEFS
EMOTIONS
CHOICE
POSITIVE ACTION
GOOD OUTCOME
HARMFUL ACTION
BAD OUTCOME

Worksheet 1

SESSION 3: HOW THOUGHTS AND FEELINGS AFFECT BEHAVIOR

Activity: Your Choice

Get into pairs, and work together on Worksheet 1. Use a real situation, and fill in the blanks about the positive and negative results of choices. How could the results affect the choice you will make next time? Spend some time discussing how you would change your thinking to arrive at a more positive outcome.

Another reason why Learning Concept III doesn't always work is that the negative results can strengthen our beliefs and thought habits. We smoke weed, we get in trouble, and this may strengthen our belief that "I am no good." So we smoke again to get rid of that negative feeling. It becomes a cycle where we repeat and continue the actions despite the problems that occur. To see what we're talking about, look at Figure 3. Every time a choice is made and bad outcomes result, the action may stop, but it might also strengthen the negative thoughts that led to the choice. But if a positive outcome happens, then the action and the thoughts that lead up to that action become strengthened.

Activity: Who Makes The Choice?

For this skit, we will need four volunteers. At your counselor's suggestion of an event, such as a chance to commit a crime or being offered a joint or having the opportunity to deal some drugs, the first person will state an automatic thought (the thought habits/reaction), such as "the joint will make me feel good." The second person will then state the beliefs and attitudes behind the reaction, that "weed isn't harmful and makes me happy." The third person will choose an action based on the beliefs and thought habits, like "take the hit," and the fourth person will say how the action chosen had negative or positive results, either getting high and happy or getting caught by the cops and going to jail.

The group will then discuss how each step decides the choices given to the next step and how the result could strengthen or weaken the thoughts, attitudes, beliefs, and feelings that caused the reaction. The thought habits are that "weed will make you feel good," which are supported by deep-seated beliefs and attitudes.

How can this pattern of thoughts, beliefs, attitudes, and feelings be altered?

Putting It Together

- Think about the principles that were just given. How did the principles work together in helping Mary and Jarrod make their decisions?
- What are the specific thoughts and emotions that led up to Mary's and Jarrod's decisions?

SESSION 3: HOW THOUGHTS AND FEELINGS AFFECT BEHAVIOR

- Think about an action that led to a positive or negative feeling and how that helped you make a choice the next time.
- Think about your thoughts, feelings, and emotions that led to a positive result and how that made you feel.
- Which learning concept is likely the best way you learn?

Using the Program Guides and Tools for Change

Use the Pathways Change Scale (PCS) to indicate your levels of knowledge and skill about how we learn and how thoughts are related to our feelings and actions.

Understanding the relationship between having thoughts, taking drugs, and committing crimes.

0	1	2	3	4	5	6	7	8	9	10
Low					Medium					High

Understanding the three rules of learning and how they relate to your patterns of thinking and acting.

0	1	2	3	4	5	6	7	8	9	10
Low					Medium					High

Having the ability to use the information in this session to change or manage harmful patterns of thinking and acting.

0	1	2	3	4	5	6	7	8	9	10
Low					Medium					High

SESSION 4: UNDERSTANDING DRUG ABUSE AND PATTERNS OF DEPENDENCE

Objectives

- Review Session 3: How Thoughts and Feelings Affect Behavior.
- Talk about how we see substance abuse and drugs.
- Learn some basic facts about substances and their effect on our bodies.
- Discover the two paths to addiction.
- Apply the paths and cycles to yourself.

Jarrod's Story: *We started doing pills all the time, pretty much every weekend. We didn't go to parties much because we couldn't afford it, but Mary and I were happy just being together—just as long as we weren't with each other for a couple days after we had taken some pills. I wanted the feeling all the time, the feeling of freedom and the ability to belong without the worry of rejection.*

I never really understood why I felt so low for a couple days afterward. How could something that makes me feel so good end up bad for me? Every time I felt so down I thought about how I didn't want to ever feel like that again, but then the weekend would come and Mary and I would party again.

Mary's Story: *I popped a pill again before school. My day floated by in endless pleasure… A party tonight… I'll take Jarrod. We'll have a fantastic time! I can feel it!*

Thinking Back

Last session we began talking about how our thoughts, actions, and feelings are all sitting together in a meeting in our head and how we are part of the meeting as well. Even though our thoughts and feelings control our actions, not the outside world, we control our thoughts and feelings. And although sometimes our thoughts can become distorted, it still means that we have power and freedom over the choices we make.

We also started talking about how we learn behavior. There were three concepts that we covered, all of which help to strengthen or weaken our responses the next time the same choice has to be made.

Activity: The Concepts of Learning

Let's take a moment to remember what those concepts are and how they help learning. Separate into three different groups, each one representing a learning concept. Try to be in the group of how you think you learn best. Get together with your group, and discuss how to **act out the learning concept.** Then act it out for the other two groups.

SESSION 4: UNDERSTANDING DRUG ABUSE AND PATTERNS OF DEPENDENCE

Now that we know how our thoughts and feelings can affect our actions—and how learning can sway whether we make that decision again or not—let's talk a little about drugs and addiction.

Thought and Discussion: What is addiction, and what causes it?

Basic Things to Know About Drugs

1. Definition of Drugs

A drug is something we use to change how we feel, think, or act.

2. Drugs Affect Both Our Minds and Bodies

When we take drugs, it changes how our body talks to itself. It also changes and releases the chemicals in our brains that help control our thoughts and feelings.

Activity: How Much We Know

We'll stop here for a moment so that you can take the drug knowledge test. Discuss your answers and why you chose them.

3. There Are Four Basic Categories of Drugs That People Take to Get High

- Drugs that slow down our brains are called sedatives, or downers. Drugs like alcohol, quaaludes, and Xanax are downers.
- Drugs that reduce pain while providing an intense sense of pleasure and euphoria are called narcotics. Some drugs in this category are heroin, OxyContin, Demerol, and Percodan.
- Drugs that speed up or excite our brains are called stimulants or uppers. Some uppers dramatically speed up our bodies and minds, like cocaine and meth, while others like caffeine speed us up in a less obvious manner.
- Drugs that alter our perception and sense of reality are called hallucinogens. Mescaline, peyote, LSD, and PCP are placed in this category. Marijuana is often placed in this category as well.
- To see the different classes of drugs, look at Table 1.
- How about cigarettes? What category would you place them in?

Table 1

DRUG CATEGORIES & WITHDRAWAL EFFECTS

	Physical	Psychological
NARCOTICS * Heroin * Codeine * Morphine	watery eyes runny nose cramps nausea loss of appetite yawning tremors chills sweating	irritability panic anxiety
STIMULANTS * Meth * Cocaine * Caffeine	cravings tiredness headaches	depression paranoia disorientation aggression apathy (meth) anxiety irritability
DEPRESSANTS * Alcohol * Barbs * Xanax, Valium, etc.	loss of appetite muscle tremors insomnia sweating hyperactivity	anxiety delirium psychosis altered perceptions
HALLUCINOGENS * MDMA * Marijuana * LSD	hyperactivity (marijuana) loss of appetite	depression anxiety irritability delirium paranoia
NICOTINE * Cigarettes * Chewing Tobacco * Pipes	cravings headaches indigestion diarrhea sore throats increased appetite fatigue coughing nausea insomnia	irritability depression restlessness feelings of frustration and anger lack of concentration anxiety

4. Drugs Affect Us Directly and Indirectly

- The drug effect during use (the direct effect) is what happens when we are on the drugs, which may be physical or mental. Smoking marijuana can make us feel physically tired or drained while it causes us to laugh.
- The indirect effect is what happens after the drug is gone. Our bodies begin to start missing the drug when it's gone, like not being able to sleep when we haven't used in a while.

5. Different Drugs Have Different Effects (Direct and Indirect) on Us

- How a drug affects us depends on the drug, and the direct effects are usually opposite of the indirect effects. Cocaine speeds us up so that when we are not on cocaine our system slows down and we are tired and depressed. Alcohol slows us down, but when we aren't drinking our system speeds up and we can't sleep.
- Both effects can cause problems.

Activity: How Drugs Affect Jarrod

Take a moment to look back at Jarrod's and Mary's stories. What were some of the direct effects of the pills? What were the indirect effects? Which category of drug do you think the pills that Jarrod and Mary took belonged to?

6. When We Take Drugs, Our Bodies Become Toxic

Drugs poison our bodies. When the drug (and that does include alcohol) leaves the body, the body has to try and return to normal. Sometimes this can cause the body shock, which is what we call withdrawal. Depending on the drug and how much was in the body, the reaction can be so strong that the body quits or goes into seizures.

7. Tolerance for Drugs Can Increase, Causing You to Become Physically and Mentally Dependent

As we keep doing the same drug, we may need more and more just to get the same feelings, or the same amount will give us less of the feelings we want. This is called tolerance. The ability to grow tolerant depends on the drug, but all drugs can cause us to need more. You used to get a buzz off of one beer or a couple of hits, but now it takes two or three beers or a whole joint to get the same positive feelings. This is called tolerance and is one reason why we become dependent on drugs.

8. Mixing Drugs at the Same Time Can Increase the Strength of One or Both

One drug we take may get stronger because another drug is in our body. Drinking alcohol and smoking weed together causes our minds to become much more confused than if we used one drug alone. People have died after combining alcohol and narcotics or other sedatives.

Specific Drugs and Their Effects

Nicotine/Tobacco

- Found most commonly in cigarettes and other smoking items, tobacco is grown and harvested.
- Symptoms of use can include smelly hair, clothes, and breath; coughs; shortness of breath; and poor athletic performance.
- Consequences include addiction; emphysema; chronic bronchitis; heart disease; and cancer of the lung, voice box, throat, bladder, pancreas, kidney, and mouth.

Marijuana

- Known as weed, pot, grass, skunk, Mary Jane, and reefer, just to name a few, marijuana is a drug that is grown and has distinct leaves.
- **Immediate Effects:** Euphoria; relaxation; slowed reaction time; distorted sensory perception; impaired balance and coordination; increased heart rate and appetite; impaired learning, memory; anxiety; panic attacks; and psychosis.
- **Long-Term Effects:** The possible consequences of regular, long-term marijuana smoking include the following: cough, frequent respiratory infections, increased risk for cancer, mental health decline, and addiction.

MDMA

- Known as Ecstasy, E, X, and by a number of brand names, MDMA is part mental enhancer and an upper that releases serotonin in the brain and is often in pill form.
- Symptoms of use include trancelike states, euphoria, increased pulse rate, and excitement of the senses—usually touch, taste, and smell.
- Consequences of use can include impaired judgment and coordination, deep depression and anxiety, sleep disorders, and states of confusion.

LSD

- Lyseric acid diethylamide, often going by the name of LSD, acid, or whatever the substance is taken on such as blotter or pez, is a chemical substance that is often found in its original form as a liquid.

- Symptoms of use include trancelike states, excitation, euphoria, hallucinations, insomnia, and often increased sense sensitivity, especially of visual stimulants.
- Consequences of use can be violent behavior, impaired judgment and coordination, self-inflicted injury, paranoia, depression, anxiety, and unpredictable flashbacks.

Methamphetamine

- Most commonly known as meth, crystal, or ice, this drug can be found in powder or rock form and is an upper.
- Symptoms of use include tremors, excitability, insomnia, sweating, dry mouth and lips, weight loss, paranoia, and in some cases hallucinations.
- Consequences can be weight loss, nutritional deficiency, chronic sleep problems, paranoia, anxiety or nervousness, severe depression, violent behavior, and death from heart failure or suicide.

Other Drugs of Abuse

Inhalants

- Inhalants include solvents (paint thinners, gasoline, glues); gases (butane, propane, aerosol propellants, nitrous oxide); nitrites (isoamyl, isobutyl, cyclohexyl), laughing gas, poppers, snappers, and whippets.
- Consequences include stimulation, loss of inhibition, headache, nausea or vomiting, slurred speech, loss of motor coordination, wheezing, cramps, muscle weakness, depression, memory impairment, damage to cardiovascular and nervous systems, unconsciousness, and sudden death.

Anabolic Steroids

- Anabolic steroids include Anadrol, Oxandrin, Durabolin, Depo-Testosterone, Equipoise*:* roids, juice, gym candy, or pumpers.

Dissociative Drugs

Ketamine

- Ketamine is known as Ketalar SV, cat, Valium, K, Special K, vitamin K.
- Consequences include feelings of being separate from one's body and environment; impaired motor function, analgesia, impaired memory, delirium, respiratory depression and arrest, and death.

PCP and Analogs

- Phencyclidine, or PCP and analogs, are also known as angel dust, boats, hogs, love boats, and peace pills.

- Consequences include feelings of being separate from one's body and environment; impaired motor function, analgesia, psychosis, aggression, violence, slurred speech, loss of coordination, and hallucinations.

Salvia Divinorum

- Salvia divinorum is also known as Salvia, Shepherdess's Herb, Maria Pastora, magic mint, and Sally-D.
- Consequences include feelings of being separate from one's body and environment, impaired motor function, euphoria, slurred speech, confusion, dizziness, and distorted visual perceptions.

Dextromethorphan (DXM)

- Dextromethorphan (DXM) is found in some cough and cold medications. It is also known as Robotripping, Robo, and Triple C.
- Consequences include feelings of being separate from one's body and environment, impaired motor function, euphora, slurred speech, confusion, dizziness, and distorted visual perceptions.

Source: National Institute on Drug Abuse

Activity: Passing the Buck

Get in a circle—if you aren't in one already—and pass around the ball your counselor will give you. The first person will begin by saying which drug of abuse they are—for example, "I am heroin." Then hand the ball to the next person who will say what direct effects can come from the drug. The next person will be the indirect effect. Have all the people representing the direct effects stand together and all the indirect effects form a separate group. As the ball goes around, more drugs will be added together, showing how toxic (poisonous and deadly) drugs can be when added together in our systems. Do any members of the group know someone who died of a deadly drug combination?

Alcohol

Alcohol is considered a drug, and it's one of the most used and most dangerous drugs, so we'll get a little in-depth about alcohol. Drinking and driving is the leading cause of death in the 15- to 20-year-old age group. Just one drink is enough to be convicted of driving while impaired, which means you are put on probation, lose your license, and have to take classes for your drinking. How many in the group knows someone who has gone through the experience of a DUI?

1. Alcohol is a downer, which means it slows down our system and makes us tired.
2. One drink contains about one-half ounce of pure alcohol. One can of beer, one glass of wine, and one mixed drink are all considered one drink, despite the differences in size.

3. Although the alcohol level depends to some extent on the weight of the person, the number of drinks, and the time it took to drink the drinks, it takes about half of 1% of alcohol in the blood to kill a person.
4. Alcohol dissolves in water, so about 98% of alcohol is broken down by the digestive system and the rest leaves through breath and urine. That means most of the alcohol does not leave your body when you go to the bathroom.
5. Adult drinkers are classified by how many drinks they have on one occasion. How does the following adult classification apply to teenagers?
   a) Light drinker: one drink
   b) Moderate drinker: two to three drinks
   c) Heavy drinker: four to five drinks
   d) Excessive drinker: six or more drinks
6. How many times we drink is also grouped this way:
   a) Infrequent: Less than once a month
   b) Occasional: Less than one time a week
   c) Frequent: one to three times a week
   d) Consistent: four to five times a week
   e) Daily: six to seven times a week

Activity: A Glance at You

Take a moment to look at the previous labels, and assess what kind of drinker or drug user you think you are. How many drinks does it take for you to begin to get a "buzz"? How many before you get sloppy? Go around the group, and share how much you think you were drinking or taking drugs before treatment. Why did you drink as much as you did? What do you get from alcohol? What are your thoughts about drinking and driving?

Activity: Passing the Buck for Alcohol

Refer to Activity: Passing the Buck for instructions.

7. Females and people who weigh less, are tired, or haven't eaten tend to get more drunk. That doesn't mean that if you are fatter you can drink more. More body fat actually keeps the alcohol from breaking down and may increase the amount of alcohol in the blood. Because females have more body fat compared to men, sometimes it's harder for their bodies to get rid of alcohol. They may feel the effects of alcohol at lower doses than men. But just because you don't act as drunk as your friend does not mean you don't have the same level of alcohol in your system. Some people develop ways to act more sober than they are; this is called behavioral tolerance.

SESSION 4: UNDERSTANDING DRUG ABUSE AND PATTERNS OF DEPENDENCE

Drinking and Your Body

Liver: When you drink a lot, or even moderately, fatty tissue builds up in your liver. The fatty tissue gets itself between the healthy cells and cuts off the blood supply, leading to dead cells throughout your liver. The body replaces the dead cells with scar tissue, and when that happens it's called cirrhosis, which stops your liver from working properly.

Stomach and Guts: Have you ever gotten a cut and someone put alcohol on it to clean it out? It made your skin and the cut burn really badly. Well, this is what alcohol does to your stomach. The alcohol burns holes in the lining, which gives your stomach what we call ulcers.

Heart and Blood: Heavy drinking, especially when you drink and smoke together, can increase your blood pressure, the amount of pressure on your veins from the blood moving through them, and can cause heart problems.

Brain and Nerves: Your brain has a way of keeping small bits of alcohol out of it. But when there is a rush of alcohol, the fence is broken and the brain cells can be hurt or killed by the alcohol. When you are sober, your ability to think quickly and clearly and to feel comfortable can also be affected if your brain has become damaged by alcohol.

Activity: A Chain of Destruction

Form two teams, and sit down facing each other on the floor. All but the first people in each line have their eyes closed. The counselor flips a coin as many times as necessary until it lands on heads. Then the race begins. The first people (who have their eyes open) tap the next person and so on until the tapping reaches the end of the line, at which time the last person to get tapped raises his or her hand. The first team done is the winner. This is how our brains work when they send information. Only the messengers are electrochemical signals rather than hands.

Next let's see what happens when the brain is compromised by alcohol or some other drug.

After your counselor secretly designates one person in line who can't function or do their job, the coin is flipped and the race begins. Only this time, the impulse stops, and the "nerves" at the end of the chain do not get tapped. This is what can happen when too much alcohol gets into the brain; the brain connections become damaged. After the winning team is announced, everyone opens their eyes and the losing team is informed about the person (neuron) who didn't function.

Pathways to Addiction

Since everyone is different, there are also different ways to get addicted or hooked on drugs.

SESSION 4: UNDERSTANDING DRUG ABUSE AND PATTERNS OF DEPENDENCE

The Mind–Action Cycle

Remember the concepts of learning that we talked about in Session 3? Well, Learning Concepts I and II play into this idea of addiction. If we believe that marijuana will make us feel good—and it does—then we will do it again. If we believe that marijuana will take away negative feelings, such as pain or worry—and it does—we will do it again. Check out Figure 5 to get an idea of how this looks.

Figure 5: **AOD Use Increases Problems in Thinking and Behavior**

Substance Use Mental Expectation ▸▸ **Turns on Positive Events:** Euphoria, Relaxation, Warm feelings, Warm memories, Positive mood, Improves thinking, Positive relationships ▸▸ **Substance Use & Strengthened Expectation**

Substance Use Mental Expectation ▸▸ **Turns off Negative Events:** Reduces tension and stress, Blocks out negative memories, Blocks out negative self-thoughts, Copes with stress ▸▸ **Substance Use & Strengthened Expectation**

If you expect, or believe, that positive feelings will come from using a drug and it happens, then the drug use and the thoughts about the benefits of taking drugs have been strengthened and become what we called earlier an action habit. Positive feelings can include feeling powerful, energized, relaxed, or happy.

But say you expect to turn off a negative feeling. If you do a drug with that thought and the negative feeling gets turned off, then that also can lead to an action habit. An example of that may be you can't deal with the worry of the future so you smoke marijuana. For a while it makes you forget, and you feel better.

The Mind–Body Cycle

Earlier in this session we talked about the direct and indirect effects of drugs. We may use alcohol or weed for the direct effects, which are relaxation and reduction of negative feelings. But when the drug leaves our system and our bodies go into shock, we begin to feel the indirect effect, which is the opposite feeling. We call this the rebound effect. For alcohol and marijuana, the indirect or rebound effect would be lack of sleep, stress, and tension, which is likely the reason why we did it in the first place. Because these feelings are uncomfortable, we may use the drug again to reduce the negative feelings, almost as if the drug were a medicine that could cure the indirect effects. In order to keep yourself on balance, you have to keep taking the drug. It seems as if the only other option to doing more drugs is to wait out the discomfort until your body can return to its normal, pre-drug state, which sometimes can take a while. This cycle also works for uppers as well as downers. After coming off an upper, you will likely get really tired and depressed and crash. To keep yourself from getting tired, you keep taking the drug. The cycle of use continues until an addiction is formed. Figure 6 shows us how that might look.

SESSION 4: UNDERSTANDING DRUG ABUSE AND PATTERNS OF DEPENDENCE

Figure 6: **Mental-Physical Addiction**

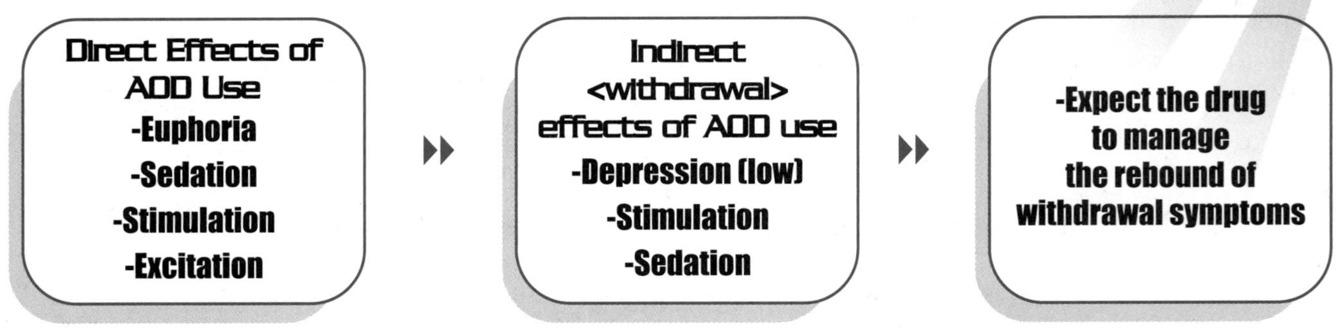

The Harmful Cycle of Abuse and Dependence

So far what we've explained is shown by **Points A through C** on Figure 7 (p. 53). And many people stop at **Point C** with the action habit. But sometimes we have problems because of our drug use. You get caught smoking marijuana (**Point D**). So you have to go to court and your parent(s) is really upset with you, which causes worry about what's going to happen.

When you get home from court, you go to your room and smoke a joint to deal with the stress from the adults who are now on your back (**Point E**). This gets you in more trouble (**Point F**), which gives you more to worry about and causes you to want to smoke even more (**Point G**). Now you're smoking marijuana because of the trouble caused by your having smoked marijuana. Consider the following saying: "The man takes a drink, the drink takes a drink, and the drink takes the man."

Forming a Habit and a Pattern of Dependence

The next activity is designed to show how your brain becomes damaged through repeated use of a mood-altering drug—in this case, cocaine. Keep in mind that all mind-altering drugs affect the brain's internal communication system.

Activity: Cocaine in the Brain

There are eight volunteers. One person represents cocaine, three represent the presynaptic neuron, three represent the postsynaptic neuron, and one person represents a beautiful sunrise. A container (clear bowl or glass) of small packages of sugar symbolize the synaptic vesicle, which contains many molecules (the sugar packets) of the neurotransmitter dopamine.

The six people who represent the neurons arrange themselves in two lines of three with a 3 foot space between them (the synapse). The sensation is a beautiful sunrise.

		BEAUTIFUL SUNRISE					**COCAINE**	
pre	1	2	3	synapse	post	4	5	6

At one end (presynaptic terminal)—triggered by sensations from the sunrise—person #1 makes a motion and taps person #2 on the shoulder, who taps #3—who is standing at the synapse. Then #3 **reaches into the synaptic vesicle** and takes out one of the sugar packets (dopamine) and **moves it across the synapse** giving it to person #4 who then taps #5 who taps #6 who exclaims, **"Whoa!"** waving his or her hand in ecstatic delight (showing a natural sense of joy that might come from seeing a beautiful sunrise).

When #4 sends the message on, he or she hands the neurotransmitter (sugar packet) back to #3, who replaces it in the synaptic vesicle. Then #1, at the presynaptic neuron, starts the process again. Practice this two to five times until it runs smoothly.

In comes cocaine. . . The message comes in normal fashion—i.e., #1 taps #2 and so on. The dopamine (sugar packet) crosses the synapse; however, this time when #4 attempts to give it back to #3, cocaine steals the sugar and hands it back to #4 (blocks the re-uptake of the dopamine), and #4 sends the message in the usual fashion by tapping #5. As soon as #4 taps #5, **#4 attempts** to return the sugar packet to #3, **but again cocaine takes it and hands it straight back**. Then #6 is saying, "Whoa! Whoa! Whoa!" really fast (excess dopamine).

Then #3 is just sitting there with the remaining sugar packets in the synaptic vesicle (the container) and **he or she doesn't need them anymore.** So #3 **empties the cylinder** and dumps the sugar packets (dopamine) on the floor. The police officer then removes the cocaine and then the neurotransmitter (sugar packets) can no longer be accessed from the cylinder. Withdrawal comes when the cocaine is no longer available, and the pleasure derived from the excess dopamine is no longer there because the nerve cells felt that the dopamine molecules were **no longer necessary.** This leads to **cocaine withdrawal.**

With some modifications, the same model could be used to explain withdrawal from other drugs like caffeine, methamphetamine, Ecstasy, or nicotine. Now let's do one more exercise, this time showing the various ways that people deal with the rebound or withdrawal effects of various drugs.

Activity: Dealing With Drug Rebound Or After-Effects

For this role-play, we will need three to nine participants who will play the part of direct effects, indirect effects, and withdrawal managers. Everyone will line up, with the direct effects in line first, followed by indirect effects and withdrawal. A drug will be chosen, and the direct effects will each describe some effects of the drug. The indirect effects will then say what happens when coming off the drug. The withdrawal managers will then give one or two solutions as to how to deal with or prevent the indirect effects.

SESSION 4: UNDERSTANDING DRUG ABUSE AND PATTERNS OF DEPENDENCE

Putting It Together

- What were some of the direct and indirect effects of the pills on Jarrod? How did they affect Mary?
- What cycle of addiction do you think Jarrod and Mary fit into the best? How did the drugs affect their decisions?
- How do drugs affect your mind and body now, and how will drug use affect your mind and body in the future?
- Which pathway to addiction might be closest to your use?
- How do the learning concepts play a role in addiction?

Using the Program Guides and Tools for Change

Use the PCS here to indicate your understanding of how drugs become addictive and how they create chemical imbalances in the brain.

0	1	2	3	4	5	6	7	8	9	10
Low					Medium					High

Indicate the degree to which you will be able to use the information presented in this session to make healthier choices about alcohol and other drug (AOD) involvement.

0	1	2	3	4	5	6	7	8	9	10
Low					Medium					High

With your counselor, complete your Self-Portrait (SP) Section 1: Alcohol and Other Drug Assessment.

With your counselor, begin to develop the areas in your Plan for Change (PFC) that correspond to the factors that you identified in your SP.

SESSION 5: CRIMINAL CONDUCT AND THE INFLUENCE OF DRUGS

Objectives

- Review Session 4: Understanding Drug Abuse and Patterns of Dependence.
- Understand the thinking habits that can get us in trouble.
- Understand the cycles of negative behavior.
- Understand how drug use and criminal conduct (CC) work together.

Jarrod's Story: *One night there was a huge party that we went to. Of course we took some pills, but we took more than our normal amount because it was a special event. Boy, did we have a great time that night.*

When it came time for us to go home, Mary was still really messed up. She asked me if I could drive us home since we both were going to get in trouble if we were late. I didn't really think that I was all that messed up, and besides, I would have done anything for Mary.

I was too messed up to drive. I got us into an accident and ended up killing Mary and a passenger in the other car. Now I sit in this metal box, waiting out my sentence for manslaughter.

Mary's Story: *Popped a pill again before school today. My day floated by in endless pleasure—until I met Jarrod. He was sitting all alone, looking like an old version of myself. It made me sad for a moment. I had to share my dope with him. I knew that I could change his world!*

The Discussion of Drugs

In Session 4, we talked about the four different types of drugs and how they can affect our bodies. We also began talking about the effects of alcohol (also a drug) on our bodies and our minds. What are the four basic categories of drugs?

After we learned more about drugs in general, we discussed how drugs are used to either give us positive feelings or get rid of negative feelings. But it is when we apply the concepts of learning to drug use that we begin to understand how addiction can occur. When drugs give us feelings we want or get rid of feelings we don't want we begin to do them more. But problems and negative feelings come out of drug use, so we continue to do them to get rid of the negative feelings. The learning concepts don't just apply to drug use, though. They can also apply to getting in trouble and being involved in criminal activities.

Getting In Trouble and How It's a Cycle

Just like drug use, getting in trouble is a learned process. Getting in trouble and having problems is a way to deal with our worlds inside and outside of our mind. Stealing something from a store may cause positive feelings, because we now have something we want and we've gotten away with something. But it can also be used to turn off negative feelings, like skipping school because it stresses us. In turning on positive feelings or turning off negative feelings, our actions get strengthened and form thought and action habits, like "I don't need money. I can just steal it." Just as smoking marijuana can lead to problems and smoking more, actions that we do in the world around us can lead to problems. How could Figure 7 be applied to developing a habit of crime and violence?

As shown in Learning Concept III, when we get in trouble for problems we cause, we sometimes stop doing those actions. But remember that we talked about how negative results can strengthen our negative thought habits and beliefs? The same idea applies to getting in trouble. If we're always getting in trouble, our thought may be "the world is against me." That thought will help choose our actions (because remember our thoughts, feelings, and actions are always together in the meeting in our minds), and if the action turns out negative, then it just makes the thought stronger. If we rely on old negative thought habits to deal with the problems from our actions, we are likely to get into even more trouble.

Activity: How Negative Thoughts Lead To Bad Outcomes

Form a circle, facing inward toward each other. You will be given two objects, spaced evenly in the circle. You will pass the object to the person next to you. One object represents beliefs, and the other represents negative results. The purpose is to get both objects in a neighbor's lap while avoiding having both objects in your lap. When a person finally has both objects in their lap, they will give one example of a negative result and the belief that led to the action and was strengthened because of the negative result. Then start passing the objects around again.

Here is an example of this belief: "Nobody messes with me cause I'm so tough and I've got to prove it to get respect." Because of this belief you get into fights; when you beat someone up, you get approval from your friends and you feed the negative belief about how tough you are and how proving it to your friends is the way to earn respect.

What would be alternative ways of thinking and acting to gain respect (self-respect and respect from other people who are important in your life)?

What Do We Mean By Negative Behavior?

Getting in trouble means putting yourself at risk of self-harm or harming others and becoming a focus of the legal and criminal systems.

- **Legal trouble** means going against a law of a city, state, or country (e.g., doing drugs); and also means going to court.
- **Moral trouble** means going against what people or a religion see as right or wrong, like stealing or disrespecting your parents.
- **Social trouble** means going against something a culture or community believes in, like treating elders with respect or playing fair (not cheating).

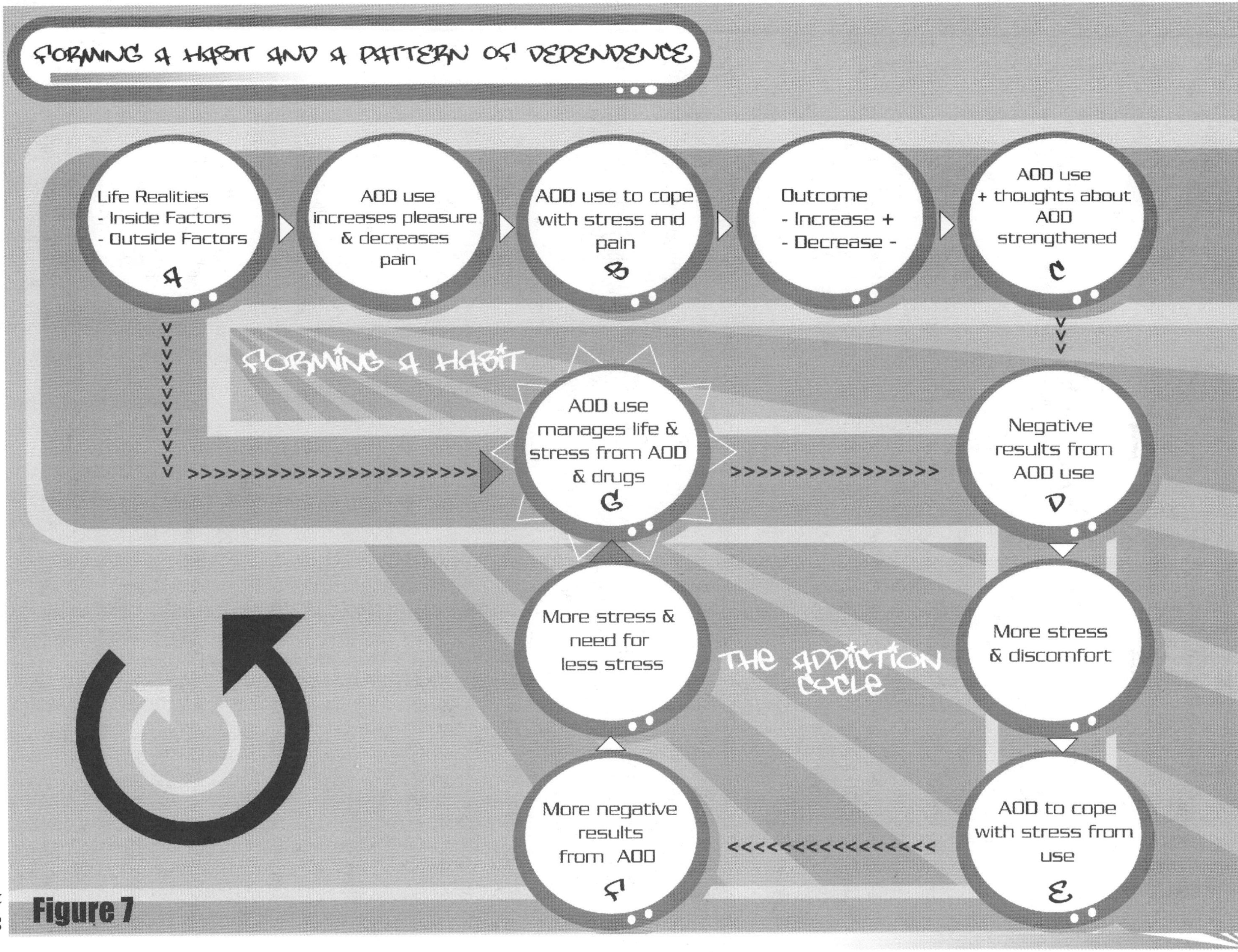
FORMING A HABIT AND A PATTERN OF DEPENDENCE
Life Realities
- Inside Factors
- Outside Factors
A
AOD use
increases pleasure
& decreases
pain
AOD use to cope
with stress and
pain
B
Outcome
- Increase +
- Decrease -
AOD use
+ thoughts about
AOD
strengthened
C
FORMING A HABIT
AOD use
manages life &
stress from AOD
& drugs
G
Negative
results from
AOD use
D
More stress &
need for
less stress
THE ADDICTION CYCLE
More stress
& discomfort
More negative
results
from AOD
F
AOD to cope
with stress from
use
E

Figure 7

SESSION 5: CRIMINAL CONDUCT AND THE INFLUENCE OF DRUGS

- **Psychological trouble** is when we do something that causes us to have negative thoughts or feelings about ourselves.
- **Self-harm** is when our actions cause damage to our body or brain.

Activity: Jarrod's and Mary's Trouble

Jarrod and Mary got in trouble because of bad decisions they made. What kind of trouble do you think best fits their situations? Is there more than one type of trouble that could apply? In what way is just doing drugs getting in trouble?

Risk Factors

There are certain situations, thoughts, and patterns of behavior that we have participated in during the past or in the present that are considered risk factors for continued problems, into our adulthood, with AOD abuse and criminal activities. Some of the things we can control and some of the things we cannot. But we can always control how and what we think about the actions and situations. The first six items on Worksheet 2: Rating Self on Risk Factors have already happened to us (Risk Factors That Can't Be Changed), while the others are parts of our personality and life situation that put us at risk at the present moment (risk factors we can change). These are the things that we can really do something about.

Activity: Your Own Risk Level

Fill out Worksheet 2 with your level of risk, and then discuss with the group how you may be able to deal with the risks. What risks are stronger in their influence on your actions? Are there risks that everyone has in common?

Thinking Filters

Remember the green sunglasses that distort our thoughts? When we get in trouble, it is usually because we have thought habits that have become distorted or are errors in our thinking. Worksheet 3 lists some of the distortions in reality that we may have that led to problems.

Activity: Recognizing Harm-Directing Thoughts

Fill out Worksheet 3, and discuss how the **harm-directing thoughts affect your life** and how you may use your thoughts and freedom of choice to change the errors. Do you have some errors in common with someone else? How do the harmful thoughts conflict with some of your values like freedom, respect for others, and family? Can you commit to some different ways of thinking and acting that might lead to more positive outcomes?

Rating Self on Risk Factors

Worksheet 2

Check or Rate the Risk Factors as to How They Apply to You

Risk Factors That Can't Be Changed	None	Low	Moderate	High
Past Involvement in Crime				
Negative Family Situation				
School Problems				
Early AOD Use				
Involved with Delinquent Friends				
Isolation From Peers				
Risk Factors That We Can Change	**None**	**Low**	**Moderate**	**High**
Antisocial/Criminal Friends/Peers				
Have Criminal Role Models				
Self-Centered Thinking				
Criminal Thinking				
Criminal Beliefs				
Lack Social/Relationship Skills				
Have Angry/Aggressive Attitude				
Have Angry/Aggressive Feelings				
Act on Spur of the Moment				
Don't Have Family Closeness				
Go Against Authority/Rebellious				
Get Rewards Through Doing Crimes				
Blame Others for Your Actions				
Lack of Good Logical Thinking				

Worksheet 3

MANAGING HARM-DIRECTING THOUGHTS

Mindfulness, Commitment, and Behavior Change

HARM-DIRECTING THOUGHT	FREQUENCY never, sometimes, a lot	VALUES	COMMITTED ACTION
Examples:			
I need drugs to cope			
I am entitled to take what I want			
Others feelings are not important to me			
I can't trust anybody			
I can't live without . . .			
I can't live without a lot of money.			
Want what you want right now			
Thinking about criminal things			
Seeing things only your way			
Blaming others: Victim stance			
Think: "I feel screwed."			
Don't need anyone			
I need drugs to cope			
Demand from others but don't give			
Put things off			
Self-Identified Harm-Directing Thoughts:			

SESSION 5: CRIMINAL CONDUCT AND THE INFLUENCE OF DRUGS

Patterns of Trouble

Just as there is a pattern of AOD dependence, there is also a pattern of problem behavior. There are external forces (e.g., influence of group leaders and friends) and internal pressures (e.g., hurtful past memories) that lead to problems and trouble. We make our mental choices according to those events. The choice gives us a positive or negative reaction or response, and then we make a decision as to how we are going to act. Let's say you see something you want, but you don't have the money for it. An internal event may be that you think, "I will never be able to afford this thing." This makes you feel frustrated and angry because you can't have it, so you decide to steal it. This is an example of how an internal event has led up to legal trouble. Figure 8, shows us how this cycle begins and where it likely ends. But there are ways you can change the cycle:

- The first thing you can do is to change your mental reaction, or thought habit, about what is going on around you. Instead of thinking, "I can just steal it," it is more positive to think, "I would rather pay for it because I would feel better." This change makes your thought more **pro-social.**
- The second thing you can do is to change your actions. Choose not to do something you know would get you in trouble. You may think about stealing something, but instead you just walk away.

Events That Set Off the Criminal Conduct Cycle

Third, you can avoid putting yourself in the situation. If you know smoking weed will get you in trouble, then don't hang around places that have weed. This is considered preventing the action.

Activity: An Avoidable Situation

You will be given a situation by your counselor that could have negative results, such as vandalizing property. Think about the thoughts and actions involved with the situation. One by one give an alternative to the negative thought or action, such as "instead of thinking it doesn't matter, I could think . . ." or "instead of breaking that window, I could . . . ," or give an example of how you would avoid the situation. Keep doing this until everyone has had a chance to offer an alternative, and then discuss how you can put the alternatives to use in an actual situation.

We are not able to hide ourselves from all situations, though. So keep in mind that true change comes when you handle the mental habits and reactions. Change can only happen when you take control of your thoughts and feelings and make the choice out of your free will. This can lead to positive outcomes.

Using Drugs and Negative Behavior Have Strong Effects on Each Other

Using drugs and drinking alcohol are illegal, but there is also a connection between the two actions in which one causes the other. There are several ways using drugs can get us in trouble:

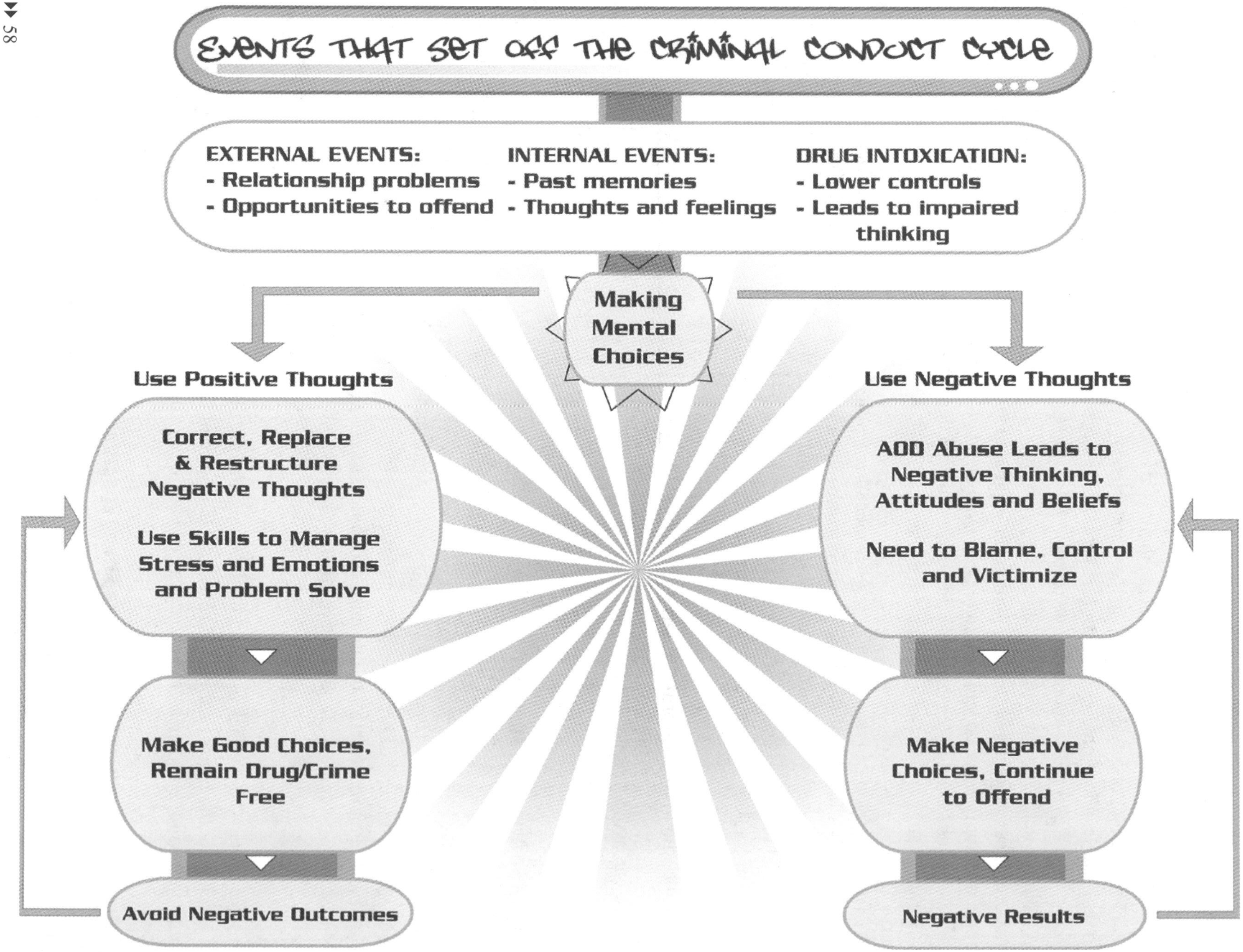
EVENTS THAT SET OFF THE CRIMINAL CONDUCT CYCLE
EXTERNAL EVENTS:
- Relationship problems
- Opportunities to offend
INTERNAL EVENTS:
- Past memories
- Thoughts and feelings
DRUG INTOXICATION:
- Lower controls
- Leads to impaired thinking
Making Mental Choices
Use Positive Thoughts
Correct, Replace & Restructure Negative Thoughts
Use Skills to Manage Stress and Emotions and Problem Solve
Make Good Choices, Remain Drug/Crime Free
Avoid Negative Outcomes
Use Negative Thoughts
AOD Abuse Leads to Negative Thinking, Attitudes and Beliefs
Need to Blame, Control and Victimize
Make Negative Choices, Continue to Offend
Negative Results

Figure 8

SESSION 5: CRIMINAL CONDUCT AND THE INFLUENCE OF DRUGS

1. Using drugs lowers our self-control, stops good judgment, and gets our thoughts into distorted views (like seeing with green sunglasses on).
2. Drugs are often found in situations that can be problematic (like someone might be carrying a weapon).
3. Drug use can stop us from having positive mental habits and often can lead to losing control over our thoughts.
4. Drugs can distort how we think and feel. They can stop us from feeling guilt or fear before doing something we know is negative and could get us in trouble.

Activity: Seeing How Distortion Works

For this exercise, you will need to get in pairs or groups of three. Take a moment to look at the following phrases. As a group, try to figure out what the phrases say. Write the following reorganized phrase in your workbook, and then get back together as a large group. How did the change of spaces within the phrases change the meaning? Did the phrases make more sense before or after you rearranged them? How does distortion rearrange your thinking?

Ifi tswo rthd oing, I tswor thdoi ngri ght. ______________________________
Yo urmi ndc anma ket hewh olew orl dch ange. ______________________________
I fiam tole arn, the nimu stbe sho wnhow. ______________________________

Putting It Together

- Out of the four types of trouble (legal, moral, social, and psychological), which one(s) do you think most applies to Jarrod's situation? What about Mary's situation?
- How did the drugs affect Jarrod's and Mary's ability to make decisions? How did they distort their thinking?
- How do drugs affect your thinking and behavior?
- What are some of the ways your thoughts can become distorted?
- How might you be able to avoid drugs and trouble by controlling your thoughts?

Drug Test

1. (T or F) Alcohol is a deadly poison.
2. (T or F) A can of beer, a glass of wine, and a mixed drink all have the same amount of alcohol.
3. Define a *drug*.
4. How do drugs work?

5. What are the general kinds of drugs?
6. Define *tolerance.*
7. (T or F) Mixing two drugs in the body at the same time may increase the strength of one or both drugs.
8. Of the following, who will get more drunk: the person who just ate or the person on an empty stomach?
9. (T or F) Bigger people, or people with more fat, can drink more alcohol before getting drunk.
10. Define *drug addiction.*
11. List three negative effects of marijuana.
12. What are the dangers of using Ecstasy?
13. What are long-term effects of acid use?
14. (T or F) Coffee and cold showers can help you sober up.
15. (T or F) It's more dangerous to drive drunk than to drive high.
16. (T or F) "Natural" drugs like pot and shrooms are less dangerous than chemical drugs made in labs.
17. (T or F) You feel more depressed when coke wears off than you did before you used it.
18. (T or F) Children in families with alcoholic parents are three to five times more likely to become alcoholics themselves.
19. (T or F) Smoking cigarettes relaxes you even when you aren't used to smoking.

A web-based test on the effects of drugs, which would be great to discuss with members of your group and your counselor, can be found at http://drugfactsweek.drugabuse.gov/iqchallenge.php.

The Hooked on Nicotine Checklist

First answer the following questions about cigarettes, and then answer the same questions for alcohol or any other drugs that you may have used.

An answer of *yes* to any one of the questions indicates that addiction has begun:

- Have you ever tried to quit smoking but couldn't?
- Do you smoke now because it is really hard to quit?
- Have you ever felt like you were addicted to tobacco?
- Do you ever have strong cravings to smoke?
- Have you ever felt like you really needed a cigarette?
- Is it hard to keep from smoking in places where you are not supposed to, like school?

When you tried to stop smoking (or when you haven't used tobacco for a while) did you do the following:

- Did you find it hard to concentrate because you couldn't smoke?
- Did you feel a strong need or urge to smoke?
- Do you feel nervous, restless, or anxious because you couldn't smoke?

Using the Program Guides and Tools for Change

Indicate the degree you will use the skills taught in this chapter to change your thinking and behavior around AOD abuse and CC.

0	1	2	3	4	5	6	7	8	9	10
Low					Medium					High

Indicate the degree to which you understand your risk factors (past and current) for progression of AOD and CC into adulthood.

0	1	2	3	4	5	6	7	8	9	10
Low					Medium					High

Indicate the degree to which you understand how certain events can set off the CC cycle.

0	1	2	3	4	5	6	7	8	9	10
Low					Medium					High

Indicate the degree to which you understand and can identify your personal set of harm-directing thoughts that may result in AOD abuse and crime.

0	1	2	3	4	5	6	7	8	9	10
Low					Medium					High

With your counselor, complete the following components of your SP:

2. Family, Parents, and Living Environment
3. Emotional and Psychological Issues
4. School Achievement and Adjustment
5. Relationship With Peers
6. Harm-Directing Thoughts and Criminal Conduct

With your counselor, begin to develop the areas in your PFC that correspond to the factors that you identified in your SP.

Jarrod's Story

I feel so lonely here. I shouldn't be here. This is not where I belong.

I have always felt lonely . . . isolated. Maybe it has something to do with my dad leaving when I was really young or maybe that my mom never has time for me because she's always working. Or maybe it's because I just never really felt like I belonged with anyone my age. I've had friends, but I've always been on the outside—or better yet, like I was trapped in a glass box.

Up until my freshman year, I thought that's how everybody felt. But then high school started. Suddenly everyone else was involved in a whole different world. I was still in my glass box as all my old friends grew and met new friends and left me behind.

Then I met Mary. She was 16, older than me, but really friendly. I was sitting on the lawn at school, in my own thoughts, when she walked up and asked me for a light. I didn't really smoke, but I had this thing for fire so I had a lighter I let her borrow. Next thing I knew she was sitting down and talking to me. We talked for only a couple of minutes, and then she ran off to join her friends, but for a moment I felt like I was a person.

I hadn't seen her for a couple of weeks when I ran into Mary again. I was downtown, sitting in the park and staring at the grass when I looked up and saw her smiling down at me. The sun suddenly came out, and her hair was like a golden halo. She sat down and stared at the people walking around for a minute. Then she looked at me and asked me if I partied. I looked back at the ground before I quietly admitted I didn't have friends I could go out with. She smiled and said she would like to take me to a party this weekend if I didn't think my parents would mind. My heart stopped as I watched her open the door to my glass box, and I said yes.

That Friday night Mary picked me up at my house around 8:00. I had told my mom I was staying at one of my old friend's houses, and she didn't really ask much more. Mary's car was crowded with her friends, and we all squeezed in tight to drive to this party out in the middle of nowhere. Despite the crowd in the car, I felt isolated and alone until we got there and then Mary took my hand. While we were waiting in line, Mary took a couple pills out of her pocket and gave me one. I knew what it was, but at that time I didn't care and besides, what would one pill do? So I took the pill and waited. I was in a corner, isolated from everyone around me, when gradually my body began relaxing and my mind began feeling free. Mary, who was watching me closely, laughed and grabbed my hand, pulling me into the crowd. And for the first time in my life, I didn't feel like I was somewhere I didn't belong. Everybody was happy, and they let me know that I was deserving of love.

I was the last one to be dropped off the next morning, and all I could do was sit in Mary's car in a daze. We hadn't rubbed backs, or made out, but I'm pretty sure we had held hands the entire night. With a "see ya later" I was on the curb in front of my house, watching as she drove away. And despite feeling sweaty and sleep deprived, I was the happiest I had been for as long as I could remember.

Although it was hard to remember that a day later. Suddenly I felt as if the world was ending, like I was on a roller coaster through the pits of emotional hell. My mom noticed something was wrong and tried to talk to me a couple times, but then she just left me to myself in my room.

From then on, Mary and I spent pretty much every day together, just hanging out after school. It wasn't like we were dating. We were just really close to each other. It was about a month or so before the next party, and once again there were pills. But we were happy and together, and feeling comfortable and relaxed around people was important to me. And being with Mary was the most important. I didn't think about the down.

Slowly we began doing pills more often. We began doing them in small groups, and sometimes it was just Mary and I, listening to music and talking about worldly things while we held each other's hand. We always made sure to stay away from each other the 2 days following, though. No one wants to be around another person going through a down—especially if you are too.

One weekend there was this huge party that we decided to go to. To make it extra special we both took a couple more pills than usual. It was about 5:00 in the morning when we had to go home. Mary was pretty out there and told me she couldn't drive and begged me to drive for her. I thought I could do it, and I would do anything for Mary. So I began driving. Somehow I ended up on the left shoulder, and we crashed into another car. I had to sit there in pain as Mary slowly died.

The passenger of the other car ended up dying too, a young mother with two kids. I couldn't stop crying during my court hearing, but it didn't matter. Two people had died, one of whom was the most important person to me in the world. And now I'm back in my box, except this time it's metal with iron bars while I wait out my sentence for manslaughter. I cry every night in pain, emotional and physical, and I have never felt lonelier in my entire life.

Mary's Story

January 21

I went to that shrink again today. What a quack! He told me I'm "depressed." Wow, it took him that long to figure that one out. Whatever. I guess I'm going to start taking some pill that will help me feel better. I'm not convinced, but I guess I don't have much to lose. Someone told me they got worse! What's up with that?

February 14

Still depressed, just in case you (or anyone else) cared. I've been taking these pills for 3 weeks now and haven't noticed any difference. The natty drug pusher told me to be patient and that I will need to wait 6 weeks to even see if they are working. This was not part of the deal. What's the point.

March 3

Went to the quack again today. Felt depressed when I got there and GREAT by the time I left! I met this guy in the waiting room just as we both leaving from our appointments. I must've looked pretty down 'cause he asked if I wanted something that would really pick me up—and did it ever!

March 4

What a difference from yesterday. I'm so tired, so depressed I can't even write. Later.

March 29

I quit taking those pills from the quack. The pills I found in the waiting room work much quicker. I'm meeting with that guy tomorrow at the mall—I can hardly wait to enter euphoria again!

April 8

I have found heaven. It's so intense I can't take these pills every day, but I feel so alive when I'm on them. Nothing bothers me. It's like I'm floating on a cloud.

May 16

I popped a pill again before school today. My day floated by in endless pleasure—until I met Jarrod. He was sitting all alone, looking like an old version of myself. It made me sad for a moment. I had to share my dope with him. I couldn't let him suffer anymore. I knew I could change his world. . . . I hope it works as well for him!

June 15

A party tonight—I'm taking Jarrod. He's such a doll! We will have a fantastic time. I can feel it!

Chapter Three:

Talking About Yourself and Listening to What Others Say

GOALS OF THIS CHAPTER

- Learn the importance of developing good communication skills.
- Begin using tools to help you become aware of your thoughts, feelings, and actions.
- Share some deeper stories with each other.

CYNTHIA'S STORY

SESSION 6: LEARNING COMMUNICATION SKILLS

Objectives

- Review Chapter 2: Building a Knowledge Base.
- Understand the importance of good communication.
- Learn how to talk about yourself and how to be open to receive feedback (to consider what others think about what you are saying).
- Learn how to make it easy for others to talk to you and to hear your feedback.
- Learn the tools of awareness: autobiography, journals, and thinking reports.

Cynthia's Story: *My dad used to beat me—and beat me bad. My mom tried to protect me when she was home, but she wasn't always home. Besides, she got beat too, and when she didn't have her alcohol, she was likely to throw me out of her way. My brothers were never home, so I never really had anyone to talk to or tell about the beatings.*

I used to dream of being an actress or doing something special to get away from my family. But I ended up running away from them, and now I'm out on the street making a lousy $20 to let some old fat and sweaty man touch me. The memories of my dad and my mom don't seem so bad now. I used to try to save money to get out, but then I realized that there is no point to goals and that this is the life I'm stuck with.

Up to This Point

So far we have learned about change and how our *mind* controls our actions. Although our *attitudes, thought habits,* and *beliefs* are what control our actions in the outside world, we are the ones who have control over our thoughts. *We have freedom* in the choices we make and the actions we take. Everyone sees the world differently because of their past and their opinions, but *everyone has control* over the thoughts that come from how we see the world.

We then learned about drugs and alcohol and how these can *poison our bodies* and gain *control over our thoughts.* Of course, using substances usually doesn't occur all by itself. Getting in trouble and committing crimes are usually tied to using drugs, even if it's just the fact that drugs are illegal. By taking part in these *negative* actions, doing drugs, and committing crime, sometimes we strengthen the negative thoughts that got us there in the first place. By using the learning concepts we talked about in Session 3, we begin to get an idea of how behavior *continues* despite negative feelings and results.

So now that we have gotten to know each other a little bit and we have an idea of the basic concepts and principles behind learning, substance use, and negative behavior, it is time to start *sharing something* about ourselves with each other, as well as be able to see ourselves from another person's view.

What Is Communication?

Talking to another person is considered *communication.* But there are actually *two kinds of ways* to show our feelings and thoughts to others:

1. The first is *nonverbal communication,* also known as *body language.* This is how we "talk" without using words. The *tone* of our voice, the way we *move* our body and hands, and the *expressions* we have on our face are all part of nonverbal talking. Sometimes our body language is *different* than what we are saying with words. This causes us to be misunderstood, and to be clearly understood, we should use the body language that *agrees* with our words.

Activity: Let Your Body Talk

Get into **groups of three** and sit in slightly separate parts of the room. **Attitudes** and **situations** will be handed out, and as a group come up with a way to get the other groups to **guess what the attitude and situation is.** You **cannot** use words to talk about your situation, only **body language** and **facial expressions.**

For example, the group situation might be getting arrested with the attitude as anger and unfairness. While acting out the arrest, use your **facial expressions** and **hand movements** to betray the anger and frustration of being innocent. Then take a moment to talk about some of the wrong guesses the groups may have come up with. What could have made the other groups think that? What could your group have done to get the message across clearer?

2. *Verbal communication* is how we talk when using words. When using words, though, we have to make sure that the other people understand what we mean. Remember **Principle 2** in Session 3? Everyone sees the world *differently,* meaning we have different opinions, attitudes, beliefs, and values, so that what we *assume* to mean one thing may mean something very different to *another person.* Opinions are often not right or wrong, but they do affect how we see and understand.

Clear and *honest verbal communication* can help others understand the point we are trying to make as well as help us to understand our own thoughts. When we understand ourselves, we can begin changing the thoughts that hurt us and other people.

Activity: Building Blocks Of Communication

One person will stand up and **choose** from a bag a piece of paper that has some shapes drawn on it. Then, with **words only** and no hand or body movements, the person will **describe** what is drawn on the piece of paper. Each person of the group will **draw** what the person standing up is describing without asking questions. Then have a **second person** stand up and describe **the same drawing,** with each person making a second drawing based on the second description. **Compare** the two drawings with the original shape. How do different words and descriptions aid in drawing the picture? How would you have described it differently? Notice that, depending on the words chosen, the picture can turn out differently. It is important to choose your words when trying to communicate with another person.

Opinions Are Not Facts

Sometimes the same words can have *different* meanings, like music. Music is defined as *arranged sounds to create something that has a beginning and end with a pattern of rhythm.* But when someone says *good music* to us, we may think of different things. One of us may *think* of rap while another may hear heavy guitar. The definition of music is the fact of what we think is good music is *opinion.* In order to communicate clearly, you would not only say, "Music makes me feel good." You may want to say, "When I listen to rap music, it makes me feel good." Even if the other person's opinion is different, the more specific you can be, the better the chance they will understand what you mean.

Let's See Ourselves Through Communication

There are *two ways* that we participate in talking with other people: (1) *talking about you* (self-oriented) and (2) *talking about them* (other-oriented). Both are important in talking with other people to *understand and be understood.*

Active Sharing: Talking About You

When talking about *you* with another person, there are actually two things involved: (1) *self-disclosure* and (2) *receiving feedback.*

Self-disclosure means *talking about yourself* and not the other person. It involves using *I* when talking and sharing with someone—your counselor or group—about *your* past and current thoughts, feelings, and actions. Self-disclosure does *three things* that can help you change.

1. It puts your *thoughts into words* so that you can hear them. By saying the words out loud, you are really disclosing to yourself, making you more aware of what you think and who you are.
2. It allows others to see *who you are* and also allows them to tell you (give honest feedback) about how they see you.
3. It opens *channels of trust* and helps others to tell about themselves. It is important for us to remember to use *I* when we are self-disclosing, and not *you.* When we use the word *you,* we are *really* talking about *the other person* and not our own thoughts and *feelings.* When we are in an argument with someone, the sentence usually begins with *you* because we want to *blame* or tell the other person what he or she did to upset *us.* But the whole point of self-disclosure is to talk about us, so we want to avoid using *you.*

Activity: Cynthia's Sharing

Get into pairs or groups, and take a look at Cynthia's story. Did Cynthia have anyone she could share her story with? Are there people at school or outside of her home that she could have talked with? Was running away her only option?

SESSION 6: LEARNING COMMUNICATION SKILLS

Receiving feedback means listening when someone else is talking to you about you and how he or she sees you as a person. *Feedback is the other person's opinion and not necessarily true,* and we want to keep that in mind so we can *avoid* getting defensive. When we get defensive about what someone else's opinion is, we hear *feedback* as *blaming,* and then both people end up getting hurt. The point is to *see ourselves* from outside, not to get angry or hurt with another person.

Take a look at Figure 9. This is a picture of how talking about ourselves can help us to change. When we share ourselves with another person, that person gives us feedback as to what they see and think about us. We not only hear ourselves talk but then we hear ourselves in the other person's feedback. This helps us to talk more about ourselves and to become more *aware* of who we are.

Encouraging Others Through Active Listening

When we do this, it means getting people to talk to you and then you share how you see them. There are two skills involved to encourage others to talk with you.

1. **The open statement or question.** An open question allows for the person to give us more than a *yes* or *no* answer. Instead of saying, "So, do you like rap music?" you might say, "Hey, what do you like about rap music?" This opens the lines of communication so that other people may feel open to telling you about them. An example of this is "So what's been going on?" or "What've you been up to today?" We know we hear people ask others, "What's up?" and then not even wait for the answer. The important thing here is that we do wait for an answer, and then we listen to what the person actually says.
2. **The feedback listening skill.** This is when we reflect back what we hear and observe about what the other person is communicating—e.g., "I hear you saying that you're so frustrated with your dad that you feel like never speaking to him again," or "I see you as angry," or "It sounds like something's really wrong." These are *active listening skills* where we hear what the other person says and then *reflect back* what they are saying. We serve as a kind of *mirror* so the person can hear what they were telling us.

Activity: Hearing Ourselves

Pair up, and use the skills of **self-disclosure** and **feedback** to talk to each other about a situation that is **important** to you. First decide which one of you will be *self-disclosure* and the other *feedback,* and after a couple of minutes, switch roles. Then get back into the large group. One at a time have the feedback person say what **they heard** about the situation, and then have the sharer tell the group what they heard about themselves. Does hearing what another person has to say change what you think? Does it help to hear what others say?

Understanding Our Own Thoughts

Becoming *aware* of ourselves does not happen just by talking with other people and hearing what they have to say about us. We also have to *become aware* of what we are thinking at any moment in order to

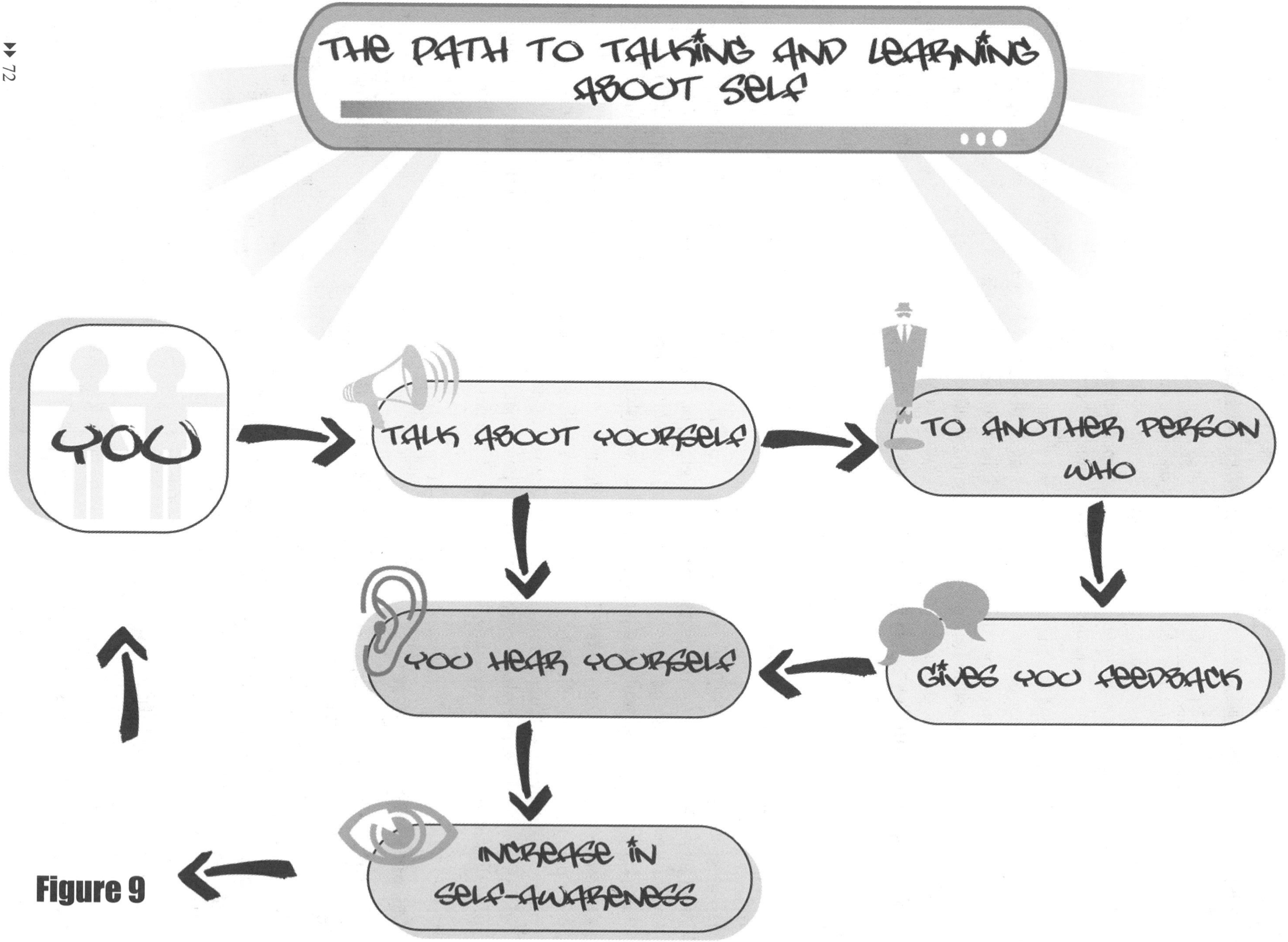
THE PATH TO TALKING AND LEARNING ABOUT SELF
YOU
TALK ABOUT YOURSELF
TO ANOTHER PERSON WHO
GIVES YOU FEEDBACK
YOU HEAR YOURSELF
INCREASE IN SELF-AWARENESS

Figure 9

have *choice* over our actions. There are *three* tools that will help you with the process of *controlling your thoughts and actions:* **(1) autobiography** (telling your story), **(2) journal,** and **(3) thinking report.** These tools will help you in *gaining awareness* of yourself and your thoughts. One of the most important parts of understanding your own thoughts is to recognize thinking errors.

But First—Problem Thinking

Earlier in Session 2 we talked about *thought habits*—how they are *automatic* even if there is an error in them. Even though these thoughts are not based on fact, we *use* them to help us through hard times and problems. If your parent looks angry when they come home from work, your first thought may be "What did I do wrong this time?" Your parent may not be angry with you at all, but that was your *thought habit.* These *errors* in our *thinking* can cause a lot of problems though. If you automatically think your parent is angry with you and for no reason, then you are more likely to act hurt and angry with them. Take a moment to look back at Worksheet 3 in Session 5. Which of these thoughts do you consider to be errors in your thinking or "harm-directing thoughts"? We all have them, and the quicker we become aware of our *personal errors,* the sooner we can make positive changes in our lives.

Activity: Whose Error Was That?

One at a time, **choose a situation** out of the bag. Once everyone has a situation, **read** it out loud to the group. Within each situation, there is a harm-directing or unhealthy thought pattern that causes the action to end as it does. For example, one situation could be a kid walks into a store. There isn't anyone around, the clerk is in the back, and the kid is by himself. The kid originally came into the store to buy a soda, but when he didn't see the clerk his thought habit was "I can just take the soda." The clerk catches him, and he gets arrested for shoplifting. You are to **pick** out the **error** in thinking in each situation, and then give an **alternative** way of thinking so the situation ends better. The kid thinks of just taking the soda but then decides that is wrong and he should just pay for it. He spends the $1 to get the soda and doesn't get arrested.

Tools for Change

There are *three* important parts to our minds: (1) *memories,* (2) *responding to now,* and (3) *our dreams about the future.*

- **Memories.** It is through our memories that we write our story about ourselves. But our *memories* come from our daily experiences, so our memories are decided by how *we choose* to live each day. It is true that things happen to us outside of our control, but we always have a choice in how we handle what happens. So how *we choose* to handle what happens also decides our memories. The *autobiography and* Program Guide 1: Telling My Story (TS) will help us to understand where we have been so we can choose our paths in present and future.

- **Responding to now.** The *journal* and *thinking reports* will capture our responding to now. Three important parts of responding to the present are *thinking, feeling,* and *speaking.* All three of these are the glue of our mind that help us to reason and learn, which then *help us to organize* our present and awareness of now.
- **Our dreams about the future.** Imagining, setting goals, and planning are how we map out our future. But to make the map possible, we have to *know* where we've been (memory) and where we are now. Our journals and thinking reports help us *plan for* our future.

Activity: Cynthia's Memories

Take another look at Cynthia's story. How did her future dreams affect her decisions, if at all? What were her memories before she ran away, and what are her memories now because she ran away? How are her memories decided by her actions? Use as specific detail as possible when answering the questions.

Activity: Dreaming of the Future

Take a moment to write down a future goal of yours. How will that goal be made possible? What can you **do** or **avoid** in order to obtain that goal? What steps should you take right now to begin achieving your goal?

We will use three tools in trying to become *aware* of ourselves in the past and present and give ourselves something to look forward to in the future. The three tools are (1) *writing your story* (autobiography), (2) *keeping a journal,* and (3) *using a thinking report.* During the remainder of the program, we ask that you use these tools to describe your life experience and to record your current thoughts and dreams for the future. You may be asked to discuss the *progress* that you are making on *keeping a journal* and on *your autobiography* at the beginning of each session.

Writing Your Story

We will write our stories over the next couple of weeks. This story *represents* our history and is made up of our memories and past experiences. We can't really know where we are now unless we *understand* and *know* our history. There may be experiences that you may not want to share with the group. If something comes up that is troubling or upsetting to you, it would be a good idea to talk privately with your counselor.

We realize not all of our history and past are pleasant, but it is important to see that both our negative and positive experiences have *come together* to make us who we are. It is not easy to write your history, but it is important in order to *take control of your change.*

You won't have to write your story from scratch. You may use information that you have already put down in TS (Program Guide 1). Here is an outline we would like you to follow.

SESSION 6: LEARNING COMMUNICATION SKILLS

- Describe the family you grew up in.
- Describe your childhood from your first memory through now.
- Describe your level of school completed, any work skills or background, and relationship experiences as well as your hobbies.
- Write your history with substance use and/or getting in trouble.
- Describe what brought you into this program.

Keeping a Journal

You will use your journal to write down your *thoughts, feelings,* and *actions* on a daily or weekly basis. This will help give us an idea of how we think and feel over time. It is helpful to include the situation, your feelings, your thoughts, and what you did in the situation. Did you handle it well, or could you have done it differently? It is important to be *honest* and use the journal as a way to express yourself. Once again, if something comes up that is upsetting, it would be wise to ask for some individual time to discuss this with your counselor.

Using a Thinking Report

A thinking report will help you to pay *attention* to your thoughts and actions. The *first step* in taking control and changing is learning to pay attention to our own thinking.

Here are some basic things to include:

- **Event.** *Describe* in a few words the situation. Try to follow the *facts* and describe what you see but not what you thought or felt.
- **Thoughts.** Describe and write down any *thoughts* you might remember. Don't worry about explaining, blaming, or making excuses; just write down what you thought at that moment.
- **Feelings.** Make a list of all the *feelings* you had: nervous, angry, excited, etc.
- **Attitudes and beliefs.** What attitudes and beliefs are *related* to this event?
- **Outcome.** Write down what your *action* and *behavior* was as a result of the event. Then think about and write down the thoughts, feelings, beliefs, and attitudes that all added up to your action.

The first step in taking control and changing is learning to pay attention to our own thinking.

Putting It Together

- Cynthia ran away because she didn't feel like she could talk with anyone. How did her future goals—or lack of direction—affect her decision?
- How did Cynthia's life, memories, and goals change with that one choice of running away?
- Think about some opinions you have. How might those opinions affect your actions?
- Remember one situation that turned out negatively for you. How did thinking play a part in the decision that was made? How could have changing your thoughts changed the results of the situation?

Using the Program Guides and Tools for Change

Use the Pathways Change Scale (PCS) to indicate your understanding of the importance of good communication.

0	1	2	3	4	5	6	7	8	9	10
Low					Medium					High

Indicate the degree to which you have learned the basic skills for effective communication.

0	1	2	3	4	5	6	7	8	9	10
Low					Medium					High

SESSION 7: SHARING YOUR STORY

Objectives

- Review Session 6: Learning Communication Skills.
- Share a deep emotion that you have been holding on to.
- Share your thinking report about your past substance use.
- Retake the tests you took when you entered the program, and compare your scores from then and now.
- Increase your awareness of past criminal offenses by logging them all, and relate this with your recorded legal history.
- Review the thinking report that dealt with one offense.
- Share a deep emotion that you have been holding on to.

Cynthia's Story: *It really hurt me, being beaten and thrown about by my parents. It was like I was a rodent or some unwanted pest that should be punished for existing. I used to be close with my older brothers, but then they got older and started hanging out and staying at their friends' houses. I felt abandoned by my parents, my brothers, and the world.*

So when it came time for me to start selling myself to make money, I didn't really think too much about it. After all, there really wasn't much to me. Don't get me wrong. I still dream of something different. But my reality is this, and there isn't anything that can change that.

A Look at Last Time

Last session we spent some time learning about communication, both *verbal* and *nonverbal,* and how it is important to communicate *clearly* to others. How do the two kinds of communication differ from each other? Which is most effective in getting our point across to another person? We also learned about *active sharing* and *active listening.* We then learned about how *our choices* can decide what our *memories* will be later on in life. It is also important for us to keep our *dreams* in our minds so that our choices will be in our *best interest* and those we *love and care* about. Finally, we learned about the three tools for becoming more aware of the thoughts and events that shape our feelings and actions: (1) *the autobiography,* (2) *journal,* and (3) *thinking report.*

Activity: A Skit in Time

Get into groups of three or so, and create a skit in which memories and future goals interact with the thoughts, feelings, and choices made. Have one person represent **memories and future goals,** one person represent **thoughts and feelings,** and the third person represent **choices.**

The **first person** will mention a **memory or future goal**. Then the **second person** will state the **thoughts and feelings** that come from the memory or future goal. The **third person** will then say the **action chosen** based on what the other two people have said. For example, one future goal may be to go to college. The thought may be "I need to study in order to get a scholarship," and the feeling may be excitement over what the future might bring. The action is then to study and focus on school to make the goals a possibility. Is it better to make choices from memories of the past or goals of the future?

Dig a Little Deeper

Although we discussed *trust* in Session 1, it's now time for us to dig deeper and *trust* each other a little more. This will not be easy for most of us and a lot harder than the sharing games we've done up to this point. But it is really important for us to get an *honest look* at ourselves, in terms of our thoughts and feelings, as well as our choices. In Session 2, we talked about how it is hard to change because *we hold on to our view of ourselves.* At this point, we may continue to hold on to some parts of our old views of ourselves. But this can cause thinking errors and often makes us ignore our past errors in action. But *you have decided* to be here, to continue on with the program, and now *you are ready* to take on even more challenges in telling and thinking about your life.

Activity: Cynthia's Pain

Cynthia speaks in her story about the feelings she had while living with her parents and later when she was living on the streets. What do you think is Cynthia's **view of herself?** Why is it hard for her to change that? What feelings and emotions does Cynthia have, and how do they affect her decisions and goals?

Sharing a Deep Emotion

Now we will ask you to take a look at a *deep emotion* that you have carried around with you. The emotion might be hurt, anger, betrayal, or deep sadness. Take a moment to think about that emotion.

Activity: Letting Go of Pain

Get into **pairs** or **groups of three.** Share with the others a **deep emotion** that you have carried around with you. **Describe** how that emotion has helped you to make choices, such as anger at your parents has made you want to fight everybody. Be sure to use your best communication and listening skills from the last session. Take a moment to **listen** to what the other person is saying to you. What emotions do you have in common? How can talking about and sharing this emotion help ease the pain and help you make better choices?

SESSION 7: SHARING YOUR STORY

An Honest Look at Substance Use

Take some time and *look honestly* at your substance use. You may be asked to retake some of the questionnaires that you took when entering the program. The counselor will assist you in making *your profile.* Use Worksheet 4: Your Test Scores to compare the scores from before you entered the program and now. How are they different, or are they the same? Then take a moment to fill out Worksheet 5: Recording Problem Episodes From Alcohol and Other Drug Use about *negative results* or *problems* that have come out of your using *substances.* These should be specific episodes of your life with a tie to substance use.

A Walk Down Memory Lane

We all *want* to feel like we are *good people* doing good things. Even some of us who have long histories of getting in trouble have a hard time looking at our past offenses. Most of us haven't even looked at how substance use and criminal conduct (CC) have worked together in our past.

Keeping in mind the *honesty* of this session, fill out Worksheet 6: Criminal Conduct Log Work Chart. Right now you are only to fill out the *first four columns.* Review this log in class as well as compare it with your recorded legal history.

After you have compared and reviewed, fill out the *last column* of the worksheet. Write no if *substances were not involved* in the situation. Write *B* if you used before the offense. Write *D* if you used during the offense. Write *A* if you used after. If all three apply, write *BDA.*

Activity: An Unfinished Thought

Sit in a circle. The first person will **choose an incomplete sentence** out of the bag. The person has to **complete the sentence** with their own thought or experience. Go around the circle until everyone has completed two to three sentences. Remember to **listen** to what the other group members are saying and possibly what you have in common with them. Which sentence was harder for you to finish? Which sentence was easier for you to finish? Is it harder to share deeper emotions, or is it easier to pretend you don't care?

Putting It Together

- Cynthia's lack of self-worth was created by her feelings about the situation at home. How do those emotions control her actions now?
- Deeper emotions often cause us to choose actions that are negative. How do your emotions influence you?
- Why is it hard for us to talk about our deeper emotions? What emotions did you have a problem sharing?

Worksheet 4

YOUR TEST SCORES

NAME OF TEST	1ST SCORE	2ND SCORE	HOW ARE THE SCORES DIFFERENT?
1.			
2.			
3.			
4.			
5.			
6.			

Worksheet 5

RECORDING PROBLEM EPISODES COMING FROM AOD USE

DATE	DESCRIBE THE PROBLEM OR NEGATIVE EPISODE

Worksheet 6

CRIMINAL CONDUCT LOG WORK CHART

ARREST DATE	NAME OR TYPE OF CHARGE	CONVICTED	PROBATION	TIME SERVED	RELATIONSHIP WITH AOD

For the last column, use the following:

Put **(B)** if you drank or used other drugs before the offense.

Put **(D)** if you drank or used other drugs during the offense.

Put **(A)** if you drank or used drugs after the offense.

Put **BDA** if you drank or used drugs before, during, and after the offense.

SESSION 7: SHARING YOUR STORY

Using the Program Guides and Tools for Change

Use the PCS to indicate your ability to share the facts about your past patterns of substance abuse and CC.

0	1	2	3	4	5	6	7	8	9	10
Low					Medium					High

Indicate your ability to share emotions with people that you trust.

0	1	2	3	4	5	6	7	8	9	10
Low					Medium					High

With your counselor, complete your Self-Portrait (SP) on the following sections:

7. Thinking and Feeling Patterns

8. Other Areas

9. Motivation and Readiness for Treatment

With your counselor, begin to develop the areas in your Plan for Change (PFC) that correspond to the factors that you identified in your SP.

Don't touch me. I hate it when people touch me. I know that's my job. You don't have to tell me that. Just do what you have to do and leave me alone.

Did you know I was once a princess? I had my sparkling tiara, a long silky dress, nice shoes, and jewelry. Okay, actually it was a cheap Halloween crown, one of my mom's worn-out nightgowns, her scratched high heels that I nearly broke my ankle in, and plastic crap my mom bought at some drugstore. But in my mind, I was a princess and I controlled my whole world. I never noticed the dirty floors of our trailer or the fact that my brothers rarely came home when I was in my world.

But that was when my dad wasn't home. Because when he was home, I was a mouse—and not even the kind that squeaks. I was a mouse that hid in my room behind my dolls. It wasn't so bad when he came home sober. For the most part, he would ignore me and yell at my mom because the house was a mess and yell at my brothers for being lazy pieces or something like that. But when he came home from drinking, he would shake the trailer with his yelling and throwing things. For the most part he beat on my mom, since she usually pushed me into my room when she heard him coming. But sometimes she was gone when he came home. And not even my door would stop him from coming in and hitting me while I cried and screamed.

Tell my mom? What good would telling my mom do? She got beat more often and harder than I did. Besides, when she had her alcohol, she was a zombie that didn't even know who I was. Sometimes I couldn't even stand to look at her, to have her turn those vacant eyes my way. When she wasn't drinking, though, she turned into some demon from the pits of the underworld and was worse than him. If I didn't want to get thrown at a wall, I had to be quiet in a corner far from her eyes. Telling my mom was not something I could even attempt to do.

So I dealt with it. As far as I knew, everybody's daddy did this to them. It was just a normal event in a normal family that does the normal things that we did. I dealt with it until I was 12, and I couldn't deal with it no more.

One night, after my mom passed out but before the monster came home, I stuffed my backpack with my most treasured things and I left. I only meant to be gone for the night—spend the night away and then maybe go back when everyone was sleeping. But as I sat and shivered on a sidewalk not too far away, I got scared. I would probably get beat by both of them, and beat bad, if I went home because I had been out all night. That scared me even more, so I stood up and started walking. I didn't really know which way to go, so I just started walking toward the lights and kept walking. Ideas and dreams of getting a job and my own place or becoming an actress or marrying a prince and never seeing my parents again floated through my head and lulled me into not feeling the cold or the pain.

A week on the streets taught me that no one wants to hire a 12-year-old girl. Once again my world was shattered, and so I settled down into begging and feeling like the scum I am. One night I was walking around an all-night convenience store, hoping for some food, when I bumped into a girl who looked like she was looking for someone. I mumbled "sorry," cause I didn't really have the energy to do much more, when she stopped me and said I looked hungry. She asked how long I had been on the streets. At that point, I think it was around a month, and she took me back to her hotel room. She gave me a little something, a candy or something, and told me she was looking for a roommate if I was willing to work. I told her that no one would hire me. I had already tried, and besides, I had no clothes or anything. And she said I didn't have to work a regular job to make money. I had in my possession something that men would pay for.

So the next night I was standing on the corner with her. At first I didn't know what to do. But then I noticed it didn't seem to matter whether I knew what I was doing, and it seemed that me being really young made me more money. So now I had a place of my own and a job to pay for it. For a time I tried to save every dollar, except what I had to pay for my room and the little I ate. But after a while my dreams began to fade, just as the memories began to fade. Being beat by my dad didn't seem as bad as doing what I had to do for some lousy $20. But I can't go back now.

And every time some dirty man touches me, I shudder and cringe. I hate when people touch me. But it pays the bills and I have nowhere else to go.

Chapter Four:
Backsliding to Drugs and Crime

GOALS OF THIS CHAPTER

- Learn what relapse and recidivism (RR) mean.
- Discuss the process of RR.
- Learn the warning signs of RR.

TYLER'S STORY

SESSION 8: IDENTIFYING TRIGGERS AND YOUR HIGH-RISK SITUATIONS

Objectives

- Review Chapter 3: Talking About Yourself and Listening to What Others Say.
- Develop skills to identify warning signs for negative or criminal behavior.
- Develop skills to identify warning signs for substance use.
- Increase your understanding of the connection between substance use and negative behavior.

Tyler's Story: *I'll admit it. I started doing heroin at a party. I didn't know exactly what it was, and I didn't really care. I feel that you only live once, so I try different things, and besides, my ex was at the party stressing me. What I didn't realize was how hard it was going to be for me to get off heroin.*

So finally I was clean after months in a program, when I ran into an old friend. I wasn't too worried because she had nothing to do with my using. But her boyfriend did. I started hanging out with him again, and before I knew it, I was back at that house, stoned out of my mind, and taking a bump.

Sharing Our Stories

In our last session, we spent some time sharing a deep *emotion* that we have been carrying around for a while. We then took a moment to see how that emotion may have led us to act out *negatively* or make choices that did not end well for us.

You were also asked to retake some of the admission questionnaires you had already taken and to record a log of your negative behavior. The point of this was to not only show the possible changes you have *already started* but also to share how *substance abuse* (drug and alcohol) and *negative behavior* (criminal actions) tend to *work together.*

Although we have all participated in negative behavior, most of us tend to avoid or pretend the past did not happen. Just as there are *harm-directing thoughts* that when followed cause us to make the wrong choices, there are also errors in *how we look at the past.* The criminal log is an effort to remind us of the things we did wrong—and how they went wrong—so that we may *make the choice* to not go back to that life.

With our *past* in mind, it's time to move *forward* in our change and focus on how to live comfortable and responsible lives without the use of drugs or participation in criminal activities.

What Are High-Risk Situations?

In Session 5, we discussed certain things in your life that are *risk factors.* For a memory jog, take a look at Worksheet 2: Rating Self on Risk Factors. These factors cause a person to be high-risk (HR) for substance abuse and criminal conduct (CC). But *situations* can be HR as well. These HR situations are usually the *HR events* that have led us to use alcohol and drugs in the past.

The events may even trigger your old patterns of *thoughts* and *feelings* about needing the substance in order to deal. An example of this may be that after a hard day at school when you think everyone is stressing you, you may feel like you *need* a joint just to relax.

The craving and urge from a situation like this may lead us to a thought like "I cannot cope without the use of substances." These *stressful situations,* or even happy situations, like when you do something well and feel the *urge to celebrate,* can lead us back into our previous use.

The *HR situations* do not just apply to substance use though. It can also apply to criminal or other behavior. This type of situation makes you think or feel like you want or need to be involved in getting in trouble with drugs or crime while it increases your impulse. Situations like this could be just hanging out with old friends who you used to get in trouble with. Another could be allowing yourself to be in a situation that has led to you committing a criminal act.

Activity: The Situation at Risk

When looking at Tyler's story, what were some of the **HR situations** he was put in? Did he have a choice to be in the situations or not? What could he have done to avoid the situations?

So Then What Is High-Risk Thinking?

HR thinking for substance use involves the *thought habits,* the thoughts that automatically jump into our head that lead to the use of substances. The thought habits can be *set off or triggered* in HR situations, or it could be the other way around, where the thinking leads you into HR circumstances. The *thinking* often takes place when we feel scared or when we believe that we aren't being treated fairly and may also be tied with *cravings* and *urges* to use the substance. An example of a thought habit may be "I'm stressed, so I need to smoke a joint" or "No one cares anyway, so I may as well drink."

Just as HR situations are *similar* for CC and substance use, HR thinking for crime is similar to HR thinking for substance use; it involves using the old thought habits that lead you to participating in negative behavior and usually takes place before the behavior itself. They may even be set off by HR situations or could lead you to HR situations. "I deserve better" or "It doesn't matter anyway" or "Nobody's going to get hurt" are thought habits that lead us to fall back into negative behaviors. Even thinking about participating in negative or criminal behavior is an example of HR thinking.

Activity: The Thought of the Situation

Get into groups of three or four, and develop a skit in which the **HR thoughts interact** with the **HR situation.** An example may be there is marijuana smoking going on at a party. The HR thought is "Weed can't hurt me, it'll be fun, and everyone is doing it anyway." Think about how **thoughts** can either give in to the situation or change the situation.

Come up with an **alternative** thought that might counteract the HR situation, such as "If I smoke pot, I could end up going back to jail" or "If I smoke, then I will probably act stupid and might get in trouble." Do your skit in front of the larger group, and then ask if they can distinguish between the positive or HR thought.

SESSION 8: IDENTIFYING TRIGGERS AND YOUR HIGH-RISK SITUATIONS

Relapse and Recidivism: What Are They?

Sometimes we think that *relapse,* or going back to using substances, only occurs once we start *using* again. But that's not necessarily true. Relapse actually *begins* when we put ourselves in a situation that has led to use in the past. Relapse also can mean *going back to thought habits about using substances* as an option for dealing with HR situations. Let's say you get angry at the school system and want to break some windows or pull a prank, and your friends are egging you on. Instead, you begin thinking that smoking a joint will help you calm down and forget. To deal with your friends pressuring you to act negatively, the *thought habit* is "I need to smoke a joint." But just because you think the thoughts does not mean you have fully *relapsed.* Just as with everything, there are *stages.* The *early stage of relapse is thinking about using* but not going back to your habit of use. A *full relapse* is when you go back to your previous level of use, which led to problems.

Recidivism means reoffending. Recidivism happens when we start having the thought habits that lead to *destructive or criminal behavior.* It also happens when we start to put ourselves in situations or act a certain way that in the past has led to committing a crime. Recidivism does not mean getting caught or even choosing the action. Just as with relapse, recidivism happens in *stages* with the *full recidivism* happening when you actually *commit a crime.* It is important to remember that recidivism begins when you allow any of the risk factors from Worksheet 2 to play a dominant role in your life.

The Causes of Relapse and Recidivism

Relapse usually begins when we feel like *we don't have the power or strength* to deal with a feeling or problem. Try to find out what situations cause you to want to use the substance and what you are *thinking* and *feeling* at the time. This allows you to *take control away* from the drugs and *have the strength* to manage the situation without a substance that changes how you act, think, or feel. By understanding how we *think* and *feel* about these HR situations, we can figure out what causes us to use substances and participate in behavior that is harmful to others. Then we can figure out ways to deal with these situations without being *weakened* by the problems that come with substance use and criminal behavior. Here are some possible triggers, or causes, for RR:

- Conflict with another person.
- Social pressure, or hanging out with peers involved in substance use and trouble.
- Unpleasant feelings: stress, depression, anger, and guilt.
- A change in self-image: from being a person who doesn't use to being a user; from the image of living free of trouble to one who gets involved in trouble; from a person who is incarcerated or in a restricted living situation to someone who is back home or in the community.
- Being in a situation where you previously used drugs or were involved with criminal activities.

SESSION 8: IDENTIFYING TRIGGERS AND YOUR HIGH-RISK SITUATIONS

Activity: A Discussion About Tyler

Something triggered Tyler the **first time** he tried heroin. What was his **trigger?** What was the **trigger** when he **relapsed** back into his heroin use? Were the triggers similar or different in how they affected Tyler? How could he have avoided his first use and his relapse episode?

Activity: Your Own Triggers

Let's take a moment to fill out the Relapse/Recidivism Log in Worksheet 7. Take each of the triggers that were previously mentioned and write down a **specific event** that applies to you. Then write your **thoughts** and **feelings** and your **response,** either positive or negative. Then use Worksheet 8: Coping Skills to write down how you dealt with or **would now deal with** each of the events.

Activity: Once Again—A Cycle

Just as there is a pattern to substance use and getting in trouble, there is also a **pattern to relapsing or going back to negative behavior.** There is a way to gain control over the pattern of our RR, though. Worksheet 9: The Relapse/Recidivism Calendar is meant to help you understand your pattern of substance use and criminal behavior. You will not only be able to see the patterns of your problems but you will also be able to see further into **how substance use and crime go hand in hand.** In filling out the worksheet, use **straight lines** to show sober and positive periods of your life, and use **wavy lines** to show when you were using substances or committing criminal acts. Hold on to this worksheet because you will be doing more work on it in the next session.

Putting It Together

- What was the HR situation for Tyler, and how did it affect his decisions? What were Tyler's triggers?
- What are some of your warning signs for getting in trouble with criminal activities?
- What are some triggers that cause you to want to do substances?
- How will knowing your pattern of use and negative behavior help you to change?
- Describe how RR are gradual processes of erosion.

Using the Program Guides and Tools for Change

Use the Pathways Change Scale (PCS) to indicate your levels of knowledge and skill to prevent relapse to alcohol and other drug (AOD) abuse and returning to criminal activity.

SESSION 8: IDENTIFYING TRIGGERS AND YOUR HIGH-RISK SITUATIONS

Indicate the degree to which you have increased your understanding of the connection between substance use and harmful or criminal behavior.

0	1	2	3	4	5	6	7	8	9	10
Low					Medium					High

Indicate the degree to which you have developed skills to identify warning signs for substance use.

0	1	2	3	4	5	6	7	8	9	10
Low					Medium					High

Indicate your level of skills to identify warning signs for harmful or criminal behavior.

0	1	2	3	4	5	6	7	8	9	10
Low					Medium					High

1. With your counselor, review your Self-Portrait (SP) Section 6: Harm-Directing Thoughts and Criminal Conduct.
2. With your counselor, complete your SP Section 7: Thinking and Feeling Patterns.
3. With your counselor, continue to develop the areas in your Plan for Change (PFC) that correspond to the factors that you identified in your SP.

Worksheet 7

RELAPSE/RECIDIVISM LOG

Below are four situations that are often seen as high-risk situations which can lead to relapse or reoffending. Write in specific situations that apply to you. Then write down your thoughts and feelings. What was the action you took? Discuss the positive and negative outcomes. Describe at least one situation in each category. What thoughts would lead to better outcomes?

TRIGGERS	THOUGHTS/ FEELINGS	BEHAVIOR + −
1 : CONFLICT WITH ANOTHER PERSON		
2 : SOCIAL OR PEER PRESSURE		
3 : AN UNPLEASANT FEELING		
4 : AN CHANGE IN SELF-IMAGE		
5 : FAMILIAR PLACE OR SITUATION		

Worksheet 8

Coping Skills

Write a short description of how you have coped or now cope with the situations outlined in Worksheet 7. Write a statement for each of the five situations.

1) Conflict with another person
2) Social or peer pressure
3) An unpleasant feeling
4) A change in self-image
5) Being at a place that triggers memories of crime or substance abuse, including alcohol.

Worksheet 9

The Relapse/Recidivism Calendar

(Adapted from Gorski, 1993)

Use this exercise to examine your AOD abuse and criminal activities. You will gain insight into how your AOD and legal problems are related. Write in the dates of your first serious attempts to stop AOD abuse and criminal behaviors. Use a **straight line** to indicate periods of sober and resposible behavior. Use a **wavy line** to indicate periods of relapse or recidivism. When you come to the next session, describe the series of events that led to AOD relapse and to criminal involvement.

Year		Jan	Feb	Mar	Apr	May	Jun	Jul	Aug	Sep	Oct	Nov	Dec
	AOD												
	Crime												

Year		Jan	Feb	Mar	Apr	May	Jun	Jul	Aug	Sep	Oct	Nov	Dec
	AOD												
	Crime												

Year		Jan	Feb	Mar	Apr	May	Jun	Jul	Aug	Sep	Oct	Nov	Dec
	AOD												
	Crime												

SESSION 9: LEARNING HOW TO STAY CLEAN AND AVOID TROUBLE

Objectives

- Review Session 8: Identifying Triggers and Your High-Risk Situations.
- Understand the idea of RR erosion.
- Understand the thoughts and actions that lead to RR.
- Learn to avoid RR by seeing the thoughts, feelings, and attitudes that trigger your use and CC.

Tyler's Story: *I didn't really want to do heroin again. I remembered the pain I went through while I was on it and while I was trying to get off of it. But I started hanging out with my old friends again. After a while, I went to the house with my friend, and when I was smoking weed, I took a bump. I didn't really think it was a big deal. I thought I could control it, and besides, I knew it would make me feel good. But then the next morning, while I was withdrawing, I became confused and angry. I wasn't clean anymore. I no longer had the months of sobriety at my back. The next time I was offered a bump, I took it. After all, I had already used once. What would one more bump do? I would quit after this one. But one turned into another and another. If I wasn't clean anymore, then I was a user. So I might as well use and enjoy myself. But I still felt like crap.*

High-Risk, Triggers, and You

In the last session, we spent some time learning what RR means, which is *going* back to the actions or thoughts that either lead us to use substances or cause criminal behavior. Remember, RR *does not* happen all at once but occurs in stages that begin with the *thought habits* first and then end with a return to our old harmful and destructive patterns.

There are also *triggers* that can make the *old thought habits* come back to us. The triggers can be anything from *outside conflict and pressure* to *inner feelings and changes* in our self-images.

But because there are *stages* and different *triggers* to relapse and recidivism, that means the process happens slowly. Since the process occurs in stages, that means we can *change* or *stop* the relapse before it becomes full blown. But to stop the relapse, we have to be *aware* of how and why it begins in the first place. That is what this session is about, *learning* the how and why so you can have *control* over stopping RR.

Activity: Tyler's Trap

Tyler started falling into some **HR situations** and **HR thinking.** What were the thoughts that caused Tyler to fall back on his old habit? What were Tyler's triggers and what stage of relapse is Tyler in now?

SESSION 9: LEARNING HOW TO STAY CLEAN AND AVOID TROUBLE

What Is Relapse/Recidivism Erosion?

Because RR is a *process,* that means there is a sort of erosion within our mind that happens with RR. Just as rain *erodes* away the topsoil, which contains the good stuff for growing and nurturing plants, RR begins the erosion of the topsoil of our mind, which contains the good stuff for us to grow and mature. But this doesn't happen quickly; rather, RR erosion can happen over a long period—even *years*—so that we can't really see it happening, even if a relapse episode seems spur of the moment.

Figure 10: The Relapse/Recidivism Erosion Process, gives us some idea of how the erosion happens. It's a slow *decline* in our positive selves until the relapse episode happens. It is then a *choice* of whether we continue back to our old selves in a full relapse or if we stop the relapse. But it is in *your control* whether you decide to relapse or not. Fill in the lines on Worksheet 10 to describe Tyler's RR process and how he might have stopped the erosion before reaching a full-blown RR episode.

Activity: Your Own Path

Take a moment to think about some possible RR episodes in your life. **Draw** on the right half of a piece of paper an **action that you were participating in when you relapsed.** Now **think** about what happened **before** the action. For example, you were hanging out with some friends at the park and ended up smoking some marijuana. Before you relapsed, you may have been thinking you were bored, or you were stressed out about something.

Think about your own situation and these questions:

- Did someone say something, or were you going somewhere?
- Write the thought or feeling that led up to the relapse in front of it (left side of paper).
- What led to that thought or feeling? Did something happen? Draw or write that event?

Try to trace back your thoughts and feelings to the initial choice that led to your being in a HR situation. Notice how many things happened before the action of relapse. This is the **erosion of RR.** It doesn't start with the actions but rather the thoughts, feelings, and choices before the action. Create an **Erosion Skit** where a person gradually loses their self-control and returns to drugs or crime. Rerun the skit, and model how the situation can be prevented.

Steps to Relapse/Recidivism

Just like the steps to change, there are *steps* for RR. But unlike the steps to change, the steps to RR are *negative* and move us *backward* rather than forward. We have to keep in mind what we talked about in the last session. RR does not mean committing the act. RR starts with the thought habits that lead to the actions. Take a look at Figure 11: The Relapse/Recidivism Model, which shows the steps to RR described in more detail on page 102.

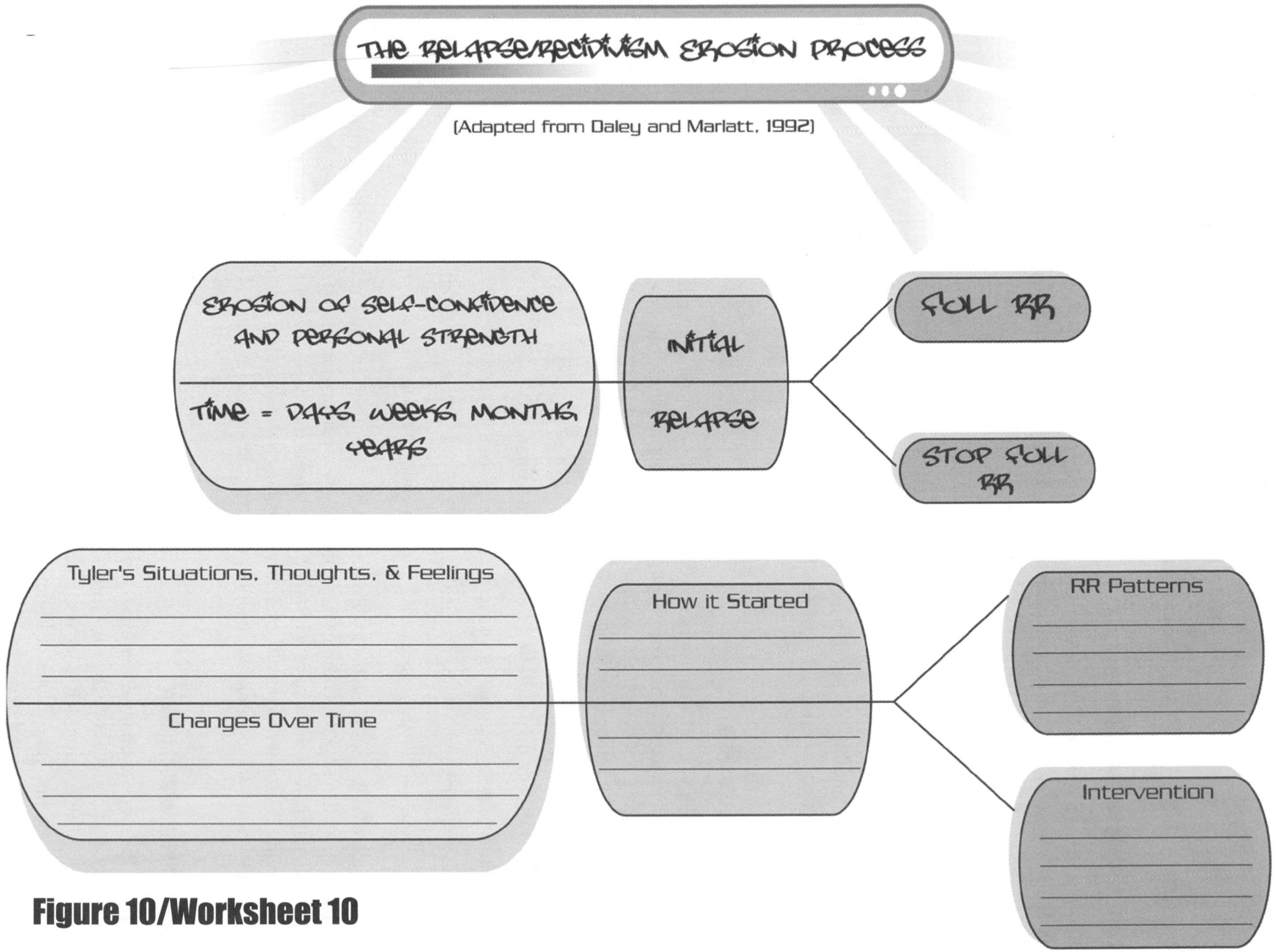

Figure 10/Worksheet 10

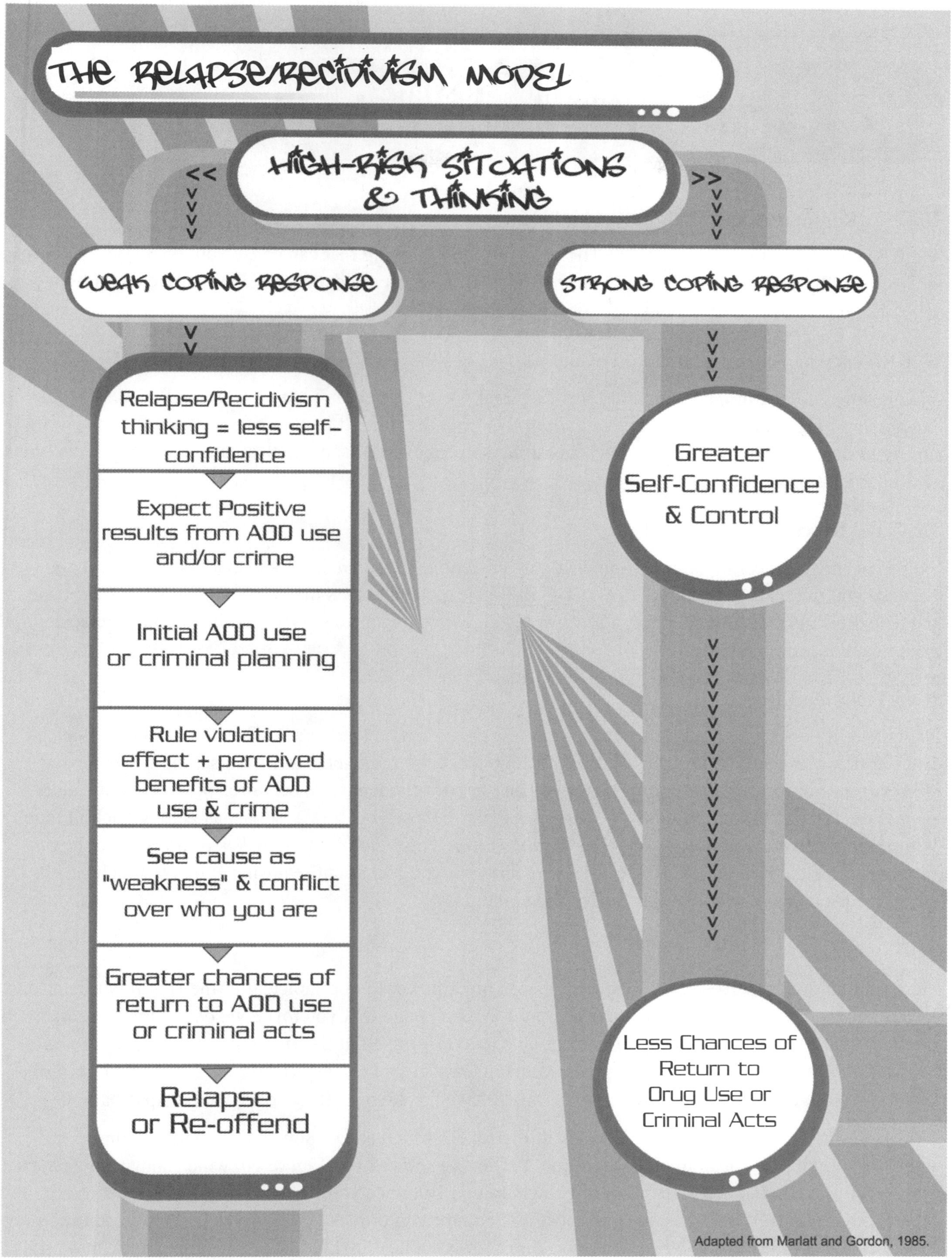
THE RELAPSE/RECIDIVISM MODEL
HIGH-RISK SITUATIONS & THINKING
WEAK COPING RESPONSE
STRONG COPING RESPONSE
Relapse/Recidivism thinking = less self-confidence
Expect Positive results from AOD use and/or crime
Initial AOD use or criminal planning
Rule violation effect + perceived benefits of AOD use & crime
See cause as "weakness" & conflict over who you are
Greater chances of return to AOD use or criminal acts
Relapse or Re-offend
Greater Self-Confidence & Control
Less Chances of Return to Drug Use or Criminal Acts
Adapted from Marlatt and Gordon, 1985.

Figure 11

SESSION 9: LEARNING HOW TO STAY CLEAN AND AVOID TROUBLE

High-Risk Situation and High-Risk Thinking

We talked in the last session about the HR situations and thinking that can cause you to *feel* out of control or weak and by doing that increasing your risk for RR. Keep in mind, though, that you are the only one who has *control* over your actions.

Self-Efficacy or Sense of Personal Power

This is how we cope or deal with stressful situations. This is *based* on your *memories* of success or failure, how *others* judge and influence you, and your *feelings* at the time. It is your *personal sense of power* or ability to manage a given situation, such as asking someone out or staying clean at a party where everyone is drinking or doing drugs.

Expected Outcome

This is what we *expect* to happen from choosing an action. If you *choose* to smoke a joint, it is likely because you *expect* it to make you feel good. But the expected results may be completely *different* than the actual results. When you expect a *positive* result from using a substance, the likelihood of relapsing, or going back to using, goes way up.

Rule Violation Effect

We talked in Session 2 about how our views of ourselves can be *challenged* when we decide to change. But our new views are *good* for us and *help* us to choose the right actions. But in setting our new views, we set *rules* for ourselves so that we don't go back to our old identity. When a relapse occurs, it causes *confusion.* We like to think of ourselves as "clean" or "honest," but a relapse means getting back in touch with our old selves, which was *using* or a *troublemaker.* This *conflict* often makes us go back to the *old view,* which is the rule violation effect. How much *guilt* you feel about relapsing and how much you *blame* yourself will decide the *strength* of the violation.

Self-Blame

How we think of ourselves and our role in relapse gives power to our choice after the first relapse episode. If you believe the relapse is due to your *personal weakness* and that you *lost control,* then you are likely to *continue down* the path of relapse. If you are able to stop yourself at the first relapse episode (i.e., the *initial violation* of the rule you have set for yourself), and if you can see clearly the *internal and external factors* that are related to your fall, then you might have the strength to get off of the relapse path.

Now is probably a good time to take a look at Figure 12, which shows how giving in to seemingly unimportant urges can lead to an RR episode. Earlier we showed you Figure 10, which shows how relapse and recidivism can happen after years of being straight. But once you have an RR episode, it does not mean you are forever lost to using substances and committing crimes. *You have the ability to control* your thoughts and actions, and *you can choose* to move toward a healthy life instead of falling back into using and criminal behavior. We will cover this idea in more depth in future sessions.

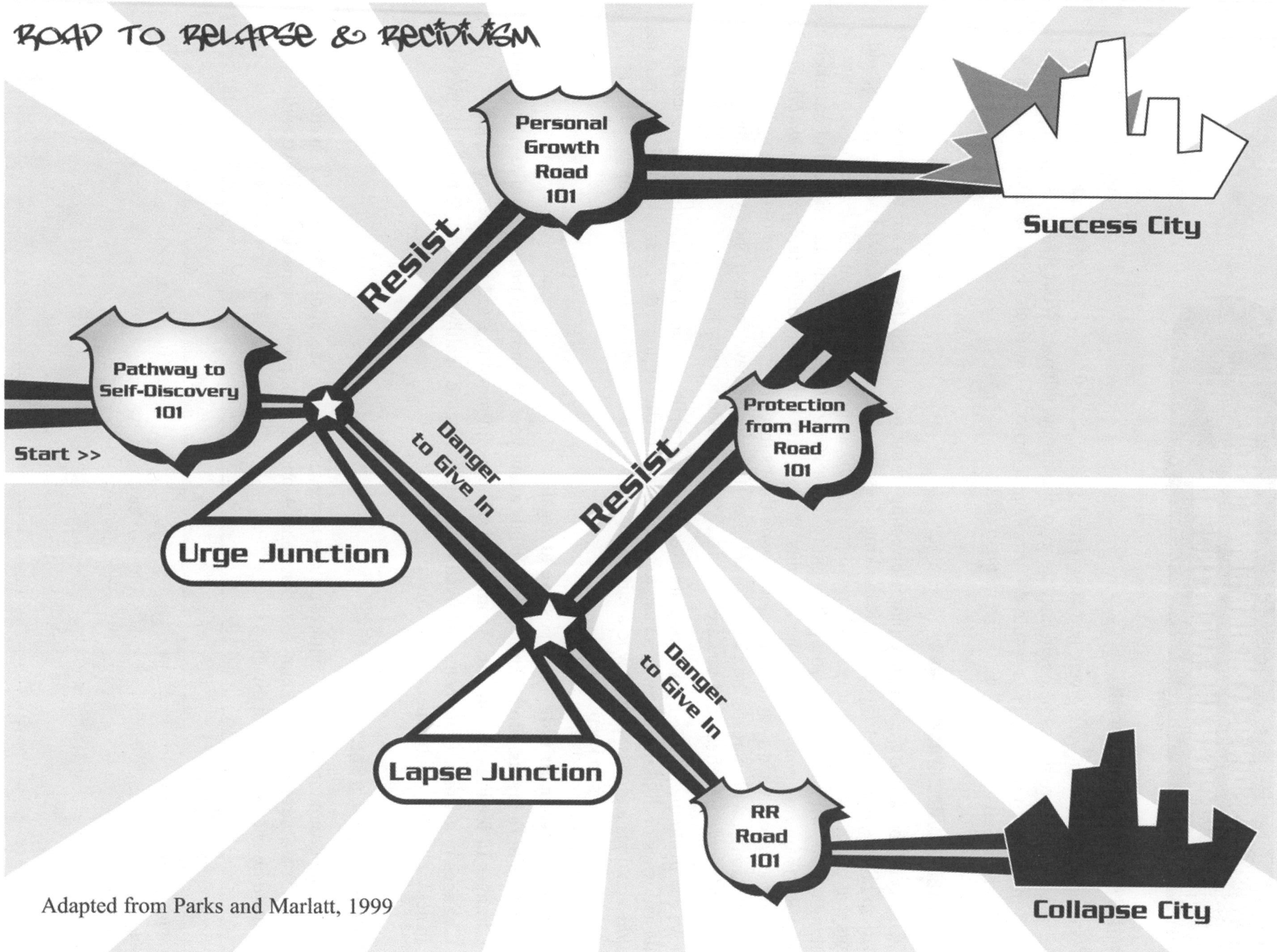

Adapted from Parks and Marlatt, 1999

Figure 12

SESSION 9: LEARNING HOW TO STAY CLEAN AND AVOID TROUBLE

Activity: Tyler and His Erosion

Look at the steps that were given, and then reread Tyler's story. How do any of the steps play into his relapse? Were there things he could have done to prevent his relapse? What was the step that had the most influence in whether Tyler would do drugs again or not? How could Tyler have stayed on the "Pathway to Self-Discovery," as shown in Figure 12?

Clues to Relapse/Recidivism Erosion

We tend to fall back into the *negative* (harm-directing) thinking and beliefs when we find ourselves in HR situations. Stress is a huge trigger for HR thinking. It is not always possible to avoid people, places, and things that might increase our urges and cravings for AOD and crime. When you take *control* of your thinking to *deal* with a situation, you will begin to feel a *sense of power* in your decisions and are likely to avoid RR. If you *lose control* over your thoughts, though, you will likely begin feeling *weak and insecure.* The weakness, combined with thoughts about *good* things that might happen if we took a drug or got some fast money, will increase the chance of relapse. If you don't have control, once you relapse you will feel the *rule violation* effect, and you are very likely to continue to relapse.

But we can *avoid* the relapse by pulling ourselves away from HR situations and HR thinking. There are skills and ways of thinking that we can use to build up the nurturing topsoil of our mind. We take part in *healthy* activities and *trust* people who are healthy, and we are always *aware* of the warnings. Here are some of the warnings to keep in mind.

- **Changes in your attitude.** From positive to negative
- **Changes in thoughts.** From thinking confidently about your decisions to thinking you're out of control
- **Changes in feelings and moods.** From an up and hopeful mood to a sad or depressed mood
- **Changes in actions.** From being involved in activities that are healthy and positive to being involved in activities where substances are involved

Activity: Charting a Change

As a large group, **draw** a table with two sides that everyone can see. Along the left side, **write** out thoughts, attitudes, beliefs, feelings, and actions. Along the top, put the signs for negative and positive on each side of the dividing line.

	–	+
Thoughts: **Attitudes:** **Beliefs:** **Feelings:** **ACTIONS:**		

SESSION 9: LEARNING HOW TO STAY CLEAN AND AVOID TROUBLE

Together **think** of a situation that involves relapse or recidivism. In the **negative column,** write out the harm-directing thoughts, attitudes, beliefs, and feelings in an HR situation. Then write the **action** that is a result of this pattern of thinking and feeling. Now do the same for the **positive column.** Compare the results and how each thought, attitude, belief, and feeling affected the action chosen.

Discuss the different ways you can control your thoughts and feelings in order to prevent a negative outcome (i.e., relapse or recidivism). Now do the same for the other; for example if you did a chart for relapse the first time, now do a chart for recidivism.

Putting It Together

- Tyler's relapse began by hanging out with old friends. Can you trace Tyler's story through the different steps? How might Tyler have changed his relapse in each step?
- What were some of the thoughts that led to Tyler's relapse?
- RR is a process that can happen over a period of years. Do you recognize yourself in any of the stages?
- What are some of the thoughts that can lead you to RR? What are some of the thoughts you can use to prevent RR?

Using the Program Guides and Tools for Change

Use the PCS to indicate your levels of knowledge and skill to prevent AOD relapse or a return to criminal activity.

How much you understand the process of RR erosion										
0	1	2	3	4	5	6	7	8	9	10
Low					Medium					High
The degree to which you now understand the thoughts and actions that could lead you to RR										
0	1	2	3	4	5	6	7	8	9	10
Low					Medium					High
Have learned skills to avoid RR by changing or managing the thoughts, feelings, and actions that trigger your AOD use and CC										
0	1	2	3	4	5	6	7	8	9	10
Low					Medium					High

- With your counselor, review all the sections of your SP that might be important for preventing relapse and reoffending behaviors.
- With your counselor, continue to develop the areas in your PFC that correspond to the factors that you identified in your SP.

TYLER'S STORY

The world is a painful place to be. And I am filled with that pain. When I was younger, I was never the person to stick out much. One look at me and people usually didn't look again, unless they were the type to search out people like me. And I liked that. I liked being a loner for the most part, staying home to write and play my guitar when everyone else was out drinking and being stupid. I didn't get involved much in the drama and shallowness of high school. I always considered it a waste of time.

That's not to say I didn't have friends. I had a few—just enough to be a normal kid, I suppose. I got along with everybody, and most people got along with me. I just didn't enter myself in any popularity contests, which was definitely different than my parents. But they had their agenda, and I had mine.

So one of the few nights I went out, a couple of friends and I were at some older guy's house partying. While most people were drinking, I was sticking to smoking the occasional bowl that got passed my way. I'm not much of a drinker. My ex-girlfriend was there and creating a lot of drama that I didn't want to be part of. Life is depressing enough as it is, so I was just about to leave when my friend suggested we go in the back room and smoke a joint before I left. The guy who lived in the house came with us. After all, you should share with the host, and while we were puffing it up, he offered us some powder. Although I didn't know what it was, and I wasn't much of a user, I took a bump. I always thought you only live once so you might as well experience it all. Later I learned it was heroin, but by then I thought I had seen a little bit of heaven.

By the time that hit kicked in, I was swimming through the clouds of apathy. I didn't feel a thing, and I was better for it. I still left the party—that didn't change—but as I floated through the crowds and brushed past my ex, I was in a state of nirvana. I'm not sure how or when I got home, but I barely waved to my parents on my way down to my bedroom, closed the door, put on some music with a heavy bass beat, and was lost…until the next morning.

That was when I found out just how much pain there can be in one human body, mind, and soul. But that didn't stop me the next time, though, or the next. The high was just too perfect to even think about the low. Next thing I knew I was freebasing just to get a high. Of course, that was when my parents took me to rehab. It was a full 3 months in an inpatient treatment program, learning how to change my thoughts and actions. And it worked.

I went back to school, although a different one this time. Everyone decided I should make different friends to help keep me sober. I was deep into my guitar and had started making plans to go to school for music theory. Life was getting back to how it was, and I was once again a clean guy who had dreams and goals—for a while. About 6 months later, I ran into one of my old friends. She asked me if I was okay, and we started talking about the old days. We hung out the rest of the afternoon, and I didn't think anything of it because she was not a friend who was involved in my using. We decided to hang out again, but the next time her boyfriend, who was there the first night, was there. I thought there was nothing to worry about. After all, I was strong and clean by now. But a couple of weeks later, I ran into him again, and he asked me to come to this party with him. Not to worry, I thought, he would never do anything to put me at risk.

Except that he did. And I fell. It was at the same guy's house as before and almost the same situation as before. Stoned out of my mind, I took a bump. I thought that I was strong enough to control it this time.

But I wasn't. The next morning, as I was going through withdrawal, I was confused and angry. I was no longer clean and sober for almost a year. I would not be clean for a couple of days. And I had enjoyed it. I wasn't sure who I was or what was going on anymore.

So the next time I did it again. I figured, hey, I don't have those months of sobriety anymore, so what would one hit do? One hit turned into another and another. And each time was an excuse to do it one more time. And one more time meant that I would do it one more time and then quit. But the quitting never came.

And now I sit here in the dark, plucking at strings that should have been changed months ago, never seeing the sun or my parents except to go out and buy more. And I will buy more, just to avoid the pain of living and the pain of my body letting go.

Chapter Five:

Making a Commitment to Change

GOALS OF THIS CHAPTER

- Understand what it takes to move from Phase I to Phase II.
- Utilize the program Tools (CB Map, STEP Method, Relaxation Skills, Mental Self-Control Skills) and Program Guides (Telling My Story [TS], Master Skills List [MSL], Self-Portrait [SP], Plan for Change [PFC], Stages of Change Scales [SOC], Thinking and Action Pattern Charting [TAP]).
- Think about how far along we are in the change process.
- Describe our targets for change.
- What do we want from here on?

MIKE'S STORY

I've thought about changing. I really have. I started drinking when I was young, I can't even remember when. I never really thought my drinking was a problem, or something that needed to be changed. But then one night, I was at a party with some friends. We had all ditched school to start drinking early, and by 9 o'clock we were all hammered.
I had never felt sicker than I had the next morning. As I was sitting in the bathroom, puking my guts out, I started wondering what had happened, how I had gotten home, where the hell my car was and why my fist was all bruised and bloody.
I called the friend who I thought had gotten me home. I guess I had gotten a little too wild at the party, making a fool of myself, and as I was walking past the garage of the house, I guess I punched it. A cop had stopped us and I had a court date for MUI and public intoxication.
M.U.I.
Court date: February 15
But I didn't think anything of it. So I kept drinking. And it kept happening. Almost every weekend was a blur or some non-existent action of my body.
My girlfriend broke up with me. She said she couldn't be with a guy who drank so much and made an ass out of himself and her. My friends avoided me.
I didn't want to drink anymore. My mom was actually kind of helpful. It was really cool to think that other people were willing to share and help me if I asked.
So I think I want to stop drinking. In fact, I know I want to stop drinking. Besides, pretty soon, they're going to put me on probation, then I'll have to take tests every couple of days. I don't get the warm and numb feelings anymore, and it's just not fun.

Ikera's Story

SESSION 10: DEVELOPING YOUR PLAN FOR CHANGE

Objectives

- Review Chapter 4: Backsliding to Drugs and Crime.
- Discuss the stages of change (SOC).
- Discuss which stages of change you are in.
- Explore tools for changing your thoughts and actions: CB Map, STEP Method, Relaxation Skills, Mental Self-Control Skills.
- Develop your Self-Portrait (SP) and Plan for Change (PFC).

Mike's Story: *I think I want to change. In fact, I know I want to change. Drinking just isn't fun anymore. I drink all day long—even at school because I bring in a pint and sip on it between classes and during lunch. My girlfriend broke up with me. I guess during my blackout periods I make a real ass out of her and myself. My friends don't like drinking with me anymore. I think they are embarrassed to be around me when I drink.*

When it got really bad I decided to sit and think about what I get from alcohol and why I drink so much. I don't know why, but the urge to drink until I can't drink anymore is really strong. My mom has been a lot of help, though. I guess she used to drink a lot, and now she's cut way back. I even asked my ex and my friends about what I do when I drink and how it makes them feel. I never realized there were so many people who were willing to help me.

Ikera's Story: *I want to stop using—really I do—but it's scary. Using is what has kept me sane over the past few years—kept me in some control of my feelings and my memories. Using is also what has dragged me to the edge of insanity and has caused so much shame. A month ago, I think I hit my bottom. I don't know how long it had been since my last shower. I was starting to get desperate and ready to sell myself to anyone who would have me when this lady sat down and just started talking to me. I followed her right to the teen rescue center.*

Some days, I really hate sobriety. I want to give up a lot. Sometimes the pain and the memories are just too much to bear, and I think about using. But at the end of the day, I feel so proud that I didn't give in—that I was able to be strong and deal with all this shit without checking out.

Relapse and Recidivism: Staying Clean

Last session we spent some time talking about the triggers for relapse and recidivism (RR). To review, a relapse is when we participate in the thinking and actions that lead to substance reuse. Recidivism is the thoughts and actions that lead to returning to criminal conduct (CC). Remember, just the thought itself is considered part of the process of RR.

We talked about how triggers, usually high-risk (HR) situations and HR thinking, can result in urges and cravings to participate in destructive patterns of behavior. These triggers can be anything from conflict and stress—or even good feelings (like wanting to celebrate)—to being around old friends and old situations where we used to participate in the action we are now trying to avoid. Although it may not always be possible to stay away from HR situations, we do have control over our thoughts, and that in itself can help prevent RR.

Activity: Taking Charge of Cravings and Urges

Break into groups of two or three and discuss possible RR situations that you have faced in the past month. Take some time to discuss what happened and how it may have been different depending on your thoughts. For example, someone may have offered you a drug or suggested doing a crime. The craving was to get high, to get money, to get even . . . or whatever, but your thought was "I am already in trouble—been there, done that—and I really want my freedom." Because you have power over your thoughts, you resisted the drug or criminal activity and controlled yourself through the craving and urge.

With your partner/group, develop a skit with the RR situation that you think shows the process the best. After performing the skit, discuss in the large group about what was done right in the situation and what may have been done differently to have a better outcome.

Recognizing Your Stage of Change

In Session 1, we discussed the three phases of this program: Phase I: What? Challenge to Change: Deciding What to Change; Phase II: How? Commitment to Change: Using the Tools for Change; and Phase III: Now! Ownership of Change: Calling the Shots. Each of which is related to the stages that people experience when deciding to change a negative habit or destructive pattern of behavior. Now it's time to look at where you are in the process of changing important areas of your life.

We will complete SOC (Program Guide 5) to clarify where we stand now on changing alcohol and other drug (AOD) abuse and criminal activities. Remember, you can be at different SOC for different problem areas. For example, you may be 100% ready to stop criminal activity but not at all ready to quit smoking cigarettes. Let's review the SOC.

Phase I: What? Challenge to Change: Deciding What to Change

This is the phase where we start thinking about change and looking at ourselves to see where and what changes need to be made. In this phase, you are open to getting information about yourself and your problems. The early phase of this stage is about building self-awareness, while the latter part is about taking greater risks in talking about yourself and your problems to others. You have met this challenge when you commit to continued treatment with the desire to learn how to be free of substance use and crime. The basic ideas are thinking, self-awareness, sharing about you, and being willing to commit yourself to further help.

SESSION 10: DEVELOPING YOUR PLAN FOR CHANGE

Phase II: How? Commitment to Change: Using the Tools for Change

You have made the commitment to work on improving the quality of your life and are now open to talking about your problems and what changes need to be made. You are now making a genuine effort to change your thoughts, attitudes, and beliefs, and you have been able to go a while without using drugs or getting into trouble. You are now involved in learning and using the skills of thinking and acting to keep yourself away from using substances and participating in criminal activities. It is in this stage when you begin to assert your control and freedom over the thoughts and actions that lead to problems. You actively practice skills for control over negative thoughts and feelings, getting along well with others, and being a responsible member of your community.

Phase III: Now! Ownership of Change: Calling the Shots

When you reach this stage, you are now making changes because you want to and not because "they" (the system, parents, or others) want you to. You feel strongly about your distance from substances and criminal behavior, and you have replaced your negative thinking with positive alternatives. The skills to control your thinking have become an important part of your everyday life. You can recognize when you are on the road to relapse or reoffending, but are able to stop the RR progression at the thinking part. You are here because you want to be.

Activity: Mike's and Ikera's Desire to Change

When looking at Mike's story, do you think he wants to change? Why? Is he ready for change? Do you think Mike will be successful in his effort to quit drinking? What stage of change is Mike currently in? What are some of the specific signs that Mike is ready to change his pattern of drinking? What things can Mike do that will help him to move forward in his effort to change?

What about Ikera? Is she at the same stage of readiness to change as Mike? What are some of the signs that Ikera is ready to change? Are there any indications that she is not quite ready? What are some of the things that Ikera might do to become more committed to the change process?

Our Desire to Change

You are now at the point where you are likely to have made a very positive decision—to continue on the road to change. You have learned and worked hard and are now ready to become committed to the action phase of treatment: Phase II: How? Commitment to Change: Using the Tools for Change.

How do you know if you are ready for change? That is a big question that we all ask ourselves, and we are the only ones who really know the answers. Some of us may still be here mostly because we have to be. That is fine; just be honest about how you feel concerning change. Here are a few signs that may show you that you are ready for change:

- You are open to people telling you (giving you feedback) about your drug use and criminal behaviors.
- You see that you have problems in your behavior and substance use.
- You talk about what you want to change and often hear yourself say that you can change.

Change *does not happen all at once* nor does it happen easily. There will be times that you will feel that it's not worth it, or it's just too hard to change. But that is what you will be learning in Phase II, the skills to deal with everyday situations so that you aren't stressed or worried about what is going to happen and have confidence in dealing with your HR triggers in positive and healthy ways. Of course, the first step in targeting and learning how to change is to focus on your thinking.

Activity: Where Am I in the Change Process?

Complete the SOC (Program Guide 5) to get some ideas on where you stand in the change process for AOD abuse and criminal activities. You will have other opportunities to complete this Program Guide during your treatment. Rate yourself on each statement as honestly as you can, knowing that you may change your ratings at a later time.

A very important indication of your readiness to change is making progress on the SP (Program Guide 3) and the PFC (Program Guide 4), which we will work on during this session. If some group members are farther along in Phase I, they may share elements of their SP and PFC to newer group members, giving their ideas about how to think creatively and positively about the process of making changes in your life.

Activity: Looking at Yourself and Planning for Change

- Turn to TS (Program Guide 1). Following your counselor's direction, begin filling out selected sections on your own.
- Next turn to the MSL (Program Guide 2) and update your ratings on the various skills that you have studied so far.
- Work on your SP (Program Guide 3) and PFC (Program Guide 4) together with your counselor.
- The PFC will take some time and careful consideration, as it will involve specific problems, needed changes in thoughts and actions, and specific treatment activities that will be helpful to you in changing the problem. Try to be complete, and identify as many problems as you can for each main area. Your counselor will give you examples on how to complete the PFC, which will set important guidelines for the next phases of your treatment. You will modify your PFC as you discover more information about yourself. Your PFC will help you set goals and change targets for Phases II and III of your program. You will continue working on your PFC in other group sessions and during individual meetings with your counselor.

SESSION 10: DEVELOPING YOUR PLAN FOR CHANGE

Before graduating from Phase I, you and your counselor will have a meeting to finalize your SP and PFC. During your last Phase I session, you will share this information with the group. When you accomplish this, it means that you have successfully completed Phase I: What? Challenge to Change: Deciding What to Change. You have taken on the challenge of identifying what areas of your life are specific targets for change and how you will work on self-improvement for the remainder of this program.

You are soon ready to begin Phase II: How? Commitment to Change: Using the Tools for Change. Congratulations!

Ways to Change

The first steps in the process of change are completed by becoming aware of **what** we would like to change and the **thinking and action habits** that cause our problems. Now it's time to seriously begin to learn how to use the tools for changing the thoughts that lead us into problematic feelings and actions. These will become your target thoughts and target actions. These are thoughts and actions that you recognize as causing problems in your behavior and ones that you have decided that you want to change. Below are the five basic steps for changing target thoughts and behaviors.

1. **Pick the thoughts** that lead to feelings and behaviors that are problematic.
2. **Describe attitudes and beliefs** behind the thought.
3. **Set goals** on how you would like to think or act. To set a goal, we have to stop and think what we want the new behavior to be. You may feel uncomfortable about changing, and that's okay, but once you have set a goal, live up to it.
4. **Pick one or more action methods** you will use to change the thought or behavior. We will cover these next.
5. **Change the target behavior.** If you really want to change, you will.

Action Methods for Changing Negative Thoughts and Behaviors

When we talk to ourselves, we are really teaching ourselves new ways to do things. Here are four ways to teach ourselves to change:

1. **Thought stopping:** If we have an automatic thought—for example, "I don't trust him"—then we are able to stop this thought by thinking, "I can be open to hear what he or she is trying to say. I am not going to think this way." We may still not completely trust the other person, but we have interrupted our thoughts and made ourselves think something different.
2. **Their position:** By taking responsibility for our actions and then placing ourselves in the other person's position, we can develop respect for the other person and a sense of control over our lives.

3. **Positive thought:** When you begin thinking negatively, replace the thought with something positive. Instead of thinking, "I need that jacket," think instead, "I'm ready to graduate this phase of my treatment." If you train yourself to think positively, then your behavior begins to reflect that.
4. **Arguing with yourself:** Every time you have a thought that you know will lead you into trouble, argue with yourself. By saying "That's stupid" or "That's not true," you can stop yourself from thinking and then acting on negative thoughts by showing yourself how the negative thought actually doesn't make sense. For example, the thought "I would like to get high and feel great" can be countered by "Taking this drug will only make me feel worse in the long run."

The list of mental self-control and change skills, shown in Table 2, can be used throughout the program and in real-life situations to gain control over how you think about potentially risky or harmful situations.

Table 2 Mental Self-Control and Change Skills

Name of Skill	*Description of Skill*
Thought stopping	Stopping thoughts by shouting "stop" or visualizing a stop sign or slamming on brakes.
Accepting	Accepting the thoughts and not changing them. "It's okay to think this way sometimes."
Shifting the view	Changing how you think about someone: "She's bossy" to "She's just trying to help me."
Thinking "their position"	Saying the other person's view to yourself: "They're saying. . . ."
Thinking "taking responsibility"	Thinking "What part of this is my fault, my responsibility?"
Planting a positive thought	Replacing negative with positive thought: "It's not working" to "It will work out just fine."
Having a thought reward	Rewarding thinking that leads to good outcomes: "I'm proud I did that—good thinking."
Exaggerating or overstating the thought	Changing your thoughts of worrying about the job: "I'm going to worry myself sick for 50 hours."
Conditioning: making thoughts weaker	Thinking about doing a crime: Imagine being put in a jail cell and "hearing" the door slamming.
Conditioning: making thoughts stronger	Thinking about positive outcomes when deciding not to use drugs.
Going to court with your thoughts	Thinking "I want to steal." Get evidence that it doesn't make sense, then make a verdict.
Coping statements that affirm "I can handle it"	Repeating statements that increase self-mastery and confidence: "I've solved bigger problems."
Using relaxation skills	Using muscle relaxation; imagining calm scenes, having mental–physical focus, using deep breathing.
Using thought replacement	Replacing angry thoughts with positive thoughts.

SESSION 10: DEVELOPING YOUR PLAN FOR CHANGE

Activity: Changing Together

Your counselor will hang some paper on a wall where everyone can see it. Then, as a group, think of one thinking error from Worksheet 3: Managing Harm-Directing Thoughts that is common to the group. Using the example here as a model, write down the thought on the paper, and underline the common pattern of problem thinking. Underneath the thought, separate the paper in thirds, and on one side, write down the attitudes and beliefs that are behind the thought or behavior that is going to be changed. On the other side of the paper, write down a couple of goals and things that you would like to happen or what you would like to think. Then in the middle third, write down a thinking or action method. Select the mental self-control skills from Table 2 that would be helpful in changing the thought or behavior.

- Each person in the group will select *two* of their own negative thinking patterns from Worksheet 3: Managing Harm-Directing Thoughts.
- Use the mental self-control skills in Table 2 to develop alternatives to the problem-generating thoughts.

HARM-DIRECTING THOUGHT *"I want what I want right now."*		
Attitudes and Beliefs	**Methods of Change**	**Goals**
"I'm entitled to take things that aren't mine because I've been abused." "So what, they deserve it. They would do the same thing to me." "Gotta have respect, no matter what."	Their position, arguing with yourself Taking responsibility Thought stopping	Freedom: "I am trustworthy" Being fair; not hurting others Avoiding harm; staying alive

Visualizing Change

1. The STEP Method for Self-Management

Figure 13 provides the framework for the STEP Method. This serves as the first line of defense in any "hot" situation. It is used when there is *little time* to consider the underlying beliefs, rules, attitudes, and values that activate unhealthy automatic thoughts and actions, as defined in the CB Map for Learning and Change.

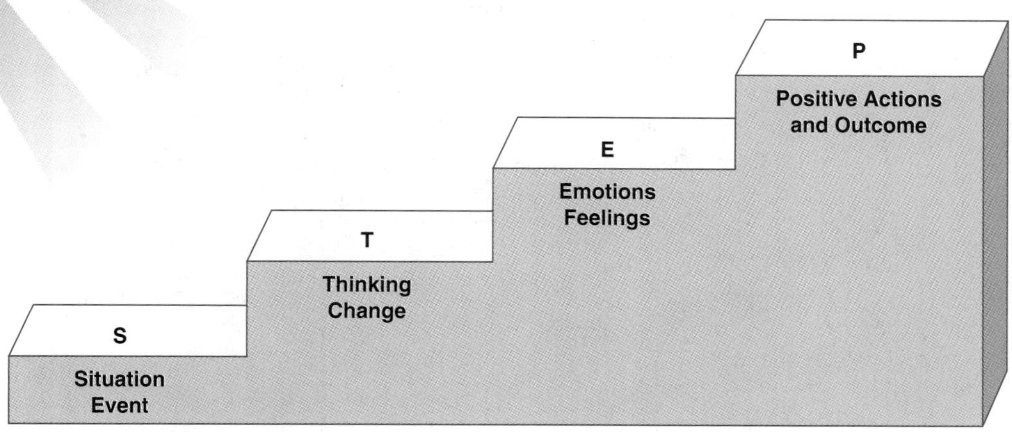

Figure 13 The Step Method

We use STEP when working on changes to bring about positive actions and outcomes in "hot" situations. For example, let's focus on a situation (S) that leads to negative thinking (T).

An example might be getting out of a residential placement and meeting old friends who are quick to offer an opportunity to use a drug or to commit an "easy" crime. We need to think quickly. How can we change our automatic, knee-jerk thoughts of "I won't get caught" or "Yeah, do it!" to more responsible and protective thoughts? How can we have thoughts and beliefs that lead to positive emotions (E) and positive actions or behaviors leading to positive outcomes (P)?

In the CB Map, the action or behavior could be positive (leading to a good outcome) or negative (leading to bad outcomes). Now we want our thoughts and actions to work swiftly and effectively. We want the outcome to be *positive*: prosocial behavior, drug-free living, and positive relationships with others and our community.

2. Pathways of Learning and Change (CB Map)

First introduced in Session 2: The Power of Thought, the CB Map (as shown in the following figure) represents the basic change model in the *Pathways to Self-Discovery and Change (PSDC)* program. The key to positive growth and change is understanding how our past reactions (thoughts, feelings, and actions) to HR situations have sometimes resulted in serious problems. Essential to the change process is an openness to recognizing, modifying, and better managing the underlying beliefs, attitudes, and value structures that support harm-directing (irrational or unhealthy) patterns of thoughts, feelings, and actions.

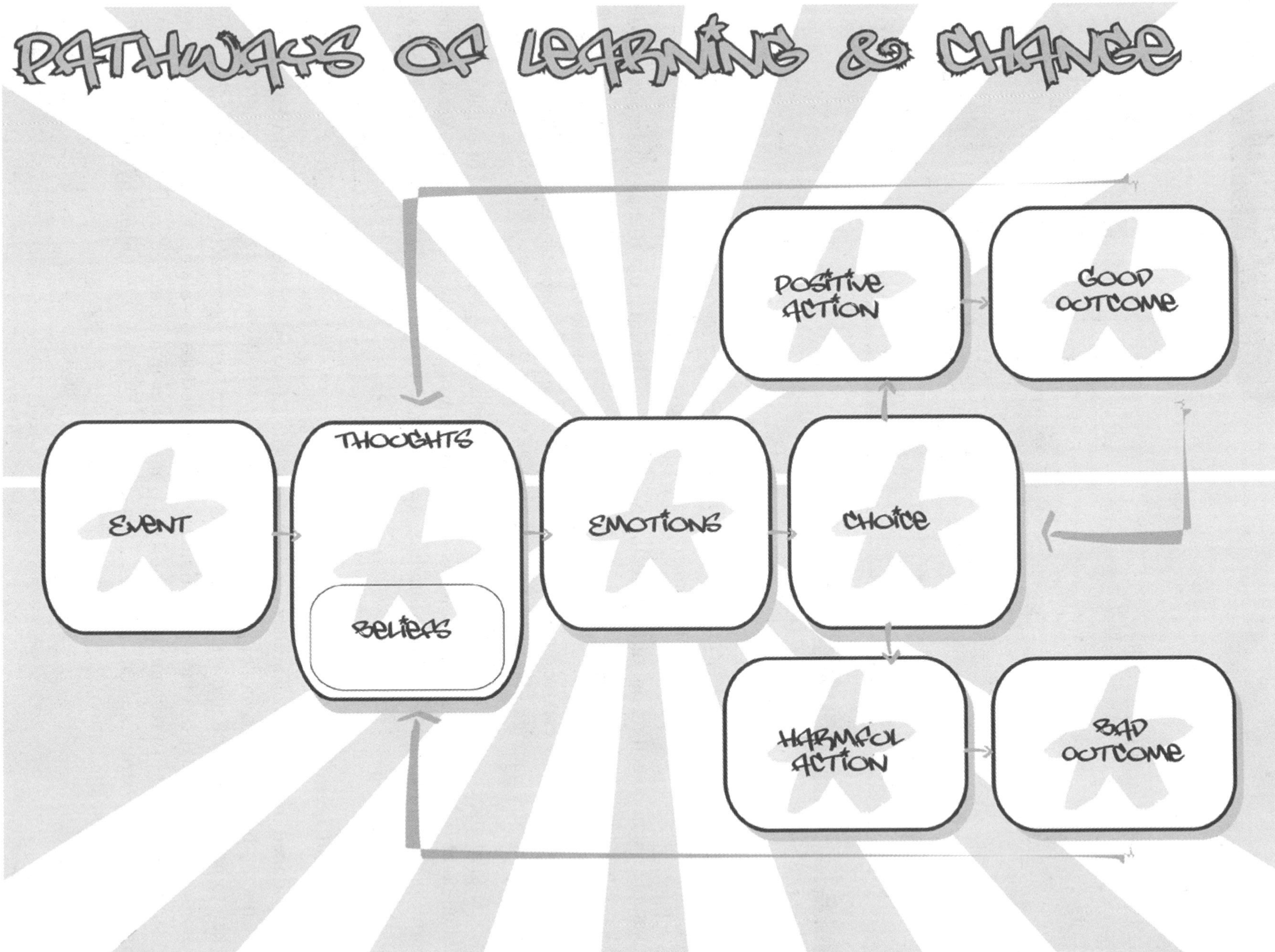
PATHWAYS OF LEARNING & CHANGE
EVENT
THOUGHTS
BELIEFS
EMOTIONS
CHOICE
POSITIVE ACTION
GOOD OUTCOME
HARMFUL ACTION
BAD OUTCOME

Figure 1

Activity: When to Look Back and When to "Step Up"

Your counselor will lead a review discussion of two tools (STEP Method and CB Map) for developing positive responses to trigger situations. You will practice and rehearse these techniques to improve self-control over thoughts, feelings, and actions. Table 2, which presents a list of mental self-control skills, may serve as a cheat sheet to use when called upon to discuss how you will manage HR situations and the automatic thoughts.

Using Relaxation Skills to Cope With Difficult Situations

Another critical set of tools for managing HR situations is the broad array of relaxation skills shown in Table 3.

Table 3 Relaxation Skills

Skill Name	*Description and Approach*
Calm Scene Relaxation	Close your eyes, and imagine walking on the beach, watching the sunset, and laying by a stream in the mountains.
Body Relaxation	Eyes closed, focus on parts of your body and tell them to relax; my arms are heavy, my hands are warm, I am relaxed. Go through all your body parts. Practice relaxing thoughts: "I feel relaxed. I am calm. I am feeling soothed. I feel quiet."
Calm Breathing	Close your eyes and focus on your breathing. Breathe slow and steady, in and out for 5 minutes. Breathe into your stomach, making your stomach rise and fall. Let the air out completely. As you breathe, imagine your heart breathing in and out, taking in oxygen and breathing out stress. As you let out the air, feel yourself sink into the chair.
Deep Breathing	From normal breathing, make each breath deeper until you breathe deep five times, Breathe in through your nose and out through your mouth, puckering your lips and blowing out slowly. After five deep breaths, go back to normal breathing. **Do no more than five deep breaths at a time.**
Muscle Relaxation	Close your eyes, put your hands on the chair arms, and breathe normal and steady. Take about 10 minutes for this exercise. Tighten each muscle group for a few seconds, and then gradually let the muscles relax slowly. Do each two times. First, squeeze your eyes closed and then relax the eye muscles. Then, squeeze your hands on the chair arms, and gradually let the muscles relax. Squeeze your arm muscles, and let them go gradually. Don't squeeze real hard, but tighten them up and then relax them. Go through all of your muscles, your shoulders, your stomach, your thighs, legs, and toes. Squeeze gently but tightly. At the end of this exercise, with your eyes closed, think of a calm scene. Take your time.
Stretching Relaxation	Stretching lets the tension go out of the muscles and hooks the parts of our body together. **If you have a medical condition, check with your doctor first before doing stretching exercises.** Lay on you back, and pull one knee to your chest, stretch the leg back, and do the same with the other knee. Pull both the knees to your chest. Do these several times. Do several situps, but do them easy and slow. Feel the muscles stretch. Lay on your stomach, and push your upper body up by your hands and arms. Do it gently. Lay on your side, pull your leg to your chest, then straighten it out and swing it slowly back. Feel the back muscles stretch. Always be gentle and slow. Do this on the other side. Now, come up with other stretching exercises. Get a book on stretching.

SESSION 10: DEVELOPING YOUR PLAN FOR CHANGE

Skill Name	*Description and Approach*
Active relaxation	Walk 15 minutes a day. Swing your arms for a while. Put your hands behind your back, and walk for a while reflecting on how good you feel. Do as much lifestyle walking each day as you can. Get a set of Shouxing balls or a soft ball, and do hand exercises each day. Work out a couple times a week by playing a sport or going to the gym.
Grounding	Grounding focuses on the outside world and on the now, not the past or future. Describe what is around you: sight, sounds, colors, temperature, objects. Say or read out loud a saying, such as the Serenity Prayer. Think of something funny. Examples: The chair is wood, the kids are playing in the yard, the wall is green, there is one window, the sky is blue, the breeze is cool. This will help you focus away from your stress.

Sharing Our Story

Change is promoted by sharing our story (self-disclosure) and listening to feedback.

Now that we have reviewed the SOC, decided we want to change, and began to cover general ways that we can change behavior and thought, let's take a look at how being in this group helps us to grow and change.

We have discussed how talking about our thoughts and feelings and the feedback we get from others are important parts of learning about ourselves, while they also help us to build trust, friendship, and support. Yet there are many parts of our lives that we have still not shared. The part of our lives that we know about but that others don't is called our *hidden area*. The part that others see but we don't is called our *blind area*. The part that we don't know about ourselves and others don't know either is called the *unknown area*. Finally, there are things that we see and know and that others also see and know; this is called our *free* or *open area*.

The Johari Window, as shown in Figure 14, gives us a picture of what these areas look like. It is our goal to make the *free area* larger and shrink the *blind, hidden,* and *unknown areas.*

Activity: Learning About Myself and Sharing With Others

Create a Johari Window using four poster-size pieces of paper. As a group, write in some of the things that you have shared with each other in the *free area*. In the *hidden area*, think of some general things that people tend to hide from other people, and in the *blind area,* write some general things that only other people may see. Then as a group, think of ways to be able to move the things from the *hidden* and *blind areas* to the *free area* of the window.

On a separate piece of paper, create your personal Johari Window. Are the methods you are using realistic for your life? Are there certain things that you have hidden in the past that you would like to be in your *free area?* How are you becoming more aware of elements in the *blind area?* Are the methods you are using realistic for your life? What about parts of your mind that nobody is aware of in the *unknown area*?

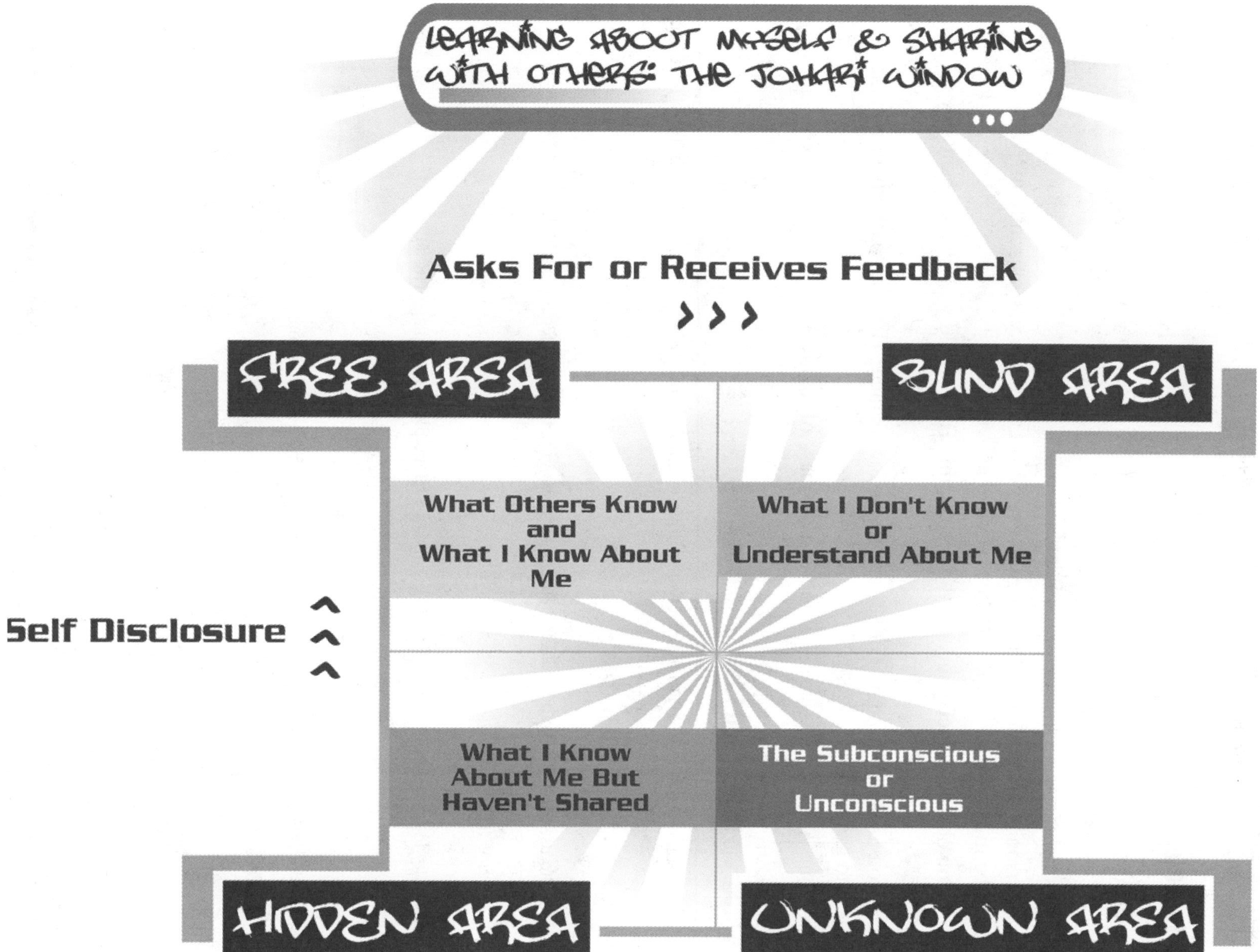

Figure 14 The Johari Window

SESSION 10: DEVELOPING YOUR PLAN FOR CHANGE

Putting It Together

- Mike wanted to change, but at first he wasn't sure. What SOC do you think Mike is in? Do you think he is ready to change?
- Where do you think Ikera is according to the SOC?
- The only person who can decide to change is you. What SOC are you currently in? Which stage would you like to be in? For AOD problems? For criminal activities?
- How have you changed since you started the program? How would you like to change by the time you are done?
- How have you used the Program Guides and Tools for Change? How has participation in the group helped you to grow and change?
- What are your views about entering into the next phase of treatment?

Using the Program Guides and Tools for Change

Use the Pathways Change Scale (PCS) to indicate your ability to utilize the *PSDC* Program Guides and Tools for Change.

0	1	2	3	4	5	6	7	8	9	10
Low					Medium					High

Rate your ability to use the CB Map and STEP methods for managing thoughts, feelings, and actions.

0	1	2	3	4	5	6	7	8	9	10
Low					Medium					High

Indicate your ability to use Table 2: Mental Self-Control and Change Skills to manage HR situations.

0	1	2	3	4	5	6	7	8	9	10
Low					Medium					High

Rate your ability to use Table 3: Relaxation Skills to remain calm in "hot" situations.

0	1	2	3	4	5	6	7	8	9	10
Low					Medium					High

Rate your progress in expanding the *free area* of your Johari Window. Indicate your ability to use the CB Map for managing thoughts, feelings, and actions.

0	1	2	3	4	5	6	7	8	9	10
Low					Medium					High

With your counselor, continue to work on your SP and PFC.

MIKE'S STORY

I've thought about changing. I really have. But sometimes it is so hard to think about changing when all I want to do is have fun.

I started drinking when I was young. I can't even remember when. I'm sure I was drinking even before my first memory of drinking, but like I said, I can't remember. So everything was fine for me, I guess. I never really thought my drinking was a problem or something that needed to be changed. I liked how it made me feel, ya know? All warm and numb without a care in the world.

I still didn't think much about it when I started taking pints to school. I would steal them from my mom's liquor cabinet or get my friend's cousin to get it for me. I kept it in my pocket, and since I preferred schnapps, I didn't really have to worry about the smell ratting me out.

But then one night I was at a party with some friends. We all had ditched school to start drinking early, and by 9 o'clock, we were all hammered. All I remember was going to this one girl's house and getting myself a beer from the tap. The next thing I knew, I was stumbling along the sidewalk with one of my friends trying to hold me up. I sat down on the curb, and then all of a sudden I was home. I had never felt sicker than I had the next morning. As I was sitting in the bathroom, puking my guts out, I started wondering what had happened, how I had gotten home, where the hell my car was, and why my fist was all bruised and bloody. That was just the beginning of my nightmare.

When I called the friend who I thought had gotten me home, I didn't like what he had to tell me. My car was fine, I guess. Someone had driven it to my house while I was stumbling home, and it should be out on the curb. But I guess I had gotten a little too wild at the party, throwing things around and making a fool of myself. It took all my friends to drag me out of the party, which I insisted on not leaving because I wasn't done drinking, and as I was walking past the garage of the house, I guess I punched it with all my strength. The mystery of the bloody knuckles was solved.

Of course I couldn't remember any of this. But when he told me that a cop had stopped us and that I had a court date for a MUI and public intoxication, I thought he was just messing with me. I thought I would have remembered something like that—until I reached into my pocket and pulled out a ticket. What a freaking night.

But I didn't think anything of it. I thought maybe I had some bad alcohol or it was because I hadn't eaten anything or something. So I kept drinking. And it kept happening. I needed to drink more in order to feel buzzed, yet I was still blacking out. Almost every weekend was a blur or some nonexistent action of my body with my mind gone.

My girlfriend broke up with me. She said she couldn't be with a guy who drank so much and made an ass out of himself and her. My friends started avoiding me. I would ask them if they wanted to do something, and they would ask if I was going to drink. I usually said yes, and they usually said no. And the truth was I didn't want to drink anymore. I couldn't remember if I had any fun, or if I met some cool people, or really anything.

I started talking to my friends and my ex about the things I did when I was drinking, just to get an idea of how I looked to other people. Then I spent a lot of time in my room, by myself, thinking about why I liked drinking so much and why I felt the need to drink to the point of blacking out. My mom was actually kind of helpful. I guess she used to drink a lot. That's probably where I got my first drink, but she had cut way back. It was really cool to think that other people were willing to share and help me if I asked.

So I think I want to stop drinking. In fact, I know I want to stop drinking. Besides, pretty soon here they're going to put me on probation, and then I'll have to take tests every couple of days, and then I won't be able to drink. It's time anyway. I don't get the warm and numb feelings anymore, and it's just not fun. I don't even know why I started drinking in the first place, even if I could remember my first drink.

IKERA'S STORY

I want to stop using—really I do—but it's scary. Using is what has kept me sane over the past few years, kept me in some control of my feelings and my memories. Using is also what has dragged me to the edge of insanity and has caused so much shame.

Mom says I was always an angry kid—a temper like my dad's. I don't really know when it started, but it's always been there and I've been getting in trouble for it my whole life. When I'm high, though, I'm suddenly mellow. My anger disappears, and I'm like not bothered by anything. The downside of being mellow is that I also stop caring about the things I should care about—mostly myself.

A month ago, I think I hit my bottom. I don't know how long it had been since my last shower—to think of how I must have smelled and looked at that point. On top of the stench, I hadn't had a fix for a day and was shaking bad. I must've looked totally schizo sitting on that corner with my sign and empty coffee can. I sat there for what seemed like all day but never pulled in enough donations to get my fix. I was starting to get desperate and ready to sell myself to anyone who would have me when this lady sat down and just started talking to me. Honestly, I don't remember much of what she had to say to me in that first meeting, but she must have said something good because I followed her right to the teen rescue center—just across the street from my chosen corner.

I don't know how long I was there before my memory began to kick in, but as soon as I realized where I was my anger came back full swing. That same woman sat my angry butt in a chair and began talking to me about changing my life, about getting sober. I had heard it all before, and I didn't want to hear it again, but I sat and listened anyway—something was different this time. I think mostly I was tired and ready to give up, but I haven't yet.

Over the past month, I've been angry at a lot of things but mostly myself. In some ways, it feels kinda good to be angry again. At least I care about something now. I've been trying to talk about my feelings and learning about where all that anger came from in the first place. I know I don't have it all figured out yet, but I understand myself more now than I ever could high.

I know now that I have a lot of reasons to be angry—I mean my life was messed up before I ever started using. Those things never should have happened to a little kid, not to anyone. And there's no excuse for it. But I've also learned that I've done more damage to my life than anyone. I never solved any problems by using, but I sure did create some. Worse than that, I hurt a lot of people in the process. Some of them, well, I still think they deserved it. Guess I should work on that... But most of them were innocent—just like me.

Some days, I really hate sobriety. I want to give up a lot. Sometimes the pain and the memories are just too much to bear and I think about using. But at the end of the day, I feel so proud that I didn't give in—that I was able to be strong and deal with all this shit without checking out. All those people who hurt me, ya know, it's like I'm showing them all how much they didn't hurt me, how much they can't control me. Every time I succeed, I feel that I'm proving everybody wrong.

Sobriety is tough, but I'm getting a lot of support. I just started going to group counseling and have even tried some of those 12-step meetings. It just helps to talk to other people who understand what I am going through. They keep reminding me that sobriety is the key to really living. I don't think I was really doing that before—I was just surviving. I want more than that now.

PHASE II

HOW?

COMMITMENT TO CHANGE: Using the Tools for Change

Chapter Six:

Basic Communication Skills

GOALS OF THIS CHAPTER

- Review basic skills to communication.
- Learn how to start conversations.
- Practice the skills of active sharing and active listening.
- Learn and practice assertive problem solving.

CRYSTAL'S STORY

SESSION 11: GIVE AND TAKE WITH OTHERS

Objectives

- Review Phase I and your Plan for Change (PFC).
- Review and discuss basic skills to communication.
- Learn how to start conversations.
- Practice how to give and receive compliments.
- Learn and practice the skills of active listening and active sharing.
- Share and receive feedback about a deeper part of yourself.

Crystal's Story: *My parents don't understand me. I don't think they'll ever understand me. I got in trouble for shoplifting, and all they did was yell at me. I tried telling them that they didn't pay enough attention to me and that they don't give me the things I need to feel good about myself. But they got all upset and said I was blaming them for something that wasn't their fault. After all, I was the one who shoplifted.*

It just seems like every time I try to talk with them we end up fighting. I try to tell them how I feel, but they get upset like I'm always blaming them. Or sometimes they try to tell me what they hear me saying. I know what I'm saying, and it's not like I blame them for everything. I'm just trying to get my point across. I don't think they listen to me . . . so I just don't listen to them.

The Program So Far

In Phase I, you were asked to make a decision about change. We spent some time covering the three phases of change, and then you were asked where you thought you were and where you wanted to go. We then had you develop your Self-Portrait (SP) and PFC, which presents your change goals and resources to make changes during treatment and on your own. As you continue through this program, you are expected to modify your PFC as you learn more about yourself and develop improved ideas about how you wish to continue on your journey of self-discovery and change.

Many come to this program because they are court ordered or for some other reason they have to be here. But you have all fulfilled the requirements for completing Phase I of Pathways to Self-Discovery. This means that you have used the Program Guides and have made an active choice to learn and practice the Tools for Change. You have made a commitment to making change an important part of your life. In some ways, the journey of self-discovery is similar to, though *much better than,* taking drugs. Understanding ourselves while gaining freedom and control over our lives is *extremely exciting* and you *feel different*—only this time in a very positive way.

You have made a commitment to making change an important part of your life.

SESSION 11: GIVE AND TAKE WITH OTHERS

Activity: Thoughts About Change

Make a large circle in which everyone can see everyone else. Go around the circle, and one by one **talk about** your **interests, desires, and concerns with change.** Some of you may still think that it isn't fair that you have to be in the program, but most will agree that we have learned a great deal so far. Be genuine, and tell everyone **what you think about being in the program** and how it may or may not affect your life. Be sure to listen to each other, and when appropriate, give some helpful feedback. Offer constructive advice about how the person who is talking about him- or herself may be able to achieve what they want from this program and life.

Let's Talk: Improving the Skill of Communication

In Session 6, we took some time to learn about communication. After we discussed *verbal* and *nonverbal* communication, we took some more time to learn about the two sides to talking with someone: (1) *self-disclosure (active sharing)* and (2) *active listening.*

Active sharing, where we talk about ourselves to someone else, is a very important part of talking with another person. But *active listening* is just as important. After all, communication can't happen with just one person.

Active Sharing

Active sharing is when we share or talk about ourselves to another person. The sharing involves two skills that can help you communicate more easily.

The first skill is using the **"I" message.** This means talking about you, using four basic parts to talk about:

- I feel . . . because . . .
- I need . . . because . . .
- I think . . . because . . .
- I do or I act . . . because . . .

The purpose of using *I* when sharing with others is exactly that: We are *expressing ourselves* and not *talking down to, blaming,* or *talking about* the other person. This is not like bragging because you are *sharing something* about yourself. As was shown in Figure 9: The Path to Talking and Learning About Self, when we talk about ourselves we usually learn more about how we actually think and feel about important parts of our lives. What is *most important,* though, is rather than saying things like "You make me feel . . ." or "You are so selfish . . ." we can improve our communication by taking *personal responsibility* for our thoughts, wants, needs, feelings, and actions instead of placing blame or making demands on others to take care of us. We can explain the reason for our "I" statements by using the word *because*—for example, "I feel sad *because* I am going to be lonely when you leave."

The second skill when trying to actively share something about yourself is *being open to feedback from others.* Sometimes it's hard to hear what others have to say about us, but it is important to hear ourselves through their point of view. The important thing to keep in mind is *not to get defensive or angry.* People give you feedback on the basis that you have given them permission to tell you what they think. And although it's easy to get angry when we hear something negative, it is our responsibility to listen to what people are telling us and to *make our own decisions* (without becoming defensive or angry) about whether the information is true and helpful.

We always have *the options* of disagreeing with, or not believing, what is being said.

Activity: A Voice of Blame

Crystal has a hard time talking with her parents. She thinks they are always repeating stuff to her without really listening to her point. How do you think Crystal could **improve communication** with her parents? How do you think she can better get her point across? What kind of **messages** does Crystal use when trying to talk with her parents? Does she use the **"I"** or **"you"** forms of communication?

Just as we tend to push away or *get defensive* (sometimes we *strike out* at the person who we think is being critical of us) about *negative feedback,* we often don't accept *positive feedback* either. We may push away the compliment because we might feel afraid of getting *too close* to someone, or sometimes we *don't think much of ourselves* so we think the compliment is a lie, or maybe we think the person is trying to *set us up* so they can get something from us.

Active Listening

Active listening is when we are on the other side of the conversation. That means we listen to what the other person is saying. There are ***two key skills*** in active listening:

1. **Invite the person to share** by using open statements or questions such as "Tell me about . . ." or "How are you?" We don't want to use questions that can be answered with a *yes* or *no* answer because that does not tell us much about the other person.
2. **Reflect back what you heard** the other person say: "I hear that you are saying you are upset."

It is important for us to keep an *open mind* and *channel* when actively listening. Our attitudes, beliefs, and feelings tend to influence everything we hear and see around us. But when we are actively listening, we set aside those influences so we can be open to the other person. It is helpful to remember to *not let our own thoughts interfere* with hearing what someone is trying to say.

SESSION 11: GIVE AND TAKE WITH OTHERS

When we discussed communication in Session 6, we also learned about *nonverbal talking,* or *body language.* In order to be a good listener, we need to pay attention to the body talk of the other person. Paying attention to the posture, facial expressions, tone of voice, personal space, and body movement of the other person can help us to better understand and learn about that person. Most importantly, when we listen to another person, we should let the person know we *hear* and *understand* what they are saying. By making eye contact, nodding our head, reflecting back what we hear, and also actively sharing about ourselves, we let the other person know that we are listening to what they have to say.

Activity: Crystal's Listening Skills

Crystal says that her parents never listen to her when she talks to them about what she is thinking and feeling. But as we just discussed, listening works both ways. What can we say about how Crystal listens to her parents when they are talking to her? What evidence do we have that Crystal might be open to what her parents tell her?

The Gift of Gab

Now that we know the two basic elements to a conversation—(1) ***active sharing*** and (2) ***active listening***—it's time to practice starting a conversation. Interacting with other people can be difficult, especially if we *don't feel comfortable* or *haven't developed the skill* to start talking with another person. Often we use alcohol or drugs to loosen ourselves up so that we feel more comfortable with other people, but by using substances, we are really keeping ourselves away from other people. In order to feel comfortable talking with another person, we first have to learn the art of conversation.

Conversations do not have to be long or just about "important" topics. Sometimes just talking about the weather can be interesting to both people. When starting a conversation, it can be helpful to keep these things in mind.

- It's okay to talk about yourself.
- Listening to the other person is just as important as talking.
- Observe your situation, and see if the people around you are interested in similar things.
- Use open-ended questions: questions that can be answered with a *yes* or *no* do not lead into talking. An example of an open-ended question is "Tell me some things about how your day was today."
- Communication and talking can be powerful, and it helps us to feel more connected to the world around us.

SESSION 11: GIVE AND TAKE WITH OTHERS

Activity: The Art of Conversation

For this activity, you will need to separate into groups of three or more but no more than five people. Using the **conversation skills** we have previously discussed, ask each other **questions** about your life, families, hobbies, etc. Be sure **not to use** *yes* or *no* questions. As you listen to each person talking, write down things that the whole group has in common. For example, a person may ask another about what they did today before coming to the program. While the person is answering, they may say something about a member of their family. If everyone in the group has a brother or sister, write it down. After a short while, get back into the larger group and share what your group found it had in common. The group with the most in-common things written down by the end of the activity wins.

Deeper Sharing: When Good Communication Skills Make a World of Difference

Recall the Johari Window (Figure 14) that we learned about in Chapter 5: Making a Commitment to Change. We will now see how the communication skills that we have been learning and practicing are vital when we want to share important parts of our lives.

Activity: Sharing a Deeper Part of Yourself

Move into a circle where you can see everyone. Your counselor will have a beanbag or a ball, and he or she will say one **honest and deep thing** about himself or herself such as being concerned about a child's welfare or being scared about a parent dying. They will pass the bag to another person—any person within the circle. The next person will **give feedback** to the counselor, such as "I hear that you are afraid, and it's causing you to not do what you want to do." After giving feedback to the previous person, they will **then share** something important or meaningful about themselves. The bag will be passed again, and the next person will give feedback and then share. This will be repeated until **everyone in the group** has given feedback, shared, and gotten feedback.

Complimenting and Strengthening Others and Being Open to Hearing Praise

We have all been working hard in this group to develop the skills for *self-discovery* and *change.* Let's use the remainder of our time in this session to show our appreciation of all the good work we have been doing as individuals and as a team. *Giving* and *receiving compliments* are important parts of sharing and communicating. It also helps us to see the positive things about ourselves. Here are a few tips for giving and receiving compliments:

- Be very specific about what you are complimenting a person for. For example, instead of saying, "Good job" you might offer, "I am impressed at how you have been helping the group to move in such positive directions through your upbeat attitude and helpful comments."
- Take time to listen to the praise.
- Do not deny the praise.
- Though you may not agree, tell how the compliment makes you feel good.

Just as receiving compliments is important in sharing ourselves, *giving compliments* is important in listening and sharing with other people. Everyone likes to hear something positive. Giving compliments is like giving feedback, except that we focus on the *positive aspects* about the other person. The most effective way to give a compliment is to know the person through listening to what they have to say.

Activity: It Takes One to Know One

By now we should know each other pretty well, so stand up and move around the room. Go up to each and every person in the group and **give them one compliment.** Make the compliment honest and sincere and something specific that you truly think about the other person. Then allow the other person to compliment you. Remember and use what we just talked about in giving and receiving compliments. Listen to the compliment, do not deny it, and let the person know how it makes you feel. Make sure that you give at least one compliment to every person in the group—and be specific about what you are praising the person for.

Putting It Together

- Crystal gets into fights with her parents often. What are some of the problems that Crystal has with her *sharing* and *listening skills,* especially with her parents? How might she better communicate with her parents? Think of some specific examples or situations that will help Crystal be a better communicator.
- Think of some past conversations you have had. Were they good conversations? How did you start them? What did you learn from them?
- How can conversations help you change and develop?
- How did the deeper sharing and giving and receiving of compliments bring you closer to some members of the group?
- When we gave everyone compliments, what did you discover about what people appreciate about you?

SESSION 11: GIVE AND TAKE WITH OTHERS

Using the Program Guides and Tools for Change

Use the Pathways Change Scale (PCS) to indicate your ability to utilize the active listening skills (open questions and reflective listening) presented in this session.

0	1	2	3	4	5	6	7	8	9	10
Low					Medium					High

Rate your ability to use the active sharing skills ("I" messages and openness to feedback) taught in this session.

0	1	2	3	4	5	6	7	8	9	10
Low					Medium					High

SESSION 12: ASSERTIVE SKILLS DEVELOPMENT

Objectives

- Review Session 11: Give and Take With Others.
- Discuss the four ways people deal with conflict.
- Learn and practice the skills of being assertive.

Crystal's Story: *I couldn't believe it. My friend just took some expensive makeup and put it in her purse. I had a really bad feeling about it, and I said we shouldn't do it. But she just looked at me and asked if I was scared. I said* no *and that I just didn't want to get caught or get anyone hurt. She said that no one gets hurt from shoplifting. The store absorbs the cost, and we get what we want. So I stole, and we got caught.*

When my mom came to pick me up, she was furious. She didn't say a thing to me until my father came home. And then everything snapped. I tried talking to them, but they got mad at me and called me a spoiled brat and grounded me. I went to my room and slammed the door. When they called me down to dinner, I ignored them. In the morning when it was time to go to school, I ran out the door without even talking to either of them. They deserve to be punished. They got the silent treatment for a long time after that.

Reviewing the Art of Conversation

In the last session, we discussed the basics of talking with another person. There are two people involved in a conversation: (1) the *active sharer* and (2) the *active listener.* Although conversations can happen in a group setting, the two roles will always be played by someone. We showed how by using *open questions* and *observing* what is going on around you, starting a conversation can be done without much effort. After looking closely at the characteristics of effective communication, we discussed how *active sharing* and *active listening* are especially important when talking about very personal experiences, even some that you hardly ever share with anyone.

Activity: Practicing Talking Skills

Break into pairs, and try to pair up with a person you haven't had much conversation with up to this point. Take some time to get to know each other and have a good conversation. Remember to ask each other **open-ended questions** and practice **active listening** when the other person is speaking. Also keep in mind the **"I" message** and being **open to feedback.** Try to have as much of an in-depth conversation as you can in the time allotted. Then, after returning to the larger group, share what you learned about the other person during your conversation. What **did you learn** that you didn't know about the other person? What **did you share** about yourself?

SESSION 12: ASSERTIVE SKILLS DEVELOPMENT

Managing Conflict

Unfortunately, conversations cannot always be positive or easily done. Sometimes talking can be used as means to *try to convince us to* do something that is not good for us or that we don't necessarily want to do. Sometimes people around us become overly aggressive; they may do or say things that don't seem right. Some examples are feeling pressured to get in a car with a drunk driver, or being pressured to have sex with someone, or someone in your family is yelling or playing loud music when you are trying to study. In all of these situations, assertiveness is a skill that can protect us from harm or from making bad situations worse.

Most importantly, by being assertive, we maintain our self-respect and are confident that we are doing our best when it comes to managing conflict or disagreements with other people.

Before getting into what assertiveness means and how it can be helpful, we will first go over *three common ways* that people deal with problems or conflict, which don't usually work. In fact, sometimes these ways can get us in more trouble than before.

Ineffective Styles for Dealing With Conflict

Flight

Avoid the problem or be passive, usually giving in to what someone else wants at the expense of giving up our own rights.

For example, let's say you don't like people smoking in your car. By being *passive,* you would let another person smoke in your car anyway, just to avoid the disagreement or conflict. But by allowing the other person to smoke, you are *giving up your rights* to decide the rules of your car, and your car smells like smoke all over and the smoke gets into your clothes, which you don't like, and into your lungs, which disgusts you even more.

Fight

We may strike out by attacking others verbally or even by using physical aggression. The *aggressive person* protects their rights but gets what they want at the *expense* of another person. Others pay at the will of the aggressive person.

In the previous example, the *aggressive person* is the one who insists on smoking in the car. All they care about is smoking, *despite the wishes, rights,* and *desires* of the owner of the car or the other passengers. If challenged, the *aggressive* smoker may strike out by shouting, "It is my right to smoke when and where I want, and people who don't want me to smoke have no business offering to take me anywhere. In fact, they should just stay away from me. Let me out!"

Fake

This style is called "passive–aggressive." The person does not necessarily avoid all the problems, but they are indirect about getting what they want. Because the passive–aggressive person does not express his or her needs in a way that other people can respond to, nobody is completely satisfied in resolving the conflict.

Using the previous example, the passive–aggressive smoker who is denied permission to smoke in the car might demand frequent emergency stops to the toilet (while everyone has to wait) so they can satisfy their smoking habit. Meanwhile, everyone, including the smoker, is held up an extra half hour because of the frequent stops, and everyone is upset when the ride is finally over. Another scenario might be that the passive–aggressive person agrees not to smoke in the car but says, "It wouldn't matter if I did because the car stinks anyway."

Activity: A Method of Dealing

As a group, take a look at Crystal's story. What method of **dealing with conflict** did she use with her friend? What method of dealing did she use with her parents? Were the methods different? Which one worked out well for Crystal, if any of them? Why did Crystal use those methods? What **method do you use** in dealing with conflicts or problems? Give examples of how you might have used each style: **flight, fight, or fake** in dealing with conflict.

None of these ways gets a positive result or meet the needs of the person in a healthy manner. In fact, these ways of dealing with conflict tend to drive others away. Because they feel *isolated* or *distanced* from others, some people lean on substance use and criminal actions in order to *satisfy unmet needs* for closeness, dealing with conflict or stress, or even to gratify needs for power and control.

Activity: Flight, Fight, or Fake

Break into groups of four. For this activity, you will need to **create a skit** that involves the three options that were previously described for managing conflict: **flight, fight, or fake.** Have one person **offer the situation,** such as setting fire to an abandoned building. The first person represents the **flight** method of dealing, which would be to quietly go along or leave without anyone knowing. The second person will be the **fight** method, which for our example would be to destroy the lighter/matches or attack the person suggesting the situation. The third person will be the **fake** method, who says that they would do it but the other people are so stupid that they would be sure to get caught. Perform your skit for the rest of the group, and allow them to guess which response each person is playing.

Choosing the Healthy Option

Fair

How do people deal with conflict in a positive manner? By learning how to be assertive or being **fair.** The assertive person stands up for their rights but does not get something at the expense of another person. A lot of our problems come from the struggle of getting our needs met. Learning to be assertive can get your needs met but not by making other people suffer for it.

SESSION 12: ASSERTIVE SKILLS DEVELOPMENT

Assertiveness is something that doesn't have to be hard or complicated. Here are 10 key ways to be assertive:

1. *Recognize your rights* in a situation without trespassing on the rights of others.
2. *Know how to clearly state your opinion* and what you want.
3. *Consider the needs of others* as you get your needs met.
4. *Be flexible and give,* yet still make your situation known.
5. *Avoid blaming* or using "you."
6. *State how* you think and feel *by using the "I" message.*
7. Be focused on your *goals.*
8. Become part of the *solution.*
9. Stick with your decision. Don't continually ask, "What might have been?"
10. *Confront* the *problem* and not the other person.

The word *FACTS* will help you to remember some of the basic ideas of how to be assertive:

F—Be *flexible.*

A—*Avoid* blaming.

C—*Concentrate* on achieving your goals.

T—*Tell* what you think.

S—Offer win-win *solutions.*

An assertive driver would insist on not smoking in their car and calmly *state their reasons.* The person who is being assertive might suggest pulling over once during the hour-long trip or stopping somewhere so the smoker could have a break if they wanted to. Assertive people find solutions that *meet as many people's needs* as possible.

Activity: The Fair Response

As a group, discuss and decide on several different situations in which you might have to use one of the four responses. Then decide on a couple different assertive, or fair, responses to the situations at hand. For example, the situation is **whether or not to get into the car** of someone who has been **drinking.** One possible assertive response might be "No thank you, I think I'll walk, because I don't want to be in danger of being involved in an alcohol related accident." Another assertive possibility might be "I don't think it's safe for you to be driving. I don't feel like visiting a hospital tonight. Let's take a cab." Be careful that the responses you think of are assertive are not aggressive.

Suppose you are on probation and you go to your friend's house. In front of four other friends, he or she offers you a bag of weed so you can have some smoke and get some easy money. Discuss the different options of **flight, fight, fake, and fair** in this situation.

Using Worksheet 11: Pathways of Learning and Change, take an event that you recently experienced in which you used one of the three **ineffective** options for managing conflict. Then describe how the situation would improve if you were to use an **assertive** (fair) response.

Putting It Together

- Crystal uses more than one method in dealing with her conflicts. Which methods does she use? How does she use those methods in resolving her conflicts?
- Which of the ways to deal with conflict do you most often use? Give examples.
- Try to remember some past conflict you had. How could it have been resolved if you had been assertive?
- When looking at your thinking report, what happens when you use one of the three methods of dealing other than assertiveness?
- Take a look at your PFC. Are there areas that you might need to work on as far as assertiveness is concerned?
- Review your SP and PFC. What will you work on this week? Share this with the group.
- Do you want to add to your PFC?

Using the Program Guides and Tools for Change

Use the PCS to indicate your understanding of the four methods described in this chapter to cope with conflict (i.e., fight, flight, fake, or fair).

0	1	2	3	4	5	6	7	8	9	10
Low					Medium					High

Rate your ability to use the skills to be assertive as presented in this chapter.

0	1	2	3	4	5	6	7	8	9	10
Low					Medium					High

- Consider the elements that you have included in Program Guide 1: Telling My Story (TMS). Are there some areas of your life where the use of assertiveness skills would lead to improved outcomes?
- Have a look at Program Guide 2: Master Skills List (MSL), and update your self-ratings on active sharing, active listening, starting conversations, giving compliments, and assertiveness skills.
- With your counselor, continue to work on your SP and PFC. How can assertiveness fit into your PFC?

Pathways of Learning & Change

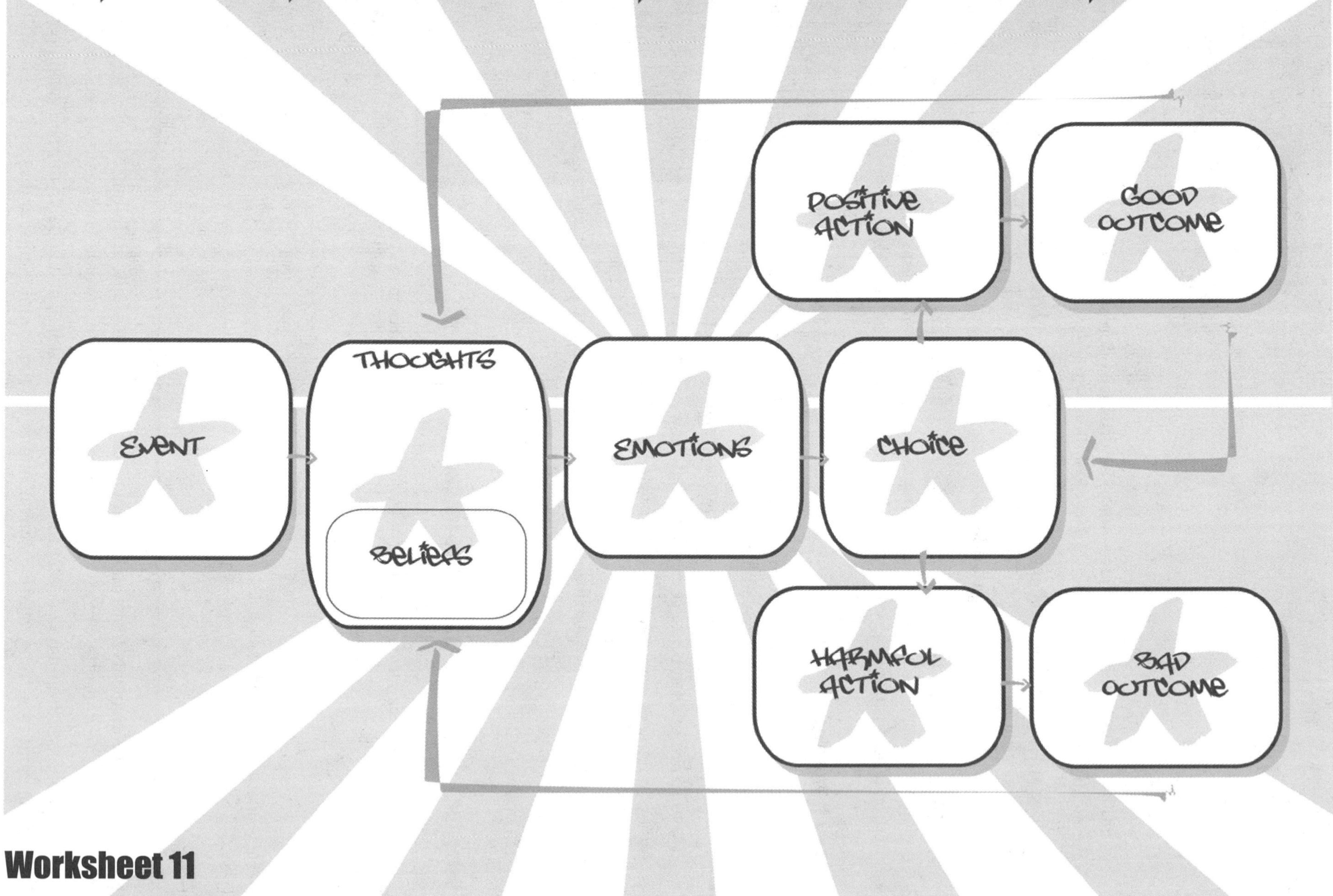

Worksheet 11

Crystal's Story

Life is not fair. I'm always getting in trouble for things I didn't even want to do, and when I try to explain myself . . . forget it. No one listens to me anyway.

So this one time my friend and I were walking through the mall. She was looking for a specific shirt that she wanted to buy, so we were just browsing through the stores. We went into a Walgreens to get some candy when we decided to look at the makeup. My parents don't really like me wearing makeup because they think I am too young for it, but it's sometimes nice to just look and see what the new trends are. So my friend started pulling some expensive makeup off the shelves, and with one glance around, she put it in her purse.

This really kind of scared me. I told her maybe we shouldn't be doing that, and she looked at me and asked if I was scared. I said no I wasn't, even though I kind of was, and I said that I don't want to hurt anyone or get caught. She called me a chicken and said that if I didn't steal the makeup I would never get to wear any. Besides, according to her, no one gets hurt in shoplifting. The company absorbs the cost, and we get what we want.

I didn't really want to, but I ended up taking some lip gloss and foundation and putting them in my purse. I had a really bad feeling about it, but I figured she was probably right. She's so much more mature than I am. We were walking out the door, and I thought we would actually get away with it, when the security guard stopped us and asked us to open our purses. Suddenly my heart dropped into my stomach, and I thought I was going to get sick.

Needless to say, he pulled us into the security office and then began to call our parents. While we were waiting, my friend began to freak out and cry. She started saying it was my entire fault, that if I hadn't slowed her down she wouldn't have gotten caught. Ha, some maturity. I reminded her that if it hadn't been for her stupid idea to shoplift, we would have never done something that we could have gotten caught for.

Her dad and my mom came to pick us up from the mall. The guard didn't call the cops since he released us to our parents, but we aren't allowed back into that Walgreens forever. I've never been eighty-sixed from a store before; it felt like some judge just descended a sentence of life on my head. And my mom was furious. She didn't talk to me the whole way home. When we got home, she sent me to my room to wait until my dad got home. And then the shit hit the fan.

When I walked into the room, there was an eerie and dead silence—the kind that reminds you of walking into an abandoned house that's supposed to be haunted and that flutters at the base of your heart like butterflies. Before one word was spoken, I was shaking in my shoes and getting goose bumps.

Calmly, almost too calmly for my tastes, my dad asked me why I took that makeup without paying for it. It was like something snapped in me, and immediately I said that they didn't let me wear makeup and the only chance I would have to wear it would be to take it from a store and keep it in my locker. My mom got a dead look on her face and said that it is not their fault I stole and that my not wearing makeup had nothing to do with this. By that time, though, I was in a whirlwind of emotion and tears. Suddenly I yelled that they never spend time with me and that I want so many things that I never get and that it wasn't fair that everyone else got to wear makeup and wear expensive clothes and get to drive their parents' car at 14 and do whatever they wanted, and I was stuck in a cage and treated like a child. My father snapped. He started yelling that they fed me, clothed me, made sure a roof was over my head, and the thanks they get is a little girl yelling at them and blaming them for a stupid mistake she made of her own free will. I told them they didn't understand, they would never understand what I go through, and they never even try. I told them it's like they don't even love me. My mom stood up, and with a look that could kill a serviceman, she called me an ungrateful brat and said that I was grounded. I stomped up to my room and slammed the door.

And that was that. When I was called down to dinner, I ignored them. Slowly, I began to go around them but not very often. And when I did, I didn't talk to them. I can't believe my mom called me a spoiled brat, and they deserved to be punished for yelling at me. I guess eventually things got back to normal. Actually, I don't even know what normal is, was, or if it will ever be that again. I just know that for some reason I get into situations where I get into trouble when I don't even want to be there. And my parents never understand and never will understand.

Chapter Seven:
Avoiding Trouble and Playing Fair

GOALS OF THIS CHAPTER

- Learn to recognize cravings and urges.
- Discuss ways to control our desires.
- Understand negotiation and compromise.
- Learn skills to avoid and get out of high-risk (HR) situations.

ANTHONY'S STORY

TERESA'S STORY

SESSION 13: MANAGING CRAVINGS AND URGES ABOUT CRIME AND SUBSTANCES

Objectives

- Review Chapter 6: Basic Communication Skills.
- Learn how to avoid HR situations—people, places, and things that might cause you harm.
- Develop the skills to deal with cravings and urges when you can't avoid trigger situations.

Anthony's Story: *I ended up in the hospital with a bullet in my leg. But I guess that isn't all that bad, because my best friend ended up dead. We were members of a gang that controlled our neighborhood, and at first it was great—all the money and cars and more than that, the power and fear we had over people. It was incredible. This was the dream life coming from the place I did.*

While sitting in my hospital bed, I used to think about all the fun I was missing out on. But my best friend was dead. A gang counselor said that if there was a time to get out, it was now. And I guess he's right—my friend's memory deserves more than for me to end up dead, too. But sometimes I think of the life and the partying, and I want it so bad I can feel it in my chest. I just know it's time to get out, and talking to the counselor helps me a lot.

Teresa's Story: *I grew up dirt poor. I would hear that stupid ol' saying in my head "You are what you eat," and I certainly wasn't going to be garbage. I was poor, but I deserved more. I guess that's where it all started. So I started stealing food, and I got this rush whenever I took something from the store. What else could I get away with? Soon I was taking resellable merchandise—whatever would sell on the streets. To make a long story short, I got caught, and when that happened they were able to connect me to a number of other recent thefts. I'm coming up on my release day, and I know I don't want to come back, but I'm so afraid that I won't be able to help myself when an opportunity presents itself. I wasn't able to turn my back before, and I'm so afraid I won't be able to do it now either.*

Looking Back at Assertiveness

In the last session, we discussed *assertiveness* and other ways to deal with conflict. Although there are *four ways* to deal with problems that arise in our lives, *being assertive* is the only way we can ensure our needs are being met without interfering with someone else's needs.

In order to be assertive, we sometimes need to say no to the people we like and care about. That doesn't mean to attack them or to be mean to them but merely telling them no and why we feel the way we do.

SESSION 13: MANAGING CRAVINGS AND URGES ABOUT CRIME AND SUBSTANCES

Activity: Remembering as a Group

As a group, **draw a chart** on the flip chart paper. You will have three HR situations down the left side and the four methods along the top. For each situation, **fill out each top method.**

For example, being **offered marijuana among a group of friends** is the first situation. The first method is to be **passive,** then **aggressive,** then **passive–aggressive,** and finally **assertive.**

Create **your own situations,** and with your counselor, fill in how to respond passively and then what the results are. Fill in the following for each method: **passive, aggressive, passive–aggressive,** and **assertive.** After filling out the chart, take a moment to look at the results. Which method seems to deal with each situation the best?

Situation	Passive	Aggressive	Passive–Aggressive	Assertive
1. OFFERED WEED RESULTS	**"I really shouldn't but what the hell?"** *Caught with dirty UA*	**"You've got some f—k'n nerve. I'm gonna flush it in the toilet, a—hole."** *Fight breaks out*	**"I'd smoke it, but your stuff always stinks anyway."** *Bad feelings all around*	**"I'm not interested, and just being near this can put me in jail. So don't put me in this situation ever again. See you later."** *Feel good about yourself. Don't overreact.*
2.				
3.				
4.				

Sometimes saying no is not the most difficult part. There are HR situations like being offered marijuana as in the previous example that can pose real problems in relapse and recidivism (RR) prevention. Situations are not the only difficulty we face in changing, though. Often *our thoughts* can cause us the most severe problems, and our thoughts are what cause HR feelings, which we refer to as *cravings and urges.*

What Are Cravings and Urges?

A *craving* is the desire to *take a substance* or *participate in criminal activity,* and it is something that will be a part of your life. Although cravings are uncomfortable, they don't last all that long, and they are something that you can overcome.

SESSION 13: MANAGING CRAVINGS AND URGES ABOUT CRIME AND SUBSTANCES

But cravings don't usually stop at the desire. They begin to move into what we call *urges.* While *cravings are the mental desire* for something, *urges are the actual physical symptom,* like tension or stress, and sometimes even moving toward the thing desired. Let's say you want to smoke a joint because you are hanging out with old friends you used to smoke with. The event triggers the craving for the weed, and you start thinking about how good it might feel. The urge is when you can feel in your body the desire, and you may even begin searching for someone who can supply you with a joint.

Activity: Anthony's and Teresa's Cravings and Urges

Take a moment to look at Anthony's and Teresa's stories. Do you think Anthony has a **craving** for his previous life, or do you think it has moved into an **urge?** What is some of the **evidence** in the story that points to one or the other?

How about Teresa? She got busted and spent time in jail. Do you think she is ready to quit stealing? Is she having **cravings** and **urges** for money and "the good life" before being released? How can we tell from the information presented in the story?

Can you think of any cravings or urges you have had recently?

Cravings may be *triggered by events* around you, such as hanging out with old friends or a stressful situation, and then they trigger the physical urge. The urge then may trigger memories and psychological symptoms, such as feeling good, enjoying something you want, and having fun when you are high. Urges happen pretty quickly and then drop off, but the best way to prevent an urge is to ***stop the craving.***

Activity: Everyday Urges

As a group, go around and discuss a **craving or urge** you have had in the past week. What was the situation or the thoughts that caused you to crave something? Did the craving become an urge? Were you able to stop it, and how? If you weren't, why not? How would you better deal with it next time?

Things That Can Trigger Cravings and Urges

There are certain common HR situations that often *trigger* or *cause cravings,* which may lead to *urges* and *relapse.* Here is a list of some common triggers for *relapse to drugs* and returning to *criminal activities:*

- Being around substances or places where you used to drink or take drugs.
- Feeling like your life situation is changed, such as getting out of a correctional placement.
- Seeing other people using and being invited to join in.
- Being with people who use or are involved with crime.
- Certain emotions, including tiredness, stress, anger, frustration, and excitement (like when we want to celebrate).

Ways to Manage Cravings and Urges

Although the situations that were just given are something that can happen every day, there are five primary ways to manage the cravings and avoid the HR situation:

1. ***Sharing with*** family, friends, or someone you trust about the craving and asking for their support.
2. ***"Toughing it out"*** and getting control of the craving by bearing with the discomfort. It will go away. Here's how you can tough it out:
    - *Notice* how you experience the craving. What are your *thoughts* and *feelings* about the craving? *Where* does it occur in your body?
    - Identify the thoughts that are keeping the craving alive.
    - Challenge your HR thoughts using the mental self-control and change skills in Table 2.
    - Is it still a *craving,* or has it become an *urge?* Remember, urges are when your *physical body* begins to feel it and you take actions to fulfill the craving, such as searching out a friend who can smoke you up. You can still turn things around.
3. ***Talk yourself down.*** When the craving becomes an urge, *focus on your body* where you feel the urge. *Talk to yourself,* and *take control* of your actions figuring out alternative ways to feel comfortable.
4. Practice ***"urge surfing."*** Ride out the wave, and you can relax at the shore.
5. ***Find another activity*** that will distract you from the craving or urge.

Control over thoughts leads to freedom and strength.

Activity: What Triggers Us?

As a group, think of several different **real-life situations** or events that will trigger you to have a craving or an urge. Share these **triggers** with each other. Are the triggers the same or different for different people? Now think of different ways that you might **avoid the events** or situations that can cause a craving or an urge. If it is not always possible to avoid these situations, what are some of the **positive things** that you can do to cope with urges and cravings?

Complete Worksheet 12: Dealing With Cravings and Urges. This is an important task. The plan you make for this exercise will help you to deal with cravings and urges for a long time to come.

Worksheet 12

Dealing With Cravings and Urges

Make up a plan to deal with an episode of craving. Pick two or three of the strategies in class, and describe how you would use them when you feel tempted to relapse.

1. List your cravings or urges.

2. What activities would you choose to distract you?

3. Who might you call for help?

4. What mental self-control skills from Table 2 did you use? Thought stopping? Shifting the view? What others?

SESSION 13: MANAGING CRAVINGS AND URGES ABOUT CRIME AND SUBSTANCES

Mind Over Matter

Remember at the beginning of the program when we talked about how substance use and getting into trouble are usually done on impulse? Well, the same idea works with cravings and urges. Usually the *craving occurs* and we are already *on the move* to *fulfill the urge* before we realize what we are doing. Through ***self-talk,*** we can begin to *control our impulses.*

When trying to talk yourself out of an urge, it is helpful to *remind yourself* of the *bad things* that have happened because of using or committing crimes. Then start *thinking of the good things* that come out of *being clean,* like being able to do what you want or go where you want. The most important part of dealing with cravings and urges is to remember to *stop and think* about *what you have to lose* by using *substances* or committing *crimes.* Keep your *positive goals* in front of you as your guide.

Activity: The Role of Mind

Break into smaller groups of about three people. Create a **skit** in which one person has a **craving** and **an urge. By role-playing positive** or **negative thoughts,** the others either try to **convince or stop** the person (without any physical contact) from fulfilling the urge or craving. The first person has to either **decide to participate** in the negative behavior or **refuse,** depending on the strength of the arguments.

Returning to the stories of Anthony and Teresa. How **might Anthony control** his cravings to return to his life as a gang member? What would Anthony have to lose by returning to the gang? How might Teresa manage her cravings and urges to have money and feel the rush of getting away with a crime.

Now fill out Worksheet 13: Loss of Joys and Pleasures, and think through what it would mean to you if you gave in to some of your cravings and urges.

Putting It Together

- While in the hospital, Anthony has *cravings* and *urges* to be back in the gang. When approaching her release date, Teresa is thinking about whether she can give up stealing. How is each of them dealing with their cravings and urges?
- Think of one specific situation in which you had a *craving that became an urge.* How did that situation affect you? What was the outcome? How could have the outcome been different?
- When you aren't able to avoid the situations, *how can you deal* with the urges? Which of the five ways works best for you?
- Take a moment to look at your *autobiography.* How have *cravings* and *urges* influenced you in the past? Do you think you can control them?

Worksheet 13

LOSS OF JOYS AND PLEASURES

What are your joys and pleasures, and would you lose them if you committed another crime or relapse back into full alcohol and other drug (AOD) use?

List ten pleasures and joys that you have in your life. Make these your top pleasures and joys.	Would you lose them if you reoffended or relapsed?	
	yes	no

SESSION 13: MANAGING CRAVINGS AND URGES ABOUT CRIME AND SUBSTANCES

- Use Worksheet 14: Pathways of Learning and Change to describe how you would use "thought stopping" and "self-talk" skills to prevent a HR event from leading to a craving and urge for drugs and crime. How would you use the STEP method to resist a craving or urge?

Using the Program Guides and Tools for Change

Show your level of understanding of what you would give up if you returned to substance abuse and criminal activity.

0	1	2	3	4	5	6	7	8	9	10
Low					Medium					High

Rate your ability to use the skills taught in this lesson to manage cravings and urges for alcohol or drugs.

0	1	2	3	4	5	6	7	8	9	10
Low					Medium					High

Indicate your ability to use the skills taught in this session to manage cravings and urges for criminal activity.

0	1	2	3	4	5	6	7	8	9	10
Low					Medium					High

Pathways of Learning and Change

Complete this picture. Take an event that you recently experienced. Then note your automatic thoughts that came from that event. Then note your feelings and beliefs. What was your behavior? Fill in the rest of the boxes. What might happen if you decide to change your thoughts and beliefs?

Worksheet 14

Pathways of Learning & Change

Complete this picture. Take an event that you recently experienced. Then note your automatic thoughts that came from that event. Then note your feelings and beliefs. What was your behavior? Fill in the rest of the squares. What might happen if you decide to change your thoughts and beliefs?

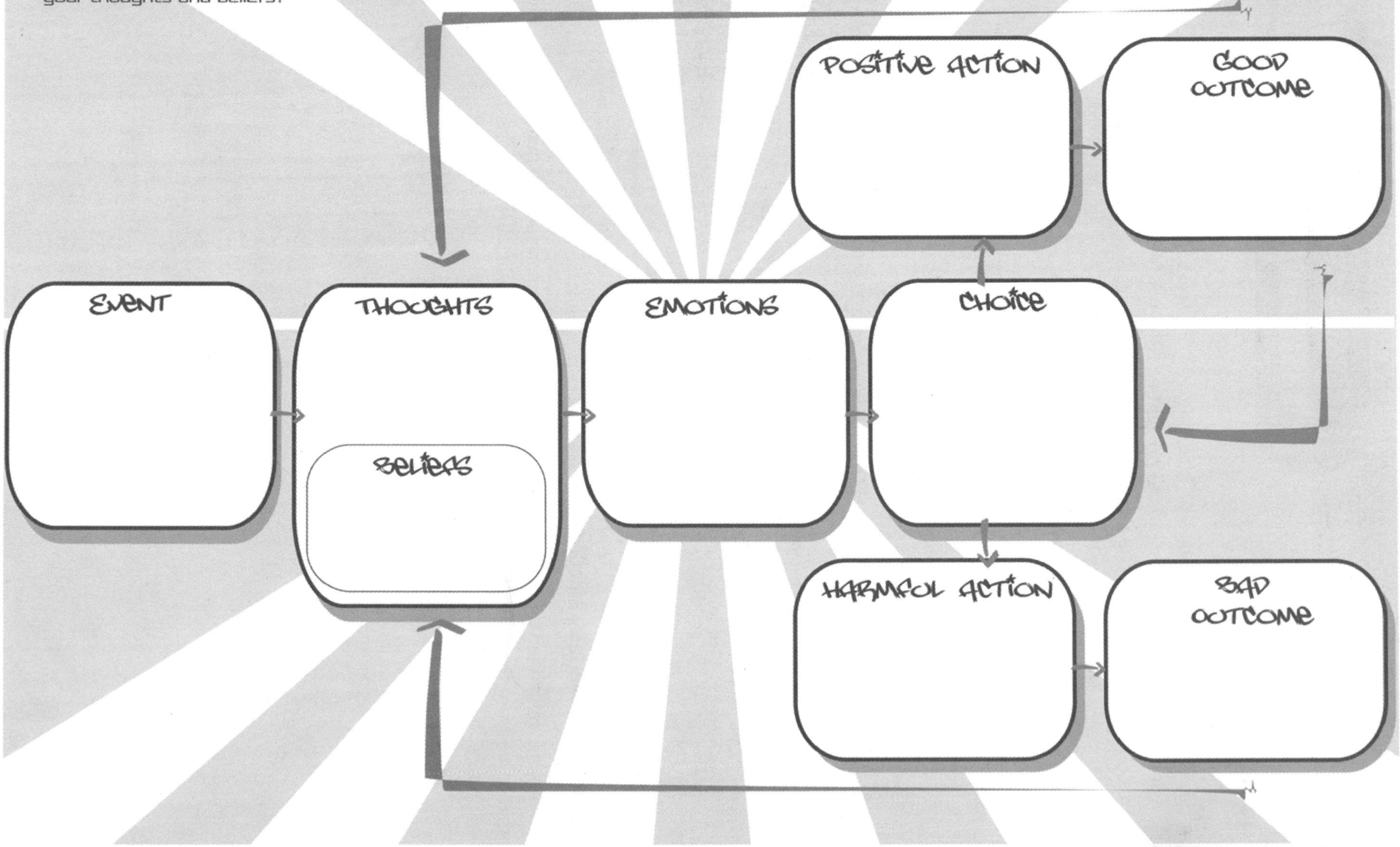

SESSION 14: HOW TO BARGAIN AND WHEN TO SAY NO

Objectives

- Review Session 13: Managing Cravings and Urges About Crime and Substances.
- Learn the process of negotiation for getting your needs met while treating others fairly.
- Review important information from Chapter 4 on RR prevention.
- Learn and practice refusal skills to deal with HR situations.

Anthony's Story: *My mom has gotten a second job to move us out of the neighborhood. I guess that is probably a good idea. I'm not sure how I'll be able to say no to the crew when all I really want is to be part of the power. I want to be the one feared, not the one who is afraid. But I want my best friend's death to mean something, even if it's just getting me out of the situation. It's going to be a hard struggle, but I guess in the end it will be worth it.*

Teresa's Story: *I mean, what was I supposed to do? Give up the influence of having money and power? Every time I thought about stopping, I would find myself in some new opportunity, and that feeling would go off deep in my gut and I just couldn't help it: I would steal, and I would feel triumph and joy and tell myself that was the last time. Of course, that was until the next opportunity came up. Now that I'm coming up on my release date, I'm scared that I won't be able to make it without going back to my old self.*

Up to This Point: Cravings and Urges

Last session we spent some time discussing *cravings* and *urges.* While cravings are the *mental event,* usually because we are in certain situations, *the urge* is the physical symptom, like tension, and the *movement toward the negative action,* such as drug use or committing a crime.

After going over certain events that may begin the chain of fulfilling cravings and urges, we went over several different methods that may help us to avoid the relapse or return to criminal conduct (CC): (1) *sharing with family or friends,* (2) *toughing it out,* (3) *talking yourself down,* (4) *urge surfing,* and (5) *finding another activity.* Which of the five do you think is most effective for you? Why? Often, all five methods are useful.

Activity: The Skill to Avoid

As a group, think of a **situation** that is really **hard to avoid.** Spend some time thinking of a si
that you are likely to find yourself in that might create a craving or urge. After a review of th

SESSION 14: HOW TO BARGAIN AND WHEN TO SAY NO

different ways to avoid RR, decide **which one(s) are best** for the situation that the group decided on and why. What makes that way better than the others? How effective would the others be for the same situation? Spend some time talking and debating about how to **avoid relapse and reoffending.** Notice that not everyone will agree on the same method; each person is different with their own ways of dealing with things.

Now that we know about how to manage *cravings* and *urges,* it is time for us to push forward into the actual skills that will help you *avoid the situations* that may trigger these thoughts and feelings.

First we will go over another *lifeline to freedom* and strength—**negotiation skills**—because although not all situations are HR, most situations can become HR when we begin to *have a conflict* with others and *fail to settle our differences* in a fair and honest manner.

We know that *not all situations are negotiable,* however, and that is why after reviewing the skills that we learned to *prevent* RR we will also be learning another powerful tool known as **refusal skills.** These are specifically designed for situations where there simply is *no room for bargaining.* Actually, even entering into a discussion about how you might come over to the *side of temptation* might only weaken your resolve and increase the likelihood of relapse or reoffending.

Dealing With Conflict

Ever get into an argument with a parent or teacher because they are *asking you to do something you don't want to do* or they *aren't giving you something that you want?* Conflict between people is unavoidable. Everybody sees the world differently (Principle 2 of Session 3), and often everyone has their own agenda built around their opinions. As we have discussed earlier, opinions are neither right nor wrong, so how do we work with people in a way that everyone is satisfied? This is called *negotiation.* It's when a deal is struck between people so that we are confident that the solution is fair and everyone's needs are being met. We call this a **win-win** situation. One person doesn't have to be "right" and the other "wrong"—both come out feeling good.

But negotiation is a difficult goal to reach. Sometimes people don't want to negotiate; there is too much involved, or they view the situation as nonnegotiable. In order to know when it is okay to negotiate and how to negotiate without stepping on someone's toes or moving into their personal space, we need to learn *negotiation skills.*

Negotiation—A Win-Win Solution to Conflict

Negotiation, which is the *ability to discuss and compromise* in order for the people involved to get what they want, is a way for all of us to resolve conflict and be happier in our lives. In order to do that, we first need to learn the different skills involved in negotiation.

SESSION 14: HOW TO BARGAIN AND WHEN TO SAY NO

Let's say we want our parents to help us buy a car. There are some steps to follow in order to negotiate successfully:

- **Ask.** The first step is to ask if they would be willing to help buy a car.
- **Find out why.** If the answer is no, then the next step is to ask why they won't. Make sure to listen and hear the reasons the other person is offering for not giving you what you want.
- **Repeat the reason.** "So the reason you don't want to help me buy the car is. . ." Let the other person know that you have heard them and can see where they are coming from.
- **Compromise.** It is this step that makes negotiation possible. Offer the other person something they may want, or suggest a middle ground. For example, we offer to pay half of the car and work off the part the parents are putting up. In a **win-win** situation, everybody wins.

Activity: A Skit of Success

Break into groups of two or three. For this activity, you will need to come up with a situation in which **compromise and negotiation** are the main themes. After you have written and practiced the situation, perform for the larger group. Did your negotiations seem realistic? **What steps** did you use? Do you think the situation was resolved to the **benefit of everyone,** or do you think that something wasn't fulfilled in the negotiations?

Dealing With Money

Most of us are interested in *having* money to get some things that we want. Sometimes we *rely on our parents* or *friends* to help us out, especially if we are not working or are earning too little when the need arises. We all know that people get "funny about money."

Negotiation to get what we want is only possible if the *other person is sure that we will do our part* as well. This is where some difficulty can come in. What happens if we offer to pay back the money put up, but *our word is no good* for the other person because of past mistakes? Here are three skills that will make compromise a little more realistic.

1. **Pay your debts.** If our parent has a problem lending us money because of past debts, then we might say, "How about I set up a payment plan with you?" If you *pay off your previous debts,* it is easier for people to compromise.
2. **Use collateral.** Offer to set up a situation that *benefits the other person* and gives them a reason to trust you. An example is "If I don't make my payments to you, then you can take away the car."
3. **Give references.** Offer people who will *back up your word* and give their reputation for your sake. If our mom doesn't believe we will pay back the money, we may want to use our father as a reference. It is important to *not use* someone as a reference without consent.

SESSION 14: HOW TO BARGAIN AND WHEN TO SAY NO

Activity: A List of Negotiations

Take a moment to write down a list of **things you want.** Write two or three things you would like to have but things that you must negotiate with another person for. Next to the items on your list, write down **who would be able to give it** to you. For example, one item that you feel you should be able to negotiate for is a new pair of shoes. The person to negotiate with is your parent. Take some time and think of **ways to negotiate** with that person for the item you want. Share with the group a few things on your list. Are you able to negotiate for everything you want? How does **compromise** play into your negotiations? Will you have to use a reference or collateral in your negotiations? Can you realistically negotiate for everything you want?

Life does not always make it easy to sit down with someone in order to negotiate. Most of us do not own corporations or have boardrooms in order to isolate and focus on the negotiation. So what do we do if the person we are trying to negotiate with is upset, busy, or too distracted to hold a discussion?

- **Offer to help.** If we offer to *help a person in a difficult situation,* the other person will likely be more open to helping us in our situation.
- **Ask to talk later.** Sometimes the time is not right to ask for certain things. *By asking to talk later,* we are able to set up a meeting time in which both people will be more able to focus.
- **Wait for a better time.** Instead of trying to set up a meeting, sometimes it is *better to just wait.* If your mom is busy with the baby, it is better to just wait until the baby is put down for a nap and your mom has time to relax.
- **Ask someone else.** Most of our problems and needs can be met by more than just one person. If the person you are trying to negotiate with is too upset or distracted, it may be better to *ask another person.*

Activity: Distracted Compromise

As a group, make a list of situations that may make it **difficult to compromise.** Write at least three situations, and then go back through the list and **offer suggestions** for how the compromise and negotiation may be **successfully** completed. Make sure to have an open discussion, and try to come up with as **many solutions** to the difficulties as possible. The outcome we want is that both sides are winners.

Informed Negotiation

Negotiating for what we want is often like a debate. There is a lot of back-and-forth before both people reach a compromise that will satisfy both. One of the *worst things* that can happen when in negotiation is *to not be informed.* Learn and know about what you want and how you intend to get it before putting it on the table. Going back to our example, if we didn't have any idea of where we would get the money or how we would pay back our parents, the likelihood of them compromising with us is unlikely. But if we approach them with what we want, how much it will cost, and what we are willing to do for it, in realistic terms, then compromise is more likely.

Of course, information flows both ways. If the other *person is vague* about what they want from the situation or why they don't want to compromise, *ask them for more* information. It's not a good idea to get demanding or angry, but ask them if they can help you understand *their point of view* and why they don't want to agree. Remember our communication skills. When you are trying to get more information, use the *active listening* skills and *really listen* to what they have to say before offering feedback. Active listening leads to **win-win** outcomes.

Of course, some areas are *nonnegotiable,* especially areas where another person's rights are being infringed upon. The best thing for you to *know is when to quit.* Some things are not meant to be, and then there are always other things you can negotiate for.

Activity: A Bag of Negotiation Skills

Form a large circle with your group. Your counselor will have a beanbag or ball that will be passed among members of the group. Your counselor will toss the ball to a person in the circle, and that person will begin by **saying something they want.** The group will then ask the person who or whom they will **negotiate with** in order to get that. After every answer, the group will ask **more questions** or offer difficulties that may arise in the negotiations.

For example, we want a new car. We will negotiate with our mom. What if she is too busy to talk with us? We can **offer to help** her while we try to talk with her, or we can ask her if she will **talk with us later.** What if she says no? Offer some **collateral** or a **compromise** that will help her as well as get us the car, like we will drive our younger sibling to and from school. What if she asks how much it's going to cost? We will have done some research first, and we will offer her how much it will cost and a plan on how to pay for it. After the person with the ball has **successfully made their case on** all problems the group can think of for the negotiations, the ball will be passed to **someone else** in the group, and the new person will tell the group something they want and who they will negotiate with. Continue doing this until everyone in the group has practiced the negotiation skills.

One area that is *completely nonnegotiable is any situation that brings you into contact with criminal activities or substance use.* It is important and beneficial for us to know how to negotiate with other people in order to smoothly move through most conflicts, but when in a HR situation where you are being tempted or urged to do something you know is dangerous or harmful, negotiation is not applicable. That is when *refusal skills* come into play.

SESSION 14: HOW TO BARGAIN AND WHEN TO SAY NO

Review of Relapse and Recidivism Prevention

In Sessions 8 and 9 in Chapter 4, we learned about HR situations and how to spot when RR may occur. Here are some important terms to remember from those sessions.

HR situations are the situations that have *led to substance use* or *criminal behavior* in the past. When in these situations, we may think or feel that we need the substance or be involved in negative behavior.

HR thinking has to do with the *thought habits* (remember, the automatic thoughts) that lead to using substances or criminal activity. This also includes the thoughts that may put us in HR situations for use and trouble.

Relapse starts happening when you engage in HR thinking or situations that have led to use in the past. It doesn't start with the actual action but with the thought habits leading up to the action.

Recidivism starts when you involve yourself in the thinking or *thought habits that lead to criminal behavior*. It also happens when you take part in actions or put yourself in HR situations.

Activity: Anthony's and Teresa's High-Risk Thinking

Teresa discusses the feelings of triumph and pleasure she got from stealing. Anthony discusses the struggle he has with the thought of not being part of the gang anymore. Do you think they are participating in HR thinking that could lead to relapse or reoffending? Is Anthony able to avoid getting back into gang activity? How? What about Teresa and her cravings and urges for money and thrill seeking? How might they successfully change, despite their thinking and urges?

Remember that RR does not start with the action, but begins way before, with the *thoughts in our mind* and how we choose to manage them.

When we control our thoughts, we control our feelings and actions and vastly reduce our chances of RR.

When and How to Say No

We know that not all situations are avoidable. Things happen *outside of our control,* but we are the ones who have control over our own actions and decisions. As with everything we want and like to do, *being able to refuse* to take part in substance abuse and criminal behavior *begins with practice.* This also requires you to be aware of the HR thinking and situations you can become involved in.

SESSION 14: HOW TO BARGAIN AND WHEN TO SAY NO

Here are some keys to using refusal skills:

- **Saying no** without hesitation and in a firm, clear voice.
- **Looking at the person directly** and not avoiding their eyes—this lets them know that you do not want to participate.
- **Not feeling guilty** for refusing. You won't hurt anyone's feelings by refusing, but you will hurt yourself by accepting.
- **Choosing to take part in something different:** take a ride; go to a movie, etc. Ask the person to stop asking or putting pressure on you. A friend will understand and give you room.
- **Letting the person know** what you have to lose by accepting.
- **Not debating** with the person. After saying no, change the subject. If you debate the subject, it means you are persuadable and debating with yourself.
- **Not making excuses.** Excuses mean you won't now but you might later.

Activity: Anthony's Refusal

It seems like Anthony has **mixed feelings** about change. Why does he want to get out of the gang, and why doesn't he? Could any of the previously listed **refusal skills** help him if his friends ever confront him? Why or why not? How might Anthony be successful in refusing?

Activity: The Role of Refusal

In groups of three or four, create two skits in which a person has to **refuse their friend's offer** of **something that is bad** for them—e.g., two people want to take some drugs and go to a movie. The third person has to refuse the offer without rejecting their friends. In order to do that, the third person may say, "No, I'm still on probation, and if I get caught I will have to go to jail. We can all go to the movie straight, though."

In the first skit, the refusal person **will not use the refusal skills** that were previously listed and end up doing what they were trying to say no to. In the second skit, have the refusal person use the skills that were previously listed to **successfully refuse** without being aggressive or angering the friends.

Knowing the Situation

Learning the skills of refusal also means that *you know when to use* the refusal skills. In order to do that, we have to understand in what situations our weakness lies and then figure out how to control our own actions.

Activity: My Own Difficult Situation

Take some time to fill out Worksheet 15: List of High-Risk, Difficult Refusal Situations to **identify the situations** you think may cause you **problems with refusing.** Then mark whether the situation fits in

SESSION 14: HOW TO BARGAIN AND WHEN TO SAY NO

refusing substances or **criminal behavior.** Then get into groups of two or three to discuss ways that you **can refuse** in the situations that will be hardest for you. Put some effort into it, because the more comfortable you are with them here means the more comfortable you will be with them in a real situation.

Putting It Together

- After reviewing the *negotiation skills,* do you think you negotiate well? How do you compromise with people like your parents and friends? Can you work for **win-win** outcomes?
- Teresa is thinking about the money and thrills she got out of committing crimes. How might she manage her HR thinking about returning to a life of crime?
- Anthony has a hard time deciding if he wants to change. What *signs of recidivism* does Anthony exhibit? How might Anthony *avoid returning* to the gang and his life of crime?
- In order to use the refusal skills, we first must know that we are in a HR situation. How might you become aware that it is a HR situation?
- What refusal skills might work best for you?
- Think about how hard it may be for you to say no to a friend. Think about how you might do that without hurting them or yourself?
- Review Figure 11: The Relapse/Recidivism Model. How can it be helpful to you to avoid relapsing or reoffending?

Using the Program Guides and Tools for Change

Rate your ability to use the **negotiation skills** taught in this session to create a win-win solution to conflict.

0	1	2	3	4	5	6	7	8	9	10
Low					Medium					High

Indicate your ability to use the **refusal skills** taught in this session to *refuse* to take part in substance abuse or criminal behavior.

0	1	2	3	4	5	6	7	8	9	10
Low					Medium					High

- Review your Self-Portrait (SP) and Plan for Change (PFC). What will you work on this week?
- Do you want to add something to your PFC?
- Review your Master Skills List (MSL). Update your self-ratings for the following: managing urges/cravings, preventing relapse, managing high-risk (HR) exposures, using refusal skills, using conflict resolution skills, and using negotiation skills.

Worksheet 15

LIST OF HIGH-RISK, DIFFICULT REFUSAL SITUATIONS

List all situations. Then check if they apply to AOD abuse, CC, or both. These situations are both high-risk (HR) to relapsing into AOD abuse or going back to CC. They are also difficult situations to say no in.

HIGH-RISK, DIFFICULT REFUSAL SITUATIONS	FITS ALCOHOL AND OTHER DRUG ABUSE	FITS CRIMINAL CONDUCT

Anthony's Story

Living on my block is dangerous. And if you don't belong to a group, you are dead before you are old enough to move away. Of course, if you do belong, you are dead before you can legally drink. I was jumped in when I turned 12, about two years ago. There was no debate or any pro and con talk in my head about joining. It was what you did, and that is exactly what my best friend and I did. But you have to understand. It seems like the best life to live coming from where we come from. Man, we saw those guys growing up, and they always had money and clothes and gee'd-up cars. It's true we would hear about kids dying and gunshots and shit, but what does that matter when those guys had brand-new clothes all the time and we were wearing hand-me-downs that would be rejected from the Salvation Army.

So when we were 12, we got jumped into the gang that ran our block. I hear different stories about different gangs doin' different things to get a person in. I even hear about girls having sex with all the members. It was nothing like that. We just had to take on a couple of guys and get bloodied up. And at the time it was worth it. Because when we were done, we had a crew at our back. No matter what went down, we knew they would be there.

I started off running stuff for the crew—just deliveries and breakin' shit every once in a while. But as I got older and proved my loyalty, I started getting more jobs and more inside knowledge. I guess we had this big thing with a neighboring gang—territory wars and shit. All I know is that sometimes things would get heavy. But I never worried. I had a couple hundred people who would step up for me because I was part of a crew. I never worried about no cops or any rival gang doing nothing, because we were a force to be reckoned with. I could walk by the school and throw rocks and break all the windows, and nothing would get done about it because people were afraid. And as I got older, I began to feel the power of fear. I was never afraid, but everyone was afraid of my friends, so that meant I had power and they didn't—money and power and all the things I wouldn't have without a membership.

My best friend and I had a good life for once. And just because we were part of a crew didn't mean we weren't a pair no more. I knew this kid from way back before I could remember. We wore Pampers together. We knew where we were from and where we were, and that's all that matters. The gang had us doing different shit. He wasn't much for chaos and destruction. He had smarts. So they had him training for some business shit. I don't know. I was the one who broke stuff.

About a month or so ago, my bro and I were walking down the street, minding our own business. I think we was gonna get some ice cream or something when suddenly there were screeching tires behind us and gunshots. Suddenly there was a tearing, fiery feeling in my leg and I fell. I couldn't stand. I couldn't move. I had never felt so much pain in my life. I heard my friend go down too, but it was different. I could hear a wheezing, breathless sound. I crawled over to him. He was facedown, and I tried to turn him over. They had shot him in the back a couple of times, and I think one got his lung because it sounded like he was breathing through his back. I tried to stop the blood as a bunch of people swarmed around us. I couldn't talk or look at any of 'em. I only saw my friend and so much blood. When the ambulance got there, they separated us because they were gonna take him Flight for Life to some better hospital than the general. I heard he died before he even left the ambulance.

So I'm about to leave the hospital now. They kept me here for so long because I guess the bullet pierced some major vein in my leg. They were worried it would hemorrhage if I moved too early. I've also had some depression. I keep thinking I'll see my friend, and it never happens. I dream about him a lot. Not many of the crew have been by. They are weird about any cop involvement, so I've been alone most of the time. There was this gang counselor who kept coming to see me. In fact, he was here just this morning. He kept talking about how he knew where I was coming from, about how he had been there, and about how it was time to get out. But how do I say *no*? All that money, all those clothes and women. And more than that, the power and protection. If I turn my back, I am alone. If I want to break a window, the cops will be all over me. And damn, I want the power and money. The chance to be more than a nobody. I want it so bad I can feel it in my chest and bones. The memories of the parties and the life are more real to me than the bullet in my leg.

Then I think about my friend . . . and all the friends who have been lost along the way for some higher purpose of one person that most of us don't even know. My mom's gotten a second job to move us, and maybe the counselor is right. If now is not the time to get out, then I will die in. And I think my friend's memory deserves more than for me to go back into what killed him. If I have to make a life the hard way, it will be worth it knowing it was for him.

Teresa's Story

What can I say? I grew up poor—not just kinda poor—welfare and food stamps poor. It seemed like we never had enough to eat. I would be so angry walking to school, seeing other kids with lunches packed, throwing away half-eaten apples and Pop-Tarts while my sister and I were starving. There were times I was tempted to pick that thrown away food right out of the garbage, but I would hear that stupid ol' saying in my head "You are what you eat," and I certainly wasn't going to be garbage. I was poor, but I deserved more.

I guess that's where it all started. I wanted to eat, so I started stealing food. I guess technically the food I was taking wasn't mine, but it wasn't garbage either. And besides filling my empty belly, I got this rush whenever I took something from the store—that butterflies-in-your-stomach feeling. When you have it, it's almost enough to make you sick, but once you know you are in the clear, that sickness turns into triumph and joy. There's nothing better in the world! It didn't take me long to figure out that I was good at being sneaky. In over a year of stealing random groceries, I was never caught once—not even close. By the end of that year, I wasn't getting the butterflies anymore—it was just the same ol', same ol'. And besides, if I was that good at stealing food, what else could I get away with? I mean, there were a lot of other things in this world I wanted—things beyond what I needed just to survive. The other kids at school had lots of expensive things, brand-name clothes, new CDs, and phones and shit. Just because my momma had a minimum wage job and dad was long-gone didn't mean I deserved to suffer.

I started small, you know, makeup and other little things I could easily stuff up my sleeve or into a small purse. I got that old feeling back, and I was able to get my sister and I all the things we had wanted for so long. Since I was getting away with it, I just kept pushing the limits. Soon enough, I was taking resellable merchandise—whatever would sell on the streets. I mean, having goods is nice but having cash is having power over my life. With money, I was able to buy anything my family needed. It felt good to know that I could take care of us in ways that momma couldn't.

After a couple of years, it all started to catch up to me, though. I guess I just started to look suspicious. The cops started cracking down on stolen goods in the pawn shops, and I was a suspicious customer—a 16-year-old girl with hundreds of dollars of stuff every couple of weeks. But I didn't want to give everything up, you know? I mean, what was I supposed to do, just give up that money, give up a chance to have things I had never had? A chance to provide for my family? Give up the influence of having money and power? Talking about it now, the answer seems obvious, but then, it was inconceivable. Every time I thought about stopping, I would find myself in some new opportunity and that feeling would go off deep in my gut and I just couldn't help it—I would steal, I would sell it, and I would feel triumph and joy and tell myself that was the last time. That was, of course, until the next opportunity came up.

To make a long story short, I got caught, and when that happened, well, shit hit the fan. I was selling a brand-new MP3 player to an undercover on the street. Eventually, they were able to connect me to a number of other recent thefts. Luckily, I was still charged as a juvenile, but with that many felonies, I was going to have to do some time in a correctional facility. So, here I sit.

I'm coming up on my release day, and I know I don't want to come back, but I'm so afraid that I won't be able to help myself when an opportunity presents itself. I wasn't able to turn my back before, and I'm so afraid I won't be able to do it now either.

Chapter Eight:
Responsibility to Others and the Community

GOALS OF THIS CHAPTER

- Define value, moral, and community norms.
- Understand your own set of values and morals.
- Discuss moral dilemmas and how they help us change.
- Learn about empathy and its role in interaction with people.

45

HUNTER'S STORY

MARIAH'S STORY

SESSION 15: UNDERSTANDING VALUES AND MORAL DEVELOPMENT

Objectives

- Review Chapter 7: Avoiding Trouble and Playing Fair.
- Learn prosocial values.
- Understand your own set of values and morals.
- Discuss what you see as the morals and rules of the society around you.

Hunter's Story: *People are weak, and if you let them, they will feed off of you—like parasites. And bums are the absolute scum of society—dirty, filthy, mooching little parasitic mites that beg for my hard-earned cash. I can't even drive yet, but I have a job. Why can't they get a job?*

My mom used to give money to the bums downtown. She wouldn't buy me a piece of candy, but she would give them change with tears in her eyes. My dad would get mad at her. He said she was encouraging them and keeping them from getting off their lazy asses and becoming a part of decent society. Dad says they're like alley cats. You feed one of them and the next day there are 20 at your doorstep.

Mariah's Story: *When I saw my brother, I told him about an accident some of my friends had gotten in. I had tried to talk them out of driving that night—none of them were in any shape to get behind the wheel—but they just wouldn't listen to reason. There was nothing left for me to do. When I was telling my brother this, I expected him to totally back me up, but he told me I should've called someone—even the cops! Now, I guess I just don't know what's right anymore. Everything I believed before just seems upside down.*

How to Bargain

In Session 14, we discussed and learned about negotiation skills and refusal skills. Conflict often comes up when we are dealing with other people, especially when wants and needs are involved. Since everyone has a different opinion—and opinions are neither right nor wrong—sometimes it is difficult to get what we want from the people around us. That is when negotiation comes into play. Once we have learned to negotiate and compromise, it is easier to work with people toward a common goal.

Activity: Means of Negotiation

Take a moment to review the **negotiation skills** for **win-win** outcomes that we covered in Session 14: How to Bargain and When to Say No. Go through a **thinking report** *(situation, thoughts and beliefs,* *feelings,* and *actions),* and see if there were any cases where you negotiated or if there were any situations that negotiation would have worked for. Break into groups of two or three, and share with your group members the situations in your thinking report that would have **(1)** been more successful with negotiation, **(2)** successfully used negotiation, or **(3)** did not successfully use negotiation. Then discuss with each other how each situation could have been more successfully resolved to arrive at a **win-win** solution.

There are, however, situations in which *negotiation skills* are not useful or would actually do more harm.

High-risk (HR) situations, or situations that put us at risk for recidivism or relapse, are situations where we should not use negotiation. Rather, refusal and avoidance are better suited for dealing with these situations in order to keep us from doing something we don't want to do.

Activity: Steps of Refusal

As a large group, make a list of the **refusal skills** covered in the last session. Think of situations in the past month that required refusal skills. Which of the refusal skills did you use, and how successful were you at avoiding relapse and recidivism (RR)? If the skill was not successful, what possible options do you have for next time? Review your Self-Portrait (SP) scores on harm-directing thoughts and criminal conduct (CC). If they were high, this session is especially important to you.

Making Personal Choices About Right or Wrong

Our choices about what is worth bargaining for, what is worth living (or dying) for, and what should unquestionably be rejected or refused depend on our personal values or goals, what we think is right or wrong, and if we think certain actions can get us in trouble with those in authority. Before we move into this session on *taking personal responsibility for our actions,* we are going to define certain ideas and words that we will be using.

- **Values.** These are things that we see as *worthwhile* or that mean a lot to us. These become *guiding principles* of our life. An example of this may be *loyalty* to friends and family. Others might be to have a *comfortable or exciting life.*
- **Personal Morals.** This is what we see as *right* or *wrong* in relation to other people or society in general. An example of a moral is whether or not harming or killing another human is right or wrong. Following the Golden Rule is another example of a personal moral standard of conduct.
- **Community Norms.** These are *rules,* or *guidelines,* that we live by. This is about what the people in our community consider right or wrong. Sometimes norms are formal (as in legal regulations); or they can be informal (as in public opinion). Robbery or vandalism falls within legal norms. Being

respectful to others is an example of an informal norm. In other words, common norms refer to the actions that are *valued* by our community, such as safe driving, as well as those that will be *punished,* such as minors in possession of alcohol or driving under the influence.

- **Prosocial Thinking.** This is thinking and acting in such a way that we take part in and build positive family, community, and social relationships.

Activity: Hunter's Values

Break into smaller groups, and take a look at Hunter's and Mariah's stories. What **values** do you think Mariah and Hunter are exhibiting? What sort of **morals** does Hunter have, and how do they agree with prosocial thinking, if at all? What are some of the values you share with Hunter? What are the conflicting morals and values the Mariah is facing?

Activity: My Own Values

Take a moment to look at Worksheet 16: Values, Morals, and Norms. In the first column, from the list of values shown here, write in **five of your values,** ordering them from most to least important (a list of things that people value is shown next). Be sure to include some of the things that are most important to you and some that are least important. They could be love, friendship, family, or any number of things that you place high, medium, or low values as to their importance in your life.

Sometimes you might live up to your values, and sometimes you might not. Just place a check in **no, sometimes,** or **yes** according to whether you think you are living up to your values or not. Then, as a group, make a list of some **common values** that are held by the majority of the group. What values are common in the group? Which values do the group follow, and which values do the majority of the group not follow?

Things That People Value

Comfortable life	**Equality**	**Exciting life**
Family security	**Freedom**	**Happiness**
Inner harmony	**Mature love**	**National security**
Pleasure	**Salvation**	**Self-Respect**
Sense of accomplishment	**Social recognition**	**True friendship**
Wisdom	**World of beauty**	**World of peace**

Worksheet 16

Values, Morals, and Norms

List of Your Five Most Important Values	Do You Follow These Values?		
	No	Sometimes	Always

List of Your Five Most Important Morals	Do You Follow These Values?		
	No	Sometimes	Always

List of Your Five Most Important Community and Society Standards	Do You Follow These Values?		
	No	Sometimes	Always

SESSION 15: UNDERSTANDING VALUES AND MORAL DEVELOPMENT

The Values of the Program

In the beginning, we started this program with the idea that thoughts cause and interact with feelings and actions. We also discussed that the very basis of our thoughts begins with our beliefs and attitudes. During the process of this program, we have not necessarily tried to teach you any particular morals or values. Yet throughout our program we have been trying to give you some very important ideas that have something to do with values and morals.

- **Change.** We have talked about and taught you the value of change. The skills you have been learning are meant to help you value and understand change.
- **Freedom and control.** A lot of the skills we have been trying to teach you have the end goal of gaining freedom and control over your life.
- **Building positive relationships with others and your community.** We have mentioned this once or twice before, but this essentially means being prosocial, which is the opposite of being criminal or antisocial.
- **Concern for others.** This is a clear goal of this program.

Activity: Hunter's and Mariah's Values

Take a look at the last two values of the program (positive relationships and concern for others), and then compare that with Hunter's story. How does Hunter show these values, or does he? Would it be possible for Hunter to learn to accept the last two values, and why or why not?

Will Mariah be able to change her value of not ratting on others? How does the value of concern for others conflict with value on not telling on her friends, even when their lives and the lives of others might be endangered?

Activity: My Morals

Take some time to fill out the part of Worksheet 16 that covers *your moral beliefs*. List **five morals** that are important to you and that you feel you would like to live by—e.g., *do not harm others, respect people's property, be faithful, don't have sex before marriage, keep your word.* Then check whether you live up to each of those morals using no, sometimes, and yes. If you have any questions about what a moral is, look at the definition that was previously given or ask your counselor. Which morals do you follow, and which morals do you tend not pay to attention to?

SESSION 15: UNDERSTANDING VALUES AND MORAL DEVELOPMENT

Activity: Standards Of Conduct

Use **Worksheet 16** to list **five basic norms or standards of conduct** that your community lives by—for example, *don't steal, don't do drugs or drink alcohol.* For this activity, you can get into small groups if you would like. Then check whether you don't, sometimes, or do live by those community norms. Which community norms do you agree with, and which do you think are pointless? Why?

The Dilemma of Values

Sometimes a conflict can occur between our values and our morals. This can happen when what we value goes against what our personal morals are or even the norms of the community. An example of this may be that one of your values is loyalty, which means you are very loyal to your friends. But what if your friend wants you to break into a house? The value of loyalty to your friend is now coming into conflict with your moral against breaking and entering or even the community moral of upholding the law. Can you be loyal to your friends and at the same time be a responsible citizen? Can you achieve a **win-win** situation?

It doesn't have to be that complicated, though. It could be a value of expensive clothing or cars or wanting a lot of money that is in conflict with the moral of not stealing. For some people, our values can compete and come into conflict with our morals on a regular basis.

Activity: Competing Minds

Take a moment to look at **Worksheet 16.** Do any of the values you listed go against or conflict with the morals or the basic community norms you listed? If a value conflicts with a moral or norm (community standard of conduct), then put the number of the value next to the norm it conflicted with listed on your worksheets. Then as a group, get together and discuss some of the values that conflict with the morals and norms. Write these down, and then discuss why they conflict and how you can possibly deal with each so they don't conflict or there aren't any problems arising from the conflict.

Where Do Values and Morals Come From?

So now that we have talked about values, morals, and standards of conduct (which are the rules and expectations of society), we are going to take a moment to look at how our values and morals develop.

Although television and other forms of media have some influence on how we develop, the values we usually get from those media are related to the standard of conduct for the society around us. It is important for us to remember that what we see on television is meant to entertain; they are not to be rules of living.

SESSION 15: UNDERSTANDING VALUES AND MORAL DEVELOPMENT

So where do we get our *values* and *morals?* Usually the *people closest to us,* such as our parents or family members, are the ones who teach us our values and morals. We may even get them from our neighbors, friends, and the people we see every day, but most often they come from the people closest to us and those who are around us all the time.

But our values are not always positive or healthy. Because of the influence of others on our values and morals, negative things can develop within our belief system. Sometimes our beliefs and values can cause harm to other people and ourselves. In order to avoid harming those around you and your community, thinking about and becoming aware of your values and morals can help you to be more aware of what some of your core beliefs are, and then you—and only you—can decide if they should change.

Activity: The Growth of a Value

Break into groups, and begin discussing Hunter's and Mariah's stories. Who do you think **Hunter got his values from? Where did Mariah get her values from?** Why do you think that? Are Hunter's values a positive influence in his life, or do you think his values will cause him problems? Why? Would it be possible for Hunter to change his values in his current environment? Are his values helping him to become a responsible citizen? Does it make sense for Mariah to reconsider some of her values and moral standards? Which ones?

Activity: The Belief of Me

First get into pairs and review Worksheet 1: Pathways of Learning and Change (Session 3). Use a **real situation,** and fill in the blanks about the **positive** and **negative results** of choices. How could the results affect the choice you will make next time? Spend some time discussing how you would change your **thinking** to arrive at a more positive outcome.

For this activity, which looks at different people's values and beliefs, the room will be separated into two parts, with one side representing *agree* and the other side representing *disagree*. The far side of each part will be the strongest you can feel, and the closer to the middle, the less absolute your value or belief is. The counselor will then begin to read off beliefs, and you will go to each side of the room that represents how you feel about the issue. For example, the phrase is "All drugs should be legalized." Depending on how you believe about the issue, you will move to the area of the room you think represents your stance. Then one at a time you will say one to two sentences on why you take a certain stance on a value.

SESSION 15: UNDERSTANDING VALUES AND MORAL DEVELOPMENT

AGREE			DISAGREE		
Strongly Agree	Middle Zone	Slightly Agree	Strongly Agree	Middle Zone	Slightly Disagree

Do our values and morals help us to reach win-win outcomes? Does the community gain from our values and morals?

Putting It Together

- Hunter shows some really strong values, but are his values positive or negative? What do you think Hunter's morals are? What are Mariah's values and morals? How do their behaviors match up with community norms?
- Our morals and values are taught to us by the people closest to us. Where did Hunter and Mariah get their values?
- Values and morals are the basis of our belief systems. What values do you hold about the world around you? What morals do you have?
- Take a moment to look at your worksheets. Who do you share your values with? What values and morals do you have in common with your parents or people closest to you?
- What values and morals do you have that are different from the people closest to you?
- Do any of your values and morals show up in your autobiography, and which ones are they? How do they affect your choices?

Using the Program Guides and Tools for Change

Rate your understanding of values, morals, and community norms.

0	1	2	3	4	5	6	7	8	9	10
Low					Medium					High

With your counselor, continue to work on your SP and Plan for Change (PFC).

SESSION 16: UNDERSTANDING AND PRACTICING EMPATHY

Objectives

- Review Session 15: Understanding Values and Moral Development.
- Continue looking at morality and values.
- Understand the difference between sympathy and empathy.
- Learn to consider the position of other people. Learn empathy.

Hunter's Story: *One day my space filler and I were walking around downtown when I ran into this girl. My "friend" told her to watch out, and I was just about to say something rude to her when I looked into her eyes. There was something soft and weird about her eyes. I could see that she was poor, but I didn't know how poor. She began telling me that she lived in a car with her family. She was looking for a job or for money, but she kept talking about how hungry she was. I felt bad for her—I really did. But I also know that feeding bums encourages them, and she was a bum, no matter how good looking she was. But I bought her a couple hot dogs, enough to feed her family, too. But then I left. I didn't want to be around her anymore. I won't feed bums anymore, and I can't believe I did it that one time.*

Mariah's Story: *My mom beat the idea into my head not to be a tattletale. A couple years ago, my brother got ratted out. This snitch, Sasha, got caught with a bag at school. She was taken to the principal's office, the cops were called—the whole thing. Turns out, Sasha totally sold out. My brother took the fall on his own. He's serving a 3-year sentence for drug dealing on school property. I got to see him a few weeks ago when my family went for our monthly visit. I told him about the accident some of my friends had gotten into after a night of heavy drinking. I tried to talk them out of driving, but they wouldn't listen and there was nothing I could do. My brother told me I should have called someone, even the cops! Everyone is blaming me for the accident, saying, "I should've done something"—even my own brother!*

Our Last Session

Last session we began to define and discuss values, morals, and standards of conduct. **Values,** which are a little like opinions but stronger, are our guidelines to what we consider important in life and the ideas that we hold close. An example of this may be loyalty to a friend. **Personal morals** are rules we give ourselves concerning the right or wrong of human action. One moral may be the belief that it is wrong to let another person starve. Both morals and values are things that we personally hold close and follow in our belief systems. Often our values and morals are developed and run along similar lines as family members, parents, or people who are close to us.

SESSION 16: UNDERSTANDING AND PRACTICING EMPATHY

Activity: Accepting Other People's Values

As a group, think of a **value** that is common in everyday life. Then separate into two groups according to those who **agree** with the value and those who **disagree** with the value. Sit with the two groups in a line facing each other. One by one, those who agree **will share** why they think that. The person across from them will then say why they disagree.

An example of a value for this activity would be placing great importance on doing what it takes to get a **really expensive, fancy car.** One person who agrees might say, "You need it to get respect." A person who disagrees might say, "It doesn't make you cool." Continue going back and forth until everyone has spoken once. Listen to the other people and their reasons for agreeing or disagreeing. Can you see their point of view?

Standards of conduct, also known as **community norms,** are the things that the society and group of people around us believe and follow as right or wrong behavior. Similar to values and morals, our parents and family do have a role in passing to us the community norms, but the law also impresses community norms upon us.

Common Values

Values and community norms, or standards of conduct, differ across countries, cultures, and ethnic groups. Yet all laws in all civilized nations have one value and norm in common: *the safety and welfare of people* and *the concern for people.* This concern for others, what we call **empathy,** is basic to most communities and cultures. Empathy is one of the most important values we can learn in order to change our actions and behaviors because once we begin considering other people's attitudes, feelings, and views of the world, it becomes easier to make positive choices about how to think, feel, and act. Empathy is the basis for **win-win** outcomes.

Empathy → ***Positive Thoughts, Feelings, and Actions***

Difference in Sympathy and Empathy

We often hear *sympathy* used in common language. Sympathy, however, is not what we are talking about in this session, because sympathy and empathy are different. When we have sympathy for another person, we may do the following:

- Feel sorry for that person, or pity them.
- Have compassion or caring for another person.
- Sense another person's hurt or pain.

SESSION 16: UNDERSTANDING AND PRACTICING EMPATHY

But empathy takes one more step past sympathy in our caring for others. While sympathy *means caring for or feeling sorry for* another person, empathy means *actually being able to understand and to see from that person's point of view.* Empathy is a deeper experience and a deeper emotion than sympathy because we are putting ourselves in the other person's situation. When we have empathy for another person, we can do the following:

- Take the other person's position in the present, rather than feeling badly about something that happened in the past.
- Relate to or know another person's feelings, motives, ideals, or situation.
- Feel concern for another person.
- Feel another person's pain and suffering, because we are able to put ourselves in the place of the other person—meaning we can "walk in their shoes."
- Realize, or understand what is going in internally: "I understand your pain in my heart and head."

Activity: Hunter's Feelings

As a group, take a look at Hunter's story, and then discuss whether you think Hunter felt **sympathy** or **empathy** for the girl. What is the difference between the two? Use some examples from the story to back up your opinion on whether it was sympathy or empathy. Can members of a group feel sympathy or empathy for Hunter? What are some differences between feeling sympathy or empathy for Hunter?

Activity: A Walk in Someone Else's Shoes

Worksheet 17: Practicing Feeling Empathy for Another Person has four stories telling about something that happened to another person. Carefully read each story and then **put yourself in the place of that person.** Close your eyes if you need to, and really try to think and feel what the other person in the story is going through in their situation. Then write in the second column what your feelings and thoughts were after you put yourself in that person's place. Then get together as a group, and discuss the thoughts and feelings that each of you had. Were you able to visualize and feel what was going on?

A Moral Dilemma

A *moral dilemma* is a situation where our *ideas clash* with those of other people, when a value or moral we hold is in *conflict with a rule* that is placed on us by someone else, or when two or more *beliefs* that we hold *are in conflict* with each other. In order to learn empathy, we must change our thinking. But in order to change our thinking, we often have to come in contact with a moral dilemma. So how do we recognize a moral dilemma?

Worksheet 17

PRACTICING FEELING EMPATHY FOR ANOTHER PERSON

Carefully read each brief story. Then close your eyes, and put yourself in the place of the person in the story. How does the person feel? What is the person thinking? Then write the thoughts and feelings that you had when you put yourself in the place of the other person.

Here are four stories. Each story is about a particular individual who has experienced something of great importance in his or her life. Read each story carefully.	Put yourself in the place of the person in the story. Then write down what you think the other person was thinking and feeling
John is 9 years old. He was hit by a drunk driver and was in the hospital for 2 months. He lost his right leg in the accident. He loved baseball, was a very good player, and was feeling a great deal of sadness because he knew he would never play baseball again.	
Marie, who is 35 years old, struggled all her life to make a living and support her family of four children. Her husband was killed just after the youngest was born. She works as a cook at a high school. Her oldest son is very smart and will be finishing high school this year. He wants to be a doctor, but Marie knows she does not and never will have the money to send him to college. The other day, her son came home and told her that he received a full 4-year scholarship to attend college.	
Hank, age 22, a construction worker, was leaving work when a robber hit him on the head and stole his car. The robber then drove over Hank when getting away. Hank has been in the hospital for 2 months. He has severe spinal injuries and will have to be in rehab for many months, and he may never walk again.	
Pete, who is 17, has been alcohol- and drug-free for the past year. He was out with some friends and they bet him $20 that he couldn't do six shots of tequila in 10 minutes. He did it. Then he got in his car, started to drive to his girlfriend's, and critically injured three children. The judge gave him 5 years for his third DUI.	

SESSION 16: UNDERSTANDING AND PRACTICING EMPATHY

Activity: Hunter and Mariah Face Moral Dilemmas

When Hunter meets the girl and begins to speak with her, he begins to face a **moral dilemma.** What was Hunter's moral dilemma? How did he resolve his dilemma? How did Hunter change from the dilemma, if at all? What do you think could have been done differently on Hunter's part in order to change?

Mariah also faces a **moral dilemma.** She knows that it is dangerous to drink and drive but has a conflict because her family taught her not to tell on people. Mariah always thought that being a snitch was really bad. How can she resolve her contrasting views?

Activity: The Search for a Dilemma

Break into groups of three to four people while your counselor hands out pages of newspaper. With your group, try to find at least one moral dilemma in the newspaper. Find an article where someone is doing something that is clearly wrong but they do it anyway to serve their own self-interest. Then fill out Worksheet 18, about the situation or article your group found. After you have filled out your worksheet, join the rest of the larger group. Elect a person to speak for the group, and then one at a time, share and discuss the moral dilemma your group has found. Discuss why you think it is a **moral dilemma,** and then go around the group sharing what you would feel in that dilemma and what you would do if you were in that situation.

Putting It Together

- Hunter feels sorry for the girl he meets downtown, but is he exhibiting *sympathy* or *empathy?* Why?
- How does Hunter's *moral dilemma* change him, if at all? How would you have dealt with the situation, and what would you have done differently?
- Mariah is trying to understand when it might be right to snitch on your friends. Is there a time when this would be a good idea?
- Take a moment to look at your autobiography. Were there any moments in your life that fit as a moral dilemma? What did you do in those circumstances?
- When looking at some of the conflicts you have had recently, how would empathy have helped solve the conflict to the advantage of both people?
- Often in negotiation, empathy helps us to see where the other person is coming from. Think of a situation in which you have negotiated, and think about how empathy might have helped in arriving at a fair solution.
- How does empathy help us reach a win-win outcome?

Worksheet 18

MORAL DILEMMA

Find a newspaper article that presents a moral dilemma to the people involved.

1. Describe the situation.

2. Who was the central character in the event?

3. Why do you believe this is a moral dilemma?

4. What should have been done in the situation?

SESSION 16: UNDERSTANDING AND PRACTICING EMPATHY

Using the Program Guides and Tools for Change

Show your understanding of the difference between empathy and sympathy.

0	1	2	3	4	5	6	7	8	9	10
Low					Medium					High

Rate your ability to empathize with other people, even if their backgrounds are very different from your own.

0	1	2	3	4	5	6	7	8	9	10
Low					Medium					High

Indicate your ability to discover personal moral dilemmas and to make changes in your thinking that reflect increased concern for others.

0	1	2	3	4	5	6	7	8	9	10
Low					Medium					High

- Review your SP and PFC.
- Do you need to change your ratings on your SP?
- Do you need to add to your PFC?
- Update your Master Skills List (MSL) in the areas of strengthen moral character and empathy skills.

Hunter's Story

People are too weak. And if you let them, they will feed off of you—like parasites. Most people do not even deserve to live, if you ask me.

Pretty soon I will be old enough to drive, and that is going to suck. I mean, I'll be able to go where I want without needing anyone else to get me there. Not that I ever ask my dad for a ride anywhere, though. He always says that's what legs are for. But I wouldn't want to ask him even if he did give me rides, because I can do everything on my own, and when I can't then I don't do it. But being able to drive is going to suck because everyone is going to come around and ask me for rides. People I don't even know are gonna start mooching off me, bumming around so I can be their little servant.

Nothing but a bunch of bums… And bums are the absolute scum of society…dirty, filthy, mooching little parasitical mites that hang around and beg for my hard-earned cash. I can't even drive yet, but I have a job. Why can't they get a job?

My mom used to give money to the bums downtown. She would look at them with tears in her eyes and a sickening look on her face, and she would give them money. She wouldn't buy me a piece of candy, but she would always give them money. My dad used to get mad at her. He said she was encouraging them and keeping them from getting off their lazy asses and becoming a part of decent society. My dad says they are all like alley cats. You feed one of them and the next day you have 20 on your doorstep. But my mom's gone now, left after crying and telling me she had no other choice. Said something like she couldn't live with my father anymore. Whatever, we're better off without her.

So one day a friend and I were walking around downtown. I guess you can't even call us friends. We are, um, space fillers to each other. Friends are just moochers, and neither of us wanted friends, so we became space fillers to each other. Ya know, whenever I'm bored I'll go downtown and eventually I'll run into him and we'll walk around, usually kicking or spitting at the bums or making fun of the suits. Just wasting time. After all, that's what it's like. . .just moments to waste and time to spend while waiting for the ultimate and happily satisfying day of death. That's what my dad always said when my mom asked him how his day was. What a stupid question: "How was your day, dear?" People are idiots.

Anyway, back to downtown. I was thinking about throwing some rocks at the stupid musician bums, who are a little cleaner than the average bum but still nasty insects, when I ran into this girl. She said *sorry,* and my space filler said, "Well, you should be," and I was going to say something rude when I looked at her. But then I couldn't. There was something so soft and weird about her eyes. I get the willies just thinking about how I felt when I looked at her.

So I said *hi.* She said *hi* back. I asked her if she wanted to walk with us. She said no, and that she would rather sit down. So I sat down with her on one of the steps of some building. My "friend" said he was gonna keep walking and he'd catch up with me later. I could tell by looking at her she was really poor. But I didn't know how poor.

I asked her what she was doing downtown. She said she was looking for a job or some money. Then she told me about how her dad got cancer and how they didn't have insurance so they weren't able to pay the hospital bills when he got better. And then he lost his job because he missed so many days from being sick, and now they all live in their car. I couldn't believe it. She was a bum—a good-looking and clean bum but still a bum.

That's not to say I didn't feel bad for her. I really did feel sorry for her. It would suck to lose everything, all your toys and music and stuff, because you had to pawn them for food. I really didn't know what to do. I liked her, and she was nice, and I know that it's hard when your dad nearly dies from cancer, but what was I supposed to do? I know I'm not supposed to feed them. That just keeps them from getting a real job. But I don't even let my space filler of a friend go hungry. We both work and usually get something to eat from the vendors as we're kicking and spitting together. Sometimes I pay, and sometimes he does. But this was different. I didn't want to encourage bumming, but I couldn't stand the thought of her hungry.

So I bought her a couple of hot dogs. And then I went home. I didn't really feel like talking to her after that. After all, she is still a bum, no matter how it happens that she ended up there. But I also fed her. Why did I feed her? And I even gave her enough for her family. As long as I don't have to see her again, everything will be fine. I definitely won't make it a habit of feeding bums, even the clean, young ones. It's survival of the fittest, and bums are just parasites that need to be taken out of society in order for society to be the strongest and most evolved form it can be.

Mariah's Story

Weren't you ever told not to tattle as a kid? I sure was. My mom beat that idea into my head as a kid. Any time I ran into the house to tell on my older brother, she would cut me off—"Mariah, I don't care what your brother did. You better not be tattling." She would usually follow up with the "no one likes a tattletale" threat. I guess it took me a while, but I figured out she was right, and it seems the older you get, the more important that rule becomes.

A couple years ago, my brother got ratted out. He had been hooking me and some of my friends up with weed once in a while. We probably could've gotten it on our own if we had tried hard enough, but he already knew the big dealers so it was just easier to get it from him. Anyway, this snitch, Sasha, got caught with a bag at school. She was taken to the principal's office, the cops were called—the whole thing. At lunch, rumors were flying like crazy that she ratted everyone out and the cops were going to be questioning a whole bunch of people. I tried to calm everyone down. None of it made any sense. Sasha would never do something like that. I mean, she had grown up with me and my brother. If anyone was like family, it was Sasha, and you just don't do that to family.

Turns out Sasha totally sold out. When my brother got questioned, he took the fall on his own. He was loyal, and because of it, he's serving a 3-year sentence for drug dealing on school property. I miss him so much, but he seems like a different person now. I guess in some ways it's better, but I'm not sure.

I got to see him a few weeks ago when my family went for our monthly visit. When we were there, I told him about the accident some of my friends had gotten into. It had just happened, and I was still a little shaken up by it. I had tried to talk them out of driving that night—none of them were in any shape to get behind the wheel—but you know how people are once they've been drinking . . . they just don't listen to reason. Anyway, they all piled in to go to another party. I was worried, but there was no way I was going to talk any of them out of going, so there was nothing left for me to do.

The thought had crossed my mind to call someone that could stop them from going, but outside of calling the cops or their parents, I didn't really have any options. And I wasn't going to call someone that would get those guys in more trouble. I mean, Marco is already on probation, so telling his dad or calling the cops would have just made matters worse.

When I was telling my brother this, I expected him to totally back me up. He knows better than anyone that narking on anyone for any reason is just not worth the trouble. Shows how well I know my brother, I guess. He told me I should've called someone—even the cops! I couldn't believe what I was hearing! From my own brother, nonetheless! I was pretty quiet for the rest of the visit—shocked and lost in thought, I guess. I mean, if I would have called someone maybe the wreck wouldn't have happened, but surely Mark, me, and everyone else would have been in a world of trouble.

Now, I guess I just don't know what's right anymore. I just feel stupid now. Everything I believed before just seems upside down. Everyone is blaming me for the accident, saying, "I should've done something"—even my own brother! Whatever, I guess I should have known better. Eventually everyone turns their back on you.

Chapter Nine:
Zeroing in on Harm-Directing Thoughts

GOALS OF THIS CHAPTER

- Learn what harm-directing thought patterns are and how they can control our actions.
- Discuss how to change and manage our harm-directing thoughts.
- Understand how the "entitlement trap" is a setup for harmful actions.
- Learn how to prevent negative thoughts from causing harm to ourselves and others.

GAVIN'S STORY

SESSION 17: RECOGNIZING HARM-DIRECTING THOUGHTS

Objectives

- Review Chapter 8: Responsibility to Others and the Community.
- Recognize harm-directing thought patterns.
- Realize how harm-directing thought patterns contribute to problem behaviors.
- Learn to control harm-directing thought patterns and replace them with positive thoughts.

Gavin's Story: *I knew I was going to be in trouble as soon as I walked into school. All adults hate me, but the advisor really hates me. He's always got it out for me. As soon as I saw him walking toward me, I knew he was going to say I was in trouble for something. But I was just talking to my friends, which isn't against any law or anything, so I asked him what the hell he wanted. He wasn't very nice.*

I hate going to school—not just because all adults hate me but especially the advisor. I just can't focus. Really, I'm stupid. So I let my mind wander, and then the teacher calls on me and I don't know the answer. She's so mean when she does that because she knows I'm stupid. It makes me really angry, so I talk back and she sends me to the advisor. Not that it matters, though, because he usually hunts me down for something anyway. Yeah, school sucks.

How Are Values and Morals Formed?

In Chapter 8, we began to discuss the importance of our *values* and *morals* in our dealings with the world.

We discussed how placing a value on *empathy* means that we care about what other people think and feel. While *sympathy* means pitying or feeling sorry for someone who has had ill fortune, *empathy* takes the idea one step further so we actually can imagine what it must be like to *think* and *feel like the other person—to* "walk in their shoes."

Up to this point, we have talked about how attitudes and thoughts affect our feelings and actions, but in the last chapter (Chapter 8: Responsibility to Others and the Community) we began to touch upon an even deeper part of our personality: our ideas or beliefs about *what we think is important in life* **(values)** and our personal *sense of right and wrong* **(morals).** They influence our thoughts and attitudes, and in turn, they largely influence our feelings and actions. We looked at how our being in tune with our values and morals can lead to **win-win** outcomes for ourselves and our community,

Activity: All My Neighbors

Arrange the chairs of the group in a circle, but **leave one out** so there is one too few for the entire group to sit down. A volunteer or the counselor will stand in the middle and make a statement, such as "All my neighbors who like cartoons." Everyone who likes cartoons will stand up and move to another chair but not the one right next to them. While they are moving, the person in the middle is trying to get into a chair, leaving a different person without a chair to sit in. That person will then make a statement, the group will rearrange, and then a new person will be in the middle.

Notice how, although the values are different for different people, there are often a number of people who have the same value in common. At the end of this exercise, discuss how our values are formed.

Our values and morals are usually formed as a result of the *situations* we find ourselves in and the *people* we meet when we are children. Sometimes the values and morals that we learned when we were younger are simply not in our best interest and may even have led us to hurt others. Can you think of a value or moral that you would like to change so that you can have better outcomes? Sometimes, as children, we just imitate the values and morals of our elders—for better or worse; now we can choose for ourselves.

An important way we *change a value or moral* is by being presented with a *dilemma* (an internal conflict), which puts the value or moral to the test: "Do I want to hold on to this idea of what is right or important?" It is usually *empathy for another person* that brings about the dilemmas in our morals and values. An example might be holding the belief that it's OK to steal if you can get away with it and then realizing that someone just stole your mom's brand-new music and video player.

When we see something from another person's point of view, we understand things from a different (less selfish) perspective—outside of the narrow space of our personal values and morals. The fuller view of the world can allow us to become aware of what our values really are—or if we want to change some of them—and whether they are positive or negative.

The Impact of Harm-Directing Thoughts

Harm-directing thoughts and attitudes betray our values and morals and cause bad outcomes. For example, if someone thinks "life sucks," then trying to gain *self-respect* or finding *mature love* or even living by the moral principle of being honest doesn't hold much meaning. Sometimes negative thinking is so deeply a part of us that it forms the basis of our values, morals, and beliefs about the world. For example, a negative belief like "Life is about being hurt or hurting others," could easily result in having such distorted views as "It's good to take advantage of people" and "It is not wrong to take whatever you can get."

In either case, *negative views affect our immediate thoughts* in most situations. Negative thinking often becomes a roadblock to changing our actions for the better, and the difficult thing with negative thinking is we often don't see it. Similar to our values and morals, negative thinking can become so ingrained in us that we don't see it until we are aware and in control.

SESSION 17: RECOGNIZING HARM-DIRECTING THOUGHTS

Harm-directing thoughts and attitudes betray our values and morals and cause bad outcomes.

How to Recognize Harm-Directing Thoughts

The way we think controls how we feel and act, but we have power over the way we think. We can control our thoughts and influence ourselves to make the right decisions. But first we have to learn how to be aware when we are having harm-directing thoughts. Exaggerations in what we think about and how we see the world around us set the stage for harm-directing thoughts. Here are five types of exaggerations that can adversely affect us by providing a platform for harm-directing thoughts:

1. **Expecting the worst.** This is when we *expect something negative* from everything around us, or sometimes we always count on bad results—e.g., "I know it won't work out. It never does."
2. **Putting oneself down.** This is when we think the *problem is within us,* and we constantly remind ourselves of that—e.g., "I can't do anything right."
3. **Jumping to conclusions.** We automatically assume that *bad things will happen* when we don't have proof that they will—e.g., "I know he's going to hate me."
4. **Blaming oneself.** Assuming that everything that happens is *our fault*—e.g., "I deserved it."
5. **Having a negative view of the world.** When we assume that the world is just a *horrible* place—e.g., "There's nothing to look forward to. It's just another lousy day."

Activity: Gavin's Thoughts

Let's look at Gavin's story for a minute. **What thoughts does Gavin have that are exaggerated or harm directing?** How do they fit into the categories that were just stated? Does his story have elements of all the exaggerations in thinking or just a few? Why do you think Gavin thinks that way? What kinds of exaggerations in thinking do you participate in the most?

Situations

Activity: Seeing Our Thoughts

Take some time to individually fill out Worksheet 19: Harm-Directing Thoughts and Exaggerations, using Column 1 to list **harm-directing thoughts** that you have regularly and Column 2 to label these thoughts according to the **types of exaggerations** that were just given or using the list of harm-directing thoughts in Session 5 of Chapter 2 (Worksheet 3: Managing Harm-Directing Thoughts). After you have completed your worksheet, compare your results with those of one of your neighbors. How are they similar? How are they different? Do you share some of the same errors with Gavin?

Worksheet 19

HARM-DIRECTING THOUGHTS AND EXAGGERATIONS

LIST OF HARM-DIRECTING THOUGHTS	TYPES OF EXAGGERATIONS IN THINKING

SESSION 17: RECOGNIZING HARM-DIRECTING THOUGHTS

Patterns of Harm-Directing Thoughts

Let's take a moment to return all the way back to the beginning of the program. In Session 2 (Chapter 1), we talked about how our attitudes, thoughts, and beliefs affect our actions. We then took a step further to show how our thoughts and feelings affect the actions that we choose. But we also talked about how our actions can affect our thoughts and feelings. We mention this again because it's an important part of *harm-directing thought* and how it affects our decisions.

Take an event or situation such as an adult yelling at us. This event triggers an exaggeration and harm-directing thought in our head, such as "The world sucks" or "I'm getting screwed," and that, in turn, affects our feelings and behavior. We may get angry and strike out against the adult. Each situation or event leads to a sequence of thoughts before we feel or act.

Activity: Gavin's Actions

Take another look at Gavin's story. How are his thoughts, feelings, and actions interacting with each other? How do Gavin's thoughts affect his feelings and then the actions he chooses? How do his feelings affect his thoughts about other people?

You Are in Control

By recognizing patterns of harm-directing thought, we have a chance to take control and have freedom over the events and situations that occur. Since our thoughts are in our mind, we have the ability to control or change them when they occur. As we discussed in earlier sessions, we have the freedom and the choice in every decision we make, including what we think and say to ourselves.

Activity: The Choice of Harm-Directing Thought

Use Worksheet 20: Harm-Directing Thoughts That Lead to Alcohol or Other Drug Abuse and Criminal Conduct, to list the harm-directing thoughts that you may have had that led to abusing substances or participating in criminal activities. Is there a pattern in your harm-directing thoughts? Do you use the same thoughts more often than others?

But as we said before, you are in control of your thoughts. Here are three ways you can control and change your negative thinking:

1. **Thought stopping.** Allow yourself to think a harm-directing thought. Then **stop** the thought right away. Be aware of the thought, but *tell yourself to stop the thought.* At first, just choose one

Worksheet 20

HARM-DIRECTING THOUGHTS THAT LEAD TO ALCOHOL OR OTHER DRUG ABUSE AND CRIMINAL CONDUCT

HARM-DIRECTING THOUGHTS THAT LEAD TO ALCOHOL OR OTHER DRUG ABUSE	HARM-DIRECTING THOUGHTS THAT LEAD TO CRIMINAL CONDUCT

harm-directing thought ("The world sucks"). Every time that thought happens, *be aware that you are thinking it and then stop it.* Also, recognize the kind of thought exaggeration—in this case, "negative view of the world."

2. **Positive thought planting.** Instead of just stopping the thought every time a harm-directing one occurs, try *replacing it with a positive thought.* Every time you are thinking "the world sucks," replace the thought with something positive about the world, such as "I can choose the way I live my life from now on."
3. **Self-talk.** When you become aware of a harm-directing thought, or start thinking one of them, talk to yourself about why you are having the thought and *what you can do to change or manage that thought.*

The idea behind *thought planting* is to stop the process of the thought and change where it is going to end. When an event occurs, be *aware* of the thought that is going through your mind, and *replace it* with something more positive. That, in turn, will change how you feel and the action you will take.

Arsenal of Thoughts

Although it may be possible to think of positive thoughts on the spur of the moment, it is helpful to arm yourself with some *positive thoughts so you can be ready* for when a harm-directing thought occurs. This way we don't have to struggle as much trying to replace our thoughts. Here are some suggestions:

- **Remembering good things.** What are the good things in life, *the things you do well,* and *the people you care about?* These are *always* helpful thoughts.
- **Statements of hope.** Instead of self-blaming or put-downs, *use positive thoughts about yourself:* "I am strong enough to do this."
- **Self-rewards.** When you have done something well, tell yourself that. *Reward yourself for your decision making and positive thinking:* "It was hard, but I did a really good job at coping."

The important point we are trying to make is to *talk positively to yourself.* Self-talk, or *hearing our positive thoughts* in our own head, can be very helpful in being aware of our harm-directing thoughts and being able to *change or replace* them with more positive ones.

Positive self-talk helps us to manage our feelings and actions.

SESSION 17: RECOGNIZING HARM-DIRECTING THOUGHTS

Activity: Arsenal for Control

Your counselor will have some flipchart paper up on the wall. Separate the paper into three columns, with the **first column for harm-directing thoughts,** the **second for replacement thoughts,** and the **third for the results.** As a group, think of several different harm-directing thoughts that occur throughout the day. Try to make these thoughts as close to your real thoughts as you feel comfortable. After you have listed the harm-directing thoughts, try to think of some replacement thoughts and list them in the second column. These thoughts should be realistic as well. Then discuss how the replacement thoughts may influence decisions and actions taken from that point. Write that down in the results section. How might **thought replacement be helpful for you?**

Putting It Together

- Gavin shows some exaggerations and harm-directing thoughts. What do you think are his harm-directing belief systems? Why do you think his belief systems are harm-directing?
- Which one does he use most often, and how can you tell (use evidence from the story)?
- How do Gavin's thoughts and feelings affect how he acts?
- How do harm-directing thoughts lead to bad outcomes?
- Do a thinking report (event, thought, feeling, action) when your harm-directing thinking is involved. How can this be changed?
- Of the five categories of thought exaggerations, which do you think you use most often?
- Which of the three ways to stop or target harm-directing thoughts do you think will be most effective for you? Why?

Using the Program Guides and Tools for Change

Rate your ability to identify types of thought exaggerations that you use when under stress.

0	1	2	3	4	5	6	7	8	9	10
Low					Medium					High

Indicate your skill at identifying and correcting your own harm-directing thoughts through *thought stopping*, *positive thought planting*, and *self-talk*.

0	1	2	3	4	5	6	7	8	9	10
Low					Medium					High

Review your Plan for Change (PFC). Would you like to add *"changing harm-directing thoughts"?* Why?

SESSION 18: MANAGING AND CHANGING HARM-DIRECTING THOUGHTS

Objectives

- Review Session 17: Recognizing Harm-Directing Thoughts.
- Review how harm-directing thought habits can stop us from making positive choices in our lives.
- Further recognize exaggerated thinking patterns, and develop skills to change them.
- Recognize the entitlement trap, and decide whether attitude is something that might be causing harm to yourself or others.
- Discover means to change deep-seated beliefs and attitudes that may cause harm.

Gavin's Story: *Like I told my mom, it wasn't my fault I got in trouble. The man hates me, and no matter what I did, I was still going to get suspended…just like I can't help that I'm stupid. The more I try to pay attention, the harder it is for me to focus. And the teacher should know that.*

Of course, my mom asked me about my fight—the one where I took some kid's chips and his big ol' ape of a friend came after me. But I was right in that fight. It was none of the jerk's business, and besides, I never get chips. We're poor so I can never buy those things at lunch, but don't I deserve to have snacks, too? The kid's parents are rich. They can afford to get him more. The f—ker had no business calling me a punk, and he deserved to get punched in the nose.

Review of Harm-Directing Thoughts

In the last session, we spent some time talking about harm-directing thoughts and how they can make us feel bad or choose harmful actions. These thoughts can happen automatically, and it is *only when we are aware* that we are having a harm-directing thought that we can take control.

We covered several different ways that we can manage and control our harm-directing thoughts. Although we are not able to always avoid situations or events in our life, we can be aware of the thoughts that occur. By controlling our thoughts, we can help ourselves make better decisions and feel better about our life. We also discussed *thought exaggerations*, which we also covered earlier in Phase I, that can cause harm-directing thoughts.

Activity: How I Control Harm-Directing Thoughts

Break into groups of two or three, and think of situations that have happened in the past week that involved **harm-directing thoughts.** Be honest, and share with each other what these situations were. Did you use any of the methods **(thought stopping, thought replacement, or self-talk)** when a harm-directing thought occurred? If you did, how did the method help you to change the harm-directing thoughts and the situation?

SESSION 18: MANAGING AND CHANGING HARM-DIRECTING THOUGHTS

But thought exaggerations do not just cause harm-directing thoughts. They can also be roadblocks in our desire to change. By relying on thought exaggerations, we cause ourselves to stop the change process and fall back to old habits. Now, review how you rated yourself on *harm-directing thoughts* in your Self-Portrait (SP) on thinking and feeling patterns. Rate yourself on these again. Did the ratings change? Why?

Thought Habits That Prevent Us From Doing Well

Thought habits, the *automatic thoughts* that happen in an *emotional situation,* stop us from changing and allow us to participate in harmful behavior. Here are some thought habits that can block change:

- **"I had no choice."** Spending time writing and reviewing our thinking reports should have shown us that this is rarely true, but it is one of the most commonly used excuses.
- **"Everyone thinks the way I do."** Remember Principle 2 in Session 3? ***Everyone sees the world differently,*** and because of that, no one really agrees on everything. It's easy to steal something if you think that everyone would do it if they weren't afraid, but that is *rarely* the case.
- **"I'm right, and my thoughts don't need to change."** Sometimes being right or wrong has nothing to do with the situation, but being stubborn in your thinking is an easy way to get in trouble. Every issue has two sides, and being stubborn can stop you from having freedom.

Activity: A Choice for Gavin

When looking at Gavin's story, **which of the previously given thought habits** do you think applies to his automatic thoughts? Does he participate in more than one thought habit? How do Gavin's automatic thoughts affect the decisions he makes? How might Gavin change his automatic thoughts?

Thoughts That Get Us in Trouble

Some harm-directing thoughts tend to become habits for us. They *become so automatic* that we accept them no matter what the evidence against them is. But these thinking filters are really distortions of the real situation. It's like putting on green sunglasses. Things are still what they were, but the colors are different and some shapes stick out more than others.

Activity: Labeling the Harm-Directing Thoughts

Go back to Worksheet 3 (Managing Harm-Directing Thoughts) in Session 5, in which you discovered how those harm-directing thoughts applied to you.

Now use the list in **Table 4** (Common Thinking Filters or Harm-Directing Thoughts) to **label and name the harm-directing thoughts** that you participate in. Try to use some **self-talk** in reviewing this, and try to replace some of the thoughts that you have had. For example, the label **"screwed"** may apply for feeling like the world is against you at all times. Instead of thinking that, **replace your thought** with something like "There are some people who I can actually trust" or "That's not true. There are some people that have been real good to me."

By *recognizing* the thought habits and harm-directing thoughts that we take part in, we can take control of our thoughts and change them. Just as we can change or manage our harm-directing thoughts by being aware of them, we can also change or manage our harm-directing thinking by becoming aware of the ones we use most often.

Activity: Most Often Used Harm-Directing Thoughts

Take some time to fill out Worksheet 21: My Harm-Directing Thoughts with those you participate in the most often. Use Table 4: Common Thinking Filters or Harm-Directing Thoughts and Worksheets 19 and 20 to help you with this. After everyone has filled out their worksheets, get into a group and **discuss the harm-directing thoughts you think you use the most.** Then as a group, discuss the ways you might **change or alter** the harm-directing thoughts in order to have a more positive outcome. Make sure everyone gets plenty of feedback about their thought habits, but do not blame or accuse anyone.

The "Entitlement Trap"

People who use substances or get in trouble with the law often use the **entitlement trap** as an excuse to explain away their behavior. This trap is when, because of past problems or hurt, you feel like you were the victim and you deserve some kind of special consideration, even if your behavior is offensive or harmful to others. If we think we are punished, deprived, or badly treated, we often feel like we are *entitled* to things because we have it coming to us.

Activity: Gavin's Error

In looking at Gavin's story, do you think he is using an entitlement trap as an excuse for any of his actions? Which of his actions do you think uses the trap? **How does he use the trap as an excuse?** Do you think Gavin is right in using that excuse? What entitlement traps have you used or fallen into recently?

Table 4

COMMON THINKING FILTERS OR HARM-DIRECTING THOUGHTS

LIST OF HARM-DIRECTING THOUGHTS

1. POWER THRUST—Putting people down; dominating over others
2. CLOSED CHANNEL—Seeing things only your way
3. VICTIM STANCE—Blaming others
4. PRIDE—Feeling superior to others
5. DON'T CARE—Having a lack of concern as to how others are affected
6. CAN'T TRUST—Not trusting anybody
7. WON'T MEET OBLIGATIONS—Refusing something you don't want to do
8. WANT IT NOW—Wanting what you want now and not settling for less
9. STEALING—Taking what you want from others
10. DON'T HAVE TO—Thinking, "I don't have to do that"
11. PROCRASTINATE—Putting off things until tomorrow
12. STUBBORN—Not changing your ideas
13. RIGID THINKING—Thinking in black-and-white terms; has to be one way or the other
14. CASTASTROPHIZING—Making mountains out of molehills; blowing things out of proportion
15. FEEL PICKED ON—Feeling singled out and picked on
16. THEY DESERVE IT—Thinking people have it coming; people deserve to get ripped off
17. SCREWED—Feeling that you are being screwed over; mistreated
18. SELECTIVE HEARING—Tuning out what you hear people say if it doesn't fit your thinking
19. WON'T GIVE—Demanding things from others but won't give
20. CRIMINAL THINKING—Thinking about criminal things; doing crimes
21. LYING—Lying is almost automatic for you

ADDITIONAL LIST OF HARM-DIRECTING THOUGHTS

1. ANGER—Having rage that makes you illogical and irrational
2. LONGER—Feeling separated
3. REFUSAL—Feeling that you don't have to do that
4. FAIR DESERTS—Feeling you deserve more than what you're getting: "I've been cheated."
5. THEY DESERVE IT—Thinking people have it coming
6. NO EMPATHY—Not putting yourself in another person's position
7. FAILURE TO CONSIDER HARM TO OTHERS—Having a lack of concern about how others are affected
8. SEE SELF AS GOOD—Thinking you are good in spite of having harmed others
9. NO EFFORT—Not exerting energy to achieve a goal; doing what comes easy
10. CONCRETE THOUGHTS—Not changing your ideas
11. FICKLE—Changing your mind or goals all the time
12. SEXUAL POWER—Using sex as a way to increase your self-image
13. ZERO STATE—Feeling of no value; worthy of nothing

Worksheet 21

My Harm-Directing Thoughts

Pick two harm-directing thoughts from Table 4: Common Thinking Filters or Harm-Directing Thoughts that you use a lot of the time. Or pick any other harm-directing thoughts that you use a lot that are not listed. Put the name of each harm-directing thought in the space provided. Describe how you use each harm-directing thought. Did you get in trouble? How?

1. HARM-DIRECTING THOUGHT:

Describe the situation.

____

____

How did you use it?

____

____

Did it get you in trouble? How?

____

____

2. HARM-DIRECTING THOUGHT:

Describe the situation.

____

____

How did you use it?

____

____

Did it get you in trouble? How?

____

____

SESSION 18: MANAGING AND CHANGING HARM-DIRECTING THOUGHTS

Just like harm-directing thoughts, the entitlement trap is *an excuse to commit a crime* or use substances and is not right. In fact, this trap can cause us more problems and can stop change.

Activity: Escaping From the Trap

Remember a thought that you have had recently that falls into the excuse of "entitlement." Now spend some time **arguing why that thought is not helpful** and is causing harm. Share with the group the thought and then how you argued with it. Be sure to share how it felt to argue with the thought and how you felt when you were done. Then take some time to fill out Worksheet 22: The Entitlement Trap. Be honest with yourself, and fill out the worksheet as completely as possible.

Just as we can use the *three skills* we learned in Session 17 to change a harm-directing thought, we can also use the same three skills to escape the *entitlement trap.* Here's a reminder of what those skills are:

1. **Thought stopping**
2. **Replacing with a positive thought (these are thoughts that you thought up for your arsenal)**
3. **Strong countering (self-talking)**

Activity: Entitled to Be Free

Throughout the whole program, we have been talking about how your thoughts, feelings, and actions interact to create your response to situations. But you are the one who has control over your thoughts. Break into groups of four and **create a skit** in which there is a **situation and a problem.** Give each person an **entitlement thought,** and try to show what can happen in a situation when the entitlement traps are in play—for example, a car wreck in which all the people involved think they are the victim. The situation gets out of control because everyone is blaming the other people. Make sure to let the audience know what entitlement trap is in play in your performance. One person might feel that they were entitled to turn right because they had a nicer car, even though it was the other person's right-of-way.

Then create a skit in which the **entitlement thoughts are stopped** and the situation is resolved. How can thoughts of entitlement lead to criminal conduct (CC) and substance abuse?

Putting It Together

- Gavin's thoughts often allow him to choose actions that get him in trouble. What are some of Gavin's *harm-directing thoughts?* Could he have changed the outcome of the situation?

Worksheet 22

THE ENTITLEMENT TRAP

Describe a situation in which you did something wrong because you felt like you had the right to do it. Then answer the following questions:

1. How did you justify the act?

2. Did you get away with it or were you caught?

3. Knowing what you know now, would you do it again? Why or why not?

- One excuse Gavin uses falls into the *entitlement trap.* Give an example of how Gavin uses the entitlement trap. How does it make Gavin feel about his negative actions? What would happen if Gavin didn't use the trap?
- The way we think about a situation often affects what we do in a situation. Recall some of the situations where your *thoughts of entitlement* had negative effects on your actions. Were there errors in the thought? Could you have made the situation end differently?
- Think about situations where *you did change your thought.* Did you feel more in control of the situation? How can you empower yourself more?

Using the Program Guides and Tools for Change

Rate your ability to identify your own patterns of harm-directing thoughts.

0	1	2	3	4	5	6	7	8	9	10
Low					Medium					High

Indicate your ability to use *thought stopping, thought replacement,* and *self-talk* to change, control, or manage harm-directing thoughts.

0	1	2	3	4	5	6	7	8	9	10
Low					Medium					High

Show your ability to identify and change your own attitudes of entitlement.

0	1	2	3	4	5	6	7	8	9	10
Low					Medium					High

- With your counselor, update and add to your SP and PFC. Choose a problem to work on this week.
- Update the harm-directing thoughts and patterns in Program Guide 1: Telling My Story (TMS).
- Update your Master Skills List (MSL) in the areas of change negative thinking and change thinking errors.

Gavin's Story

I hate school. I hate it so much. The only reason they make me go is because they like to torture me.

I've always had a hard time at school. I can't focus. I can't listen to the teacher. I'm stupid. So I sit there, minding my own business. Sometimes I draw. Sometimes I talk to the person next to me. More often than not I just sit and stare out the window.

But then the teacher calls on me, and I haven't been listening, and I don't know what she's talking about or what she's asking me, so I get angry. Why does she have to put me on the spot like that? She knows I'm stupid. I talk back. I get loud. She sends me to the advisor's office. And he hates me. All adults hate me.

So I got suspended this one time over nothing. I knew it was trouble as soon as I walked into school. The advisor came up to me with a look on his face. I knew I was gonna get in trouble, even though I hadn't done anything yet. I was just talking with my friends. And some of my friends like to talk. But I don't mind because I like to talk, too. But the advisor hates me, so he's always looking for a way to get me in trouble. So before he even said something, I asked him what the hell he wanted. And he told me I better watch it. I walked off. What does he know anyway?

I went to class. I was a couple of minutes late because I took the long way. Sometimes I like to wander the halls, check out the tiles on the floor. Sometimes I get to see some stuff written on somebody's locker before the janitor can clean it off. You can learn a lot by wandering the halls. But as soon as I walked in, the teacher started nagging, asking me why I was late and stuff. I told her it was none of her business, because it's not. She's not my mom. I told her so, too. She said I better sit down. I asked her why. It's not like I learn anything in her class anyway. School sucks, and it's a waste of my time. She told me to go to the advisor's office. I took off but not to his office.

First I wandered the halls some more. But then I thought that wasn't smart, and I could get caught. So I went to the park to hang out and wait for my friends. Lunch was coming up, and then I could go to the one class I like . . . art.

This one time in art class we were learning how to paint with oils. My teacher said we should get a feel for the um . . . what's that called? Oh, yeah, the medium we are using to portray our feelings. So I stuck my hands in the paint. It was kinda cool, all slippery and gooey. It was really cool feeling the paint and the canvas and trying to create something. My mom got mad that I had paint all over my clothes. That wasn't fun. Not that I get to have fun at school very often . . . I'm always in trouble.

At lunch I got in a fight. I was messing around and stole this kid's chips. I never have money because we're poor, so why shouldn't I have his? Don't I deserve chips, too? But then this big kid got all up in my face. I told him to mind his own business. He told me I was nothing but a stupid punk. I punched him in the face. Before it got too much further, all the kids separated us. He's just a stupid jerk.

By then it was time to go to art. I was happy. I was excited. It's the only thing that I can focus on. I think we were learning charcoals that day, which is only black and white, but I've seen some crazy stuff done with charcoals. But class had just gotten started when the advisor came in. I knew he was there for me. That man hunts me down sometimes, like some hunter who stalks an innocent deer. So he ended up taking me out of my favorite class to go sit down in his office—and sit and sit and watch kids and teachers walk in and out of the office. And they all stare and make snide comments. I almost got in a fight just waiting for my mom.

So I was suspended. He said something like defiance and disorderly conduct and whatever, which didn't matter, because that meant I didn't have to go to school for a couple of days. My mom was mad, but it doesn't matter because she is always mad. And I got to sit in my room, watching TV and reading comic books, and wait at the park for my friends to get out of school. Yeah, school sucks.

Chapter Ten:

Handling Anger, Guilt, And Depression

GOALS OF THIS CHAPTER

- Recognize uncomfortable or negative feelings.
- Discuss how emotional discomfort can lead to negative behavior.
- Learn steps on how to deal with angry, sad, anxious, or guilty feelings.
- Learn how to avoid violence and aggression.

TRISTAN'S STORY

I'm going to beat on her, I swear I'm going to really hurt her. But what am I going to do without her? We met two years ago, at the town fair. I think I fell in love with Audrey within the first week. Everything was great for about a year. Then some friends and I started experimenting with some harder drugs than pot. But Audrey had a hard time dealing with my drug use. Then one night my friends and I ran into her hanging out with a couple of her friends. Some guy from her class was talking to her. And I freaked out.

Before I realized what I had done I saw him with blood running down his nose like lava leaving an erupted volcano and Audrey staring at me with tears in her eyes. She helped him stop the blood and my friends pushed me into our car before the cops got called. The next morning I felt like crap. I couldn't believe what I had done. Boy did I apologize. We set a date for the next night, and everything was fine. I had a little voice in my head asking me why Audrey helped that guy when I was her boyfriend.

Everything was good for a while. Until I found out he was going to be her lab partner. I ended up drinking most of my dad's beer one night before Audrey and I were supposed to go out. As soon as I walked into her house, she started in on me being drunk for our date and how I knew she didn't like it when I was like that. I accused her of cheating. I turned around and backhanded her. I went home angry and trashed my room. She broke up with me. It's all my fault, and I'm so angry about that. I hear she is dating that guy now. I'm so hurt and angry I want to kill her. I pray I never run into them together. Who knows what I'd do.

SESSION 19: DEALING WITH FEELINGS

Objectives

- Review Chapter 9: Zeroing in on Harm-Directing Thoughts.
- Recognize your personal angry thoughts and feelings.
- Discuss how angry thoughts and feelings can lead to aggression and violence.
- Think about how anger is connected to guilt and depression.
- Learn some steps for handling anger, guilt, and depression.

Tristan's Story: *Everything was fine, and Audrey and I were in love. I started doing more drugs, which she didn't like, but they made me feel good for a little bit. But then one night I saw Audrey talking to a guy, and I got so angry that I punched him.*

The next morning I felt so bad about hitting him that I couldn't even leave my room—not to mention I was sure I had lost Audrey. I trusted her, but then I just up and hit a guy talking to her. I couldn't understand it, and I didn't think Audrey would either. I just felt so damn guilty and sad. But that didn't stop the voices in my head, whispering that she was cheating or that he was making a move on Audrey.

Review of Negative Thinking

Up until this point in the program, we have been focusing on the thoughts that can cause us to act out negatively or take drugs. In Session 17: Recognizing Harm-Directing Thoughts, we discussed how to recognize negative thoughts and how negative thoughts are automatic and affect the choices and decisions we make. Session 18: Managing and Changing Harm-Directing Thoughts began with the *exaggerated thinking* that we often fall into, leading us to substance abuse and criminal behavior.

Activity: Thinking of Errors

Take a moment to review your sessions from last week. Did you recognize any **patterns of negative thoughts** or exaggerations, and if so, what were they? What did you do to change them, if anything? Then share with the group the negative thoughts and errors you had the last week and if you were successful in using your skills to stop and change them. Go around the room until everyone has had a chance to share.

In Session 2, we talked about how our thoughts, feelings, and actions all work together in a cycle to help us make our decisions. Up until the last session, we have been discussing how *thoughts affect our feelings* and *actions* and possible ways to stop or correct our negative or distorted thoughts. Now we are going to spend some time on *feelings:* how they affect our decisions and possible ways we can control them. Review your Self-Portrait (SP) ratings for anger, depression, and anxiety. This chapter will be especially helpful for those who had high ratings.

Dealing With Anger

All of us get angry sometimes. After all, anger is a normal human emotion. But not being aware of our anger, or ignoring our anger, can often have some very negative effects on our lives and us. Although we don't like to think so, anger has been the basis of a lot of substance use and criminal actions. Often we are hurting others and ourselves by participating in these actions. Unless the harm is clearly by accident, *hurting anyone* is an act of anger.

This is not to say that anger is isolated from the rest of our mind, like some caged beast ready to spring out at any moment. There are some well-known automatic thoughts that predictably result in the very powerful and often dangerous emotion of anger.

Thoughts That Lead to Anger

- Thinking of being *shortchanged.*
- Thinking you are not being treated fairly.
- Thinking that you are the victim.
- Thinking that your space has been violated.

Notice that a lot of these thoughts that lead up to anger can fall under the category of the *entitlement trap* that we discussed in the last session. For example, "If I am not being treated fairly, then I have the right to strike out with anger and violence." By becoming aware of the thoughts you are having in the moment of anger, you can begin to take control over your anger.

Activity: Tristan's Anger and Audrey's Response

Review Tristan's story about his anger. What do you think were the **thoughts that made him angry?** There may be more than one right answer, so discuss your answers in the group and explain your reasoning. Use examples from the story to back up your opinion. How do you think Tristan could have controlled his anger?

What do you think Audrey must have been thinking and feeling? Was her decision to break up with Tristan justified? Why? When do you think it is time to get out of a relationship?

The Big Three

The largest difficulty in dealing with anger, though, is that *anger is not isolated* from our other feelings. In fact, anger is usually pretty closely tied to our feelings of *guilt* and *depression.* When we get angry, we often feel guilty or depressed. We will take a look at this cycle a little later, but it is important to know that these three emotions play heavily in returning to earlier patterns of drug abuse *(relapse)* and reoffending *(recidivism).*

Often when we are trying to recover or change our habits, we feel guilt, anger, and depression. The reason we are going to go over some of the steps to dealing and managing these emotions is because they are *high-risk* (HR) *emotions,* similar to HR situations and thinking, that can lead to both *relapse and recidivism* (RR), which in turn leads to more of the three emotions. It becomes a vicious cycle, a downward spiral with us at the bottom of it.

The Ties Among Guilt, Anger, and Depression

Emotions are something felt by all people, including the unpleasant emotions of guilt, anger, and depression. When these emotions lead to substance abuse and criminal behavior, *the situation is different.* In order to keep your freedom of choice, you must be able to control these emotions.

As kids, we were often *taught to not feel* negative emotions. Anger gets a response of "Cool it," guilt often brings out "It's okay. Don't feel bad. It's not your fault," and depression often gets returned with a fake smile and a "Cheer up. It's not that bad." Because of this, we never really learned how to deal with uncomfortable feelings. Instead, we may have used drugs and alcohol to forget or strike out with anger and violence in order release the tension. But these methods do not control the emotions; rather, they lead us into *the guilt–anger cycle.*

The *guilt–anger cycle* is something that occurs over and over again within our minds. Because we did not learn healthy ways to deal with our negative emotions, we built them up inside. When there was *too much pressure, we got high, got angry and irrational, and hurt others emotionally or physically.* But after the act was done, the decision was made, and the substance was out of our system, we often have strong thoughts and *feelings of guilt.* We don't know how to deal with the guilt, so we become *depressed,* and the whole time our anger never gets dealt with. So the feelings build up again, and then the cycle starts all over. Take a look at Figure 15: The Guilt–Anger Cycle, which shows how the cycle starts and continues. We use the term *significant other* (SO) to describe any important person in your life who plays a role in your feelings of guilt, anger, or depression. In Tristan's case, Audrey is his significant other.

Activity: Tristan's Downward Spiral

Discuss in a group Tristan's story and his **cycle of anger, guilt, and depression.** Tristan's negative actions began with the feeling of anger. How did he feel the next morning? Do you think he ever dealt with his anger? Why or why not? What was the cycle of Tristan's actions?

Activity: A Spiral of My Own

For this activity, use Figure 15: The Guilt–Anger Cycle and Worksheet 23 to begin drawing a spiral of your own. Think of a situation in which you lost your temper, and then try to think and become aware of how the situation fits into the *guilt–anger cycle.* How do your feelings fit within the cycle? How and where can you change the cycle so it doesn't end with the feelings of anger being repeated?

Figure 15

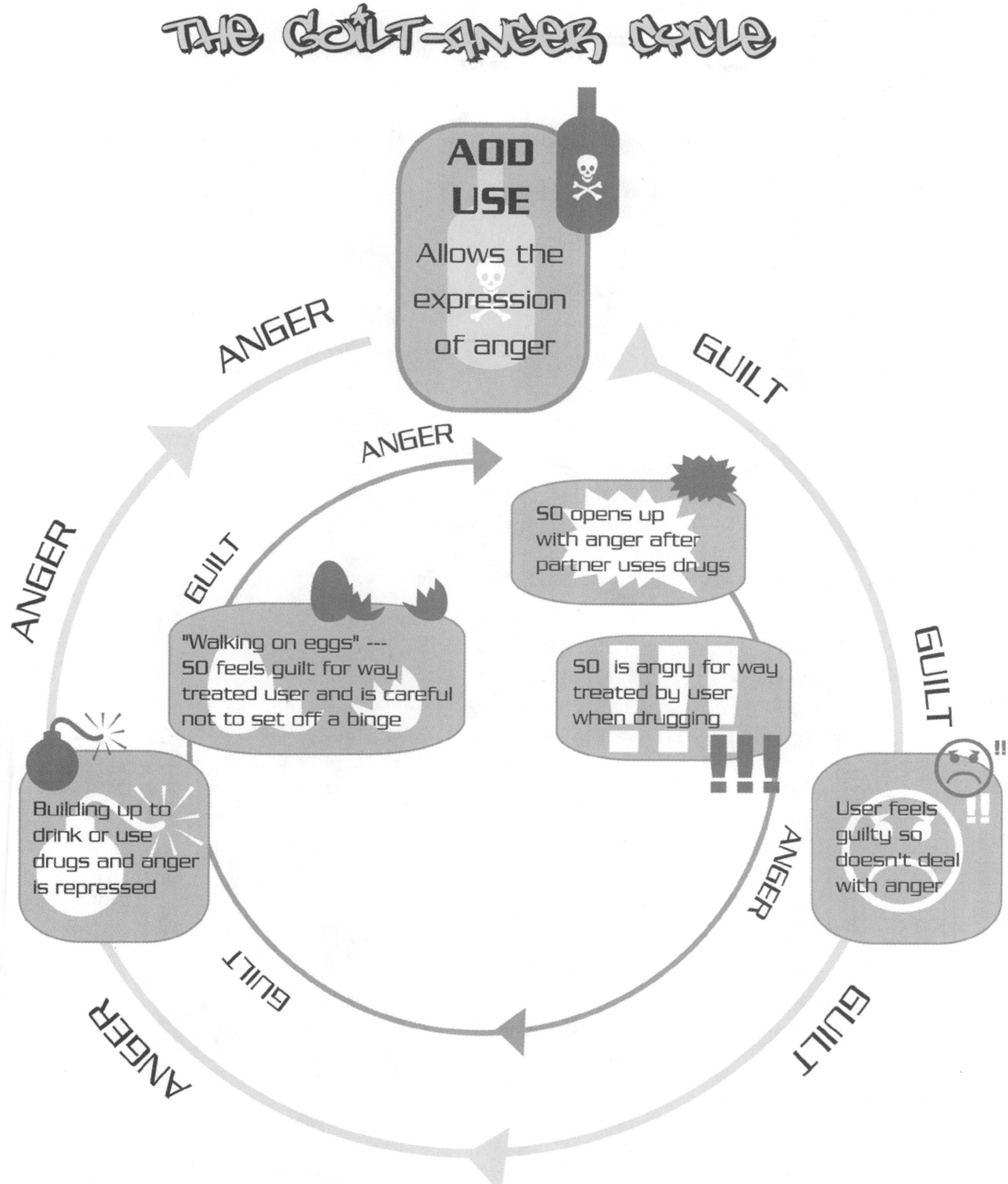
THE GUILT-ANGER CYCLE
AOD USE
Allows the expression of anger
ANGER
GUILT
ANGER
GUILT
SO opens up with anger after partner uses drugs
"Walking on eggs" --- SO feels guilt for way treated user and is careful not to set off a binge
SO is angry for way treated by user when drugging
Building up to drink or use drugs and anger is repressed
User feels guilty so doesn't deal with anger
ANGER
GUILT
GUILT
ANGER
GUILT
ANGER
ANGER
GUILT

Worksheet 23

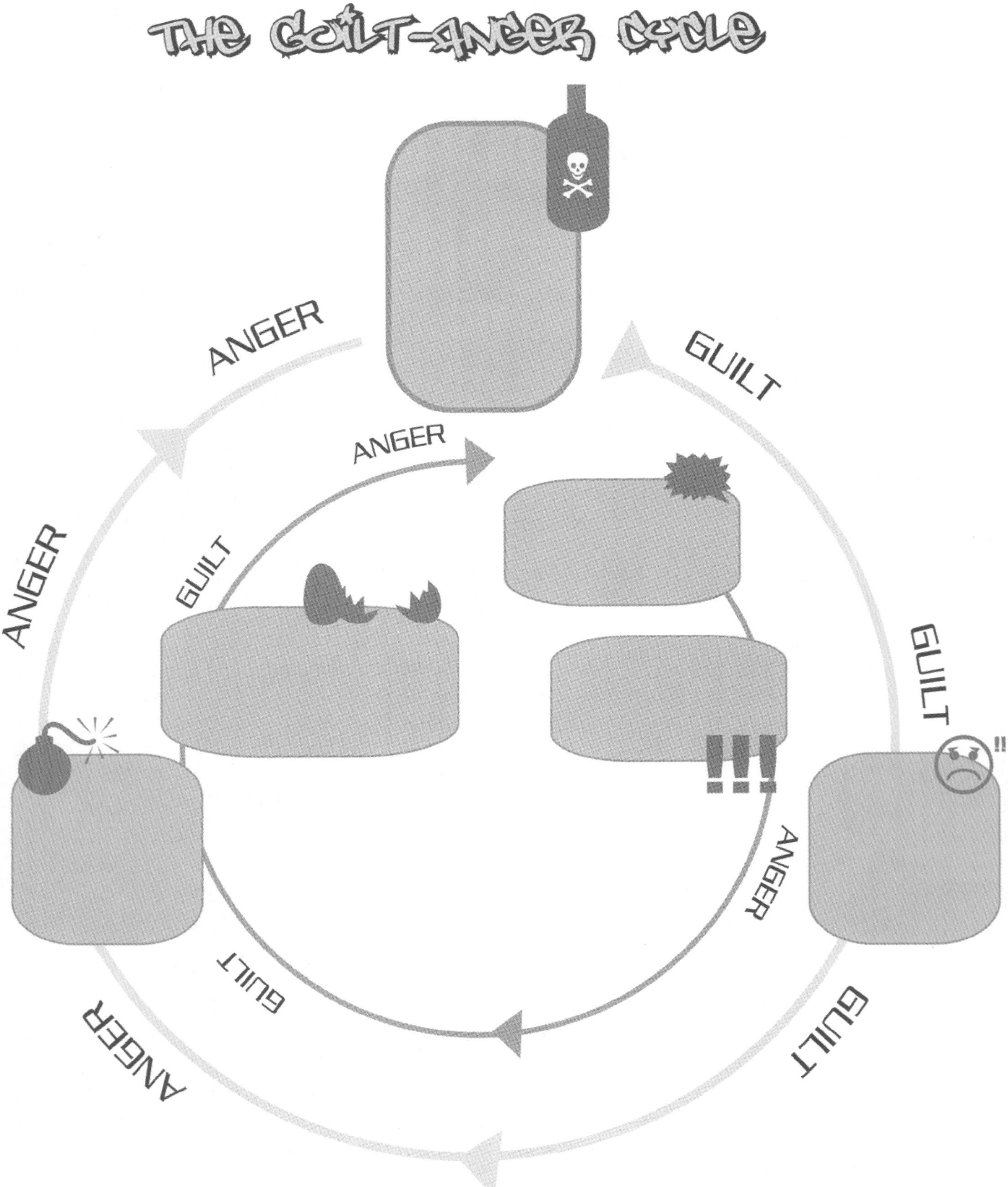

Ways to Deal With Stressful Emotional States

There are proven techniques for managing stressful emotions that have been of enormous help to people from all walks of life throughout the world. We use the word *BRAIN* to help us remember *five essential skills* to handle stressful situations.

B **Breathing.** Concentrate on focusing your attention on the area of your body near your heart. Inhale deeply for about 5 seconds, imagining the breath flowing in through your heart. Then exhale for about 5 seconds, visualizing the breath flowing out from your solar plexus (the area in the center of your body just below the middle of your rib cage).

R **Recognize and disengage.** Notice your mood and the physical signs of distress (e.g., knot in the stomach, raising the level of your voice, tenseness of muscles, flushing of face). Make a decision to "freeze the frame" of this discomfort, almost like pressing pause on your MP3 player and then moving on to a different experience.

A **Ask yourself, "Is there a better alternative?"** Is there a different way of managing the situation without getting angry, depressed, or guilty? What other thoughts might we use to change or replace the thoughts that are leading to uncomfortable emotions? In Chapter 9: Zeroing in on Harm-Directing Thoughts, we discussed ways of changing your negative thoughts. Use self-talk skills: "Why am I angry? What can I do about it positively?" Discover what thoughts are causing the feelings, and then replace them with some of your positive thoughts.

I **Input a positive feeling.** Focus on images that make you feel good. An example might be going for a walk in the woods, laughing with some childhood friends in the playground, or being on top of your game in some sport that you have enjoyed.

N **Note the changes in how you are thinking and feeling.** In a very quiet manner, notice any change in your mood, physical sensations, or negative thoughts. Maintain these positive changes as long as you can.

Activity: The Role of Anger

Break into groups of three. Together with your group, think of a situation in which all the people involved are **likely to get angry or upset.** An example might be the teacher or counselor orders a lockdown and nobody is allowed to have any time for recreation or going out of his or her room. Develop a skit that **deals with the angry situation** and uses the previously given **BRAIN** skills to keep the anger from exploding in a negative way. Perform your skit for the larger group. When watching a skit, keep in mind these questions: Is the skit believable? Is the way the anger is dealt with done in a positive manner? Did it utilize the **BRAIN** technique? Do you think it is realistic to use these skills in a real situation?

SESSION 19: DEALING WITH FEELINGS

As Always, Be Aware of Your Thoughts

We keep going over it, but it is important to remember that your *thoughts, beliefs,* and *feelings* are all in a meeting in your head. Every thought you have affects your feelings and actions. Every action you participate in will affect your thoughts and feelings. In order to learn to control and deal with your emotions, try to be aware of the thought habits, or automatic thoughts, that lead up to the emotion. Here are some examples of exaggerations in thinking, similar to the ones we covered in Chapter 9, and the types of automatic thoughts that might follow:

- **Magnifying (blowing negative events out of proportion).** "This is the worst thing ever."
- **Jumping to conclusions.** "She didn't smile at me. She hates me."
- **Overgeneralizing.** "Getting even is the only way to gain respect."
- **Self-blaming.** "I am no good anyway."
- **Expecting the worst.** "She's cheating on me."
- **Having a negative view of the world.** "Everything sucks, so I might as well take whatever I can."

Activity: The Anger in Me

Form a circle, and one at a time discuss a **situation** in the past week or two that **made you angry.** Try to share the **thoughts and feelings** that lead up to the anger, and tell the group what was the result or **action** you chose. Then, as a group, try to decide which of the exaggerated thought habits the situation fell into. Offer a way that you might have changed the situation, and listen to the feedback of the group. Go around the circle until everyone has discussed at least one situation in the past week where they either dealt with or didn't deal with anger, guilt, and depression.

A Simple and Effective Way to Deal With Anger

Perhaps the simplest way to calm down in an angry situation is to follow the **ABC** method:

A Acknowledge that you are angry.

B Back off.

C Consider your alternatives.

Believe it or not, this simple technique has actually saved lives.

Putting It Together

- Tristan became angry when he saw his girlfriend talking to another guy. What do you think his *automatic thoughts* were? How could he have changed his thoughts in order to choose a different action? How could he have used the **BRAIN** or **ABC** methods to deal with his anger?

- *Anger, guilt,* and *depression* often *create a cycle* in which the feelings keep getting stronger and nothing gets resolved. Review Worksheet 23: The Guilt–Anger Cycle, and see if the cycle plays a part in your life. How might you change this?
- Which thinking exaggerations do you use the most often? Why?
- Take some time before the next session to write up a thinking report for a situation you encountered in which you became angry. How were you able to use the **BRAIN** and **ABC** methods for dealing with anger?
- Update your Plan for Change (PFC). Do you have a new problem to add to your list? What will you work on this week?

Rate your ability to identify how your own thoughts can lead to angry feelings, aggression, and guilt.

0	1	2	3	4	5	6	7	8	9	10
Low					Medium					High

Indicate your ability to use the **ABC** method to manage *hot* situations without progressing to anger and aggression.

0	1	2	3	4	5	6	7	8	9	10
Low					Medium					High

Identify your level of skill at using the **BRAIN** method to manage *hot* situations without progressing to anger and aggression.

0	1	2	3	4	5	6	7	8	9	10
Low					Medium					High

SESSION 20: PREVENTING AGGRESSION

Objectives

- Review Session 19: Dealing With Feelings.
- Understand the different types of aggression and violence.
- Learn and practice self-control skills.

Tristan's Story: *Before I knew what happened, I had pulled the guy away from her, asked her what she was doing, and punched him, all in like a minute. The next thing I know is that he is staring at me with blood running down his face, and Audrey is looking at me with tears in her eyes.*

We talked the next morning, and I thought everything was fine. But the voices in my head wouldn't leave me alone. Why did she help him? Does she like him? Is she cheating on me? One night I couldn't handle it and drank most of my dad's beer before I went to pick her up for a date. She got angry with me and got in my face, and I ended up backhanding her. She slammed the door in my face and broke up with me the next day. And now I'm alone.

The Big Three Emotions

Last session we spent some time discussing three negative emotions that can powerfully affect our actions. They are *anger, guilt,* and *depression.* All of these emotions interact with each other in a cycle, making it hard for us to move forward and heal. By being aware of the thoughts that lead up to these emotions, we are able to control and deal with them in a healthy manner.

Activity: Thinking About Emotions

Share with the group one situation in which the **cycle of anger, guilt, and depression** played a part in how you reacted. How did you handle the situation? How might you have handled it differently? Share and offer to others ways that each person can better deal with the thinking exaggerations and the *guilt–anger–depression cycle* in order to better deal with their emotions.

Unfortunately, anger does not stop with the emotion or the use of a substance. Often it can be *verbally* or *physically* taken out on another person or an object, like in the case of vandalizing or even physical assault. This session is about *controlling your anger* so you can continue making positive choices and enjoying more freedom in your life.

What's The Difference Between Aggression and Violence?

While *anger* is an emotion we feel and is not necessarily wrong, aggression and violence are actions we participate in when we are *not able to control* our anger.

SESSION 20: PREVENTING AGGRESSION

Aggression is nonphysical behavior that *abuses, hurts,* or *injures* another person emotionally or psychologically. It can be controlled or uncontrolled. It can be calculated or happen on the spur of the moment. Consider some of the damage that aggression can do to another person:

- It can lower their self-esteem.
- It can damage their sense of dignity and self-respect.
- It can damage a person emotionally, creating fear, depression, anger, and stress.
- It can cause a person to withdraw and feel threatened.

Violence occurs when *aggression becomes physical.* Violence is everything that aggression is but *causes physical harm* and damage to things and people. It can be directed toward objects, such as smashing and breaking things, but usually relates to a person you know or who made you angry.

Violence is often directed to specific people and centers around *three primary positions* in the relationship between perpetrator and victim.

1. **Position of strength or power.** The victim of violence has power to *get in the way of* the violent person's needs or goals.
2. **Position of weakness.** The victim is *weak,* and the violent person has to maintain a *position of strength.*
3. **Position of sex.** The victim is a target of the violent person's *distorted sexual needs and drives.*

Activity: Violence or Aggression?

As a group, go over Tristan's story. Could Tristan's actions be considered **aggression** or **violence?** Use evidence from the story to support why. If you consider it aggression, think of what damage it did to Audrey. If you consider it violence, decide and think which of the three positions it would fit under. There may be more than one right answer, so **use evidence from the story** to back up your opinion.

If aggression is *not dealt with,* it often *becomes violence.* That is why it is important to deal with aggression in a positive manner. The important thing to keep in mind is that *events do not cause anger.* The *thoughts we have about the event* lead to anger and are usually caused by some problem. *High-charged* situations, similar to HR situations, are situations that usually will cause some anger or problems in our minds. Whenever possible, these situations should be avoided in order to prevent the buildup of angry thoughts and feelings.

Violence Associated With Gangs or Drugs

What *about group violence* such as *gang activities or violence and aggression around the manufacture and sale of drugs?* How do the previously stated positions *(power, weakness, and sex)* help to understand these types of violent activities?

SESSION 20: PREVENTING AGGRESSION

Activity: My Own Violence

Take a moment to fill out Worksheet 24: Managing High-Charged Situations. Write in some **emotionally charged situations** that could lead to the **expression of anger.** Then check whether or not the situation could lead to **violence.** Break into groups of three or four, and share your situations. Help each other figure out how to avoid violence in each situation.

Be Aware and in Control

Here are some of the signs that we can be aware of that will let us know when we are getting angry.

- Feeling irritable, agitated, and tense.
- Losing your temper.
- Feeling impatient; feeling like things are not going your way; feeling not in control.
- Being provoked or pushed by someone.
- Thinking and feeling you are not being treated fairly.

Skills to Avoid Aggression and Violence

When the clues begin to tip us off that we are getting angry, there are skills and steps we can take to avoid striking out aggressively or violently.

- Use ***relaxation.***
- Use ***self-talk*** to calm yourself down. Be aware of the angry thought, and use ***thought stopping*** (Session 17).
- Use ***thought replacement:*** Replace the angry thoughts with *positive thoughts.* Use the list you created in Session 17.
- ***Share*** your angry thoughts with someone without becoming aggressive.
- Use ***problem solving:*** When you begin to feel angry, try to *solve the problem.* Problem solving is something we will cover in Session 24.
- Keep in mind that the ***other person may be angry,*** too. Since they may not be reasoning well, you may be at risk.
- Use the **BRAIN** and **ABC** methods covered in the last session.
- After you successfully ***manage*** your anger, be proud and reward yourself.

Activity: Irritation Log (adapted from ART)

Take a moment and individually fill out Worksheet 25: The Irritation Log for a specific situation that you have encountered within the past few weeks. Describe the **situation** and **your reactions.**

Worksheet 24

MANAGING HIGH-CHARGED SITUATIONS

List high-charged situations that can lead you to anger or aggression. Then check if these can lead to violence.

LIST HIGH-CHARGED SITUATIONS THAT CAN LEAD TO ANGER, ANGRY THOUGHTS, AND FEELINGS OR TO AGGRESSIVE BEHAVIOR.	CHECK HERE IF IT COULD LEAD TO VIOLENCE.

After everyone has finished the worksheet, go around the group and share about your situation. Discuss what you think triggered the anger and whether you think you dealt with it well or not. Keep in mind these questions:

- Did you handle the situation well?
- How could you deal with the situation differently?
- What are your triggers to anger?

Commitment for Self-Control

Sometimes making a *promise to practice anger management* provides an excellent framework for keeping your commitment to remain in control. Worksheet 25 may serve as an important tool for keeping your anger in check.

One-Day Pledge to Remain Calm

Adapted from the Anger Control Workbook

I, ______________________________, promise to remain calm and not to lose my temper between ______________________________ (day/time) and ______________________________ (day/time). I will not become aggressive or violent no matter what stress or provocation may occur.

____ (your signature)

____ (witness)

Activity: A Moment of Self-Control

Sit in a circle, and for a moment, imagine a scene that causes you to feel angry. Take some time to imagine and begin to feel the anger the scene causes. Now begin to practice these relaxation skills.

- Take slow and deep breaths.
- Inhale slowly, in 5-second intervals, and then slowly release your breath, also in 5-second intervals.
- Repeat the breathing several times.
- Now clear your mind of all thoughts, and if a thought does occur, tell yourself, "I am relaxed." Repeat this as long as needed.

Worksheet 25

THE IRRITATION LOG

Where were you?

- ❑ Classroom
- ❑ Bathroom
- ❑ Outside
- ❑ Bedroom
- ❑ Counselor's office
- ❑ Halls
- ❑ Recreation Room
- ❑ Dining Room
- ❑ At work
- ❑ Other:________________

What happened?

- ❑ Somebody teased me.
- ❑ Somebody stole from me.
- ❑ I was told to do something.
- ❑ I didn't like what someone was doing.
- ❑ I broke a rule
- ❑ Someone started a fight with me
- ❑ Other: __________________

Who was the other person?

- ❑ Student
- ❑ Counselor
- ❑ Teacher
- ❑ Correctional officer
- ❑ Adult
- ❑ Resident
- ❑ Family member
- ❑ Gang member
- ❑ Other:________________

What was your response?

- ❑ Hit first
- ❑ Hit back
- ❑ Told a friend
- ❑ Ran away
- ❑ Ignored it
- ❑ Yelled
- ❑ Cried
- ❑ Broke something
- ❑ Was restrained
- ❑ Told counselor
- ❑ Walked away
- ❑ Talked it out
- ❑ Used skills to control anger.

If so describe skills: ___________________________

____

How do you think you dealt with it?

- ❑ Poorly
- ❑ Not so well
- ❑ Okay
- ❑ Good
- ❑ Great

How angry were you?

- ❑ Red hot
- ❑ Really angry
- ❑ Moderately angry
- ❑ Mildly angry
- ❑ Not angry at all

SESSION 20: PREVENTING AGGRESSION

After everyone has had a chance to relax completely using the skills, imagine another scene that makes you angry. This time use **self-talk** to confront and control the anger. Use your **thought stopping** and **thought replacement** skills in order to do this. Also, practice using the **ABC** and **BRAIN** methods for managing anger. Go around the circle, and one at a time say out loud the techniques that you are using. What ways seem more effective than others?

Putting It Together

- After drinking and taking drugs, Tristan became very angry, aggressive, and violent. What were some of the clues that Tristan was going to be violent? What *thoughts* and *anger management skills* might Tristan have used to calm himself down?
- Unresolved anger can lead to aggression, and aggression can lead to violence. Think about *when* you may have been *aggressive* or *violent.* Did you feel in control when you were acting out on your anger? What could you have done to stop your anger and deal with it?
- Is violence *more likely to occur* when you are with your *friends* or *a gang?* If so, what are some of the skills that you could use to change the pattern?
- Think about the *different ways to control anger* in order to avoid violence and aggression. Which way would work best for you?
- What problem area from your PFC will you work on this week?

Using the Program Guides and Tools for Change

Rate your skills to avoid aggression and violence by using the following techniques: relaxation, self-talk, thought replacement, sharing, BRAIN, ABC.

0	1	2	3	4	5	6	7	8	9	10
Low					Medium					High

Indicate your ability to follow through on your One-Day Pledge to Remain Calm.

0	1	2	3	4	5	6	7	8	9	10
Low					Medium					High

- With your counselor, update and add to your SP and PFC. Choose a problem to work on this week.
- Update your Master Skills List (MSL) in the areas of managing stress and anxiety, managing depression, anger management skills, and changing harm-directing thoughts.
- Re-rate yourself on strengths in your SP. Are the ratings higher?

TRISTAN'S STORY

I'm going to beat on her. I swear I'm going to really hurt her. But what am I going to do without her?

We met 2 years ago at the town fair, sometime around the Fourth of July, I think. She was beautiful, with long honey hair and bright green eyes with a bit of blue around the center. Always laughing and joking around, I think I fell in love with Audrey within the first week we started hanging out. We were pretty much inseparable, going everywhere together and always making our plans around each other's schedule.

Audrey had just moved to our town that summer, and in the fall, she was going to be a freshman at the school I was currently attending. Although I was older than her, it didn't matter when we were together. I think her parents had some problems with the fact that I was already 16, but they didn't stop us from dating. My dad didn't really give a rat's ass, just as long as I stayed out of his way. Everything was great for about a year.

Then some friends and I started experimenting with some harder drugs than pot. It was nothing serious, and it wasn't like I was even close to being an addict. It just made me feel better for a little while. But Audrey had a hard time dealing with my drug use. She said it made me act weird and do weird things, although I never understood what she was talking about. I was merely trying to expand my mind and spend as much time away from my violent drunk of a father as possible.

Then one night my friends and I ran into her hanging out with a couple of her friends. When we walked up, some guy from her class was talking to her. And I freaked out. It all happened so fast, but I grabbed the guy's shirt, pushed him away from her, asked her what the hell she was doing, and then turned around and punched the guy, all in like a minute. Before I realized what I had done, I saw him with blood running down his nose like lava leaving an erupted volcano and Audrey staring at me with tears in her eyes. She helped him stop the blood, and my friends pushed me into our car before the cops got called.

The next morning I felt like crap. I couldn't believe what I had done, and I definitely didn't know why. All I knew was I felt guilty as hell for doing that to the guy. After all he talks to her every day and it wasn't like I didn't trust her. All I could do was sit in the dark void of my room, not eating or anything because I was sure I had lost Audrey.

Finally, my prick of a father knocked on my door and told me Audrey was on the phone. I felt so guilty that I couldn't even talk to her. But I did and boy, did I apologize. I told her I knew she wasn't doing anything, and she said that was why she didn't like me doing drugs. We set a date for the next night, and everything was fine.

But it wasn't. I had a little voice in my head asking me why Audrey helped that guy when I was her boyfriend. Why couldn't she understand it from my point of view? Did she like him or something?

Everything was good for us for a while . . . until I found out that he was going to be her lab partner. I thought I handled it, but soon I couldn't handle the voices in my head anymore, and I ended up drinking most of my dad's beer one night before Audrey and I were supposed to go out. My dad came in while I was drinking, but he didn't say anything. He just smiled and walked out. As soon as I walked in her house, she started in on me being drunk for our date and how I knew she didn't like it when I was like that. Immediately the little voices in my head jumped up and accused her of cheating. For a second, she just stared at me and then she got in my face yelling at me about how dare I accuse her of being like that and to get out of her house. I wouldn't leave so she pushed me, and I turned around and backhanded her. She shoved me out the door and slammed it in my face. I was so angry that I went home and trashed my room.

She broke up with me. It's my fault, and I am so angry about that. I hear that she is dating that guy now. I am so hurt and angry. I want to beat her badly. Instead, I just sit and drink while thinking about what I once had and praying I never run into them together. Who knows what I'd do then.

PHASE III

NOW!

OWNERSHIP OF CHANGE:
Calling the Shots

Chapter Eleven:
Overcoming Prejudice

GOALS OF THIS CHAPTER

- Develop an appreciation for ethnicity, culture, and diversity.
- Understand the basis for prejudice and stereotyping.
- Review values and morals.
- Learn about gender roles and issues.

CONNOR'S STORY

CARLA'S STORY

SESSION 21: RESPECTING OTHERS

Objectives

- Review Chapter 10: Handling Anger, Guilt, and Depression.
- Learn the meanings of ethnicity, culture, and diversity.
- Understand the basis for prejudice and stereotyping.
- Understand and respect the rights of others.

Connor's Story: *They are all loud, obnoxious, and lazy, and they make me ill. You know the people I'm talking about. My dad grew up in this neighborhood, and he said it never used to be like this, all different ethnicities and cultures and PC crap. I can't even get a break at school. The teacher always thinks this kid is smarter because he's of this race, and the coach picks that kid for the team instead of me because he's of that race. My dad says that it's because I'm male and not the right race. The teachers and coaches say I can do anything I want if I tried, but my dad says that's just an excuse they use to make it my fault.*

Carla's Story: *Most guys are such jerks. They are loud and cocky, and it makes me sick. My mom says they are all like that. It doesn't matter what really happens. They always talk like they're "the man." She calls them lovers and leavers. One day they love you like crazy and the next day they're gone. All I know is I'm starting to not like any of them. In fact, I'm starting to kind of hate them—especially when they are so loud and messing around in the hallway. They always look at me like I'm a piece of meat, like I should worship them or something. I just glare at them.*

Review of How We Deal With Our Feelings

In our last two sessions, Dealing With Feelings (Session 19) and Preventing Aggression (Session 20), we discussed how improperly managed anger can cause a cycle of depression and guilt, which causes us to be even angrier. We learned how *automatic thoughts* and *deep-seated beliefs* can move us to *highly charged feeling states* involving guilt, anger, and depression. We become angry as the result of our immediate interpretations of a situation, usually around thoughts of unfairness, violation of territory or rights, or the thought that we are being disrespected in some fashion. Our immediate thoughts are usually guided by some deeply ingrained attitudes and beliefs about what is good or bad, right or wrong, fair or unfair. Because anger, guilt, and depression are such painful feeling states, we are easily swayed—sometimes by our families and closest role models—*to take the easy way out*—i.e., to *push these emotions aside* and avoid dealing with how we got them in the first place. As young children, we are often told to cheer up or that guilt is pointless because "it isn't your fault." Unfortunately, because these emotions are shoved aside, with repeated attempts to bury them out of view, *they have a tendency to break out* when least wanted.

As a matter of fact, we don't have any "bad" emotions. But how we *deal with our emotions* can cause problems in our life. If we don't deal with the thoughts that generate anger, guilt, or depression, they will likely build up in our minds until we explode. Have you ever shaken up a bottle of soda really hard and then tried to open it? Once the bottle is only slightly opened, the whole thing explodes because of built-up pressure. That is how our emotions are. If our anger is bottled up under pressure, once we get slightly mad we are likely to *erupt in aggression* or *violence.* It is very important to learn how to deal with negative emotions as they arise. Do not bottle them up, or they are likely to explode.

In order to cope with uncomfortable feelings, we must first become aware of the thoughts and beliefs that underlie our discomfort. When we notice ourselves feeling anger, guilt, or depression, we need to practice the skills that we learned through the **ABC** and **BRAIN** models for dealing with feelings. Remember to take some time to stop and think about why you are feeling badly and what positive thoughts can be used to help you feel better.

Of course, emotions can have a lot of influence over us in our dealings with people who seem different from us. Sometimes ideas about what people from certain races or nationalities are like, which we were exposed to as children, stir up negative emotions without any real reasons.

Activity: A Moment to Think

Take a moment to look at Worksheet 24: Managing High-Charged Situations and Worksheet 25: The Irritation Log for Session 20. Then break into groups of three, and share the **thoughts** that surround a recent situation in which ***you became angry.*** What **high-risk (HR) or harm-directing thoughts** do you recognize in each other's examples? How might the person change their patterns of negative thinking? Which of the methods of dealing with anger, guilt, or depression works best for you?

Prejudice: False Beliefs That Lead to Inflicting Harm on Others

What Is Ethnicity?

Ethnicity is a term that gets thrown around a lot in politics and the media. But what specifically is ethnicity? What does it mean to be ethnic? A dictionary would provide a definition such as "belonging to a social group on the basis of shared traits." In common terms, ethnic is usually meant to refer to a racial group living amongst a larger group who share different racial characteristics. The smaller group becomes known as a "minority." Actually, *we are all part of an ethnic group.* Religion, language, and family history are a part of ethnicity, not just our physical appearance.

What Is Culture?

While a person's ethnicity is the background traits (e.g., physical appearance, religion, family history, country of origin), a *person's culture* is their social behavior or how they act according to what they learned from society. An example might be music culture. Let's say a person listens to rap music. This person may wear clothes and speak in a manner that exhibits the *cultural lifestyle* that society and media have labeled hip-hop, rap, or any number of other labels.

SESSION 21: RESPECTING OTHERS

Because people are allowed to immigrate to this country in order to have a better life, the United States has a large *number of different cultures* in small regions and areas of the country. Consider all the ethnic groups who live or work on the small island of Manhattan or in the city of Los Angeles. This can cause some difficulties and problems. But culture can also be expanded to consider all social influence, meaning there is a *U.S. culture,* no matter how many different ethnicities reside in the United States.

Activity: Diversity Profile

According to your own beliefs and opinions, take some time to fill out the questions on Worksheet 26: My Diversity Profile. Each statement is to be filled out according to your specific values and beliefs, which come from many different places, including our teachers, families, friends, neighborhood, the region we grew up in, and our religious and spiritual backgrounds.

Generalities and Stereotypes

As human beings, we like to group things in order for us to understand and feel comfortable with them. Let's say, just for an example, that while walking one day we see a person who has *dark hair and is wearing a purple shirt.* We may note it, but we won't think about it until we see a few more dark-haired people. On seeing several people with the same color shirt and hair, we may say to ourselves, "All people wearing purple shirts have dark hair" or "All people with dark hair wear purple shirts." We have just made a *generalization* about people wearing purple shirts or people with dark hair. In some way, this will make us *feel comfortable.* The expectation of dark-haired people wearing purple shirts will give us some sense of comfort in our efforts to predict future events and understand the world around us.

One step further is a *stereotype.* A stereotype is when we begin to classify all people who look the same or belong to a certain group, and we *begin to treat them all the same.* A stereotype, similar to a generalization, gets applied to a group that may have some of the *same attributes or feature*s. When we form *negative stereotypes,* we are quick to judge people who have some characteristics of a known group (e.g., language or race) as being bad, inferior, or undesirable. So again, errors in our way of thinking can negatively influence how we think and how we act toward a whole group of people.

Using our previous example, let's say that we tried to talk with one person who wore a purple shirt and had dark hair. That person was rude to us. We may think it's just that person, but what if another person with a purple shirt and dark hair was rude to us? And another? Then we might begin to believe that *all people* with purple shirts and dark hair are rude. It may even become more spread out than that, like all people with purple shirts—no matter the hair color—are rude or all dark-haired people are rude. This does not mean our belief is true or accurate; it is just what we've learned to expect from our surrounding environment. When we reject or inflict harm on someone because of a negative stereotype, we are acting out of prejudice.

Negative Stereotype → Prejudice

Worksheet 26

MY DIVERSITY PROFILE

How we look at the world is made up of our beliefs and values; although sometimes they are given to us by the media. Our beliefs and values are based on what we hear from our parents, family, and friends or may be based on our religion or spirituality or from the region we live in. This profile will help you see your view of the world and where your beliefs and values come from.

Please Complete the following:

GENDER

A woman is characterized by: ______________________________

A man is characterized by: ______________________________

SEXUAL ORIENTATION

A family consists of: ______________________________

A relationship is: ______________________________

FAMILY

Our family traditions are: ______________________________

AGE

In my generation, we like: ______________________________

REGION

Where I live, we value: ______________________________

ETHNICITY

One of the ethnic groups that I belong to is ______________ and what makes us different is: ______________________________

What I like about my ethnic group is: ______________________________

What I don't like about my ethnic group is: ______________________________

Activity: Connor's and Carla's Stereotyping

Break into smaller groups and take a look at Connor's and Carla's stories. What stereotypes, generalities, or prejudices do you think each of them uses? What do you think causes Connor to stereotype the way he does? How about Carla? Do you think any of their stereotypes are correct, and why or why not?

Activity: The Surrounding Stereotypes

Take a moment to look over some of the items you have listed in Worksheet 26: My Diversity Profile, and think of things you do not like about your family or ethnic group. Do these fit into a stereotype or generalization? Where do you think you got these stereotypes and generalities? As a large group, list the stereotypes on a piece of paper. Then write down reasons to disagree with the stereotype. What exceptions do you make to certain stereotypes, if any? An example of an exception would be that you think dark-haired people are rude, except your one friend, who happens to have dark hair, but who isn't rude. When do stereotypes become a form of prejudice?

How Is Prejudice Formed?

As we've said before, a stereotype most often begins in a generalization, such as that all people who have certain common features will act a certain way, such as "all working-class people drink a lot of beer and watch football." Generalities come from our experience and our drive to understand the world. But stereotypes take generalities one step further. While there are exceptions to generalities and they can often be proven wrong, *stereotypes tend to go unchecked and unquestioned.* Remember, the most damaging part of forming a negative stereotype is the harm that we inflict on others through prejudice.

Need for Superiority

When people feel threatened or scared, they often strike out against that which is making them uncomfortable. By insisting that *we are better than* a group or a person, we can pretend that the group does not threaten us.

For an example, let's say we have lived in a neighborhood our whole lives and we know almost everyone there. And let's say that *we all wear orange shirts and black shoes.* Suddenly a family wearing *purple shirts and white shoes* moves in next door. We are still in the majority, and we may make a point of letting the new family know they are alone. As time goes by, however, *more* people with purple shirts and white shoes move into the neighborhood. Suddenly, we are the minority. So we act out against what is being threatened. We may feel they are taking our jobs, or ruining our schools, or changing our culture. So we begin to hate them as a group. It may even be that a purple shirt/white shoes person got promoted over us or has a bigger house. We begin to hate all purple shirt/white shoes people because we blame them for our misfortune. Can you think of any real-life examples of how this may occur?

Failure to Discriminate, to Recognize Differences

It may seem crazy, but when we do not see differences between people within a group, we become prejudiced. If we think all people from New York City are the same, we form a stereotype that would lead to prejudice—for example, some people think that everyone from New York City is aggressive and rude.

Lack of Information

Sometimes we dislike or hate another group because of the *information that is given to us* by our parents, by our friends, or by the media. Remember, some of our *core beliefs* are taught to us from a very early age, and sometimes they can become part of us without us ever really knowing it. Instead of getting to know a person as an individual, we allow ourselves to *stereotype them* according to *what we have learned.* Our father may have lost his job or a promotion might have been given to someone different from him, let's say a *purple shirt/white shoes.* Because of his feelings of rejection and anger, he may lash out against *purple shirt/white shoes* by saying, "They are lazy," or "They don't belong here," or "They only get work because they do the jobs no one else wants."

Whether we want to or not, we hear what our dad says about the other group, and it becomes a *core belief.* When we are out on the street, we will likely run into a few of the people that appear to be the way our father (or some other role model) says they are, supporting his stereotype and our generalization. The more we hear these negative stereotypes and prejudices (from parents or other role models), the more we look for the people who fit his definition and the more our generalization becomes a stereotype. At some point we may act *out of prejudice and inflict harm* on someone from the *purple shirt/white shoes* group.

Activity: The Need to Stereotype

Once again, break into groups and take a look at Connor's and Carla's stories. Where do you think Connor gets his stereotypes? What about Carla? To which of the previously given categories (superiority, information, failure to discriminate) do most of their stereotypes fit, or do they seem to fit in more than one of the categories? Why or why not? Use examples from the stories.

How could Connor and Carla get over their stereotypes? When do they show signs of prejudice? Discuss how discrimination (or recognizing differences) can make us less prejudiced.

Stereotyping can cause problems because it doesn't give people a chance to be good at what they do or be an individual and different from other people that may seem similar to the person. The fact is most of us belong to someone else's stereotype, like addict, delinquent, or gang member. And more often than not, being stereotyped works against us. Stereotypes lead to prejudice and hatred for people because of religious differences, appearance differences, history differences, or even a difference in fashion.

Activity: The Difference in Me

For this activity, break into groups according to the color of shirt you are wearing. If everyone is wearing the same shirt, break into groups according to whether you like to play sports or prefer listening to music. Give each group a name according to the means of separation, such as the "T-shirts" or possibly the "sneakers." Spend some time in your group sharing and writing down all the **differences** there are **between you and your other group members.** Try to list as many as possible. When the larger group gets back together, each person will say which other group they don't like according to an appearance (e.g., T-shirt, sneakers, dark hair, tattoos). Then that group will read the list of differences between members of their own group to the rest of the group.

Notice that when separated according to appearance, people in the small groups looked similar to each other, but when they began reading their differences, there *were more differences* than the similarity of appearance. In other words, when we *use a stereotype* to describe a person, we *omit all of the characteristics* that make them *unique* or *different.*

Appreciation of Differences

For a minute, let's try to imagine a world where everyone is the same. One morning we wake up and suddenly everyone is wearing exactly what we are wearing. They have the same color hair, and they even look just like us. We go to the movies with our friends, all of whom look just like us and say the exact same thing as us at the same time. Imagine how you would feel if you were in this situation when you woke up.

Do you feel comfortable with the idea of everyone being just like you? That is the *joy in differences.* Because we all feel and think differently (Principle 2: Everyone Sees Themselves and the World From Different Points of View from Session 3), there is change and excitement to our world. Trends change, thoughts change, and what we appreciate changes as well. Because there are so many different ethnicities, and even cultures, we can appreciate and experience things that would otherwise not exist. Different foods, sights, and experiences allow us to try out experiences that make life exciting and interesting.

Activity: Differences Within a Group

Break into smaller groups according to **ethnic or racial affiliation** (Hispanic or Latino, African American, Caucasian, etc.), and then answer these questions in your group:

- Why did you affiliate yourself with this group?
- What are some of the similarities you have with the group, outside of skin color or racial identification?
- What are some of the differences you have from the group?
- Do you have more **differences** or more **similarities** as a group?

Unfortunately, many of our *stereotypes* and *prejudice* tend to be set into our minds as *"core beliefs."* Our *values* and *morals* are *types of core beliefs* about *what is important in life* (like the value of being a good friend) and what is *right or wrong.* Since our values are our way of looking at the world, it is really hard to think about a value not being positive or in our best interest. But sometimes our values can get in the way of changing for the better or living a happier life. Remember Chapter 8: Responsibility to Others and the Community, when we talked about *moral dilemmas?* It often takes a moral dilemma in order for us to change our thought and value system for the better. Think of a *moral* that you have, such as "Slavery is wrong." But if you have a *core belief* that some people are better than others, doesn't that conflict with your morals?

We are not saying that everyone has to change their beliefs, or values; we are just saying that sometimes these may conflict with our morals, and our thinking needs to change in order to take control over our thoughts and have freedom in our lives. Are you open to changing some belief, value, or standard of right and wrong that you may have held on to for a very long time?

Activity: Difference in Diversity

Take a moment to look at Worksheet 26: My Diversity Profile that you filled out earlier in this session. What are some of the beliefs represented in your profile? What are some of the stereotypes and generalities? Go down the list, and try to think of why you think that way about certain issues. Then as a larger group, discuss each topic and belief from the different points of view. Remember to respect and value each other's opinion. Are there certain things the group can agree on? Are there certain things that everyone disagrees on? Take some time to go back and think about your answers and where they came from. What are some alternative answers?

Putting It Together

- This story about Connor shows *several different stereotypes* and generalities. What are some of the stereotypes? Why does Connor believe in those stereotypes?
- Stereotypes often begin in generalities. What are some of the generalities or stereotypes that *you believe in?* Why do you believe in them?
- What are some of the stereotypes that have been *used against you?*
- Have you ever *encountered* prejudice? What was the situation, and how did you react?
- Make a list of all the things your friends and you have in common. What are some of the differences? Would you be friends without those differences?

Using the Program Guides and Tools for Change

Rate your understanding of how the natural tendency to form generalities can lead to stereotyping and prejudice.

0	1	2	3	4	5	6	7	8	9	10
Low					Medium					High

Indicate your ability to use Table 2: Mental Self-Control and Change Skills to manage HR situations.

0	1	2	3	4	5	6	7	8	9	10
Low					Medium					High

- Update your Self-Portrait (SP). Do you want to decrease or increase any of the scales?
- Now update your Plan for Change (PFC). Have you discovered any personal stereotypes or prejudices that you would like to reconsider?

SESSION 22: GENDER ISSUES

Objectives

- Review Session 21: Respecting Others.
- Increase awareness of gender roles and stereotypes.
- Understand the external pressures that influence our view of gender and sexuality.
- Understand our personal views about men and women.

Connor's Story: *My mom always tells me that we should practice tolerance and get to know them as individuals, even though she thinks they're lazy and terrible housekeepers. Besides, what does she know anyways? All she does is cook, clean, and watch her stupid soap operas. What does she know about what's going on out in the world? I guess she did try to go to night school. But my dad said that it was either the family or her uppity education. She cried, like women do, and she whined, like women do, and then she finally decided to stay home again. It was that stupid night school that got her talking about tolerance.*

Carla's Story: *My older sister says I should practice tolerance—try to get to know guys as individuals and maybe then I might find one I would like. Even though she herself will tell you most of them are assholes—lovers and leavers, just like mom says. But who is she to talk? She's the one with two babies from two different guys. She says I should do things differently than her . . . that I should find a guy who will really respect me and live up to a man's responsibilities. Maybe they are stronger than me, but my mom says it's because the world is run by men and their brains are in their pants.*

A Reminder of Stereotypes

Last session we learned about stereotypes and prejudice. We discussed where they come from and why we have them. *Stereotypes begin as generalities,* which are helpful because they help us understand our world and put it into categories for quicker remembering. Unfortunately, when a generalization becomes a stereotype, negative things can occur, such as *prejudice* and *hatred.* They are based on our failure to see differences within a group.

So why do stereotypes occur? There are many reasons for the development of stereotypes and prejudice, but last session we discussed two of them in particular.

1. The need for superiority
2. Lack of information

Some people feel the *need to be better than others,* and sometimes that comes around because *we are threatened* or our place in the world is threatened. By using negative stereotypes, it allows us to feel better about ourselves and our position in the world. But we shouldn't have to put others down to feel better about ourselves.

Another reason for stereotyping comes about through lack of information. When we discussed values and morals in Chapter 8: Responsibility to Others and the Community, we went over how our values come from the people around us—more importantly our parents and close friends. Sometimes we are surrounded by stereotypes our whole lives, so we begin to believe and follow them without even thinking about it. Most of us don't question our values or stereotypes, so we don't usually try to find out if the information we are going off of is correct.

Activity: Appreciation of Differences

Take a moment to think about the people you were with last week. Were there any situations in which you treated someone **based on a stereotype** and not the individual? What were the situations you found yourself in, if any? Break into groups of three or four and discuss the different situations each of you had over the past week. What were the thoughts behind the situation? Help offer each other alternatives or different views of the situation in order to support the appreciation of differences.

Of course, there are some stereotypes that are so ingrained within our society that most of us don't even think twice when we say or do something. Some of these stereotypes are called *gender roles,* or how we expect men and women to behave and feel in society. In this session, we will discuss gender roles and stereotypes and find out how we think and feel about certain gender issues.

Are Men and Women More Alike or Different?

What Is Gender?

Strictly speaking, *gender* refers to male or female, based on the genitalia assigned when developing in the womb. Gender in the physical sense can become confusing, however. There are people who are termed *hermaphrodites,* which means they are born with both genitalia. There is nothing wrong with hermaphrodites, and most of them have corrective surgery in order to become the sex they feel most part of.

There is also confusion in the *mental view of gender.* Some people who think they are opposite from their biological sex are considered to be transsexual. Transsexuality occurs in both males and females, and it does not mean they are homosexual. Usually a transsexual will dress and act according to the sex they feel they are *most mentally aligned* with, disregarding the physical genitalia. Some go through *corrective surgery* in order to become the *physical gender* of the mentality they are most comfortable with.

The gender differences bring to light an issue that is prevalent throughout our society. That is the issue of *gender roles.* How are members of the male or female gender expected to think, feel, and act?

SESSION 22: GENDER ISSUES

Activity: Our Gender Stereotypes

Break into groups of three, and take a look at the List of Soap Opera Characters. For this activity, you will be helping to create a soap opera. **Your job is to name**—first and last names—all the characters in the soap opera. You will need to agree on the names as a team. When you have completed the list, return to the larger group. Each smaller group will give a report on what they named the characters. Your counselor will put a mark on each character whether the name was male or female. After all groups have reported their names, tally up the numbers and take a look at whether the majority of the group thinks the characters are probably male or female.

List of Soap Opera Characters

- A doctor who is rude to patients and thinks they are better than everyone else.
- A doctor who goes out of their way to help the homeless people of the city.
- The administrator in charge of the hospital.
- The secretary for the hospital administrator.
- The security guard.
- The janitor.
- The operating room nurse.
- The nurse who works in the new baby ward.
- A volunteer who helps in the children's ward.

How Do Men and Women Differ?

Society begins teaching us very early in life whether we are girls or boys and what is expected from us because we are a certain gender. We learn early what clothing and accessories are appropriate for males and females, and as we grow older, the expectations become more complicated and detailed. These expectations (automatic thoughts) become so ingrained that we rarely see them ourselves. They can vary from what we think people should look like (what we wear and how we do our hair), to who does the cooking and cleaning in a household, or who should go to work, or what we are expected to talk about at social gatherings. What do members of the group believe to be differences between men and women?

Activity: Connor's and Carla's Expectations

Break into groups to discuss Connor's and Carla's stories. What are the similarities between Carla and Conner in their ideas of gender roles? How are their gender expectations similar? How are they different? How did each of them form their gender stereotypes? How did Connor react when his mom tried to do **something different** from housework? What was Carla's reaction when her sister tried to tell her **try something different** with guys?

Similar to stereotypes, these gender roles become *so ingrained* that we act on them without thinking whether we agree with them or not. Similar to our values, we get them from our role models who may be parents, teachers, and friends, but even society, media, and television as a whole tend to play up to and strengthen the gender roles. The truth about how a person actually thinks, feels, and acts may be very different from typical gender role expectations. For example, some men work as highly qualified and effective nurses while some women are expert pilots who fly missions for the military.

Activity: The Role of Gender

As a large group, think and write down **all the gender roles** you can think of for both males and females. You don't have to agree with them, but think of commercials, television, and what your parents have told you to think of the roles. Once all the gender roles you can think of are written down, one by one go through them and pick out **one gender role you know an exception to.** For example, a gender role may be that "women are supposed to be the cooks for the family." If one of you knows that your father or a male friend is a better cook than your mother or another female that is a role you know an exception to. Keep going around until everyone has picked up one exception. If time allows, keep going around until there are multiple exceptions for all the gender roles. Notice that very few people you know actually fit within these gender roles.

There are exceptions to every gender role, but when a person becomes *too different* from an expected gender role, they *become labeled.* A female who is referred to as a *tomboy* is an example, but there are also instances that warrant more attention. A *transvestite* is a person who prefers to *dress* like the opposite sex. While a transsexual has the mentality of the opposite sex, a transvestite usually likes and prefers being the sex they are; they just like dressing in the opposite sex's gender-specific clothes. While a transvestite can be of either sex, the most apparent and well known are males who dress as females, such as drag queens. Keep in mind that a transvestite does not have to be homosexual. Some heterosexual males prefer to dress as females.

Transvestitism brings to light an important criticism for society, however, which is why transvestites as well as transsexuals tend to be stigmatized and looked down upon. Society and generally the world at large prefers to see things in black and white in order to avoid confusion and ambiguity. But there are many people out there who *behave differently* from what most people have come to expect as "normal." And being different is not something that is wrong or should be punished. Life is often set along a continuum, instead of just black and white; there is a lot of gray middle ground where the majority of people fall. Like we discussed in the last session, differences should be *enjoyed* and *experienced,* not shoved down and hated. And besides, as we learned in the section on stereotyping, there are many differences between members of any identifiable group.

SESSION 22: GENDER ISSUES

Labeling and stereotyping are certainly not always in reference to something as uncommon as transvestitism. A mother who *chooses to work* and have a family is sometimes stigmatized for trying to have a career. The same applies to man who prefers to *stay home with his kids* rather than work at an office. Some people call them nasty names, but that doesn't mean their choices are wrong or that they are inferior in any way. This program teaches tolerance and acceptance for people's choices, as long as they are not injuring themselves or others.

Activity: A Role Apart

Break into groups of three in order to write a skit. Act out your character in the skit according to how you think the other sex would behave. For example, the group is trying to decide where to go to eat. If you were a male, then act out your character according to how you think a female would act and react. If you are female, try to act out your character how you think a male would act and react. When other groups are performing, notice how the characters seem like they are from a really bad sitcom. Most of them are contrived and based on gender roles and stereotypes that we are taught and fed from the media from the time we are born. Then individually write or draw out some things you believe and expect from yourself and your gender. Write down all that you can think of—even some things that you do every day. Then, as a larger group, compare everyone's answers about what they expect from their gender or themselves. What are some things that everyone wrote down? What are some things that are different? What expectations do you think you unknowingly hold about your own gender?

Who Cares About Gender Roles?

The difficulty that arises from *gender roles* is that it is often used as the means of "putting a person in their place" or designating one person as better than the other person. Unfortunately, it gets drawn down the line of male versus female. The truth is that society needs both in order to function. Can you imagine a world without the opposite sex? It would get pretty boring. But by *insisting on conformity to gender roles* and stereotypes, people are not being allowed to explore their own talents or their individuality.

Activity: All About Control

Break into your discussion groups, and take another look at Connor's and Carla's stories. How did Connor and his dad **try to control** Connor's mom through gender roles? Was there any respect between Connor and his mom? Explain your answer. How would Connor's life be different if his mother would have been allowed to continue to go to school? How did Carla form her gender role expectations? How might she create difficulties in her life if she holds on to the gender stereotypes that she has formed?

It Comes Down to Respect

Respect comes in many forms, whether it is the job you work at or how much you are paid, to cultural and social pressures, to how you are treated and how you treat your friends and family. In order to get along, *we need to respect other people.* And in order to do that, we shouldn't force them into stereotypes or occupations or even clothing according to their sexuality. Everyone plays a role in society, and it doesn't have to fall along specific gender lines.

Activity: Gender Respect

Break into groups according to gender (male or female). Pick a person to record the answers, and then answer these questions:

- What do you **like** about being male/female?
- What do you **not like** about being male/female?
- What are your **opinions** of the opposite sex?
- How do you **get respect** from women/men?
- What do they need to do to **earn respect** from you?

After you have answered all the questions, get back together as a large group and share your answers. What answers did both males and females answer similarly? What were some of the differences? How will you improve your respect for the opposite sex?

Putting It Together

- Both Connor and Carla have some pretty specific gender role expectations. Where did Connor get his expectations for his mom? Where did Carla get her expectations about guys from? What do you think about their expectations?
- Gender roles are stereotypes that tend to be placed in our value systems rather early. What are some of the gender roles you expect from yourself? What are some gender roles you expect from the opposite sex?
- Although seemingly simple, once we take a closer look at gender roles, they can become more confusing. What gender roles do you think are really confusing?
- No matter the gender or sexual orientation of a person, respect is something that most people deserve. How do you show the opposite sex or people who have different sexual orientations that you respect them?

SESSION 22: GENDER ISSUES

Using the Program Guides and Tools for Change

Rate your ability to understand how gender stereotypes can result in misunderstanding and disrespect for individuals who do not fit our expectations of how they should think, feel, or act.

0	1	2	3	4	5	6	7	8	9	10
Low					Medium					High

Indicate your ability to relate positively to people who may look, feel, or act very differently from their expected gender roles—e.g., homosexual, transgender, or transvestite orientations.

0	1	2	3	4	5	6	7	8	9	10
Low					Medium					High

- Look at your thinking patterns ratings on your SP. Do some of these patterns cause you to be prejudiced? Do some cause you to make gender stereotypes?
- Update your SP and your PFC.
- Update your Master Skills List (MSL) in the area of empathy skills.

CONNOR'S STORY

Most people are so loud and inconsiderate it makes me ill—especially those kind of people. You know the ones I'm talking about.

The other night I was trying to do my homework when the neighbors were being loud and obnoxious. I guess they were having a party. They are always having a party. My dad says that's just how they are—those kind of people. They are inconsiderate, loud, obnoxious, and really shouldn't be here.

My dad grew up in this neighborhood. He said there didn't used to be all these different ethnicities and cultures and PC crap. Everyone was the same, and that's how it is supposed to be. He was raised that if you worked hard and did your job, you would be rewarded for it. No one told him that some other guy would swoop down and steal your promotion right out from under you just because the boss likes the other race better than yours or because the other guy will work for cheaper. Who knows? Who cares, except for my dad, ya know, because he's the one who's getting his job stolen and his neighborhood ruined.

So my dad says they are all like that . . . every one. And I can kinda see his point sometimes. Most of them are like that . . . all of them I've been around except my one friend. He's different. He's not like them, although I'm not sure how he turned out differently. I guess maybe he's just smarter. All I know is I'm starting not to like any of them. In fact, sometimes I feel a kind of hatred toward them, especially when they are all loud and out in the hallway. They always give me a look like I don't belong here. My dad grew up just down the street, and I don't belong here? So I just give them a nasty look back.

My mom always tells me that we should practice tolerance and try to get to know them as individuals . . . even though she says they are all lazy and poor housekeepers. And what does she know anyways? She's not out there making a living to keep this family sheltered and fed. All she does is cook, clean, and watch her stupid soap operas. What does she know about what it's like out there?

I guess she did try to go to night school once. But then we didn't get dinner half the time, and the other half of the time she was always talking about stupid stuff. My dad put his foot down. He said it's either the family or her uppity education. My dad hates uppity people; they have no right thinking they are better than us. So she cried a lot, like women do, and whined a lot to my dad, like women do, and then finally decided she would stay home. She has no right being out there getting educated anyway. Women don't know nothing about the world . . . so my dad says. Besides, it's that stupid night school that got her started on the whole tolerance thing.

I can't even get a break at school. The teacher always thinks this person is smarter because they are this race, or the coach picks that person because they are that race, or she gets more chance to talk with her friends because she's more responsible and does her homework. Maybe he is smarter, and he is better at sports than I am, and maybe she is more responsible. But my dad says no it's because I'm male and not of the right race, and the PC crap has ruined the world. The teachers and coaches don't say that. They tell me I can do anything if I try, but my dad says that's just an excuse they use to make it all my fault when it's really their fault.

My dad's got a point. I have a right to be here, and most of them don't. And I have a right to a job when they are lazy and stupid. And I should be the one educated, not her. I have the right to do what I want to do when I want to do it, and they can't say nothing about it. And if my mom tries to tell me different, I'll hit her like my dad does. She deserves it. She can't even cook right.

CARLA'S STORY

Most guys are such jerks. They are loud and cocky, and it makes me sick—especially those kinds of guys. You know the ones I'm talking about.

The other day I was at my locker between classes, and this group of guys was being so loud. They were laughing and joking about one of the girls at our school. I guess they must have been talking about a party. They are always being rowdy and laughing about something or someone.

My mom says they are all like that. It doesn't matter what really happens. They always talk like they're "the man." She calls them lovers and leavers. One day they love you like crazy and the next day they're gone—moved on to someone else.

I kind of agree with her, except for this one guy in my history class. He knows my name, and when he says hi he doesn't call me something skanky or made up. He's different. He's not like them, although I'm not sure how he turned out differently. I guess he's just smarter. All I know is I'm starting to not like any of them. In fact, I'm starting to kind of hate them—especially when they are so loud and messing around in the hallway. They always look at me like I'm a piece of meat, like I should worship them or something. I just glare at them.

My older sister says I should practice tolerance—try to get to know them as *individuals* and maybe then I might find one I would like. Even though she herself will tell you most of them are jerks—lovers and leavers, just like mom says. But who is she to talk? She's the one with two babies from two different guys.

She says I should do things differently than her . . . find a guy who will really respect me and live up to a man's responsibilities. She only got the idea of tolerance from going through a custody battle with her exes. What does she know about what it's like for me?

I can't even get a break at work. My boss thinks that this guy can do this thing and that guy can do that thing. But since I'm a girl, all I can do is stand around and look pretty. Maybe they are stronger than me, but my mom says it's because the world is run by men and their brains are in their pants. My boss sometimes tells me I can do anything in life if I try. My mom says that's just an excuse he uses to make it my fault when it's really his.

I think my mom has a point. My rights are just the same as any guys. But trust me, if I ever get involved with a guy who expects me to do everything his way, to cook and clean, and run the house and have sex whenever he wants, I'll dump his ass before he can even think of moving on to another girl.

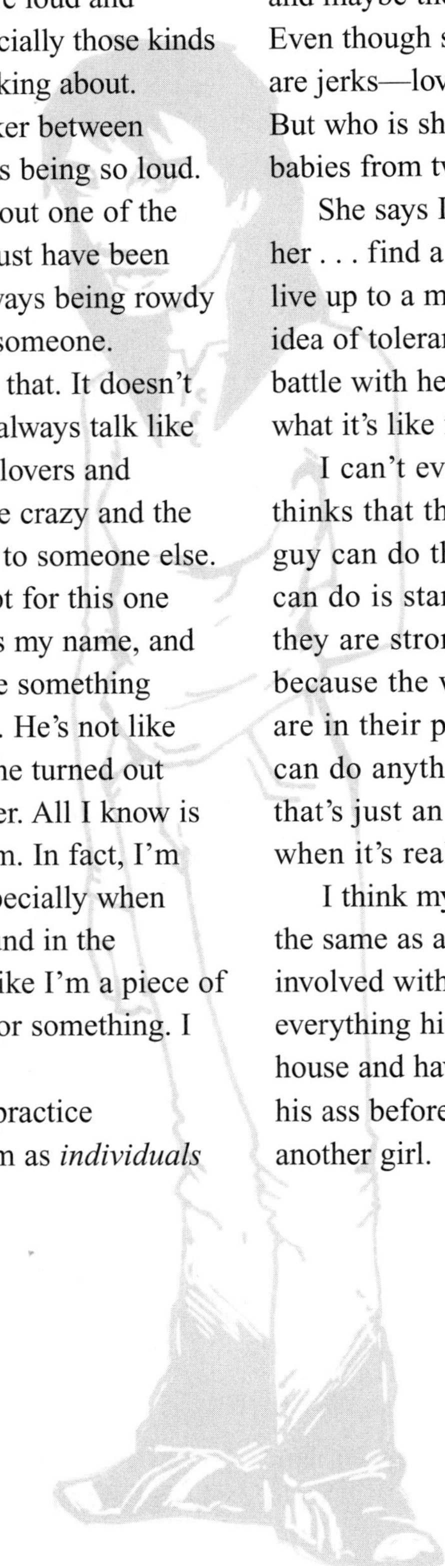

Chapter Twelve:
Building Healthy Self-Identity and Intimacy

GOALS OF THIS CHAPTER

- Discuss and understand individuality and personal identity and who you are.
- Understand the need to separate unique and different and your need to be close and part of others and having a balance between these two needs.
- Understand and apply to your life the four types of intimacy.
- Learn the risks and benefits of intimacy.
- Understand sexual intimacy and its risks.
- Make clear that a healthy self-identity and healthy intimacy are ways to prevent relapse and recidivism (RR) and live a meaningful and responsible life.

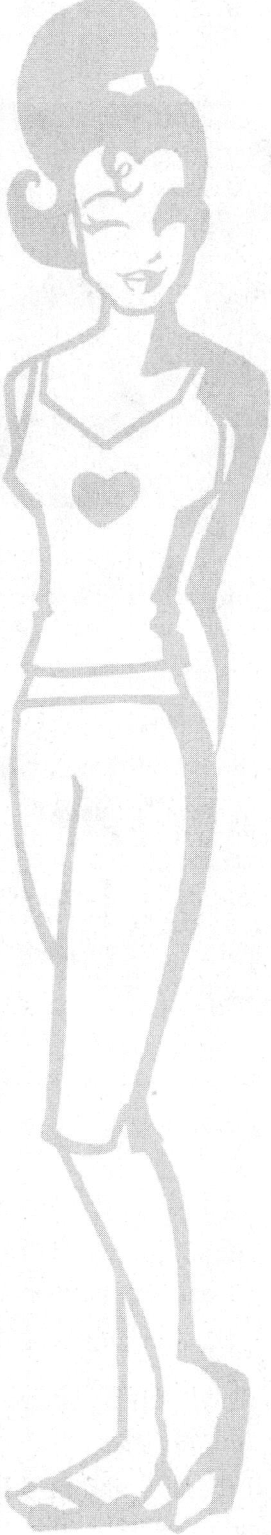

Alyssa's & Todd's Story

Todd: Alyssa and I went to a party the other night. We don't drink or use drugs. Maybe that's because I got busted at party a couple of years ago and was put into a MIP program and on probation for six months and had to attend classes. But I've got my head in the right direction now. There were other kids at the party that didn't drink and don't use drugs. Not all kids do this - most don't. But some did and were getting high on something else. Some were pretty messed up. I talked with a guy who owns his own auto repair shop. He was one who seemed to have it together.

Alyssa: I have a part-time job working in a nursery and like working with plants and flowers. It relaxes me. I haven't been the best student, but this year I'm really getting into it. I'm going to get my degree in biology and teaching.

Todd: I was going to drop out of high school two years ago but decided to finish. Want to go to Metro Automotive and Diesel School, at least for now. I love working on cars.

Alyssa: Todd and I are physically close. I think he loves me. We hug and kiss and make out. But we set the limits. We know when to stop. We decided to wait until we get married. And we don't know if we will get married. So much to do before getting to that. I feel safe with him. He would never ask me to do anything I didn't want to do.

Todd: Alyssa and I are close and our thinking is together. We want to completely trust one another and be committed before being fully intimate. We want to wait until we get married. But we're too young to get that serious. And I trust her. She would never ask me to take risks. She understands clearly what is safe and healthy. I think we have a pretty good idea of who we are, but that keeps changing. The other night when we left the party, Alyssa said, "You know, we're growing up."

SESSION 23: FORMING YOUR IDENTITY: WHO YOU ARE

Objectives

- Review Chapter 11: Overcoming Prejudice.
- Discuss identity development.
- Look at the balance between being apart and being together in a close relationship.

Alyssa's and Todd's Stories

Alyssa: *I have a part-time job working in a nursery and like working with plants and flowers. It relaxes me. I haven't been the best student, but this year I'm really getting into it. I'm going to get my degree in biology and teaching.*

Todd: *I was going to drop out of high school 2 years ago but decided to finish. I want to go to Metro Automotive and Diesel School, at least for now. I will do some of that in my senior year. I love working on cars.*

A Review of Stereotypes and Gender Roles

In the last chapter, we began discussing generalizations, stereotypes, prejudices, and gender roles. Generalizations help us understand our world, and stereotypes lead us to have closed minds about people we see as different from us. Similar to our values and morals, stereotypes are usually so ingrained in us that we are not aware of them unless they are pointed out. We discussed three reasons for developing stereotypes.

- The need for superiority
- Lack of information
- Failure to see differences

Activity: How Do We Think and Feel About Prejudice?

Think about a feature of people that you can stereotype or show prejudice around, such as brown eyes or blue jeans. Then walk around the room as a group. Show nonverbal signs of discomfort and rejection for those people who possess the feature that you decided upon. Everyone will have a different feature, but look for who is avoiding whom and what possible feature the people who were avoided have in common. Those we stereotype or who we show prejudice toward aren't aware of what we are thinking or feeling about them. What did you think and feel when certain people of the group avoided you? Did you wonder why they were being cold and rejecting? What were you thinking as you tried to avoid certain people? Was it easy avoiding all the people with the feature you wanted to avoid, or did you start wanting to make exceptions? Explain your answer.

SESSION 23: FORMING YOUR IDENTITY: WHO YOU ARE

Session 22: Gender Issues looks at the roles that males and females are expected to play in society. Look at Worksheet 26: My Diversity Profile and the activity in that session on Our Gender Stereotypes (you may not have had that session, but still look at that worksheet). Discuss whether you agree or disagree with the gender roles that are defined for your sex.

An important part of forming stereotypes—as well as how our prejudices get formed—is our values and morals. Chapter 8: Responsibility to Others and the Community covers how values and morals develop to give us a specific point of view. Although values and morals are something we pick up from our family and the world we live in, they become a major part of how we see ourselves—in other words our identity.

Values and Identity Development

As young people, we change groups and friends in a search of who we are and what we can relate to. A group may not hold the same values we do, or may go against our morals, and so we move to another group trying to fit in. "Clique bouncing" is common when we are young, as we are trying to search out our boundaries and are looking for people like us. We search for who we are by comparing ourselves with others. We try out different ways to show our self and appearances to our friends and different ways to react to others. In psychology, we call this "finding our identity."

Activity: Look at Alyssa and Todd—Who They Are

As a group, look at Alyssa's and Todd's stories. How would you describe their individual identity? Who in their life helped them to form their sense of self and identity? At this point in their lives, are they satisfied with who they are?

Separateness or Our Individuality and Closeness or Intimacy

Finding a positive identity takes place in two ways: (1) by defining who we are and what we think are positive features about ourselves and (2) by developing prosocial relationships with others and your community, which includes healthy closeness and intimacy. Abraham Maslow, a famous psychologist, pointed out two very important needs: (1) the need for separateness and to keep our own sense of self and uniqueness and (2) the need for closeness and relationship. He said that unless we have a positive sense of our own uniqueness and fulfillment, which he sees as the highest need, we will have a hard time having healthy closeness and intimacy. In the next session, we look more at closeness and intimacy. But let's look deeper into separateness and individuality and how they go along with our needs for closeness.

Individuality

One of the most important parts of our identity is our need to be separate and to fulfill our talents and our hopes and our dreams and to feel important (have self-esteem). Also, our values and beliefs tend to make up a large part of our identity along with our experiences and interests. Since no one can experience the same things in the same manner, we are all different individuals with different talents and self-needs that help shape our sense of who we are—our personal identity. Although we may belong to a certain culture or we may even hang out with a close group of friends, we are as different from other people as they are from us. In searching for an identity, most of us pick and choose from our experiences and surroundings to decide what is right for us, allowing for a unique and individual personality. We also look at both our friends and peers and at grown-ups and adults to help form who we are (our identity).

Activity: My Individual Identity

Now take a few minutes and put in the following table what you think makes up your identity. These are the ways that you carve out a role for yourself in society—for example, you see yourself as a good athlete, you work hard at your job, you have friends who break the law, you buy beer for your friends, you help your parents around the house. Remember that finding your identity has to do with fulfilling your talents. We call that self-actualization. Are their parts of your identity that go against fulfilling your talents and giving you a sense of being important? Does involvement in drugs and crime help you fulfill your talents or give you healthy self-importance?

What Makes Up Your Identity or Who You Are?

1.
2.
3.
4.
5.
6.
7.

In the group, share what you wrote in the space that makes up who you are. Did you include your talents and your thoughts about your sense of importance? Then allow the other group members to say if they think there is something they see as part of your identity that you did not list. How does your identity form your role in society? Does the role you assume help define your identity, or is your identity separate? What aspects did you have in common with another person that you may think has a completely different identity?

Activity: Look at Alyssa and Todd

Do they have their separateness and uniqueness and work at fulfilling their own talents? Does their closeness support or go against their need for separateness?

SESSION 23: FORMING YOUR IDENTITY: WHO YOU ARE

Rejecting Negativity

Many people experience confusion when they try to discover their individuality and form a unique identity. We don't wake up one morning and decide who we are going to be. This takes place slowly over a long time—testing out your thoughts, feelings, and actions and looking at the thoughts and reactions of others about you. In this journey, we often push away people who are close or who care about us. Rejection of our parents' ideals and values is sometimes an important part of defining our sense of separateness and uniqueness and our independence. Yet, this can cause a lot of problems with our family, people close to us, and the community in which we live.

Involvement in drugs and crime, which we call antisocial conduct, or going against society, may bring us feelings of closeness to the ones we are doing it with, yet it separates us and causes a lot of problems with our family, the positive people who are close to us, and our community. As we journey down the path to self-discovery and change, one of our goals will be to repair those relationships and have a positive relationship with those close to us.

In our negative and destructive path into drugs and crime, we rejected the laws of society and rules of healthy living. Rather than a prosocial role, we took an antisocial (against society) stance or role. It is okay if we choose not to take on some of the roles that society seems to say we should such as being an A student, getting a high-paying job, having a family, and owning a two-car garage. This is okay as long as your deciding not to take on these expected roles does not cause harm or danger to your mental or physical well-being or cause harm or danger to others and your community. Doing that is what we call negative identity. When we over and over short-change good and healthy chances in life for our self and others and take away our freedom and that of others, we are controlled by a failure identity.

But here is the problem: Some people like what a negative or failure identity can give them (e.g., power, drugs, making others afraid). Ask yourself, "Do I like and want that?" Crime, negative gang involvement, and substance abuse can become a part of one's identity and keep you from having closeness with healthy people who can support you and give you emotional comfort.

Many youth do not go down the path of "negative or failure identity." They take other paths that take them mostly on a positive journey. But you are in this program because you did take the "negative" path that led to a bad outcome. But now you have a choice to enter a pathway of your search for who you are, to change and discover the great and good things about yourself. Doing this will put you on the pathway that brings you good outcomes.

Activity: Another Look at Alyssa and Todd

It looks like Alyssa stayed pretty steady on the pathway to positive identify. What about Todd? Did he get off track? Now look again at the positive grown-up role models in Alyssa's and Todd's lives. Who are they?

SESSION 23: FORMING YOUR IDENTITY: WHO YOU ARE

Our Role Models

An important part of shaping who we are has to do with some of the grown-ups around us. Just as with our friends and peers, some adults are *negative* role models. They show us how to use drugs and show us antisocial and harmful ways to behave. But no matter how many negative adult role models we see, there are always some positive ones. Most people our age or grown-ups are good and prosocial.

Activity: Positive Role Models

In the following table, write down as many positive adult role models in your life. Then share one of those with the group and why you see that person as a positive role model.

List Some of the Grown-Ups in Your Life Who Were or Are Positive Role Models

1.
2.
3.
4.
5.

The Balance Between Separateness and Closeness

As we have said, two of the most important parts of our identity are being separate or apart and being close and relating to others. A healthy sense of self will be based on a balance between these two parts of our identity. When being around another person begins to interfere with activities that we may enjoy by ourselves, the relationship becomes unhealthy. Fulfilling our own talents and having time to ourselves is just as important as being close to someone and part of that person's life.

Activity: Look at Alyssa and Todd

Do they have a balance between being separate and being together? How does the separateness or being apart happen in their lives? How does the being together happen?

Activity: Looking at the Balance in Your Life

Fill out Worksheet 27: Being Close and Apart. Answer the questions about how you feel about a person close to you. Make sure you are honest about how you think and feel and how you might be able to resolve any negative things about the relationship.

SESSION 23: FORMING YOUR IDENTITY: WHO YOU ARE

In the first box in Worksheet 27, Being Close and Apart, the overlapping circles at the bottom of the page show good balance between separateness and closeness. In the next box, which indicates *you and a significant other,* draw how you see your relationship with a person. It can be someone you are in a relationship with or someone you are very close with. Put the circles far apart if you are too distant or very overlapping if you are too close or into each other's private space. How can your relationship become more balanced?

Putting It Together

- How do Alyssa and Todd keep the balance in their relationship? How does Alyssa keep her separate identity? How does Todd keep his?
- List three of the most important parts of your identity. Are they healthy? Are they prosocial, or do they go against society? Do they give you a healthy sense of self?
- Do your friends cause you to give up some of your identity and your separateness and your uniqueness?

Using the Program Guides and Tools for Change

Rate your ability to describe the things about yourself that make up your own personal identity.

0	1	2	3	4	5	6	7	8	9	10
Low					Medium					High

Indicate your ability to achieve balanced personal relationships by practicing the communication skills that you worked on throughout this program.

0	1	2	3	4	5	6	7	8	9	10
Low					Medium					High

- Review your Strengths and Resiliency scale on your Self-Portrait (SP). How important are these strengths in keeping close and intimate friends?
- Re-rate yourself. Have your strengths increased?
- Update your Plan for Change (PFC).

Worksheet 27

BEING CLOSE AND APART

QUESTION 1:
Who do you think is the person closest to you, and why do you think they are the person you feel the most for?

QUESTION 2:
What are some of the things that bother you about that person? What are the things you become angry or annoyed with about that person?

QUESTION 3:
What are some of the positive things about that person? What do you like about that person, and why do you trust them the most of all the people you know?

QUESTION 4:
What are some of the compliments you could give that person the next time you see them? How do you think they will react when you give them the compliments? Can you sincerely give them compliments?

Example of Balanced Relationship

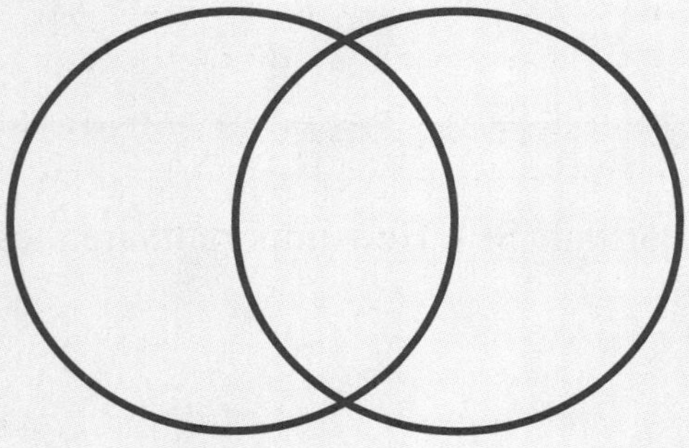

You and Your Significant Other

SESSION 24: BUILDING HEALTHY INTIMACY AND CLOSENESS

Objectives

- Review Session 23: Forming Your Identity: Who You Are.
- Learn what helps to build healthy closeness and intimacy.

Alyssa's and Todd's Stories

Alyssa: *Todd and I have been friends since we were in fifth grade. It was only in the past year that we have been going together. We will be seniors this fall. We spend a lot of time together. We go for walks, go to dances, and take the bus downtown to the art museum. We hang out with our friends together. We hug and kiss and make out. But one thing for sure, we have decided to keep our closeness and intimacy at a social and emotional level and to set clear limits as to how physically intimate we get.*

Todd: *Alyssa and I are close. But our thinking is together. We want the social and emotional intimacy to be solid before being fully intimate. Right now, we want to wait until we get married. But we're too young to get that serious.*

What is Intimacy?
Where do we learn it from?

Emotions and Intimacy

Who we are allows us to be attracted to and close with certain people who share our values, beliefs, and sense of the world. All of us have friends, family, and people who we care about. These relationships form a large part of our lives and affect everything we think and feel about certain situations and life experiences. In order to be genuinely close to another person, we need to know who we are and what we expect from the world. Emotional intimacy, or closeness, doesn't always have to be with a boyfriend or girlfriend or even our parents and family. Often we develop emotional intimacy with our friends who we are around and with whom we share the most personal parts of our lives.

What is important in developing emotional closeness is trust. This occurs on many levels and is not the same for everyone. We trust those we love and those who care about us. We trust those who would not harm or hurt us. And we trust that we can go to those persons when we are having difficulties or just need to talk. That is not to say we trust everyone we are close to in the same way or even to the same degree. Just because we do not necessarily trust a person with some of our most private thoughts does not mean that we think they will try to hurt us or that we don't want to get to know them better.

Activity: An Intimate Friend

Break into small groups, and take a look at Alyssa's story. Who do you think Alyssa and Todd are socially and emotionally close or intimate with? Why do you think that?

Are Alyssa and Todd closer and more intimate with some in their lives than others? Is Todd close to Mr. Brown? Is Alyssa close to Ms. Baker? Do we care for some people more than others?

SESSION 24: BUILDING HEALTHY INTIMACY AND CLOSENESS

What Is Intimacy?

Intimacy refers to the thoughts and feelings of knowing and being close to someone, of being part of one another, or belonging together. Healthy (sometimes called genuine) intimacy is as follows:

- Having thoughts and feelings of trust, caring, and closeness for another person or persons.
- Knowing, understanding, and respecting the strengths and weaknesses of another person or persons.
- Knowing and respecting the mental, emotional, social, and physical world of each other.

Intimacy starts with building trust, caring, and closeness. In this program, we have tried to develop a sense of trust among the group members and the program staff. Although we may get along with some members better than others, there is a level of closeness among the group. For some, the group has become like family. For others, the group has become acquaintances with whom we can share thoughts and feelings with. But the closeness we can share in this group provides a way of learning closeness and intimacy.

There are four types of intimacy that we look at in this session and the next session:

- Mental
- Emotional
- Social
- Physical

Activity: Where Do We Stand?

Break into pairs for this activity, but don't choose someone you may be close to. As a pair, find a place slightly separated from the rest of the pairs. Now begin talking to each other about how you think and feel about the person you are sitting with. Be honest with each other. If you think you don't really know the other person and can't really trust them, say so. If you think you can trust the other person, tell the person that. Then discuss how you think the two of you could increase trust in each other or be closer. If that is not possible, discuss why you think you wouldn't be able to become closer.

Where to Start?

We know that there are people in our lives who we care about and who care about us. The question really is how we can keep those close intimate friends and family. There are times when we fight with the people we care about, and disagreeing with other people is a fact of life. But there are thoughts and actions that help foster and take care of the emotional ties we develop with other people.

SESSION 24: BUILDING HEALTHY INTIMACY AND CLOSENESS

Communication

We have discussed the importance of communication several times throughout the program. The reason we keep coming back to this is because by having good verbal (talking) and nonverbal (body language) active sharing and active listening communication skills, we can support others and also get our own needs met. Imagine trying to share and become friends with a person who you couldn't talk to or communicate with. You would never know what they were thinking or feeling. Good communication will help you in several important ways:

- Feel closer to another person.
- Understand each other better and get to know each other's point of view.
- Solve problems and arguments with each other.
- Have more positive feelings and less bad feelings toward each other.
- Have a network of people who will look out for your well-being and best interests.
- Be less likely to use substances or get involved in criminal acts again.

Activity: Talking With A Friend

Looking at Alyssa's and Todd's stories, what do you think is a good example of the communication between them? What problems are they able to solve together? How do you see yourself as being able to develop the kind of closeness that they have? What problems do you think they have or will have?

To remember how to communicate well, look at Chapter 3: Talking About Yourself and Listening to What Others Say and Chapter 6: Basic Communication Skills. The key ideas are active listening and active sharing. If you can develop and maintain these two skills, then communication will become easier.

Activity: Practicing the Skill of Having Others Know That You Hear Them

Your counselor will begin with something that happened to him or her in the past week (active sharing). It can be something positive, something confusing, or something negative that your counselor had thoughts and feelings about. The person to the left of the counselor will then use the feedback skill of active listening and tell the counselor what they heard. Just do the feedback. Don't give advice or tell the counselor what to do. Just make sure the counselor knows that you heard what he or she said. After giving the counselor feedback, that person will then share something that happened to him or her and the person on the left will practice the same active listening skills. Go around the circle until everyone has shared at least one thing and given feedback.

SESSION 24: BUILDING HEALTHY INTIMACY AND CLOSENESS

The Skills of Getting Close and Building Intimacy

Good communication skills help us to remain close with the people we care about. But how do we build and keep closeness to people who we may like or would like to be more involved with or are involved with? Here are some skills and ways that we can become closer to people in our lives:

- **Don't think people can read your mind.** The only way they can know what you are thinking and feeling is if you *tell them.* It is not fair to other people to expect them to automatically know what it is you want, feel, or think.
- **Don't let things build up.** It is easy to ignore or avoid issues that may cause conflict or bad moments. If you ignore them, they get stronger—just like we talked about how anger, depression, and guilt get stronger the longer we ignore them (Chapter 10: Handling Anger, Guilt, and Depression). The same can happen between people when something bothers one or the other person. Use good communication skills to let the other person know what is bothering you.
- **Know the other person's sensitivities and what threatens them.** Good communication is knowing when it is right to share thoughts or feelings that may be difficult for the other person to hear. Everyone has their areas of threat. When you know those areas, then you are intimate with them—you know them intimately.
- **Show positive thoughts and feelings.** It is important in any relationship or friendship to express and let the other person know the good things you like about them. The positive must always outweigh the negative. Remember the skills for giving compliments from Chapter 6: Basic Communication Skills. Those help keep positive feelings between people.
- **Always work toward a win-win outcome.** When working on differences or resolving conflicts, be sure that each of you is better off. But this does not mean that you always win. Win-win means that each most likely has to give up some things.

Healthy Physical Intimacy

Something is healthy when it keeps the positive mental, emotional, social, and physical well-being of the person and results in positive outcomes. Healthy physical intimacy is more than physical contact and so much more than having sexual involvement. It respects the physical being of the other person. Each person is the caretaker of their own physical being and owns that being. That physical space goes out at least 2 to 3 feet from one's physical body. That space is sacred. Anyone entering that space must have permission. Most often that permission is not verbal. It may involve reaching out for the other person's hand, making a gesture of wanting to hug. Doing something physical together such as hiking or mountain climbing is physical closeness and physical intimacy. This is sharing a physical activity that allows one another to know the physical being of each other.

Sexual Intimacy

Sexual intimacy is only a part of physical intimacy. Meaningful sexual intimacy can only happen when healthy mental, emotional, social, and physical intimacy has been built between two people. Sexual contact by itself is not sexual or physical intimacy. The problem is that many get involved in sexual activity before they have healthy mental, social, emotional, and physical intimacy. And an even greater problem is they take part in sexual activities before a person knows who they are (identity) and what they want from life (goals).

Activity: Discuss How Alyssa and Todd Are Intimate

Take each part of intimacy. How are they mentally, emotionally, socially, and physically intimate? In what ways are they sexually intimate? In what ways are they not sexually intimate?

Activity: My Closeness and Apart Needs

First, think about your morals and values. Then, using what you have learned in the last session and this session, do Worksheet 28: My Closeness and Apart Needs. Then take a moment to think about whether these needs fit into your moral and personal values.

Remember: We Are Working on Changing Our Thinking and Our Values

This program is about change. You have taken part in actions and behaviors in the past that now you don't feel good about, such as your using drugs, having committed crimes, or having been involved in physical intimacy with someone that didn't seem right to you. But remember that this program is about change and being committed to change. With the tools and ideas of this program—and your new set of values—you have a chance to move beyond those actions. You can choose not to repeat these actions and live up to your new set of values and morals.

Healthy Closeness Takes Trust

Healthy intimacy takes trust. But how does this trust get started and continue? Here are some ways:

- Always have each other's consent and verbal permission for whatever you do together.
- Be honest with each other, and talk about what you like and don't like.
- Listen to what each other has to say.
- Treat each other as equals.
- Be attentive to each other's needs.
- Protect each other against physical and emotional harm.
- Respect each other's limits.
- Always accept responsibility for your actions.
- Decide to make sure that mental and emotional intimacy is there before taking part in any physical closeness or intimacy.

Worksheet 28

MY CLOSENESS AND APART NEEDS

In Column 1, write down some of your closeness needs, or needs you have when relating to another person or persons (e.g., going to the movies together). Then, in Column 2, write down your separateness needs—those things that you like doing separate or alone (e.g., doing computer games).

Make a List of Your Most Important Closeness Needs.	Make a List of Your Most Important Separateness Needs.

SESSION 24: BUILDING HEALTHY INTIMACY AND CLOSENESS

It Is Your Right . . . It Is Your Choice

Again, we stress that no one has the right to enter emotional and mental space without you saying it is okay. When someone does this without your permission, it is abuse. When someone takes physical actions toward you against your will, it is physical abuse. Not only do you have the right to say no but you must say no. Such actions are against the law. If you are in a relationship where you feel pressure to do things you don't want to do, say right away, "Stop, that is not going to happen." If it is upsetting, talk to your counselor, your parents, or another adult. If you feel unsafe and think you are in danger and have been threatened, call the police. A healthy relationship is a safe relationship.

What Is a Healthy Physical Closeness, and How Does It Take Place?

- It takes place after two people have developed a healthy mental, emotional, social, and spiritual closeness and intimacy.
- It takes place after there is commitment to the relationship.
- It always has the consent and permission of both persons.
- It is based on both persons being morally responsible.
- It is based on respect and trust and treating each other as equals.
- It is emotionally, mentally, and physically safe; it never involves harm.
- It always sets limits and respects each other's limits.
- Intimacy that takes place under the influence of drugs is not healthy and not true intimacy.
- It is healthy when it is part of the long-term goals of both persons and the relationship.

Activity: Healthy Intimacy

Discuss Alyssa and Todd's intimacy and closeness. Do they have healthy intimacy and closeness? Discuss how the previously given parts of healthy closeness fit their relationship.

Putting It Together

- What are your values about the four types of closeness and intimacy: (1) mental, (2) emotional, (3) social, and (4) physical?
- What are your personal goals around these four types of intimacy?

SESSION 24: BUILDING HEALTHY INTIMACY AND CLOSENESS

Using the Program Guides and Tools for Change

Rate your ability to have healthy mental and emotional intimacy with others.

0	1	2	3	4	5	6	7	8	9	10
Low					Medium					High

Rate your understanding of what is healthy physical intimacy.

0	1	2	3	4	5	6	7	8	9	10
Low					Medium					High

- Update Program Guide 1: Telling My Story (TMS) in the My Strengths and Strong Points section.
- Update your SP in the section of strengths and resilience.
- Update your PFC.

SESSION 25: THE RISKS AND BENEFITS OF CLOSENESS AND INTIMACY

Objectives

- Review Session 23: Forming Your Identity: Who You Are and Session 24: Building Healthy Intimacy and Closeness.
- Discuss and talk about the risks and benefit (value) of closeness and intimacy.

Alyssa's and Todd's Stories

Alyssa: *What I love about Todd is that he listens and lets me finish what I have to say before he talks. He respects me. I feel safe with him. He would never ask me to do anything I didn't want to do.*

Todd: *It's a give and take, and I trust her. She would never ask me to take risks. She understands clearly what is safe and healthy. She really knows what is safe. but our thinking is together.*

Review of Healthy Intimacy and Closeness

In the last session, we talked about the four kinds of intimacy: (1) mental, (2) emotional, (3) social, and (4) physical. We said intimacy involves having thoughts and feelings of trust, caring, and closeness for another person or persons. It is knowing and understanding the strengths and weaknesses of another person or persons. Between two people, it is knowing the mental, emotional, social, and physical world of each other. Healthy intimacy starts with and builds on trust, caring, and closeness. We also looked at our thoughts and actions that can build and keep healthy intimacy going, which include the following:

- Using the skills of active listening and active sharing.
- Not letting things build up.
- Knowing the other person's sensitivities and what threatens them.
- Showing positive thoughts and feelings.
- Always working toward a win-win outcome.
- Always having each other's consent and verbal permission for whatever you do together.
- Being honest with each other and talking about what you like and don't like.
- Treating each other as equals.
- Being attentive to each other's needs.
- Protecting each other against social, emotional, and physical harm.
- Respecting each other's limits.
- Always accepting responsibility for your actions.
- Deciding to make sure that mental and emotional intimacy is there before taking part in any physical closeness or intimacy.

SESSION 25: THE RISKS AND BENEFITS OF CLOSENESS AND INTIMACY

Last session we also said that sexual intimacy is only a part of physical intimacy. Healthy physical and sexual intimacy, in whatever way that it takes place, can only happen when two people have built healthy mental, emotional, social, and physical intimacy. Healthy physical closeness must do the following:

- Have the consent and permission of both persons.
- Be based on both persons being morally responsible.
- Be based on respect and trust and treating each other as equals.
- Be emotionally, mentally, and physically safe—it never involves harm.
- Set limits and respect each other's limits.
- Take place when it is part of the long-term goals of both persons and the relationship.

Activity: Look at Alyssa's and Todd's Stories

As a group, identify and discuss how they show the four types of intimacy: (1) mental, (2) social, (3) emotional, and (4) physical.

The Risks and Benefit of Being Intimate

In Session 23, we worked on identifying who you are and building who you want to be. Being intimate means that you show other people, or the other person you are close to, who you really are. You show your real self, your real identity. It's like you let people see you when you are in your old clothes, or with messed up hair, no makeup on; you open up with your thoughts. Just as there are possible risks, there are possible benefits or good that can come from being intimate: You are understood. You feel better. You learn how to dance.

Activity: Different Types of Intimacy

Use Worksheet 29: Pros and Cons of Different Types of Intimacy. In the second column, write down a couple of examples of being intimate for each of the four types of intimacy. Then write down the possible risks or what might make you vulnerable (you feel weak, hurt, exposed) that can come from the example of being intimate. Then write down the good or benefit than can come from the example. With the help of the group, your counselor will give examples on the flipchart. Here are examples:

- Mental: You tell your close friend that you don't like the way he treats girls. Risk: He gets mad and is hurt. Good: He understands my thoughts and feelings.

- Emotional: You tell your girlfriend that you get jealous when she looks at other guys. Risk: She gets mad and calls you crazy. Good: She thinks, "He wants me to be his girlfriend."
- Social: You take a risk and ask a girl to dance and she says no. Risk: You shy away from dancing parties. Good: at least you took the courage to ask.
- Physical: You go to a dance with your new girlfriend, who is a great dancer, and you don't know how to dance. Risk: You look awkward and silly and feel embarrassed. Good: She teaches you how to dance.

Activity: Sharing Thoughts About Intimacy

The group will take time to share what members wrote down in Worksheet 29. Only share what you feel comfortable sharing and at your own comfort level.

Sexual Intimacy and Personal Responsibility

The purpose of this part of Session 25 is not to give you a course in sex education or to discuss the many ways that sexual intimacy is shown or expressed. Many of you have had or most likely will have classes in this area, and most if not all of you know a lot about what is taught in a sex education class. The purpose of this part of the session is to stress that sexual intimacy is healthy only when it is built on healthy mental, social, and emotional intimacy and to stress that the many ways of being sexually intimate have their proper place in the course of life. Only you will decide on this for yourself. We want to give you some directions around this. We also want to summarize the risks that come with sexual intimacy.

Personal Responsibility—Healthy Pathways for Sexual Intimacy

Adolescence is a time when our bodies become different and our emotions are often up and down. Sexual intimacy and sexual intercourse, specifically, is a huge decision when so many other things are up in the air. So here are the positions that *Pathways to Self-Discovery and Change (PSDC)* and most responsible adults hold:

- Sexual intimacy is part of the large picture of physical intimacy. We do not consider sex just by itself as being healthy physical intimacy.
- Full sexual intimacy or intercourse should take place when one has committed to a relationship and when the person has developed healthy and mature mental, emotional, and social intimacy.
- Young people wait until they are older and fully understand the risks and outcomes of becoming sexually active. The final decision is always made by you. Just as we have freedom over our thoughts and actions, we must take personal responsibility to decide whether sex is right for us or not. But

Worksheet 29

PROS AND CONS OF DIFFERENT TYPES OF INTIMACY

For each area of intimacy, write down ways that you are at risk or are vulnerable when you take part in the four types of intimacy. Then write down the benefits or good of taking part in these four areas of intimacy

TYPES OF INTIMACY AND EXAMPLES	RISK OR BEING VULNERABLE	BENEFITS OR GOOD
MENTAL		
EMOTIONAL		
SOCIAL		
PHYSICAL		

before making any of these kind of decisions, remember to THINK. Consider the benefits and risks of any type of sexual activity.

- The biological reason for sex is for reproductive purposes. Being a teenager and a parent is not a good mix—not at all. Talk to any teenage parent, and they will tell you this.
- PSDC holds that abstinence, or not taking part in sexual intercourse, is the best and only method to be 100% sure of being safe and to prevent unwanted outcomes and 100% sure that when you make the decision to become sexually active you will have the maturity to handle the outcomes.

Alyssa's and Todd's Stories

Alyssa: *I feel safe with him. He would never ask me to do anything I didn't want to do. He really is a great guy. Oh! We are physically close, but we set the limits. We know when to stop. We've decided to wait until marriage for that.*

Todd: *Alyssa and I are close. I love kicking the soccer ball around with her. It's a give and take, like our relationship. and I trust her. She would never ask me to take risks. She understands clearly what is safe and healthy. Our thinking is together. We want the social and emotional intimacy to be solid before being fully intimate. Sometimes that's difficult when we are alone and close. but, right now, we want to wait until we get married.*

Activity: Alyssa and Todd's Level of Intimacy

Discuss Alyssa's and Todd's decisions around being sexually active. Do you agree with their decision?

What Is Sexual Intimacy?

Sexual intimacy is a part of physical intimacy. It is having mutual contact with parts of our body that brings physical and emotional pleasure. There are many different ways to express sexual intimacy, and these are seen as having different levels of physical closeness—from kissing to intercourse. However, there are many different types of physical contact between people that are not seen as sexual intimacy but are seen as being physically intimate. These include social hugging, hugging the person close to you, holding hands, putting your arms around someone to give them support, reaching out and holding a person's hands to show affection, and caring and showing that you understand.

Activity: Types of Physical Intimacy

Go around the group and have each person share an example of physical intimacy that is not considered to be sexual intimacy.

SESSION 25: THE RISKS AND BENEFITS OF CLOSENESS AND INTIMACY

Alcohol and Other Drugs and Sexual Intimacy

Alcohol or other drugs will prevent a person from making healthy and good decisions about taking part in sexual intimacy. Here is what alcohol and other drugs can do:

- Lower your ability to make good judgments about sexual intimacy.
- Prevent you from seeing the consequences or outcomes of taking part in sexual intimacy.
- Put you at high risk (HR) for having unwanted and bad outcomes.
- Prevent you from seeing how sexual intimacy fits in with the big picture of relationship intimacy.

The Dangers, Risks, and Unwanted Outcomes of Sexual Intimacy

Sexual intimacy is a part of life, but it is only healthy when it takes place within the total picture of healthy intimacy. Many young people decide to wait until they are older—when they are truly ready to accept the commitment, responsibility, and consequences of being intimate with another person—before engaging in any form of intimate sexual contact, including intercourse. However, it is important that you clearly understand the unwanted outcomes of sexual intimacy, particularly at your stage of life. We only give you a short summary of these outcomes. Remember, these outcomes are major life-changing events.

Pregnancy

Some young people may think this is not an unwanted outcome, but think about this: Are you mature enough to be responsible for the life of a baby and child? Again, talk to any teenage parent, and they will most likely tell you no. Before you become sexually active, see your doctor. If you are sexually active, then talk with your doctor about this to give you the best possible medical advice and methods to prevent the dangers and risks. If you are a teenage parent, to make this a positive outcome for you, you will need all the help, advice, and support you can get from your parents, counselors, therapists, adult friends, and health care workers. Don't be afraid to reach out.

Sexually Transmitted Diseases

Any sexually transmitted disease (STD) is serious and can be life-threatening problem. About one in five people in the United States has an STD, and 25% of new cases are found in teenagers. STDs are easily spread through most kinds of sexual contact, not just intercourse. They can lead to serious long-term problems including the inability to have children, lasting sickness, lifetime disability, and death. Ask yourself, Do you want to take this risk? Do you want to have this problem the rest of your life? Before taking part in any form of intimate sexual contact, including intercourse, think about these risks. If you have been sexually active, you should see your health care provider to be sure if you are free from any STDs.

Look at it this way: When you have sex with someone, you are having sex with everyone that person has had sex with, and you are having sex with the persons who those people have had sex with and so on.

Therefore, you may be exposed to STDs that all of those persons have or may have had. So work out the math in this problem: You have sex with someone who has had sex two other people, and those two other people have had sex with two other people. How may persons have you been exposed to? Have your group figure this out.

For more details about each STD or if you may think you have an STD, talk with your counselor or doctor or call the National STD Hotline at 1-800-227-8922 or call the Centers for Disease Control and Prevention hotline at 1-800-232-4636 (CDC INFO), or go online to www.cdc.gov/std/healthcomm/fact_sheets.htm.

There are over 20 STDs floating around. We summarize only those that are more often found.

- Chlamydia (*kluh-mid-ee-uh*): One of the most common diseases, it is a bacteria that can be picked up not just in sexual contact but through eye contact, from a towel, doorknob, or toilet seat. It can be passed from mother to baby while the baby is being delivered. The problem is that you may not know you have it: You can have the bacteria and not the signs, and even without the signs, you can pass it on.
- Genital Herpes (*her-peez*): Caused by a virus with the most common type causing cold sores or fever blisters, it can be passed on by sharing eating utensils or towels and physical contact with the body part of another person who has the disease—including kissing. It does not live outside the body for very long, so you can't get it from a toilet seat, etc. The virus hides in the body and can be caught from someone who has it but does not have the open signs or sores.
- Genital Warts: Caused by a virus like the warts found on your hands and feet (those on your hands or feet cannot be sexually transmitted), it is passed from person to person during sexual contact but not caught from a towel, toilet seat, or doorknob. If not treated, they can grow bigger and lead to cervical cancer in females. They can be treated by a doctor.
- Gonorrhea (*gone-uh-ree-uh*): Caused by bacteria and passed through sexual activity, gonorrhea is not passed on through a towel, toilet seat, doorknob, or contact with outside objects. It can be passed on from a mother to a baby. It can be treated with antibiotics. If not treated, it can cause long-term serious illness and death in a baby if the mother has the disease.
- Hepatitis (*hep-uh-tie-tiss*): Hepatitis is a virus that causes a disease of the liver but can also be caused by excessive use of alcohol and other poisons. There are different kinds of the disease, but Hepatitis B and C can be passed on through blood and bodily fluids through sexual intercourse and needles shared by drug users. It can also be passed on from mother to her baby. Some can have it all their lives yet may not show signs until later. It can cause liver cancer. Immunization for Hepatitis B has become common.
- HIV and AIDS: A serious and deadly disease, it has spread fast since it was first found in people. It is caused by the human immunodeficiency virus (HIV), which destroys the cells in the body that fights infectious diseases. It is spread through blood and bodily fluids picked up during intercourse or oral sex. It is also passed through the mother's breast milk if she has HIV but not passed on through an outside object contact such as toilet seats. There is no cure for AIDS (acquired immune deficiency syndrome), which is the result of picking up the HIV virus. Finding it and treating it early is a must

to slow it down. As of yet, it cannot be cured. It is possible to have HIV a long time before showing signs of AIDS.

- Syphilis (*siff-ill-iss*): Syphilis is caused by a bacteria that can live any place in the body. It is passed on through sexual intercourse including oral sex and from mother to her baby during pregnancy and is not passed on through contact with outside objects such as a toilet seat. It has four stages and can be treated with antibiotics if treated in the earlier stages. It goes to sleep in the third stage but in the fourth stages causes serious medical problems and death. It can be detected in a blood test and treated.
- Trichomoniasis (*trick-oh-moh-nye-uh-sis*): Trichomoniasis is caused by a parasite passed on through sexual intercourse. Unlike many STD infections, it can live on a wet towel, washcloth, or bathing suit for a few hours. It is one of the most common STDs. It is not dangerous but uncomfortable. It will often go along with other STDs. Treatment involves antibiotics.

These are some of the common STDs, but there are more out there. Talk with your doctor or counselor on how to prevent STDs. As we have said, abstinence is the best way to prevent STDs. Regular checkups and tests from a doctor are very important if you decide to become sexually active. Remember, the only sure way to prevent STDs is abstinence. And when you are ready to take part in sexual intimacy then be sure of your partner. Is he or she free of an STD? Most people who get married will do this. Before you get into a committed relationship or get married, put this on your to-do list.

Activity: Reaching Out

Each person is given a 3x5 card, and the counselor will inform the group that if you have some concerns about any medical problem related to STDs you think you have at this time, just write down "I do" and put your first name on the card and give it to your counselor. the counselor will then get back to you.

The Benefits of Sexual Intimacy

We know the serious outcomes that can come with being sexually intimate, but sexual intimacy and closeness will have good outcomes and provide positive benefits in the lives of two people who are in a committed or marriage relationship and who have learned healthy mental, emotional, social, and physical intimacy. First, it is one of the threads in the fabric of the relationship of a couple that holds them together in both good and bad times. Second, not only is it part of love but it strengthens that love. Third, healthy sexual intimacy gives a couple in marriage or a committed relationship the power and control to plan and reach not only the goals of pleasure and supporting their love but to be in charge of the creation of family beyond their couple relationship. This is what we call relationship and family planning. Not only do you have the power to be in charge of your thinking, emotions, and actions but two people together have this power.

Putting It Together

- Are Alyssa and Todd sensitive to how they can be vulnerable in the different areas of intimacy? How do they show this?
- In many ways, your group has been close and intimate. So we are going to ask you to take a risk. We are asking each person to very briefly share one type of intimacy that they feel vulnerable in and one type of intimacy that for you at this time gives you positive outcomes. Share at your own comfortable level.

Using the Program Guides and Tools for Change

Rate yourself as to your strengths or ability of handling each of the four areas of intimacy to prevent being vulnerable.

Mental intimacy

0	1	2	3	4	5	6	7	8	9	10
Low					Medium					High

Emotional intimacy

0	1	2	3	4	5	6	7	8	9	10
Low					Medium					High

Social intimacy

0	1	2	3	4	5	6	7	8	9	10
Low					Medium					High

Physical intimacy

0	1	2	3	4	5	6	7	8	9	10
Low					Medium					High

Rate your understanding of the risks and dangers of being sexually intimate.

0	1	2	3	4	5	6	7	8	9	10
Low					Medium					High

SESSION 26: PUTTING IT TOGETHER: POSITIVE IDENTITY AND HEALTHY INTIMACY

Objectives

- Review the topics of Sessions 23 through 25.
- Summarize your identity or how you see yourself, how you keep a balance between apartness and closeness, and how you see your level of maturity around the four types of intimacy.

The Purpose of Chapter 12

Remember, healthy and prosocial thinking and behavior and positive relationships with others are ways to prevent RR and to live a meaningful and responsible life.

We know that bad relationships and negative thinking and emotions are a big part of getting involved in drug use and abuse and in criminal and antisocial conduct. To continue those ways of living will only lead you back to those destructive involvements. In this chapter, we worked on these important pathways to preventing RR, becoming drug-free and crime-free, and living a meaningful and responsible life:

- Have a positive sense of who you are and how you see yourself.
- Be positive and prosocial in your relationships.
- Be involved in healthy intimacy, which means being close to; knowing; caring about; and having respect for the mental, emotional, social, and physical world of the other person and each other.

If you have a good idea of your own identity and if you understand and have the skills to have a positive and prosocial involvement with others, you have a big chance to live free of drug and crime problems.

Activity: Discussion of Alyssa and Todd's Story

What do you think the chances are that Alyssa and Todd will get involved in the use and abuse of drugs? What do you think their chances are of getting involved in unlawful activities?

Looking at Then and Now: Your Identity and Your Relationships With Others

In Session 23, we had you look at who you are, your identity. Before you came to this program, much of your past identity involved alcohol and other drugs and criminal and antisocial conduct—behavior that went against society. One of the goals of this program is to help you change that to a drug-free and prosocial identity. We also looked at two basic needs we have:

- To be apart, separate, and have your own identity.
- To be close, intimate, and in a relationship with others.

SESSION 26: PUTTING IT TOGETHER: POSITIVE IDENTITY AND HEALTHY INTIMACY

Before coming to this program, you were often involved in negative relationships that involved drug use and criminal behavior. The goal of this program has been to help you learn the skills of having positive relationships and prosocial relationships and to learn how to be involved in healthy intimacy.

Activity: Changing My Identity

We want you to look at how you changed from your negative or your drug and antisocial identity to a positive and prosocial identity. We want you to also look at how you might have changed your negative and antisocial relationships to positive and prosocial ones, and your close relationships involving healthy intimacy. Use the following table to work on this. In the first box of the first row, put down how your specific thoughts and behaviors describe your drug use and antisocial identity before this program, and in the in the second box of the first row, put down specific thoughts and behaviors that describe how you see your drug-free and prosocial identity. In the first box of the bottom row, put down examples of your drug use and antisocial relationships, and in the second box, put down examples of the drug-free and prosocial relationships you now have. With the help of the group, your counselor will show you how to do this by putting an example on a flipchart.

Changing My Identity and My Relationship With Others

DRUG USE AND ANTISOCIAL IDENTITY	DRUG-FREE AND PROSOCIAL IDENTITY
DRUG USE AND ANTISOCIAL RELATIONSHIPS	DRUG-FREE AND PROSOCIAL RELATIONSHIPS

Activity: Group Sharing and Role Play

Each group member will be asked to share one point in each box. Then your counselor will ask one group member to role-play telling someone in that person's life how he or she has changed.

Looking at Your Healthy Intimacy and Closeness

In Session 24, we worked on understanding the four types of healthy closeness and intimacy: (1) mental, (2) emotional, (3) social, and (4) physical. We said healthy intimacy involves having deep thoughts and feelings of trust, caring, and closeness for other person or persons. It is knowing and respecting the strengths and weaknesses of another person or persons. Between two people, it is knowing, caring about, and respecting the mental, emotional, social, and physical world of each other. Healthy intimacy starts with and builds on trust, caring, and closeness. We also looked at our thoughts and actions that can build and keep healthy intimacy. We go back to Session 24 and look at these again. Now let's look at your thinking and actions in each of these areas of healthy intimacy that you have right now. In the following two tables, write down some thoughts and actions that show or express healthy intimacy in each of these four areas. With the help of the group, your counselor will put an example on the flipchart.

Examples of Thoughts and Actions That Show Healthy Mental and Emotional Intimacy

HEALTHY MENTAL INTIMACY	HEALTHY EMOTIONAL INTIMACY

Examples of Thoughts and Actions That Show Healthy Social and Physical Intimacy

HEALTHY SOCIAL INTIMACY	HEALTHY PHYSICAL INTIMACY

Activity: Group Sharing and Role Play

Each group member will be asked to share one point in each box. Then your counselor will ask one group member to role-play telling someone in that person's life how he or she has been involved in one area of healthy intimacy.

Looking at the Risks of Being Intimate

In Session 25, we worked on understanding the risks of mental, emotional, social, and physical intimacy. We saw that when we are open with our thoughts and our emotions and when we show people physical actions—particularly someone with whom we have a close relationship—we become vulnerable and at risk in several ways. We may be criticized or even rejected for making a clear picture of ourselves. We also saw that when we take part in sexual intimacy, which is a part of physical intimacy, we put ourselves at risk—even dangerous and serious medical risks. We did a worksheet that had each person list the ways that they were vulnerable or at risk and the benefits of each of the four areas of intimacy.

When we involve ourselves in healthy intimacy, we make that risk less or even disappear. In the following table, for each type of intimacy, give one thought or behavior that you would see as being **healthy intimacy**. With the help of the group, your counselor will give an example on the flipchart.

SESSION 26: PUTTING IT TOGETHER: POSITIVE IDENTITY AND HEALTHY INTIMACY

One Thought or Behavior That You See as Being Healthy Intimacy in Each of the Four Areas of Intimacy

MENTAL	EMOTIONAL	SOCIAL	PHYSICAL

Activity: Group Sharing

Share with the group the one thought or behavior that you see as being healthy intimacy.

Again, We Want to Be Sure You Have a Clear Understanding of Your Rights and Safety

In Session 24, we said that you must protect your rights and protect yourself from emotional and physical harm. No one has the right to enter your emotional, mental, and physical space without you giving permission—saying it is okay. When someone does this and takes physical actions toward you against your will, it is physical abuse. Not only do you have the right to say no but you must say no. Such actions are against the law. If you are in a relationship where you feel pressure to do things you don't want to do, right away say, "Stop! That is not going to happen." If it is upsetting, talk to your counselor, your parents, or another adult. If you feel unsafe and think you are in danger, call the police. A healthy relationship is a safe relationship.

Using the Program Guides and Tools for Change

Rate yourself as to how prosocial you think your self-identity thoughts and behaviors are.

0	1	2	3	4	5	6	7	8	9	10
Low					Medium					High

Rate yourself as to how prosocial you think you will be as to your being intimate with the individual who is close to you.

0	1	2	3	4	5	6	7	8	9	10
Low					Medium					High

Based on the knowledge and skills that you have gained from the four sessions in this chapter, update the following Program Guides:

- Program Guide 1: TMS (Section J: My Strengths and Strong Points)
- Program Guide 2: Master Skills List (MSL) (Close Relationship Skills)
- Program Guide 3: SP (11: Strengths and Resiliency)
- Program Guide 4: PFC

ALYSSA'S AND TODD'S STORIES

Alyssa

Todd and I have been friends since we were in fifth grade. It was only in the past year that we have been going together. We'll be seniors this fall. We spend a lot of time together. We go on walks, go to dances, and take the bus downtown to the art museum. We hang out with our friends together. What I love about Todd is that he listens and lets me finish what I have to say before he talks. He respects me. I feel safe with him. He would never ask me to do anything I didn't want to do. We are close, but we also do our own thing. I go for walks by myself, spend time on the computer, read, and just be alone. I like that. I have a part-time job working in a nursery and like working with plants and flowers. It relaxes me. I haven't been the best student, but this year I'm really into it. I'm going to get my degree in biology and teaching.

I have three close girlfriends I spend time with. I know that Judy likes girls rather than boys, but that's okay with me. They don't drink or use drugs. There are a lot of kids who don't. To hear some people talk, you'd think that every kid does. It's not true. I have good thoughts about myself knowing I'd never let myself get into that. Believe me, I had the pressure in junior high, but I stuck to what I thought was right, and I got even more respect than the ones who got wasted.

And I wouldn't let my mom and dad down. She works at a dental office, and I look up to her. She really loves me and my older sister; and my dad runs an auto parts store, and he is a hard worker. When he comes home, he often sits down and asks me how my day went and we talk. The other night we talked about how I was going to pay my college tuition. I told him I'm saving money, and he said he'd help. Ms. Baker, my science teacher, said I might get some grants. She's helped me see that teaching biology may be a good way for me to go. and then Todd . . . I think he loves me. He really is a great guy. Oh! We are physically close, but we set the limits. We know when to stop. We've decided to wait until marriage for that, and we don't know if we will get married. We have a lot of cool things to do before getting to that, and we have a lot of growing to do.

Todd

I really love Alyssa, and we are close. What I like is I can do my thing, and that's okay with her. I was going to drop out of high school 2 years ago but decided to finish. I want to go to Metro Automotive and Diesel School, at least for now. I love working on cars. My mom really supports me in this. She's really good to me and my little brother, and my dad and I spend some time working on my old Chevy. He's a pretty good mechanic. He also works in an auto parts store.

And then there's my friend Jake. He's had his problems, but when we spend time working on cars, we have something in common.

Alyssa and I think the same. We don't drink or use drugs. Maybe that's because I got busted at a party a couple of years ago and was put into a diversion program for 6 months and had to attend classes, but I've got my head in the right direction now. I think that was partly because of Mr. Brown, my neighbor down the street. I'd work with him on his collection of old cars. In fact, I work at his auto repair shop on Saturdays. When I was charged with the MIP, I felt I not only let my parents down but Mr. Brown spent a lot of time talking with me: and he got the court to let him be my diversion probation worker.

Alyssa and I are close. I love kicking the soccer ball around with her. It's a give and take, like our relationship. She listens to me, even when talking about working on cars, and I trust her. She respects who I am. She would never ask me to take risks. She understands clearly what is safe and healthy. Our thinking is together. We want the social and emotional intimacy to be solid before being fully intimate. Sometimes that's difficult when we are alone and close, but, right now, we want to wait until we get married. But we're too young to get that serious. Alyssa and I went to a party the other night. There were other kids like us who didn't drink and don't—use drugs. Not all kids do this—most don't—but some did and were getting high on something else. We saw many different kinds of people—some having it together and some really messed up. I talked with a guy who owns his own auto repair shop. He was one who seemed to have it together. I think that Alyssa and I have a pretty good idea on who we are, but that keeps changing. We left early and she said, "You know, we're growing up."

Chapter Thirteen:
Problem Solving and Decision Making

GOALS OF THIS CHAPTER

- Understand problem solving.
- Learn problem-solving skills.
- Discuss how groups influence our decision making.
- Understand how to avoid other people's influence in order to make good decisions.

JORDAN'S STORY

Jerika's Story

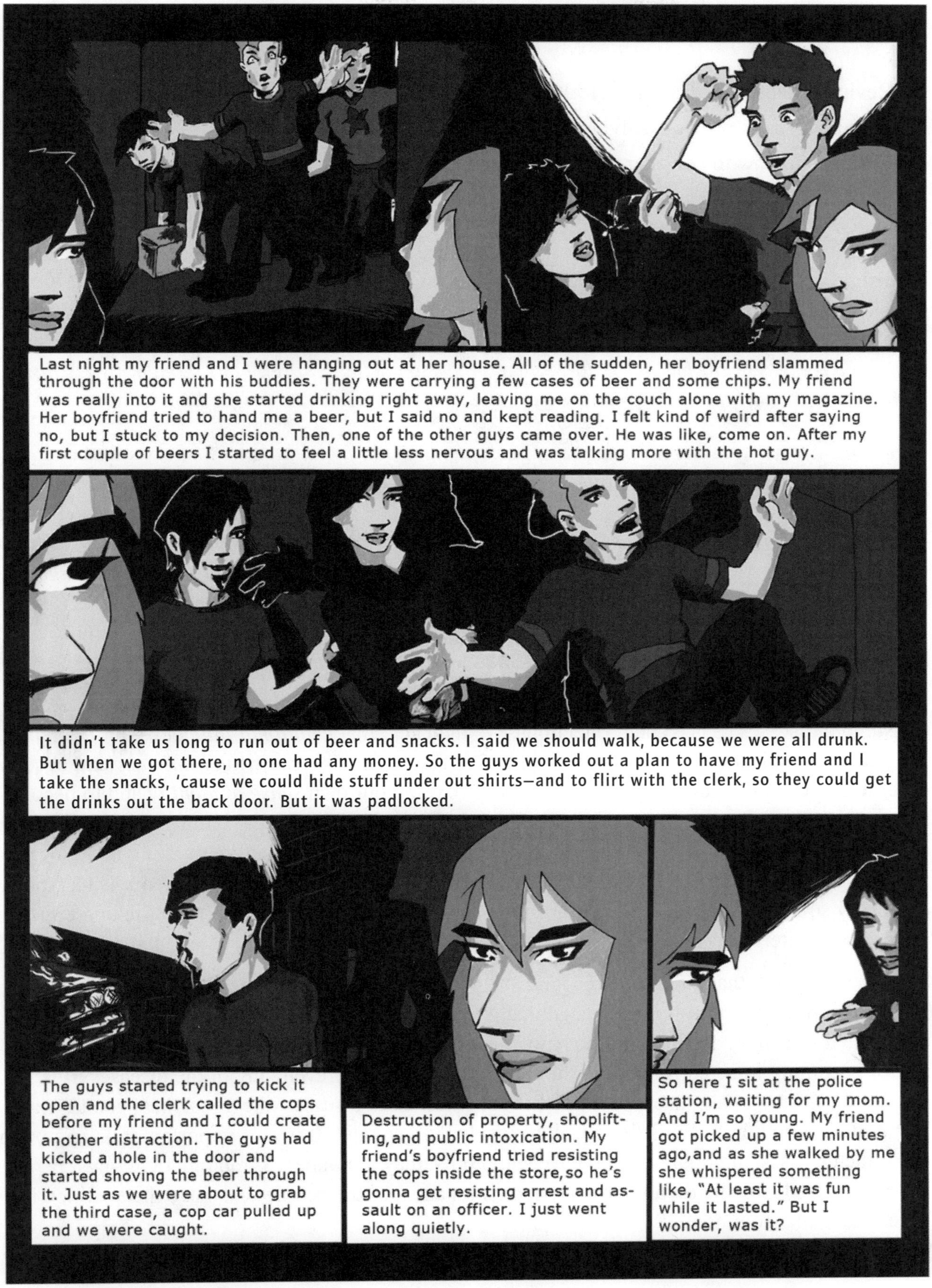

SESSION 27: PROBLEM SOLVING

Objectives

- Review Chapter 12: Building Healthy Self-Identity and Intimacy.
- Discuss steps to problem solving.
- Understand how to consider different solutions to problems.
- Learn how to cooperate and look for solutions for the good of everyone.

Jordan's Story: *So after we all got high, we were going down this alley and we were at the part where we cut across the lot of this bar when suddenly there was a fence in our way. We were like no way… no way there is a fence here. My friend's brother started pulling on the boards, saying he was gonna pull the fence down. I felt uncomfortable and my stomach got upset, but I thought it was just the drug. Next thing I know the cops are there—destruction of property and public intoxication.*

Jerika's Story: *After my first couple of beers, I started to feel a little less nervous and was talking more with this hot guy. When we ran out of beer, we decided that we needed make a run to the store. But when we got there, no one had any money. So the guys worked out a plan to have me and my friend hide stuff under our shirts—and to flirt with the clerk—so they could get the drinks out the back door. Just as we were about to grab the third case, a cop car pulled up and we were caught.*

Review of Exploring Individuality and Intimacy

In the last chapter, we began discussing emotional intimacy, sexual intimacy, contraceptives, sexually transmitted diseases (STDs), and infections. We indicated that *emotional intimacy*—built on mutual respect, communication, and trust—is vital and necessary before *true sexual intimacy* can occur. And in order to achieve intimacy, it is first necessary to develop our own *sense of identity* and to become clear about our *personal values and morals.* While the decision to have sexual intimacy is a personal choice, it is very important to have knowledge about contraceptives and STDs before thinking about becoming sexually active with another person. While pregnancy is definitely a negative when it is unexpected, and especially so for teenagers, sexually transmitted infections and diseases can have lifelong effects or result in death and often aren't noticed before they become serious.

Some people think that STDs only occur in "dirty" people or only between homosexual male partners. This is far from the truth. It is estimated that one in five people in this country have a sexually transmitted infection, and 25% of the new infections occur in teenagers. That means there is a serious risk of becoming infected if one does not take precautions to prevent any of the diseases. It is not true that females cannot pass diseases to each other, since some diseases like gonorrhea, genital warts, and herpes are carried on the outside as well as inside the genitalia. It is also important to keep in mind that a lot of the diseases, although they do have symptoms, may not appear symptomatic in most people. Diseases like chlamydia do not have symptoms for most of the people who have them, which is why they have become so common.

Activity: The Factor of Disease

Your counselor will use a flipchart, and as a group, think of the different diseases covered in Session 25: The Risks and Benefits of Closeness and Intimacy. List them down the left side of the paper and then **next to each disease, list the symptoms.** With a colored pen, mark each disease that **does not have any symptoms** for some people. With a different colored pen, mark the diseases that can have **lifetime effects,** such as infertility or scarring. With a black pen, circle the ones that have **serious damaging effects** such as heart and liver damage or death. Then mark on the right side **which ones can be cured.** Are there any of the diseases that cause serious damage or death that can be cured? How can the diseases be avoided? Can you only have one STD at a time, or can some occur together?

The only *sure means* to prevent the occurrence of STDs is *abstinence,* or not becoming sexually involved with anyone. The only other means of protection—for both yourself and your partner— is a latex condom, male or female, although they may not prevent something like warts, herpes, or syphilis if the condom does not cover the affected area. Condoms made of animal tissue, such as sheepskin, are not effective as the virus or bacteria can move through the condom skin into the other person. If a person is to become sexually active, *they must be checked by a doctor on a regular basis* in order to remain healthy, especially if a person has more than one partner. While most of the diseases can be treated with antibiotics, some such as HIV, AIDS, herpes, and hepatitis have *no known cure* and genital warts can reappear after treatment.

Becoming Good at Solving Problems

In the last chapter, we dealt with *problems that may occur* as the result of unsafe sexual actions. Although problems are a part of life and happen almost daily, most problems do not carry the *enormous weight* of those associated with unsafe sexual activity. However, most of us are here because we have not been very good at coming up with successful solutions to many different types of problems. These may include needing to get money, coping with disrespect, being upset about how you are being treated, or being invited to get high.

In fact, most of us try solving our problems in the *spur of the moment.* Sometimes we focus on *blaming the people* involved and not dealing with the problem itself. Unfortunately, that often leads us to *using drugs* in order to forget the problem or *committing crimes* in a search for a quick way to get out of a tight situation. But if we get the facts and use good problem-solving skills, then we can take pride in how effectively we can manage our lives and help others as well. People who develop good problem-solving skills don't have to turn to substances or crime in order to find a way around a difficult situation.

But in order to become good problem solvers, we first have to become *aware that a problem is occurring* and then think about the problem before we act. Sometimes that is difficult, though, because it's easier to act impulsively on feelings instead of taking time to focus on the thoughts that are happening in our minds.

SESSION 27: PROBLEM SOLVING

How Can We Tell if a Problem Exists?

One of the big things in being able to solve problems is to *know that there is a problem.* There are a couple of things we can pay attention to that will let us know when something is wrong. Most important is to pay attention to our bodies and behavior, and to keep a lookout for these signs:

- Feeling signs of stomach problems, nervousness, or depression
- Not doing our work as well
- Not acting like we want to with the people close to us
- Not getting along with people or having people avoid us
- Feeling uncomfortable with a situation

If any of these things is happening to you, it is likely that you have a problem that is not being taken care of or is being ignored.

Activity: Jordan's and Jerika's Problems

Take a moment to look at Jordan's story. What symptoms of a problem does Jordan exhibit? Why is he having the symptoms? What do you think the problem is? What about Jerika's problems? When did they really start?

Steps for Effective Problem Solving

Like we said before, everyone has problems sometimes. In fact, problems are a daily thing that happens all the time, whether it is a social situation or our thoughts, attitudes, or beliefs that are causing the problems. So then the question is how we begin to solve our problems. The first step, as in almost everything we've talked about in this program, is *knowing what our thoughts* are. Everything else is as easy as 1-2-3.

1. **Define the problem and your goal.** Identify *what is wrong.* What is it you *want* from the situation? What is your *goal,* and what is keeping you from attaining that goal? What do you need to change?
2. **What are all the facts?** What is the *information* that is important to have? What other facts or information might you need before solving the problem? Get more facts if possible. Have you *dealt with* this problem before, and if so, what did you do that time? Although the solution may have changed, if it was successful in the past, it may be a good place to start looking for a solution this time.
3. **Consider alternatives—brainstorm.** Can you think of some *different solutions?* What might other people see about the problem? Remember our discussion about empathy. How might another person feel in this situation? How does the problem look to the other person involved? Come up with *as many ways as possible* to solve the problem. They don't even have to be good solutions, just ideas on how to resolve the situation.
4. **Choose the best solution.** After taking a look at the positives and negatives, choose the solution that *best solves the problem* with the most positive outcomes or least amount of negative outcomes. Be sure

to make an effort to get the solution to work, and if it doesn't, start over. Choose several of the best alternative solutions, and begin to consider the positive or negative outcomes from using that solution. Be sure to look at the *long- and short-term results* from solving the problem in that means.

5. **Study the results.** After choosing a solution and giving it a try to solve the problem, it is important to then study the results of the solution. Ask whether the solution did what was expected of it and what the outcomes were. If the solution was successful, continue to use it and even begin applying it to other problems. Even if it wasn't successful, how can it be revised to better meet the needs of the situation?

Activity: A Moment of Problem Solving

Take a moment to fill out Worksheet 30: Problem Solving. Use a problem that is currently bothering you, and be as honest as possible. Use the previously given steps to help you answer the questions as thoroughly as possible. After everyone has filled out their worksheet, break into small groups of three or four, and **discuss your problem** with the group. Allow the other group members to offer different solutions to your problem. What are some of the group's suggestions? Have they had this problem before, and will their solution work better or worse than the one you chose? Are you able to help them with their problem and maybe offer some suggestions? What part does experience play in solving problems?

The reason that we learn and practice the *steps for effective problem solving* is so that it can become habit, allowing us to solve similar problems with ease. The more successful solutions we have in our *set of tools for change,* similar to the *arsenal of thoughts* we discussed in Chapter 9: Zeroing in on Harm-Directing Thoughts, the easier solving problems will become. The more tools we have at our disposal, the easier it will be to move through life avoiding conflict and difficulties. And the more problems we successfully solve, the easier it will be to stay away from substance abuse and crime.

Solving problems helps us to avoid drugs and crime.

Activity: A Solution to Some Problem

How could Jerika have avoided the problems she became involved in? In looking at Jordan's story, do you think he and his friends solved the problem well? How do you think things would have turned out better? What obstacles did Jordan have to overcome, and how could they have found several different solutions?

Is it likely that we can solve problems effectively when under the influence of alcohol or other drugs?

Worksheet 30

PROBLEM SOLVING

Pick a problem that you are now having. Go through the steps listed here. Use the simple steps for studying and coming up with solutions to this problem.

1. Identify or describe the problem.

____

____

2. What is your goal?

____

____

3. Give the key facts.

____

____

4. What are your alternatives? Brainstorm all of the possible solutions.

____

____

____

5. What are the possible outcomes or consequences of all these different solutions?

____

____

6. Choose the solution.

____

____

7. What do you think the outcome will be?

____

____

Activity: Creating Win-Win Solutions

When confronted with conflicts and problems, there is usually more than one person involved. This means that the skills we learned earlier about *empathy* and *communication* are vital to effective problem solving. Discuss the following steps to include other people's point of view in your problem-solving skills:

1. **Keep your attention on the problem being solved and not on the person involved.** Although it is really difficult for us to keep the other person out of it, it is the problem that we are having difficulties with and it is the problem that needs to be solved.
2. **Keep your attention on the needs and interests of the people involved and not on the positions they take.** Everyone has opinions, and quite often everybody has a different opinion when interacting with other people. The point of problem solving is not to get people to change their opinions; rather, it is for all people involved to benefit and find comfort in a problem being solved.
3. **Don't argue about the positions people take.** Opinions differ, and it's likely that most people do not agree with everyone else. The situation is not a debate about opinions but rather a problem that needs to be solved. Getting distracted in opinions merely slows down the solution process.
4. **Pick solutions that help everyone and not just one person.** If a solution only benefits one person involved, then it is likely that the problem will occur again and possibly with more negative influence and outcomes.

Activity: The Problem of the Acid River

The room will be divided into three parts, with the entire group standing on one side of the room. The middle part of the room is going to be the acid river, and there are pieces of paper about the size of a 30-inch flipchart paper (folded in half) in the river, half as many as there are group members. These represent *lily pads.* The far side is the other bank that the entire group is trying to reach by crossing the river on the lily pads. There are certain rules that may be changed by your counselor that must be followed:

- You cannot touch the floor of the room.
- There can be no sliding or inch worming on the lily pads.
- There can be no unattended lily pads. Some part of someone's body must be touching the lily pads at all times.
- All group members must arrive on the bank at the same time.
- If a violation occurs, then the entire group must go back to the beginning.

What did you learn about problem solving from the acid river game? Did the solution to the problem follow the *steps for effective problem solving* and *creating win-win solutions* that we covered in this lesson?

SESSION 27: PROBLEM SOLVING

Putting It Together

- Jordan and Jerika and their friends ran into problems. What was the problem, and how did they solve it?
- How could the *steps for effective problem solving* have been used in Jordan's or Jerika's story?
- Does the problem in both examples really begin with each person's decision to get high?
- Think of some problems you have had lately. How did you solve the problems, if you solved them at all?
- How would the steps of problem solving help you to resolve some difficulties?

Using the Program Guides and Tools for Change

Rate your ability to use the problem-solving skills.

0	1	2	3	4	5	6	7	8	9	10
Low					Medium					High

Indicate your ability to use the steps to arrive at win-win solutions when faced with problems that involve other people.

0	1	2	3	4	5	6	7	8	9	10
Low					Medium					High

- Review your Thinking Patterns ratings on your Self-Portrait (SP). Do these get in the way of good problem solving?
- Consider if you should add problem solving and creating win-win solutions to your Plan for Change (PFC).

SESSION 28: DECISION MAKING

Objectives

- Review Session 27: Problem Solving.
- Discuss the difference between fact and opinion.
- Understand the importance of propaganda.
- Learn the skills of decision making.

Jordan's Story: *I didn't really want to take a hit. When I turned around, it was all laid out on the table, and they were all taking a hit. At first I said no and that I didn't like how it made me feel last time I had tried it, but my friend said this stuff was much better and that it wouldn't make me feel like the other stuff I had tried. I still felt awkward, but his brother was like, come on, we'll have a great time, and I didn't want to be the only sober one.*

Jerika's Story: *Last night my friend and I were hanging out at her house, listening to music and reading magazines. All of a sudden, her boyfriend slammed through the door with his buddies. He tried to hand me a beer, but I said no and kept reading. I felt kind of weird after saying no, but I stuck to my decision. Then, one of the other guys came over—the one who I kind of had a crush on. He was like, come on, we'll have a great time. So I figured I'm only young once and this guy might really like me. After my first couple of beers, I started to feel a little less nervous and was talking more with the hot guy.*

Review of Problem Solving

In our last session, we began discussing the *steps to solving a problem.* We tend to jump at the *first or easiest* way to get over, without looking at the *possible outcomes* or long-term consequences. If we don't learn how to problem solve effectively, the problems will continue to come back, usually bringing other problems with them. This is similar to the *cycle of anger* that we talked about in Chapter 10: Handling Anger, Guilt, and Depression. Similar to anger, *when a problem doesn't get recognized,* resolved, or resolved well, then it will *continue to erupt* within our lives, causing us even more difficulties to overcome. After a while we become weak or are unable to control the problem, and that is when we may turn to drugs or crime for an easy way to forget or temporarily escape the problem. Review Figure 7 on Forming a Habit and a Pattern of Dependence that we covered in Session 4. This shows an important example of poor problem solving.

Unfortunately, drugs and crime merely shove the problem out of view and in the long run will cause more problems than before. That is where the skills for problem solving become an important factor in controlling and having freedom within our lives.

Problem solving increases personal control and freedom.

SESSION 28: DECISION MAKING

Activity: A Group of Problems

Take a moment to look back at the last session and go over the **steps to problem solving.** Then, individually, write a **problem situation** on a piece of paper and put it into the bag your counselor will hand around. An example of a problem may be that you want to be nice to your mom, but every time you are around her you get angry and start a fight. After everyone has finished a problem, the first person will **choose a problem** out of the bag and read the problem to the group. **As a group, use the steps for problem solving** to solve the problem written on the piece of paper. Go around the group as often as time allows or as long as there are problems in the bag. How do the problem-solving skills help in solving real-life problems? How will you use the skills to solve your own problems?

Of course, learning how to anticipate and avoid problems in the first place is a great start in how we can gain control and have freedom in our lives. One way to prevent problems is in *good decision making,* since most problems can occur from the decisions we choose. Had Jordan and Jerika made firm decisions to stay clean and sober, their other problems most likely would have never happened.

Critical Thinking and Decision Making

Just as with problem solving, often our decisions are made impulsively and are based on our *thoughts or feelings at the moment* of decision. An example might be smoking marijuana or drinking a beer. If you feel stressed or tired and you think you deserve to *really cut loose* once in a while, then it is more likely you will impulsively use the substance without even thinking about the consequences of your decision.

Critical thinking, also known as logical or rational thinking, is when we make sense out of something and get all the facts before making a decision. Often when it comes to *substance use* or *criminal actions,* we don't always get all the facts and we become swayed by emotions or *shortsighted thinking.* In order to be able to make decisions logically, we first have to make sure we take the following elements of critical thinking into account.

- **Get all the facts.** We can't make good decisions when we don't have all the correct information, so it's important we *get all the information* first.
- **Do not let your emotions make the decision.** A lot of times we make our decisions because of our feelings—*such as we are angry*—and so we punch or slam the door, or we don't like a person so we aren't going to hang out there anymore. The problem is those kinds of decisions tend to cause us more problems than before. Now we have to fix a hole in the door, or now we can't hang out with our friends because that person is going to be there. This kind of decision can do more damage to us than the thing or person we are trying to get back at.
- **Make sense of the facts.** Part of good decision making is being able to *piece together the facts* in order to *make a picture that seems correct.* The idea is not what we think or feel about the situation but what the facts tell us.

- **Are you being misled?** When we come to a conclusion because we have been swayed to the wishes or desires of another person, we have been conned or misled. When we *allow someone to convince us* of making a certain decision before we get all the facts, we are allowing that person to *con us* (notice the similarity between con and **con**trol). When a person tries to **con**vince us to take their side, sometimes telling us the truth but *more often lying* to us to tell us what we want to hear, this is called *propaganda.* Propaganda gets in the way of good decision making because we don't get all the facts or the correct facts.

Activity: A Bag of Decisions

Individually **write out a decision** that needs to be made. It can be something simple, like deciding what to eat at a specific restaurant, or it could be something complicated, like deciding to have sex for the first time. Then put the decisions in a bag and mix them up. Each person will **take a decision** and then use the previously named elements to help in making the decision. The decision should be made **based on facts** the group decides apply to the situation, and it should be to the agreement of most everyone in the group.

The Propaganda Con

Decision making, unlike problem solving, tends to take on a group atmosphere. Often there are other people around when we have to make a decision, and it is easy to be swayed by other people's desires and needs when we are trying to make a decision. But what another person wants is not always what is good for us. As we said, propaganda is when a person tries to talk us into doing something, usually by telling us something we want to hear. Here are some methods of propaganda:

- **One-sided arguments.** The one-sided argument is when the other person *plays up the aspects* that are *likely to influence* the other person to make a decision that agrees with the first person's desires. An example of this would be a friend trying to convince us to smoke a joint: "This weed is so fine and mellow. You will feel good for hours without any paranoia. And there is no way you're gonna get caught. Besides, one joint is not gonna hurt you."
- **The bandwagon approach.** This approach is *designed to make us feel left out* or *not part of the "in" group* if we do not try or do what they are selling to us. An example of this might be being offered the joint from a friend and the friend telling us when we refuse: "Hey, man, everyone is doing it. You'll be the only one not high, and everyone knows that it can't hurt you."
- **Repetition.** We often see this approach on television, radio, or even on billboards. The idea is to *repeat the product* so often that the slogans become ingrained and the specific product is the one we think of when it is time to buy something. Television ads, which might be shown four times in one hour-long program, are an example of this. Sometimes drugs are made to seem more attractive simply by the amount of times you hear about them through friends and the people you hang out with.
- **Transfer.** Advertisers, especially for alcohol and tobacco, use this approach in which they *associate the product with an attractive person* we would like to be or a fun situation that we would like to be in. One example is a beer commercial that shows everyone having fun and the guys getting really attractive females to like them.

- **Testimonial.** A testimonial advertisement is when a *famous or important person* does a commercial to promote a product. The idea behind this propaganda is the hope that the loyalty or desire to be like the person in the commercial will transfer to the product being sold. An example of this would be sports clothing commercials with a famous hall-of-fame athlete.
- **Emergency.** This is when the buyer is told that *there is a limited time* in which they can get the product at the special price or there is a *limited number of products* to be sold. An example of this would be the following: "Come on down today because the sale ends tonight at 5."
- **Bargain.** This is often used with the emergency propaganda in that they encourage a person to buy because something is *offered for free or for a reduced price.* An example would be as follows: "Buy a subscription to this magazine and you get a poster for free!"

Activity: Jordan's Decision

As a group, look at Jordan's and Jerika's stories. How do they make their decisions? What sort of **propaganda** does Jordan's friend and his brother use to convince him to use? Who do you think the decision and the propaganda benefit? What kind of propaganda does Jerika buy into?

Activity: Application of Propaganda

Take a moment to fill out Worksheet 31: Propaganda Advertisements with advertisements you have seen on television, read in a magazine, or heard on the radio. How has propaganda played **a part in your life?** Then as a group, go around and discuss how advertisements use each propaganda technique. Which ones seem more effective than others? How **can you tell** if someone is using propaganda on you? What can you do to avoid being conned into making a decision that is not in your favor? **What has been the relationship between propaganda, drug use, and criminal activity in your life?**

Propaganda and Decision Making

As we said before, group opinion tends to be involved when we try to make a decision. When the group is our friends or family, it can become really difficult to tell when they have our interests in mind or their own. Because of thoughts and feelings that can become involved in making a decision, we have to make sure we have all the facts before attempting to make a decision for ourselves.

Another thing we have to keep in mind is how propaganda and decision making play a part in our use of substances or our criminal activities. Often we are influenced to do these things by the group we are around, and they often use propaganda techniques. "Everyone is doing it" is something we hear when it comes to trying to resist substances, and the facts are that not everybody is doing it.

In fact, there are a large number of people in the country—and people you know—who are not doing drugs. Similar to this is when we get involved in crime. Sometimes we may think that we can have the lifestyle of a celebrity or have people desire to be around us if we only dress a certain way. When we don't have money to dress that way, some people might begin stealing in order to dress in a way they

Worksheet 31

Propaganda Advertisements

Describe five different advertisements that you have seen either in newspapers, the Internet, or on television. What technique or techniques did they use? Use the information that was previously given.

Ad 1
Propaganda Technique:

Ad 2
Propaganda Technique:

Ad 3
Propaganda Technique:

Ad 4
Propaganda Technique:

Ad 5
Propaganda Technique:

Ad 6
Propaganda Technique:

think is going to attract attention and respect. The truth, though, is that respect comes from who we are and how we respect other people. Stealing will only get us the attention from the cops and a negative identity (like what we talked about in Session 23).

Activity: Personal Problems Influenced by Propaganda

Individually, fill out Worksheet 32: Relating Propaganda to Your Drug Use and Criminal Conduct. For each method of propaganda, write a statement as to how that method has played a part in your using substances or getting involved in crime. An example for *transfer* would be seeing someone in the media who dresses how you want to dress. That leads you to decide to steal clothes in order to look good as well.

After everyone has filled out their worksheet, discuss as a group how propaganda affects your lives. Who has control over some of your decisions? Who do you want to have control? In what ways can you improve your decision making, and how can you avoid propaganda?

In learning how to see through the propaganda, we are able to make *decisions that are best for us* and don't fit the needs of other people using us. We all prefer to have freedom and control over our lives, and by listening and believing in propaganda without gathering all the facts, we give up our freedom and control to another person and that person's desires.

Putting It Together

- Jordan's decision is greatly influenced by his friend. What propaganda does his friend use in trying to convince him? How might have Jordan *resisted the propaganda?* How did Jerika get drawn in to making bad decisions? Were their situations similar?
- What sort of propaganda has *influenced* your decision making? Which techniques are more influential than others?
- How would you use the *problem-solving* and *critical-thinking skills* in helping to make a decision?

Using the Program Guides and Tools for Change

Rate your ability to use critical thinking when faced with a difficult decision. Be prepared to explain the reason for your rating.

0	1	2	3	4	5	6	7	8	9	10
Low					Medium					High

Indicate your ability to recognize the different types of propaganda and how they can influence some people to abuse drugs or commit crimes.

0	1	2	3	4	5	6	7	8	9	10
Low					Medium					High

Worksheet 32

Relating Propaganda to Your Drug Use & Criminal Conduct

Describe how the different types of propaganda have influenced your drug use or criminal conduct.

One-Sided Arguments:

____

____

The Bandwagon Approach:

____

____

Repetition:

____

____

Transfer:

____

____

Testimonial:

____

____

Emergency:

____

____

Bargain:

____

____

SESSION 28: DECISION MAKING

- Look at your Drug Use Patterns on your SP. Did your use of drugs get in the way of critical thinking and good decision making?
- Did propaganda play a role in your decision to use drugs or to become involved in criminal activities?
- Update Program Guide 1: Telling My Story (TMS) in the area of Relationship With Peers.
- Look at your thinking patterns on your SP. Do some of your identified Harm-Directing Thoughts cause you to make poor decisions?
- Review the section on your SP that rates our Relationship With Peers. Has propaganda played a role in your involvement with some of your criminal associates?
- Update your Master Skills List (MSL) in the areas of using problem-solving skills, using assertiveness skills, and using refusal skills.
- Update your PFC.

JORDAN'S STORY

I can't believe I did this. . . again. I should have learned from my last time, but I didn't. I listened to my friend, and here I sit again, waiting for my mom again, only this time I think it's more serious.

Last night my friend and I were hanging out at his house, playing games and listening to music. Suddenly the door slammed open and his older brother was there with his friends. They told us to move over because they needed the coffee table, and so we ended up sitting on the floor trying to finish our game while they were talking and laughing behind us. As we were playing, his brother asked my friend if he wanted any. The next thing I knew I was playing by myself.

After I had died in the game, I turned around to find powder out on the table and all three of them with rolled up bills about to take a hit. My friend snorted, coughed, and then laughed with tears streaming down his cheeks. He looked at me and offered me a hit. At first I said no. I had done it before and didn't really like how I felt afterward. My friend just said that this stuff was better and that I would enjoy it more and that it really wouldn't affect me like that other stuff. I felt kind of awkward, and I kept saying no, but then his brother was like, come on, man, we'll have a great time tonight.

So I figured what the hell. I might as well have a good time on a weekend night. Besides, I'm only young once—or so they kept telling me. A tingle began to spread over my body, and a rush went through my head just after I took a hit. And I sat back. Everyone was staring at me with dumb ass grins, but I didn't care because I felt so good. I don't know how much longer we stayed there playing video games. Time became irrelevant, and life felt like it was moving too slow and too fast all at once. My friend's brother decided that he wanted a Slurpee, and he invited us to go along with them. I couldn't seem to keep myself from moving, so I didn't think sugar was the thing for me, but I also needed to get out of the house to stop from rocking back and forth while I twitched my feet and smacked my gum.

We decided it was better to walk since the store wasn't too far away, and I knew I wasn't gonna get in a car with those guys. Maybe I would have. I dunno. So we were walking down this alley and got to the corner where we usually cut through this bar's lot, and there was a fence up. At first we were like no way, there's no way there's actually a fence here. I started walking back and forth, partly because I couldn't stand still and partly because I was looking for a way around it. We had gone down the alley because it cut five blocks off our walk, but to go all the way down the alley would mean we would have to walk back to the store, and that meant adding, like, six blocks. So we just stood there and stared at the fence.

Then my friend's brother started pulling at the fence. He's like, I'm gonna tear this thing down. I started feeling really uncomfortable, and my stomach was getting upset, but I thought it was from the drug. I thought about walking to the end of the alley and back down to the store, but then I noticed that he had one of the boards off already. So we all started pulling and pushing and swearing while trying to take down this fence that was in our way. Finally it was big enough for the older guys to squeeze through, and then it was my turn. Because I was last, I didn't notice the cops until I was on the other side staring at the guys spread out on the fence with their hands on their heads.

Destruction of private property and public intoxication were the charges. I guess my friend's brother had tried resisting them and running, so he's gonna get resisting arrest and assault on an officer, too. I just went along quietly, partly because my teeth were so clenched that I could barely speak and partly because there was nothing I could do.

So here I sit in the police station, waiting for my mom. I guess they could have shipped me straight to a juvie hall because I had a prior, but they took it easy on me because I didn't give them any hassle and I'm so young. My friend got picked up just a few minutes ago, and as he was walking by, he whispered something like at least it was fun while it lasted. But I wonder, was it?

JERIKA'S STORY

I can't believe I did this . . . again. I should have learned from my last time, but I didn't. I listened to my friend, and here I sit again, waiting for my mom. Only this time I think it's more serious.

Last night my friend and I were hanging out at her house, listening to music and reading magazines. All of a sudden, her boyfriend slammed through the door with his buddies. They were carrying a few cases of beer and some chips and told us how proud they were after getting a guy to buy them the beer—like they were real heroes. My friend was really into it and thanked her boyfriend for getting her favorite kind of chips to go along with the beer. She started drinking right away, leaving me on the couch alone with my magazine. Her boyfriend tried to hand me a beer, but I said no and kept reading. I felt kind of weird after saying no, but I stuck to my decision. Then, one of the other guys came over—the one who I kind of had a crush on. He was like, come on, we'll have a great time tonight.

So I figured what the heck. I might as well have a good time on a Saturday night. Besides, I'm only young once, and this guy might really like me. After my first couple of beers, I started to feel a little less nervous and was talking more with the hot guy.

It didn't take us long to run out of beer and snacks, and we decided that we needed to make a run to the store. I said we should walk, because we were all drunk and the store wasn't too far away. There was no way I was getting in a car with those guys. Anyway, they agreed, and we all walked the five blocks to the store. But when we got there, no one had any money. So the guys worked out a plan to have my friend and I take the snacks because we could hide stuff under our shirts—and to flirt with the clerk, so they could get the drinks out the back door. Everything seemed to be going along fine, but the back door was padlocked. The guys started trying to kick it open, and the clerk had the cops on speed dial before my friend and I could create another distraction. So we ran out of the store with the stuff we had and went around the back to see if we could pull the door open from the outside. By that time, the guys had kicked a hole in the door and started shoving the beer through it. Just as we were about to grab the third case, a cop car pulled up and we were caught.

Destruction of property, shoplifting, and public intoxication were the charges. My friend's boyfriend tried resisting the cops inside the store so he's gonna get resisting arrest and assault on an officer, too. I just went along quietly, partly because I was too shocked to say anything and partly because there was nothing I could do.

So here I sit at the police station, waiting for my mom. I guess they could have sent me straight to juvie hall because I have a prior, but they took it easy on me because I didn't give them any hassle. And I'm so young. My friend got picked up a few minutes ago, and as she walked by, she seemed so high that she didn't even know what was happening.

Chapter Fourteen:
Lifestyle Balance

GOALS OF THIS CHAPTER

- Review relapse and recidivism (RR).
- Consider the consequences of thrill seeking, drugs, and crime.
- Understand how imbalances in our lives can lead to RR.
- Develop an RR prevention plan.
- Continue discussing critical thinking and decision making.
- Learn when to walk away.

ZACH'S STORY

I can't take it anymore. About a year ago I was caught for grand theft auto. I had stolen a car from a house down the block while I was stoned. Before I knew it, though, there were cops behind me pulling me over. I kind of panicked because I knew I would get in trouble for not only taking the car, but for being stoned, too. So I kept driving. And driving and driving, all the while trying to go faster than the cops, until I bumped off the curb and ran into a tree. Grand theft auto, minor under the influence, destruction of public property, and on and on and on. My parents bailed me out. The judge looked over my profile, looked at my past record, and then ordered me into a treatment facility for six months, community service when I got out, and reparation for damages.
So here I am, going to school so I can graduate within the next couple of years, and working after school to pay back all the damages. And not doing a single thing that's fun. 'Cause when I get home from work, I'm not to leave the house. Yesterday my friend showed up at work. He asked me to take off early 'cause there was something he wanted to give me. I told him I couldn't, I had to work my full shift. But I said he could give me a ride after work if he wanted.
I told him he should take me home. He just started driving in the other direction and said I would thank him for this. At the stoplight I got out of his car. I have a year of being sober, and they say that if I'm good they'll reduce my community service time. I told my friend all that. And then I started walking away. So last night, my girlfriend called and asked why I had dissed my friend like that. I told her I couldn't be around him if he was gonna risk my chances of being good. It's just so hard sometimes, though. I feel left out and like I don't have a life anymore. To tell you the truth, if this is what responsibility is, I'm not sure I want to be responsible.

Runaway Train
When I came out of my doorway, I looked around me. Someone looked through the garbage. Was that blood on the sidewalk? Yep, the train had come through. The engine is gold; it's flashy and shiny. Young people see it, flag it down, and get on. They hear the loud music, it's pumping, it's funky. But it's a runaway train, its heading nowhere.
The engineer looks like a homeboy, dripping gold from his fingers, even his teeth. The engine is that fat wad in Hector's pocket, or the Uzi that Kareem keeps by his pillow when he sleeps. And they push you, and shove you, from the first car to the rear. And you see people lying, and stealing, and dying. And you can't hear the music, only the people sobbing and crying, "Stop the train, stop the train, I want to get off."
They're heading for prison, and jails, and for death. And everyone screaming out the windows, "Stop, stop... Don't get on this train, can't you see, can't you see!" And the young flag down the train. They can't hear the screams because the music is loud and it has shut down the brain. So, they get on, they get on the runaway train, looking for dollars, and good times, and love. What a shame. Check it out young people, last stop is death.

SESSION 29: STAYING STRONG WITHOUT DRUGS AND CRIME

Objectives

- Review Chapter 13: Problem Solving and Decision Making.
- Discuss high-risk (HR) situations and HR thinking.
- Review triggers and stages of RR.
- Learn how imbalances in our lives can lead to RR.
- Learn how to stay on the road to self-discovery and change.

Zach's Story: *I really am trying to do things right and get my life back on track. But it's not fair. I work and go to school all the time, and I don't even get to keep the money I make. And I don't have a life because my parents have put me on house arrest. I'm young, and I should be having the time of my life right now. But it doesn't seem that way to me at all.*

Yesterday my friend asked me to ditch work, and I said no, so he picked me up after work. I thought he was going to take me home, but instead he drove in the other direction. He told me that I would thank him later. At the stoplight, I got out of the car. I mean, I really wanted to go with him because lately I feel so old and like life is pointless, but I also have a drawing at home I've been working on and that I'm really into. Besides, I need to do right, and he doesn't understand that.

Runaway Train

The engine of the train always looks shiny, always holds promise of hundred dollar bills. In the first car, there's always a party, and it looks inviting. They party all night and sometimes all day. But that's a runaway train; it's heading nowhere. And once you get on it, it's running express. You see the engine, all bright and shiny. I see the caboose, all filled with death.

—excerpt from *The Runaway Train*
by Geoffrey Canada.

Review of Decision Making

In the last session, we began discussing how to make decisions that are in our best interest and consistent with our goals in life. Unlike problem solving, *decision making* usually involves a group of people, such as family or friends. Having many people involved can make it even more difficult to act in our own best interest. The important part of any decision is to keep a *realistic view* of the situation. That means keeping *emotions out of the way* and knowing the *difference between opinion and fact.*

When it comes time to make a decision, there often are other people who are trying to get what they want or need. The pressure from the other people to decide in their favor can sometimes become overwhelming.

But the best way to be able to decide in our best interest, as well as the best interest of others, is to be able to tell *what fact is and what is not.* This is where *propaganda* can emerge. *Opinions* and *fact selection* are used to try to sway a person to one side or the other. In order to think straight and make decisions that are truly in our best interest, we have to be able to see *through the propaganda* and stick to the facts.

Activity: Examples of Sway

Take a moment to look over the **different propaganda methods** listed in Session 28: Decision Making. Then write down a **situation** or **experience** you have had these past few weeks that can fall into one of the propaganda methods. Were you the one experiencing propaganda, or were you the one using it? What was the result of the situation? Break into small groups, and discuss your situations together. Is there one propaganda technique that is used more frequently than the others?

Which one do you think is most effective? Why? Help each other brainstorm about **ways to avoid propaganda.**

The purpose of *discussing propaganda* and *decision making* is that they both play a part in using substances and committing crimes. By practicing decision-making skills, we can recognize when someone is trying to sway us in a manner that is not in our best interest. This also means that we can spot the times when we attempt to use propaganda, or excuses, against ourselves.

Review of Relapse and Recidivism Definitions

As discussed in Chapter 4: Backsliding to Drugs and Crime, there are two very powerful forces that may put us in danger of returning to drugs or crime: (1) *HR situations* or (2) *HR thinking.*

1. **HR situations.** People, places, and things that put us at risk for reoffending or reusing
2. **HR thinking.** Thought habits that cause and allow us to return to substance use and crime

Certain things from our past can become a *trigger* when we are trying to avoid RR. Hanging out with *friends* we used to commit crimes with or use substances with can be a trigger that will be hard to overcome. *Emotions* and *thoughts* also can cause us to begin the erosion of RR. Feelings of anger, frustration, or even happiness can bring about the craving for a substance or lead to an urge to commit a crime. Here are some HR situations that you will need to keep an active lookout for:

HR Situations

- Conflict with another person.
- Social or peer pressure.
- An unpleasant feeling of anger, depression, or guilt.

- A change in self-image.
- Being in the presence of people, places, and things that stir up feelings of excitement about thrill seeking, taking drugs, and committing crimes.

Activity: The Runaway Train

As a group, take a look at Zach's story. What do you think about **Zach's situation?** Do you think he is **close to relapse or not?** Why or why not? What HR situations do you think Zach is finding himself in? What can Zach do to avoid those situations but still feel comfortable and happy?

Now go over the story of the ***runaway train***. What kind of propaganda is involved in getting young people to come on board? Is the poem realistic in how it portrays the train's *last stop*? Do you think Zach would be tempted to get on the *runaway train*? What kind of strengths does Zach have that might protect him from choosing a flashy and dangerous lifestyle?

Break up into groups of two, and discuss how you are likely to come in contact with a flashy and dangerous lifestyle and what plan you have made to stay out of trouble.

Stages of Relapse and Recidivism

Remember that *relapse* (returning to substance use) and *recidivism* (returning to crime) are erosions that begin in our minds. Although using drugs or committing a crime is the finale, or *end point,* of RR, it really begins with *allowing ourselves* to think the *HR thoughts* or putting ourselves in *HR situations.* Just as with change, there are recognizable stages in RR:

- *HR situations* and *HR thinking.*
- Lack of mastery skills and *loss of self-confidence.*
- *Expecting* substance use and dangerous or criminal activities to *improve your feelings or situation* in life.
- *Tendency to give up* after beginning substance use or criminal thinking *(Rule Violation Effect).*
- *Belief that you were weak* and couldn't handle the thinking or situation.
- *Backsliding* to where you were with drugs and crime before you began treatment.

For a better idea of how these work, review Figure 11: The Relapse/Recidivism Model and Figure 12: Road to Relapse and Recidivism in Session 9: Learning How to Stay Clean and Avoid Trouble. Keep in mind that *HR thinking* is the first stage of RR.

Activity: Evaluation of Personal Risk

As a group, make a list of all the **thinking skills** you have learned throughout the course of this program, such as the "thought stopping" or "positive thought arming." Then make a list of all the

action/refusal skills you have learned throughout the program. Use Table 2: Mental Self-Control and Change Skills from Chapter 5 to help guide your answers.

When the group has completed the list of thinking and action skills, individually fill out the three parts of Worksheet 33: Evaluation of Personal Risk.

First, fill out the section on ***thinking skills*** you have used in the past 3 months in order to avoid RR.

Second, fill out the section on ***HR thinking patterns*** by listing HR alcohol and other drug (AOD) use patterns of thinking and criminal conduct (CC) thinking patterns you were involved in during the past 3 months. Which **thinking skills or behaviors** did you use to deal with these thoughts?

Third, fill out the section on ***HR situations*** to list HR AOD use situations and HR CC situations you placed yourself in during the past 3 months. Take note of the thinking or action skills you used to deal with these situations.

Finally, evaluate how successful you were in avoiding the RR thinking and situations. In comparing with others in the group, did you find some situations or thoughts that most people ran into? Did you all deal with the situations alike, or did you have different ways of dealing?

Meeting Our Needs Through Lifestyle Balance

HR situations and thinking play a large role in whether we fall back into our previous use and choices, *such as getting back on the runaway train,* but there is also *another element* that has a large role in RR.

Living drug and crime free requires a *balanced lifestyle,* and life can quickly get out of balance. Too often we feel the pressure of *should* and *ought,* and we end up feeling deprived or even cheated. With the demands of work, school, and family, we often leave no time for ourselves and can become overwhelmed.

When life gets out of balance, we often begin to feel a strong desire to meet our needs right away, whether it is the need for thrills, relaxation, happiness, or material things. This can lead to *cravings* and *urges for substances* (both drugs and alcohol) and to get what we want right away through *committing a crime.* Often when this happens, especially after we made a commitment to living drug and crime free, we make excuses for what we want to do.

Relapse and Recidivism Excuses

- "I deserve more than this."
- "I work hard and don't get anywhere."
- "They have more than I do. I deserve as much as they do."
- "I deserve to have fun."
- "I have something coming. They owe me."

These thoughts *can* and *do* lead to RR. With RR, we get what we want quickly. Both give us immediate *gratification* and *reward.* The **p**roblem of **i**mmediate **g**ratification can be remembered as **PIG**.

Worksheet 33

Evaluation of Personal Risk

List up to five examples for each category to evaluate your personal risk.

Thinking Skills You Used in the Past 3 Months to Manage or Avoid Relapse and Recidivism (RR)	Action Skills You Used in the Past 3 Months to Manage or Avoid RR
High-Risk (HR) Thinking Patterns You Engaged in During the Past 3 Months	**Thinking or Action Skills You Used to Deal With Each of These Thinking Patterns**
HR Situations You Placed Yourself in During the Past 3 Months	**Thinking or Action Skills You Used to Deal with Each of These HR Situations**

But the choice we have made to indulge may be hidden. We make choices that don't seem important. This is called ***seemingly irrelevant decisions*** (SIDs). This becomes the doorway to HR thinking and situations, such as letting a friend come over when you know he's going to smoke marijuana and offer to share the experience with you or letting yourself hang out with friends who participate in criminal activity because you feel you deserve to go out and have fun.

Activity: The Exciting Life

Discuss Zach's story, and make sure to cover these questions. Has Zach made a ***seemingly irrelevant decision?*** What was the decision, and why did he think it was irrelevant? How could it have affected him negatively? What thoughts or excuses is Zach beginning to think? How might Zach combat those thoughts, and is he doing that already? What skills does Zach have to manage the PIG? Discuss the skills that you will use when your see the *runaway train* coming down the track.

Be Prepared

We can *prevent* this slide into RR. By developing a *balanced lifestyle* and arming ourselves with an RR *prevention* plan, we can help stop ourselves before we go very far down the RR road. Next are some recommendations for how to maintain a balanced lifestyle and to stay on the right track when faced with HR thoughts and situations.

Preparing for the Road to Self-Discovery and Change

1. **Arm ourselves with a self-control plan.** When we relapse or reoffend, we have made a choice to do so, and when our *lifestyles are out of balance,* we are likely to make those choices. Through this program, we have learned skills to prevent RR, which we reviewed in Worksheet 33: Evaluation of Personal Risk, but we are always faced with HR thinking and situations that can lead to RR. That is why it is important for us to come up with a plan for self-control so that we are not caught off guard every time we run into a situation. This plan is similar to our arsenal of solutions that we discussed in Chapter 13: Problem Solving and Decision Making. The figure shown on Worksheet 34: My Personal Strategies for Relapse and Recidivism Prevention will help us develop a plan for any risky situation.

2. **Maintain a balanced lifestyle.** To begin, we can achieve a *balanced lifestyle* by building in *daily activities* that can give us *positive feelings* and gratifications. That way, when we feel the need to use substances, we can immediately make ourselves feel good with a *positive activity* and thus replace the desire for the substance. An example of this may be drawing or playing music. If we set aside time every day to draw, we can turn toward our drawing and replace a desire to do drugs with interest in our art.

3. **Detach and label.** This means that every time you have a *craving* or *an urge* to use a substance or commit a crime, you remove yourself from the situation. You can also label the urge so you are aware it's happening, then ride it out and wait for it to go away. Recognize cravings and urges as thoughts and feelings that you can *detach yourself from;* in other words, they are not all consuming, and you don't have to follow them.

4. **Carefully watch the decisions that seem like they aren't important.** Remember these SIDs are the doorway into the slide to RR. The best thing to do is to be aware of what you are thinking and not make excuses. If you catch yourself thinking, "I deserve it," stop the thought and call it a "poor excuse." It is also helpful to look at the *short-term* and *long-term* good and bad parts of any decision to use substances or participate in crime. This is called a *decision window,* and it will help you to become aware of thoughts that will lead you toward RR. For a reminder of how to make a good decision, review Session 28: Decision Making in Chapter 13. Of course, the most effective means of preventing RR is to avoid the situations that are likely to lead to it.

Activity: My Strategies for Relapse and Recidivism Prevention

Develop your **RR prevention plan** by filling out the blank spaces on Worksheet 34: My Personal Strategies for Relapse and Recidivism Prevention. Try to figure out things that are realistic and that will actually help you in the case of an RR situation. Think of the things that you have confronted while in this program, and think of the things that have led to your being in this program. How might you avoid them by substituting **positive activities** and having an arsenal of **ways to cope** with negative thoughts or urges?

Break into small groups and discuss your strategies. Then have a member of your small group present the different strategies to the entire group.

Activity: Decision Window

Take a look at Worksheet 35: The Decision Window. Complete the windows for both substance use and **criminal behavior.** What do you get **right now** and **later** by not using substances? What do you miss out on by not using substances, both in the short and long run? Be sure to do the same for criminal behavior. What do you get in the short and long run by living a crime-free life?

One suggestion that may help you in preventing RR erosion is to think of RR as a highway map. This is the same map that we covered in Chapter 4: Backsliding to Drugs and Crime (Figure 12: Road to Relapse and Recidivism). During this program, you may have found yourself on this highway several times as you faced urges and cravings. You have resisted and stayed straight or abstinent, and although you may have done and thought things that brought you close to RR, you have been set on staying on *Road 101* to *Recovery City.* It may be helpful to keep this map in your mind not only to remind yourself where you want to be but also to remember that you have come so far and there is so much to gain by keeping on the right path. Whichever direction you take, though, remember that it is your choice as to your destination.

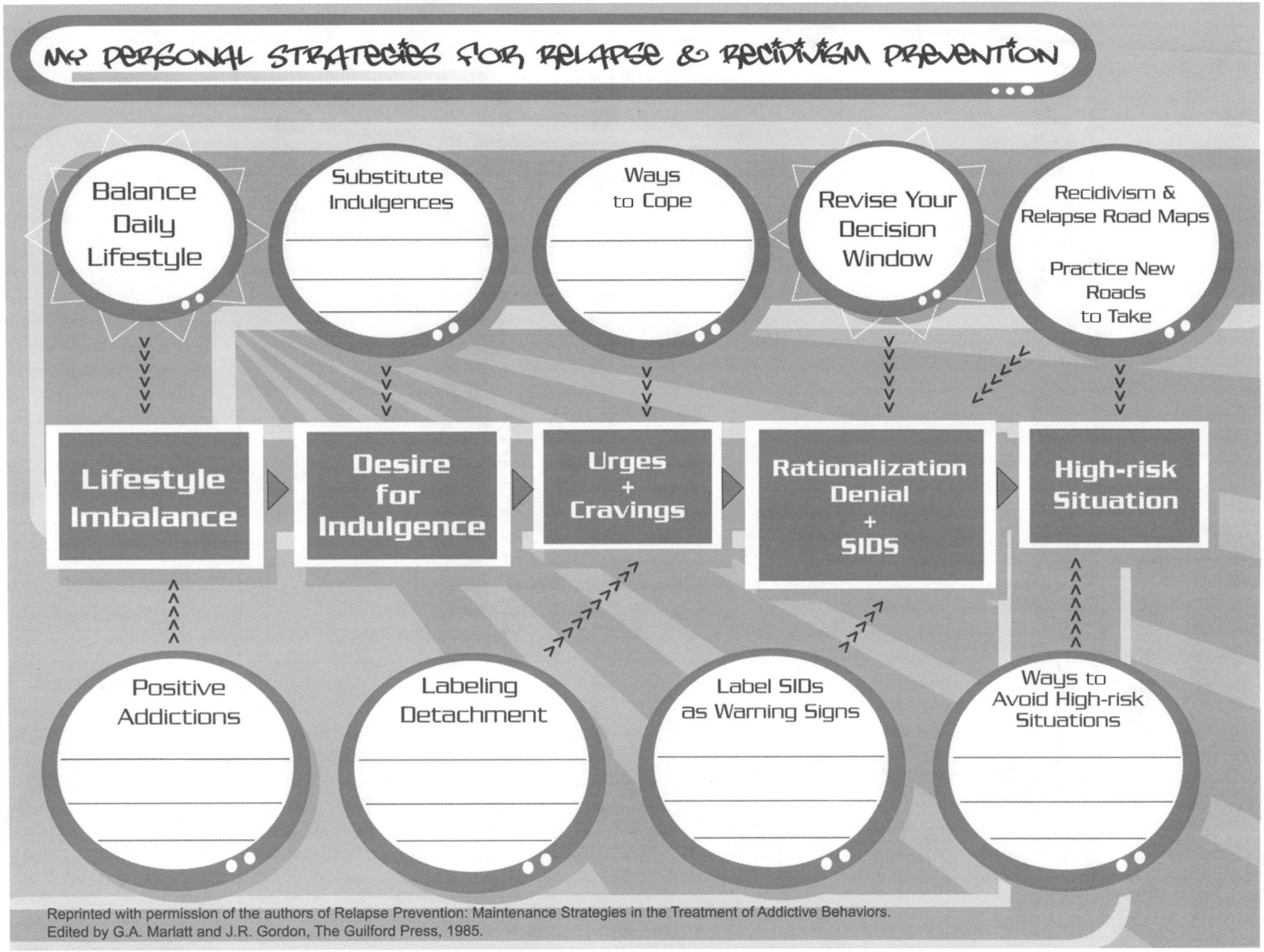

Reprinted with permission of the authors of Relapse Prevention: Maintenance Strategies in the Treatment of Addictive Behaviors. Edited by G.A. Marlatt and J.R. Gordon, The Guilford Press, 1985.

Worksheet 34

Worksheet 35

THE DECISION WINDOW

Decision Window for Alcohol or Drug Use and Abuse

	IMMEDIATE OUTCOME		DELAYED OUTCOME	
	POSITIVE	NEGATIVE	POSITIVE	NEGATIVE
LIVE AN ALCOHOL- AND DRUG-FREE LIFE				
CONTINUE TO USE ALCOHOL AND DRUGS				

Decision Window for Criminal Conduct

	IMMEDIATE OUTCOME		DELAYED OUTCOME	
	POSITIVE	NEGATIVE	POSITIVE	NEGATIVE
LIVE A CRIME-FREE LIFE				
CONTINUE TO COMMIT CRIMES AND OFFEND				

Putting It Together

- Zach really wants to *start over again,* but he's having some problems. What are some of the things that are causing Zach to become frustrated? What are some of his *thoughts* that could lead to RR?
- How is the story of the runaway train related to SIDs and PIG?
- Peer pressure tends to be a difficult HR situation to deal with. How is Zach dealing with the *peer pressure?*
- What are some of the thoughts *you catch yourself thinking* when it comes to your life?
- What are your plans to achieve a balanced lifestyle?

Using the Program Guides and Tools for Change

Rate the strength of your personal strategies for lifestyle balance and RR prevention.

0	1	2	3	4	5	6	7	8	9	10
Low					Medium					High

Indicate your ability to use the decision window to make important decisions about immediate and long-term outcomes of drug taking, thrill seeking, and a criminal lifestyle.

0	1	2	3	4	5	6	7	8	9	10
Low					Medium					High

SESSION 30: CRITICAL REASONING

Objectives

- Review Session 29: Staying Strong Without Drugs and Crime.
- Continue discussing critical reasoning.
- Review negotiation.
- Understand complaint making.
- Learn to decide the best for everyone involved.

Zach's Story: *My friend came to my work yesterday and was trying to convince me to get off early. I thought he was going to take me home, but he turned in the other direction. I wanted to go, but I knew where we were going and what we would end up doing. So at the stoplight I got out of the car. He told me to get back in, but I've had a year of being sober, and if I stay clean they'll reduce my community service. I told him that and started walking. He's my best friend, but I've got to keep an eye out for me first. It's just so hard sometimes.*

Runaway Train

And the young people see the gold engine and flag down the train. And they don't see what's happening, They don't know the pain. They can't hear the screams from the back of the train. Because the music is loud, and it has shut down the brain. So, they get on, they get on the runaway train, looking for dollars, and good times, and love, what a shame. Because it's a runaway train. It's going nowhere, and once you get on, it's going express. Check it out young people, last stop is death.

—excerpt from *The Runaway Train*
by Geoffrey Canada

Review of Lifestyle Balance

We have discussed *RR prevention* in several chapters up to this point. The reason for this is because once we are out of this program, most of us *return* to our old lives with the *same situations* that can make us think and feel how we used to. But in order to be *strong in our choices* and keep our freedom, we have to be prepared to *resist the cravings and urges* to go back to the way we were.

In order to do that, we should have a *plan that will be there* in case a situation arises unexpectedly. Last session, we discussed some *more signs of relapse and recidivism,* and we also discussed a few *more traps* that can lead us into the RR erosion pattern. Often we feel the pressure of what *we have to do* or what we *ought to do,* and we tend to think that harsh punishments and false promises are ruling our lives. This type of interpretation can lead to excuses for an action that we know will only cause us harm and negative consequences. As discussed in the last session, some common excuses are as follows:

- "I deserve more than this."
- "I work hard and don't get nowhere."
- "They have more than I do. I deserve as much as they do."
- "I deserve a good time. I've earned it."

When these excuses occur, our *choice and responsibility* for relapsing or reoffending become masked by SIDs, which begins the process of RR erosion. From our last session, Worksheet 34: My Personal Strategies for Relapse and Recidivism Prevention represents your skills to prevent the wearing away of your commitment to change. It shows a whole range of techniques and strategies for recognizing the situations and thinking habits/excuses that can lead to RR. Maintaining ownership of the change process requires using all the RR prevention strategies that you have learned in *Pathways to Self-Discovery and Change (PSDC).*

Activity: The Art of Reflection

On a piece of paper, draw situations in your life when you become **frustrated** or unhappy or that lead to **craving or urges** to participate in **substance use or crime.** Make sure to draw **facial expressions** (frowning or smiley faces) to show how you feel in the situations. Then draw some **alternative activities** that you can do to help you with those negative feelings and urges. Make sure the drawings represent you and your situation. Then go around the group and explain **what the drawings mean** and how you think you can **help yourself** get over the cravings and urges.

Of course, a major part of *avoiding RR* depends upon our *PIG* ability and our ability to make responsible decisions. SIDs can sneak up on us. We have learned and practiced skills to catch *ourselves* when we start to make *excuses for bad behavior* and *then drift into SIDs.* These important strategies and tools give us *much more strength* to avoid backsliding into old patterns of destructive behavior. An important part in *responsible decision making* is the ability to *think critically or logically* about our situation.

Critical Reasoning and Resolving Conflict

In Chapter 13: Problem Solving and Decision Making, we began discussing how to solve problems and make good decisions. We learned the importance of *getting all the facts, recognizing propaganda,* and *keeping our emotions from interfering* with a sensible decision. Because we are here in this program, all of us, to some extent, have failed to do either effectively. It is likely that we have used one or more of the following ineffective and sometimes harmful styles to deal with conflict or stress:

- **Fight.** Becoming aggressive and forceful in order to get our way, which only increases friction and conflict.
- **Flight.** Withdrawing or removing ourselves from the conflict or friction so that nothing is resolved.
- **Fake.** Going along with the other person while aggressively attacking them, leaving things up in the air.

These styles are *unhealthy,* and they usually lead us to not getting what we want or causing conflict with people around us. As we discussed in Session 12: Assertive Skills Development, **fair** (being *assertive* about what we want without attacking the other person) is the positive way to deal with any conflict. In order to be fair, though, we must use our critical reasoning.

Critical reasoning, which we started discussing in Session 28, is also considered *logical* or *rational* thinking. This means we look at the facts, *separate from our feelings* about the situation, and come up with a *resolution that benefits everyone* involved. Critical reasoning is an important part in both *problem solving* and *decision making.*

Resolving Conflict Through Win-Win Solutions

In order to solve a problem or make a decision to the benefit of everyone involved, there are certain skills that ensure an agreement can be reached and no one loses completely. This means that the result is a *win-win situation.*

- You tell the other person(s) your ideas about the problem or conflict.
- You ask the other person(s) what they think about the situation.
- You tell them why you think your idea is better or how you think the two ideas can be combined.
- You give them a chance to consider what you have said before expecting them to make up their mind.

Activity: A Debate Among Friends

Write your name on a piece of paper, and place it in a bag. If there is an odd number of people, the counselor will place his or her name in the bag as well. Randomly draw out your partner for this activity. The **two of you will sit in front of the group,** and the group will **think of a situation** for you to debate. The person who chooses the name out of the bag will be ***pro,*** or **for the situation,** and the person who had their name picked will be ***con,*** or **against the situation.** For example, the situation is **lowering the minimum drinking age from 21.**
Using the **win-win guidelines,** try to convince the other person that your side is correct. See if the debate team can arrive at a solution that includes **both people's point of view** (win-win). Remember to keep your emotions from interfering with the discussion, and be able to point out the differences between facts and opinions. Have the **group decide** whether the two people reached a solution where both sides were given fair consideration.

In order to become really effective at using the *guidelines for win-win solutions,* it is necessary to use *critical thinking* (getting the facts, recognizing propaganda, and keeping our emotions out of the picture). Here are a few more important elements to critical thinking that will benefit you in a conflict situation.

Important Elements of Critical Thinking

- **Words are important.** Our lives are filled with language and words. That is how we communicate with each other. But there can be a *breakdown in communication* if the *words* we are using *mean something different* to the other person.
- **People often don't say what they really mean.** Learn to recognize what people imply by what they are saying. Don't always *assume* you understand what is being said, and *ask questions* if you are not sure. There aren't any dumb questions, only dumb answers, so ask if they mean *what you think* they mean. This goes along with *words are important*; sometimes we don't always know what the other one is saying, but we can if we ask questions.
- **Listen to what people are assuming.** Everyone makes the mistake of *assuming something that is not true* at least once in a while. Remember to listen carefully to the feelings portrayed when a word is used, and pay attention to body language and facial expressions. Use your good communication skills (Chapter 3).
- **Fact versus opinion.** In Session 28: Decision Making, we discussed propaganda and how to recognize when it is being used. Often propaganda is used to sway us to another person's opinion. Here is how to *recognize opinion:*
  - Phrases that use words such as "In my opinion . . ." "I think . . ." or "It seems to me . . ."
  - *Emotional statements* such as "I hate that person"
  - *Extreme statements* or generalizations such as "He always does that"

Activity: The Act of Persuasion

Take a moment to look at Zach's story. What is his friend **trying to convince him** to do? What signs are there that Zach's friend is basing his argument on **opinion** and not fact? Does Zach use good **critical thinking** skills, and why or why not? Use as much detail as possible.

The Role of Negotiation in Critical Thinking

While the previously given skills help us to think *logically* and *rationally* in order to solve problems and make decisions, they will *not always* help us to resolve a situation to our liking. In fact, we will not be capable of resolving all conflicts easily or in our own manner. Negotiation, which we discussed in Chapter 7: Avoiding Trouble and Playing Fair, helps us to reach a *win-win* situation easier and with less friction. Here are some guidelines for how to negotiate to achieve a win-win solution.

Negotiation Guidelines

1. **Decide.** Decide what it is *you want and need* from the situation. Are you having a difference of opinion? Tell the other person your opinion, and then describe how you see the other person's position. Be careful not to attack or be aggressive.
2. **Listen.** Did you *understand* where *the other person* was coming from? Keep an open mind, and try not to let your beliefs build a wall against the other person.

3. **Think.** Think about the *other person's opinion* or position. What are the *options* or possible solutions that can benefit both? Your arsenal of solutions can be beneficial here.
4. **Suggest a compromise.** Can you suggest a *middle meeting ground* where both people will be happy?
5. **Discuss.** Discuss the *solutions* and *options* you have come up with, and decide which works *best for both people* involved.

Activity: The Role of Negotiation

Each person writes about a situation that **requires negotiation** in order to resolve it. Then break into groups of two or three, and randomly pick out one of the situations. Then as a group, **create a skit** in which the **negotiation is reached effectively.** The rest of the group will then discuss and evaluate how the negotiations were reached and how realistic the situation would be in the real world.

When Critical Thinking and Negotiation Fail

Sometimes *our conflicts* with other people *cannot be solved* fairly—even *through negotiation.* You may feel that someone is way out of line, *especially* at a workplace or at school. In order to *avoid negative consequences,* sometimes it can be necessary to *involve a third person.* This is not always easy, however, and can be a risk if not done correctly. Here are several steps for how to make a formal complaint successfully:

1. Find a way to *express your complaint clearly.* This means with logical thinking without an excess of emotion. Emotion will likely harm your case.
2. Find out who the *best person* to complain to is.
3. Decide on the *best time* and *place* to make the complaint.
4. Understand *how you would like to have the complaint resolved.* Tell the third person *what you want* from the situation and what you are not getting from the other person.
5. Listen to the *third person's response.* They have a more removed and objective view of the situation.
6. Try to offer *suggestions to resolve the problem* so you are taking an active part in the solution.

Activity: A Complaint Made

In Zach's story, who made the complaint? Why was the complaint made? Does Zach have a reason to make a complaint? What is the suggestion, if any, that Zach is making in order for his friend and him to hang out? Do you think his friend will respect his wishes? Why or why not?

SESSION 30: CRITICAL REASONING

In the event of conflict, it is most important to remain capable of critical reasoning. It is true that not all conflicts, problems, or decisions can be resolved to the satisfaction of all people involved. Certain situations will remain in conflict, and it becomes a *test of personal strength* to be patient and do what you can to avoid or reduce harm from the situation. We will not always get along with everyone, and not everyone is willing to negotiate and meet in the middle with us. It becomes a sign of our personal growth and change to *let some things be and walk away.*

Activity: Situations in Life

Your counselor will use a flipchart to record your answers. As a group, think of situations in your life that require **decision making, critical reasoning, negotiating,** and **problem solving.** Then, as a group, using the skills that you have practiced, think of solutions or **positive approaches** for the different situations. Are some situations easier to resolve than others? Why or why not? What solutions do you think will really work, and which ones don't seem like they would work all that well? How can you use the skills that we have been practicing to deal with some of the more difficult situations in your life?

Putting It Together

- Zach is trying to become a person who is *substance and crime free,* but his friend wants to take him somewhere that Zach knows isn't good. How did he try to tell his friend how he felt about the situation? How did Zach's friend react?
- After his friend didn't listen to him, what did Zach do? Did he have any other options, and if so, what were they?
- What situations are difficult for you? How might the skills of *decision making, problem solving, negotiating,* and *critical reasoning* help you to better deal with those situations?

Using the Program Guides and Tools for Change

Rate your ability to resolve conflict through win-win solutions.

0	1	2	3	4	5	6	7	8	9	10
Low					Medium					High

Indicate your ability to successfully use the guidelines presented in this chapter for successful negotiation when trying to resolve a disagreement.

0	1	2	3	4	5	6	7	8	9	10
Low					Medium					High

- With your counselor, continue to work on your Self-Portrait (SP) and Plan for Change (PFC).
- Update your Master Skills List (MSL) in the areas of *Conflict Resolution Skills* and *Negotiation Skills.*

ZACH'S STORY

I can't take it anymore. I am going to go crazy if I don't do something soon, and I'm afraid that what I'll do isn't going to be a good thing.

About a year ago, I was caught for grand theft auto. I had stolen a car from a house down the block while I was stoned and ended up getting into a wreck. At first I was just taking the car for a joyride. I would have it back before the owner, my parents' friend, ever knew that it was missing. Before I knew it, though, there were cops behind me pulling me over. I guess I wasn't driving straight or something. I don't know. I kind of panicked because I knew I would get in trouble for not only taking the car but for being stoned, too.

So I kept driving . . . and driving and driving, all the while trying to go faster than the cops until I bumped off the curb messing up the tires, alignment, and rims and then ran into a tree. While I sat on the curb, I couldn't believe the charges that were piling up against me—grand theft auto, minor under influence, destruction of public property, destruction of private property, resisting arrest, and on and on and on.

My parents bailed me out, and I had to meet with a probation officer before I came before the judge. She said according to my profile that I was an incipient drug addict and criminal, whatever *incipient* means. The judge looked over my profile, looked at my past record (which was just a bunch of kid stuff), and then ordered me into a treatment facility for 6 months, community service when I got out, and reparation for damages to the owner of the car and the tree.

So here I am, going to school so I can graduate within the next couple of years, and working after school at a chicken joint to pay back all the damages. And I'm not doing a single thing that's fun. I'm young, and I have all these things I want to do and no time to do them with. Because when I get home from work, I'm not to leave the house. My parents said I could consider it house arrest. I don't deserve this. I deserve to be having fun and being young while I still can. I don't even get to keep the money I earn. It all goes to other people. It's not fair.

But just because I'm not happy doesn't mean I don't want to do right. I don't want to be a common criminal my whole life. I don't want to be in the big house with all those murderers and rapists. I'm just a kid. I'm really trying to do right.

Yesterday my friend showed up at work. He asked me to take off early because there was something he wanted to give me. I told him I couldn't and that I had to work my full shift. He told me I was young and that I should be living life and no one would care if I played hooky for a day. But I said no. I couldn't do that. But I said he could give me a ride after work if he wanted.

So when he picked me up he told me he was going to take me somewhere. I told him that he should take me home. I had a drawing that I was working on. He just started driving in the other direction and said I would thank him for this. At the stoplight, I got out of his car. I really didn't want to get out, but I knew where we were going and what we would end up doing. He told me to get back in the car, and I told him I couldn't unless he was going to take me home. I have a year of being sober, and they say that if I'm good they'll reduce my community service time. Besides, I would really like to get into an art school when I graduate. I told my friend all that. And then I started walking away.

So last night my girlfriend called and asked why I dissed my friend like that. I told her I couldn't be around him if he was gonna risk my chances of being good. I like him and all, but there's a line that has to be drawn if he doesn't respect what I've got to do. He's my best friend, but I've got to keep an eye out for me first.

It's just so hard sometimes, though. I know what I've got to do. I know I did wrong and that I have to make it right somehow. But when my friends are talking about going to a football game or getting drunk at a party, I feel left out and like I don't have a life anymore. To tell you the truth, if this is what responsibility is I'm not sure I want to be responsible. But if I get less community service and into a good art school, it will be worth it.

Runaway Train by Geoffrey Canada

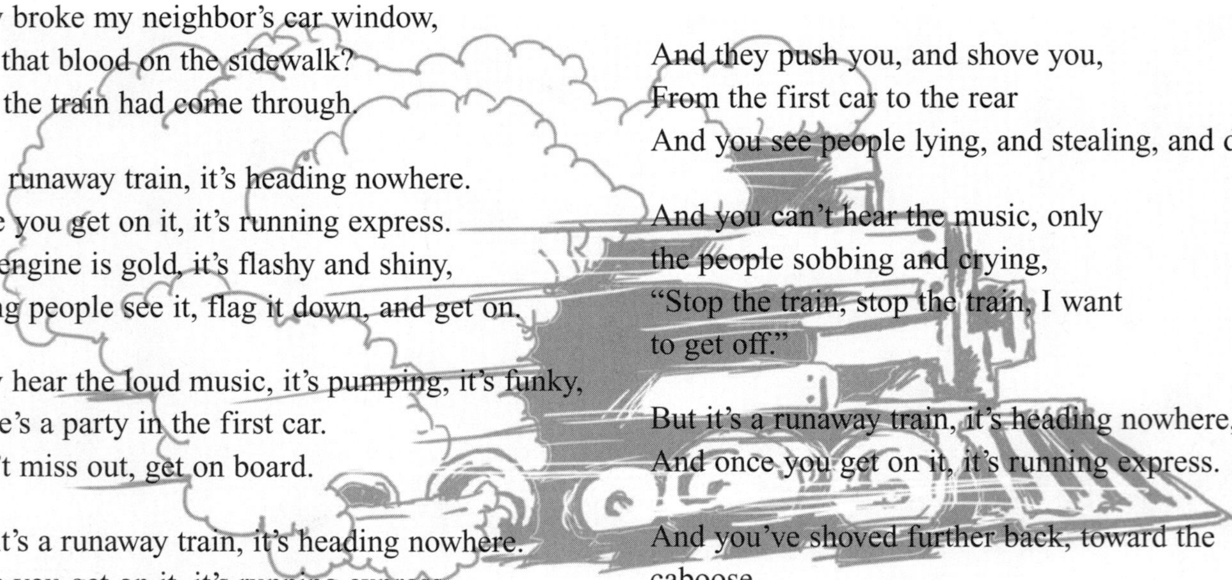

I woke up this morning, looked out my window,
Looking for signs of the runaway train.
My car was still there, no windows broken.
The train had come by, but I was spared.

When I came out of my doorway, I looked
around me.
All seemed quiet, but if you looked closely, you
could see the signs
Someone looked through the garbage,
They broke my neighbor's car window,
Was that blood on the sidewalk?
Yep, the train had come through.

It's a runaway train, it's heading nowhere.
Once you get on it, it's running express.
The engine is gold, it's flashy and shiny,
Young people see it, flag it down, and get on.

They hear the loud music, it's pumping, it's funky,
There's a party in the first car.
Don't miss out, get on board.

But it's a runaway train, it's heading nowhere.
Once you get on it, it's running express.

What runaway train? C'mon you'll see it.
The engine looks like a BMW, or an Iroc "Z."
The engineer looks like a homebody,
Dripping gold from his fingers,
His neck, his wrists, even his teeth.

The engine is that fat wad in Hector's pocket,
Or the Uzi that Kareem keeps by his pillow when
he sleeps.

The engine of the train always looks shiny,
Always holds promise of hundred dollar bills.

In the first car, there's always a party,
And it looks inviting.
They party all night and sometimes all day.

But that's a runaway train, it's heading nowhere,
And once you get on it, it's running express.

You see the engine, all bright and shiny,
I see the caboose, all filled with death.

Don't get on the train to go to that party.
Once you get on, they say, "Step on back."

And they push you, and shove you,
From the first car to the rear
And you see people lying, and stealing, and dying.

And you can't hear the music, only
the people sobbing and crying,
"Stop the train, stop the train, I want
to get off."

But it's a runaway train, it's heading nowhere,
And once you get on it, it's running express.

And you've shoved further back, toward the
caboose,
And you say, "Oh my God, there's a train on the
loose.

It's loaded with homeboys, Miguels, and the rest,
They're heading for prison, and jails, and for death.

And everyone screaming out the windows, "Stop,
stop,
Don't get on this train, can't you see, can't
you see!"

And the young people see the gold engine,
And flag down the train.

And they don't see what's happening,
They don't know the pain.
They can't hear the screams from the back of the train,
Because the music is loud and it has shut down the brain.

So, they get on, they get on the runaway train,
Looking for dollars, and good times, and love,
What a shame.

Because it's a runaway train, it's going nowhere,
And once you get on, it's going express.
Check it out young people, last stop is death.

Chapter Fifteen:

Stability and Growth

GOALS OF THIS CHAPTER

- Learn the importance of an emotional support system.
- Develop a plan for healthy leisure time activities.
- Learn how to fill our time with positive interests.
- Plan for the future.

LUKE'S STORY

Every day is a struggle. I was in a detention treatment center for about nine months after getting into some serious problems with the law. In the center, I spent a lot of time working with group therapy to change my thoughts, feelings, and actions. After my completion of the program, my probation officer, counselor, and I decided it was best that I didn't go back to my family, and now I'm out on my own. At first there was a sense of freedom, of control. I'm in a place of my own, I'm back in school, and I have a job. I don't really talk with my old friends all that much. I find myself becoming bored and depressed. When I'm not at school or work, I sit in this apartment staring at the television. What I really want to do is write.
The other day I was at my job, when a guy from my group therapy came in. He asked me to go have coffee with him. He began talking about how hard it is right now staying sober and on the right side of the law. A door opened for me. Suddenly I wasn't alone. Saturday we went into the mountains and took a small hike. He took out his guitar, and I just sat there taking deep breaths and relaxing. For the first time in weeks, I felt the urge to write. So now we make a point of spending at least one day a week together. He's convinced me to join a book club. I don't watch television much anymore. I spend that time writing. It's still really hard though. Every day is still a struggle. I just keep writing and thinking about how much better I feel now then I did then.

Lexi's Story

I was in a lock-down treatment center for nine months after some pretty serious problems with the law. My counselor and probation officer and I decided it was best if I didn't go back to my my drunk dad, psycho mom, and my little sister, who should probably be in a foster home.
I'm different now. So, it's easy for me to get lonely and depressed. When I'm not working or at school, all I do is sit in my apartment and stare at the T.V. In my dreams, I'd like to be an actress. I'd like to play roles of people with lives different than mine.
youth GROUP
A couple of days ago at work I ran into girl from my treatment group. We got coffee and she started talking about how she was having a hard time staying clean and out of trouble. She said she even feels depressed at the end of the day when she's alone. Right then I realized that I wasn't alone and I think she felt the same way. She mentioned going to church and asked if I wanted to go to a youth group meeting on my next day off. She started talking about how it's nice to meet people that are sober and to have fun just hanging out and playing games.
That Sunday we went to her youth group and when we got there the other kids were in the gym shooting baskets. We shot around with them until a lady who was in charge said it was time to play a group game. We had to tell everyone our name and act out something.
So I said my name and acted like I was on stage in a play and they all clapped, like I really was an actress. The leader said that I did a great job and so did a bunch of the kids. Since that first day, my friend and I go to youth group together. I'm getting used to the other kids and we've even been doing some skits.
One night a guy talked to some of us about getting into community theater. I got the feeling that I could do it. I'm signed up to be in the next show. I just keep practicing my lines and thinking about how much better I feel now than I did then.

SESSION 31: BUILDING COMMUNITY SUPPORT—FAMILY, FRIENDS, AND FUN TIME

Objectives

- Review Chapter 14: Lifestyle Balance.
- See how family can support your *Ownership of Change.*
- Understand how friends can support your plans for success.
- Discover how healthy ways to have fun can keep your lifestyle balance.

Luke's Story: *I was able to emancipate myself. So now I'm on my own in my own apartment with a job that pays the bills and less than a year of school left to go. But it's really hard. There is, I dunno, an empty space inside me—like something that was part of me is gone now. I started talking with a guy from my class, and we realized that we are dealing with some of the same problems. We decided to go on a hike together one day, and it was really enjoyable being out in the mountains while he played his guitar and I wrote. So now my life isn't just a job and school. Now I have things I enjoy and people I can share things with, even when I'm in the midst of an urge to do something I shouldn't.*

Lexi's Story: *My treatment team and I decided it was best if I didn't go back to my family. Since I'm almost 17, I was approved to get a place of my own. When I'm not working or at school, all I do is sit in my apartment and stare at the TV. In my dreams, I'd like to be an actress. I'd like to play roles of people with lives different than mine. A couple of days ago, I ran into a girl from my treatment group at work. She asked me to go to coffee with her. That Sunday we went to her youth group, which met at the community center. Since that first day, my friend and I have made it a point to go to youth group together. My boss even agreed to give me Sundays off just so I could go.*

A Reminder of Critical Reasoning and Its Importance

In Session 30, we continued our discussion about critical reasoning. Critical reasoning, also called logical or rational thinking, is what we use when we try to make a decision or solve a problem. Without critical reasoning, our thoughts, attitudes, and beliefs can begin to get in the way of finding a solution that works.

The first goal of critical thinking is to find a win-win situation. That means that everyone in the situation has gained something from the solution, and everyone is happy with the results. In order to do that, we must first do the following:

- Share our ideas with the other person.
- Ask the other person what they think about the situation, and be sure to actively listen to their response.
- Offer them a reason why our idea is better or a way to combine the two situations.
- Give them time to absorb and think about the information before making a decision.

It is important in this event that we pay attention to the words that are being used, especially a difference of meanings; the assumptions that both people are making about the situation; and that we know the difference between the facts and the opinions of the situation.

Of course, not every situation can be a win-win. That is when the negotiation skills we learned in Chapter 7 and Session 30 (in Chapter 14) will become useful. Finding a compromise, or a settlement, that both parties are willing to accept becomes the main goal of the problem solving.

As life has taught most of us, though, not all problems can be solved to the satisfaction of both parties. It is sometimes helpful to get a third party involved. In making a complaint, be sure to use critical, unemotional thinking with the facts and not very many opinions. It is important that the other person does not think that you are using propaganda to sway them to your side.

A Change in Lifestyle

We have worked hard on learning about ourselves and on how to change our lives to become a healthier and more responsible person in the community. Making these changes means that we are committing ourselves to staying away from drug use and criminal behavior.

In the past, drug use and criminal activities have been a large part of our life. They have taken up a lot of space in our life. They have been part of our identity—but it has been a *negative identity.* Committing to change means that we commit ourselves to replacing drug use and crime and *finding positive resources* to support our change. These resources may be in our family, in positive friends; and in fun, pleasurable, and healthy activities. This session will explore how these can become resources to support your *Ownership of Change.*

Family as a Support for Change

Some of you may think, "My family is so messed up that it can't support me in my Ownership of Change." Others will think, "Yes, my family can become a support for my change and growth." In this session, we will do a quick study of your family to see if it can become a source of support for you and, if so, to see how you can build on the strengths of that support. If you conclude that it cannot be a source of support, then we will look at ways you can find support in adult caring relationships that can take the place of your primary family.

First, look at how you rated yourself on the Degree of Family Disruption, Lack of Family Closeness, and Lack of Family Support scales on your Self-Portrait (SP). If you scored in the high or even moderate range, then you may want to ask for further help and counseling in the area of family and parent relationships. Some of you are or have been in a multifamily group or individual family therapy.

Now, let's take a look at your family. First, we will do a *family sculpture* to see how and whether your family can give you positive and healthy support for your change goals. At the end of this exercise, you will be asked to come to the conclusion as to whether you *can* or *cannot* depend on your family (or some members of your family) to support your Ownership of Change.

SESSION 31: BUILDING COMMUNITY SUPPORT—FAMILY, FRIENDS, AND FUN TIME

Activity: A Sculpture Study of Your Family

Break into two groups. Then you are asked to have members of the group **represent the members of your family.** Identify who those family members are. Then **place them in a position** to show whether you **can count** on these members to give you support in your effort to change. If a member represents your father and you cannot count on him supporting you, then put him at a distance away from you. If you have a sister that will be a positive source of support, put her close to you. Then place the family members to show whether they support each other. If you think that neither your father nor mother can be counted on to support you but they support each other, then place them close to each other but at a distance from you. When you have finished, **come to the conclusion** as to whether you will try to seek support from any of your family members or from your family as a whole. Get some feedback from group members as to what they think you should do.

If you decide that you will seek support from certain family members or from the family as a whole, then here are some ways to do this:

- **Make amends.** Take an honest look at how your involvement in drugs and criminal conduct (CC) caused problems with your family, and share with them your intent to change and that you understand the stress and grief your behavior might have caused them.
- **Use the thought-changing skills from this program.** This will lead to better outcomes in your relationships with your family.
- **Use the communication skills from this program.** Use *active listening* and *active sharing* in your desire to seek your family's support and build more positive relationships with your family.
- **Ask your counselor for at least two family counseling sessions.** If you have not already done this, for the purpose of "clearing the air," making amends, defining your needs for support and then develop a family plan to achieve this.

Ways to Find Support Outside of Your Family Unit

There are some families that are *not supportive* and would do us more harm than good in our road to a healthy life. If you conclude that, at this time, you will *not be able to count on* family members or from the family as a whole to support your Ownership of Change, then here are some ways to find support in adult caring relationships that can take the place of your primary family.

First, you may want to *further explore* whether your family can be a source of support by requesting at least one counseling session with family members to look at this issue and to *share with them* that you think you will be *unable to count on them* to support your *Ownership of Change.* If you think such a session will do more harm than good, don't do it. If you still think that your family will not be a source of support for you, you can do these things:

- Seek out and build other adult sources of support and trust, which could be *other relatives in your life* such as an uncle, aunt, and grandparent.
- Build positive relationships with *other adults* who are *good role models* and who support your goals for change. These could include your counselor or your probation worker.
- Become part of a *strong support group* such as Alcoholics Anonymous (AA), a church group, or another community group that is positive and that will support your goals for change.

Positive Friends Are a Source of Support

Friends can also be a source of support for you. Yet some of your past or current friends **will not understand and cannot support your goals for change**—*your goals to live a crime- and drug-free life.* Finding new friends who support these goals may be a very difficult part of your lifestyle change. The first important step will be to take an honest look at your friends and friendship patterns. This will give you an idea of how much change you will need to make in your friends and how difficult this will be.

Activity: A Sculpture of Your Friends

Ask members of the group to represent the **friends** you have in your life. Sort these friends into four groups: (1) those who are **involved in using (or selling) drugs,** (2) those who are **involved in doing crimes,** (3) those who **do both,** and (4) those **who are positive** and who are not and will not be involved in doing drugs or crime.

Now take groups 1, 2, and 3 and **put them at a distance from you**—as far away as you can. As you do this, say out loud the **assertiveness skills** (from Session 12) and **refusal skills** (from Session 14) you have learned in this program to distance yourself from these friends. Have the group help you with how to do this and what skills to use. Then, select some other group members to represent **positive friends**—and put them in group 4. What skills will you use to develop and build up group 4?

Trust is an important part of finding support from your family or from other family-like adults or groups. We hope that you have been able to develop trust with the people in this group as well as learned the *importance of trust* in relating to your community and society at large. Trust is a big part of developing closeness and intimacy, and trusting people who are around us will help us to live a substance- and crime-free life.

Activity: A Circle of Support

As a group, take a look at Luke's and Lexi's stories. What is the situation with Luke and his family? How has Luke been able to **build a support system** without a family? Do you think this support system is healthy for Luke? Why or why not? Where does trust fit in for Luke? In what ways is Luke's situation similar to Lexi's? How has Lexi been able to **build a support system**?

SESSION 31: BUILDING COMMUNITY SUPPORT—FAMILY, FRIENDS, AND FUN TIME

As we have said earlier, drug use and criminal activities have been a large part of your life. Without these activities, we might find ourselves being *lonely, depressed,* or *even bored.* Being lonely or bored may also cause us to have urges and cravings to participate in crime and drug use. Support from *family, caring adults, community or school groups,* and *good friends* will help us stay committed to change; replace drug use and crime; and deal with being lonely, depressed, or bored.

Another way to fill that space of drug use and criminal activities is to *replace them with healthy, fun, and pleasurable activities.* These activities will support our goals for change and will help us deal with the boredom or loneliness. Yet we might be so bent on reaching our goals for change that we get caught up in only doing the things we "should" or "ought" to do that we fail to take time to have fun and to take part in healthy play. Healthy or fun play is an *alternative* to the "grindstone" of doing what "we must" to prevent relapse and recidivism (RR). Those *shoulds* and *oughts* can lead to unhealthy ways of coping with increasing levels of stress and unhappiness. Making *healthy choices for fun living* will help us meet our *goals for change* and lead a crime- and drug-free life.

Activity: My Personal Interests

Take a moment to look at Worksheet 36. Then fill in the interest and desire you have to participate in the activities listed with a number of 0 to 4. What are some of those things that you did while on substances? Do any of these things on the worksheet have to do with crime? Can you see yourself doing some of these things in your free time?

There are four broad areas of interest that most people fall into. Although some people will be strong in more than one area of interest, most of us are strong in one area specifically. These areas are as follows:

1. Physical expression.
2. Focus on self (relaxing activities).
3. Artistic or aesthetic activities.
4. Group harmony or doing things with others.

Activity: Scoring Our Interests

Take all your scores from Worksheet 36, and then fill out Worksheet 37. This worksheet is intended to show you your specific interests, as well as how strong your interest is in each of the four broad areas. This allows you to have a guideline to what activities will keep you interested and motivated, as well as keep your boredom down and your happiness up.

Worksheet 36

THE PERSONAL PLEASURE INVENTORY

Using one of the five choices below, rate the following items as to degree of pleasure that you derive from each activity. Place the appropriate number corresponding to your choice in the blank line opposite the item. Then put the total score for each group of items.

0 = Never engaged in activity or no pleasure derived from activity
1 = Low degree of pleasure derived
2 = Moderate degree of pleasure derived
3 = High degree of pleasure derived
4 = Very high degree of pleasure derived

1. Sports
------ Playing basketball
------ Wrestling
------ Playing sports
------ Playing softball
------ Going to football games
------ Playing rough games
------ Playing football or soccer
------ Playing volleyball
Total Score________

2. Challenging Nature
------ Rock climbing
------ Canoeing
------ White water rafting
------ Camping out
------ Hiking
------ Skiing
Total Score________

3. Physical Fitness
------ Eating healthy
------ Exercising
------ Biking
------ Working out
------ Running
Total Score________

4. Romance
------ Holding hands
------ Being physically close
------ Kissing and hugging
------ Going on a date
Total Score ________

5. Soothing Sensations
------ Listening to soft music
------ Warming self by fire
------ Soaking in hot tub
------ Having back rubbed
------ Getting a massage
------ Eating at a nice restaurant
Total Score ________

6. Material Comforts
------ Making money
------ Buying clothes
------ Spending money
------ Going out for an evening
------ Improving how you look
Total Score________

7. Seeking Adventure
------ Driving to new places
------ Visiting different cities
------ Experiencing new places
------ Experiencing new things
------ Traveling to foreign cities
------ Visiting different cultures
Total Score________

8. Experiencing Nature
------ Being in nature
------ Being in the woods
------ Watching wildlife
------ Watching the stars
------ Watching the sun rise
Total Score________

9. Fun at Home
------ Redecorating a room
------ Helping around the house
------ Doing home projects
------ Having friends over
------ Hanging out in the yard
Total Score ________

10. Reflective Relaxation
------ Meditating
------ Doing relaxation exercises
------ Self-reflecting
------ Writing in a journal
Total Score ________

11. Artistic Stimulation
------ Going to the movies
------ Going to a concert
------ Creating artwork
------ Reading books
------ Writing poetry
------ Playing a musical instrument
Total Score________

12. Mental Exercise
------ Playing word games
------ Playing cards or board games
------ Solving puzzles
------ Playing fantasy games
------ Playing video games
Total Score________

13. People Closeness
------ Helping family members
------ Playing with children
------ Being with family
------ Spending time with friends
------ Instant messaging with friends
------ Being with a significant other (SO)
Total Score________

14. Religious Involvement
------ Doing spiritual thinking
------ Worshipping
------ Participating in a Bible study
------ Doing church work
------ Going to church
------ Praying
Total Score ________

15. Helping Cithers
------ Counseling others
------ Helping friends
------ Teaching others
------ Volunteering services
------ Writing letters to friends or family
Total Score ________

When you have finished scoring all your responses, place the total score for each scale on the next worksheet in the appropriate box under the Raw Score column. Then find your raw score on the row for each scale in order to find your percentile rank for that scale. The percentile rank shows you the degree of pleasure that you derive from each orientation compared with others. For example, if your raw score for Material Comforts is 17, then you enjoy this category 80% more than most people.

Worksheet 37

PERSONAL PLEASURE INVENTORY PROFILE

Name: Date:

Gender: ☐M ☐F Age:

	Scale Name	Raw Score	1	2	3	4	5	6	7	8	9	10
			Low			Low-Medium		Medium-High			High	
			DECILE RANK									
PHY EXP	1. Sports		0 2 3 4	5 6 7	8 9 10	11 12	13	14 15	16 17	18 19 20	21 22 23	24 26 32
PHY EXP	2. Challenging Nature		0 2 3 5	6 7	8	9 10	11 12	13	14 15	16 17	18 19	20 21 24
SELF FOCUS	3. Physical Fitness		2 5 6 7	8	10	11		12	13	14	15	16 18 20
SELF FOCUS	4. Romance		1 6 8 9	10 11 12	13	14	15	16	17	18		19 20
SELF FOCUS	5. Soothing Sensations		4 10 11	12 13 14	15	16	17	18	19	20	21 22	23 24
SELF FOCUS	6. Material Comforts		4 7 8 9	10 11	12	13	14	15	16	17	18	19 20
AESTHETIC DISCOVERY	7. Seeking Adventure		4 7 8 9	10 11 12	13	14 15	16	17 18	19	20 21	22	23 24
AESTHETIC DISCOVERY	8. Experiencing Nature		1 6 7 8	9 10	11	12	13	14	15	16 17	18	19 20
AESTHETIC DISCOVERY	9. Fun at Home		0 1 2	3	4	5 6	7	8	9	10	11 12 13	14 15 19
AESTHETIC DISCOVERY	10. Reflective Relaxation		0 1 2	3	4	5	6	7	8	9 10	11 12	13 15 20
AESTHETIC DISCOVERY	11. Artistic Stimulation		0 2 3	4 5 6	7	8	9	10 11	12	13 14	15 16 17	18 20 24
COLLECT HARMONY	12. Mental Exercise		0 2 3	3 4	5	6	7		8	9	10 11	12 14 20
COLLECT HARMONY	13. People Closeness		4 11 12	13 14	15 16	17	18	19	20	21	22	23 24
COLLECT HARMONY	14. Religious Involvement		0	1 2	3	4 5	6	7 8	9 10	11 12	13 14 15	16 19 24
COLLECT HARMONY	15. Helping Others		1 6 7	8	9	10	11	12	13	14	15	16 17 20
	PERCENTILE	0	10	20	30	40	50	60	70	80	90	100

SESSION 31: BUILDING COMMUNITY SUPPORT—FAMILY, FRIENDS, AND FUN TIME

The emphasis on the personal pleasure inventory worksheet is that the more we know about what we like and take interest in, the easier it will be to find happiness without drugs and crime. The best thing about these interests, though, is that they give us the choice and freedom within them instead of making us give our freedom away. Instead of believing the drug will make us happier or the crime will give us more, we are deciding what we can do to make ourselves happier and give us more.

Some of these interests, though, can be done with other people. When we share an interest with someone—or if we participate in an activity with someone—we are not only more likely to do that activity but we also grow closer to the other person. The emptiness of not using substances or participating in crime comes in part from missing the friends we used to do those things with. Taking part in an activity will also bring us in contact with more people who share the same interests as we do outside of substances and crime, allowing our circle to grow larger and our support system to become stronger. The more we share with a person, the more we are likely to trust a person. The more people we know who we don't associate with substance use or criminal behavior means, the more people we have to turn to when things are bringing us down.

Activity: Leisure Time Together

When looking at Luke's story, which broad area of interest do you think Luke fits in? What about Lexi? Keep in mind that you can have more than one area of interest. How has Luke's friend helped Luke develop a schedule that makes him feel more content? Do you think that Luke would have done those things by himself? Why or why not? How did Lexi find the support to participate in her areas of interest?

Making Time

One difficult thing is having enough time to do the things that interest us while still taking care of what needs to be done. As we mentioned earlier and in Session 29, often things that we are required to do begin to take over our lives so that we can no longer do what we want to do. This causes us to become frustrated and depressed, which often leads to problems of instant gratification (PIG) and seemingly irrelevant decisions (SIDs), resulting in RR. In order to avoid this imbalance, there are three key ideas to keep in mind:

1. **Prioritize.** Always keep in mind what is the most important thing at the moment and for the future. Instead of picking up the extra shift in order to have more money, go out for a picnic with friends. It is true the money can be important, especially in getting some of the material things we want, but our mental happiness and contentment is often more important than material things.
2. **Work out a schedule.** Set aside time every day for personal time that can be used toward an interest that is separate from things that have to be done. School and work are important but so is just one hour a day for things that interest you and make you happy.

3. **Don't overschedule.** While it is important to have a schedule in order to have personal time, make sure that you aren't on the go all the time. People need some downtime; otherwise, they can become stressed and anxious, which can lead to substance use. Leave time for relaxation and rest.

Activity: Leisure Time Activities

Break into groups of three or four, and fill out Worksheet 38, Leisure Time Activities, with all the activities you can think of outside of school and work. Then decide how many times a month the activity can be participated in and whether it replaces substance use or criminal activities. Then individually write a list of activities you would be interested in taking part in that would replace your own substance use or criminal participation. While you are writing down the activities, think of how long each activity would take and how you might rearrange your schedule in order to fit it into your life. Don't forget to place it where you think it would go in your priority list.

Putting It Together

- Luke and Lexi are having problems with sadness and loneliness. How has their support system helped each of them? What interests have they found that are more satisfying than drugs or crime?
- Who is part of your support system, and how close do you feel to them?
- What are your specific interests outside of what you have to do? How can you fit those into your schedule?
- How can you become closer to people you trust and admire?

Using the Program Guides and Tools for Change

Rate your commitment to participate in *personal interests* that will provide fun and satisfaction without the problems that come with using substances, committing crimes, or participating in dangerous, thrill seeking activities.

0	1	2	3	4	5	6	7	8	9	10
Low					Medium					High

Show your level of commitment to form a health support network to remain drug and crime free.

0	1	2	3	4	5	6	7	8	9	10
Low					Medium					High

Worksheet 38

Leisure Time Activities

List the leisure time activities that you are now taking part in. In the second column, write down how many times a month you do these activities. In the third column, check the activity that has replaced drinking alcohol and drug use time or activities.

Leisure Time Activities	Times a Month	Replaces Alcohol and Other Drug (AOD) Use

SESSION 32: PLANNING FOR THE FUTURE

Objectives

- Review Session 31: Building Community Support—Family, Friends, and Fun Time.
- Discuss the difference between work and a job or school.
- Understand how to be at your best: in relationships with family or friends, at work or school, and in your personal interests and leisure time activities.
- Plan for your future.

Luke's Story: *When I'm not in school, I bus tables for a living. It's a job, and it helps pay the bills and put cash in my pockets, but what I really want to do is write. It wasn't until we went hiking, though, that I really had a chance to write. My friend convinced me to submit some of my stuff to be published. One even got accepted, so now I'm working on my application to a school for writing, and if I keep getting my submissions accepted, I can quit my job. Now there is a chance that I can do what I want and what I'm good at for the rest of my life.*

Lexi's Story: *So I'm signed up to be in the next show, and the director says that I have real talent. She says that if I get through the production and decide to do more, she'll spend some time helping me prepare individually. Maybe she'd even write me a recommendation for the theater program at the local college—once I graduate high school, of course. It's still hard to stay focused on my dream, and I have to keep reminding myself that I won't achieve it if I'm using. I still miss some of my old friends and the old times, but I'm not as lonely as I used to be. I just keep practicing my lines and thinking about how much better I feel now than I did then.*

A Look Back at Support and Leisure Activities

In Session 31, we discussed some of the difficulties that will be facing us once we're out of this program. Up to this point, we have been learning and practicing knowledge and skills that will help us maintain the change and growth that began in this program. In Session 29, we began talking about how, even when we think we are doing the right things by working all the time, we can be setting ourselves up for an RR episode. So in the last session we started discussing how we can avoid the loneliness, depression, and boredom that can come from a lack of balance in our lifestyles.

In order to maintain a balance in our lives, there are certain things that we must make an effort to develop and maintain:

- A support system that consists of family or friends, as long as they are people we trust and care about.
- Activities that we can become interested in mentally and physically that do not involve substance use or crime.
- A schedule of priorities so we always know what is most important to us.
- Personal time to take us away from the things that have to be done sometimes, even if they are not fun.

As long as we have these things set into our schedules and lives, then it will be easier to maintain balance and control in the changes we've made to our lives.

Activity: My Balance

Take a moment to fill out Worksheet 39: Personal Time. List the interests or activities that you did this past week. Then write down the time on the day that you did the activity and how you felt after the activity was finished. How did you schedule your time this past week? Do you think you included enough interests, or do you think you did only what you have to do?

Break into groups of three and four, and compare the activities and time spent on them. Who spent more time on things they enjoy? Compare how people feel when they are doing things they enjoy. How can you help each other schedule more interests? What are some of the common interests you have?

Another aspect of maintaining balance is understanding our strengths and weaknesses in order to find a future path that will help us maintain our new control and freedom. In order to do that, we must first know what our interests and abilities are, separate from our jobs or school, and how to develop our work into something we are happy doing.

A Difference in Terms

Productive and meaningful work, doing something that we enjoy, is a strong alternative to substance use and crime. Although school is considered work, it is often not something that we think expresses ourselves and who we are. In fact, many people work to pay bills or buy things or because we have to, not because we see it as a productive and healthy aspect of our identity. Often work and job/school mean the same thing, but in truth there is a difference between our work and going to school.

Our work (a combination of our interests and abilities—Luke's work is writing and Lexi's is acting) is a physical or mental activity and effort that is directed toward accomplishing or gaining something. Work is made up of our talents and desires in order to practice our skills and earn a livelihood. We own and control our work; it is ours and ours only.

School is just given to us in order to find and fulfill our work. One example of a person's work may be art. Let's say that you like to draw, write, or play guitar. That is your work. But if you only go to school to socialize and you are not in any classes that help develop your skills, then school is not giving you a healthy place to fulfill your work. Your work, art, writing, guitar, snowboarding, etc., is a way to define your lifestyle.

Worksheet 39

Personal Time

First, write down several pleasant activities that you believe you would enjoy doing in the next week. On the following chart, plan 30 to 60 minutes each day that you reserve as your own personal time. Make the time for this in advance. When the time comes, decide which of the things from the list that was given in the A Look Back at Support and Leisure Activities section you want to do and take time to do it. Write down what you did and how it felt to do something for yourself.

Healthy Activities

____

____

____

____

	Personal Time	Activity and Recreation
Monday		
Tuesday		
Wednesday		
Thursday		
Friday		
Saturday		
Sunday		

Activity: Story of Work

Break into pairs or groups of three in order to write two short made-up stories: One will be about a person who enjoys their work, their interests, and abilities and the other will be about a person who is unhappily involved with their job or school. Be sure to include what each person is thinking or feeling in their situation.

Effectively Working

It would be nice if everyone could find a job or classes in which they can do their work in the best manner possible. And the truth is, we can find a school or skills training environment that supports our work. But it is not something that falls into our laps.

In order to find a situation that fits our work, we first must be effective in developing our work. Dr. Stephen R. Covey is famous for what he calls the *seven habits of highly effective people,* and the following list summarizes his findings.

These habits can help us develop our work to the best of our ability, and then open doors to find the classes, school, or job that fits our work.

1. **Take a positive approach.** Take responsibility for your life by having a personal vision of what you want to accomplish. Set goals for yourself.
2. **Have your long-term goals in mind.** After you have set goals, achieve them. Take personal leadership of yourself, and know that no one will get you there but yourself.
3. **Do what is most important first.** Prioritize. You manage your time, energies, and focus in order to achieve your goals. This is considered personal management.
4. **Think win-win.** Even work like art and professional sports include working with other people in the job situation. Remember what we talked about in decision making and problem solving, and think of how to solve every situation to the best of everyone involved.
5. **Understand other people's points of view.** In Session 16, we talked about empathy: putting yourself in other people's shoes. To effectively work with other people, we must first understand where they are coming from.
6. **Combine your resources.** The whole of something is more than the sum of its parts, meaning going to school as an artist isn't a means of living unless there are mentors, advisors, and professors/teachers. By working together with other people, we can go further than by ourselves.
7. **Achieve a lifestyle balance.** This means keeping yourself in balance physically, mentally, emotionally, and spiritually. Refer back to Session 31 to remember how to maintain balance.

SESSION 32: PLANNING FOR THE FUTURE

Activity: Work Versus Job

In Luke's story, he mentions that his job is busing tables, but writing is really what he likes to do. What is Luke doing to further his goals? What goals has Luke set for himself? Of the just-listed seven habits of effective people, how many has Luke achieved for himself? What can he do to make himself more effective? What kind of education will most likely prepare Lexi for the kind of work she will enjoy throughout her life?

So How Do We Know What Our Work Is?

Now we know how to work effectively in order to achieve our goals and find a situation that matches our talents and desires. But we will begin to figure out what it is that we consider our work. As we've said, work does not have to mean your school or job. Our work can be drawing, playing an instrument, learning, thinking, or even building something or tearing something down. Whatever we desire to do that will benefit us in healthy ways and makes us content and excited to do it can be considered our work.

Activity: And My Work Is. . .

Take a moment to fill out Worksheet 40: What is Your Work? in order to identify what your work is. First, **give a name to the work you do.** It can be anything from *rap artist* to *basketball player*, but first a name must be given to it. Then think of all that is contained within your work. All that is physically, mentally, and emotionally involved in your work should be written down. An example is your work as a student. Being a student means you have to take notes, listen to the teacher, respond to questions with thoughtful answers, think about what you have learned, apply it to the outside world, and try to come up with other ideas based on what you have learned. Break into groups of two or three, and discuss with each other your individual work. How can each of you apply the seven skills to your work? What job or school goals can you think of that your work can be applied to?

It is okay—and actually really important—for us to feel pride in our work. We don't have to like our situations, but we can love our work and what we do with ourselves. Make sure you can feel the power and freedom in having pride in what you do for work and how it makes you feel.

Matching Work With School

So now we have an idea of what our work is, where our talents lie, and what we want to do with ourselves. The difficult thing now is finding classes, a school, a training program, or a job that we can align with our work in order to feel mental well-being and to achieve our goals. Not only does finding a situation that matches our work help us achieve our goals but it also plays a major part in building and maintaining a healthy lifestyle. When we are fulfilled through what we are doing with our lives, there is a lot less risk or desire to search for that fulfillment through negative means. The following are skills that

Worksheet 40

WHAT IS YOUR WORK?

First, give a name to your work. The following are some examples: Artist, Writer, Poet, Scientist, Family Provider, Athlete, Student. Then write down everything you think of that defines your work or the important parts of your work. Use extra paper if you run out of room in this Worksheet.

NAME OF MY WORK:

LIST WHAT DEFINES YOUR WORK OR THE IMPORTANT PARTS OF YOUR WORK

can help us get into the school or a situation we want that matches our work. Keep in mind that school can be considered a job, and some schools require the same application process as a traditional job.

1. **Developing a resume.** A resume describes your work history and your desire for work. In order to be effective, it has to be neat, typed, and accompanied by a cover letter. For school purposes, this can be part of your statement of purpose. Try not to leave large open periods of time. Explain periods of inactivity with phrases such as "I was searching for a situation that defined me."
2. **Filling out the job/school application.** This is where you emphasize your personal strengths and strong skills. In a school application, it can be helpful to say that you are good at writing, or you like participating in class, or you do something that will set you apart from other applicants.
3. **Doing research.** This means finding schools that are specifically designed to reach your goal. Keep after it until you succeed, and make sure to use your support system (family, friends, counselor, etc.) to help you with the disappointment if you don't get accepted and then get inspired to try someplace else.
4. **Developing telephone skills.** The telephone is used to set up interviews, discover information needed, and to present yourself to a future employer or school. Make sure to introduce yourself to the person who answers the phone, ask to speak with the specific person to answer your needs, and then introduce yourself again to the next person. Make sure that the person you are speaking with knows who you are and the purpose of the phone call.
5. **Interviewing.** Both companies and most schools interview before hiring or accepting prospective candidates, and it can be important to be prepared. In order to be prepared, rehearse for the interview and keep in mind that you are trying to sell your work and your purpose. Know that just because you are not selected to be in one school does not mean there isn't one that is just as good, if not better, still out there waiting for you.
6. **Setting goals.** Most important, in all of what we have been trying to teach, is setting goals for where you are going and where you want to be. Use long-term and short-term goals in order to set a plan that is realistic. Keep in mind that the goals have to be realistic in order to be achieved.

Activity: A Plan for the Future

Individually work on Worksheet 41: School and Work Plan for the Next Three Years in order to set a **plan for your future.** Be sure to include short-term goals as well as long-term objectives in your plan. Think about how you might go about things in order to achieve your objectives. Then get into a circle with the larger group, and one by one, discuss your **individual plans for the next 3 years.** Are the goals realistic? What is the person going to do tomorrow or the next day to begin achieving the goals? What is the order in which things have to be obtained, or what are the separate objectives that can be attained at the same time? Remember, only you have control over what you do. You may decide to change your goals at any time. What is important is that you begin to think about planning for a healthy and happy future.

SCHOOL AND WORK PLAN FOR THE NEXT THREE YEARS

List your specific objectives for education, school, and work for the next 3 years.

LIST SPECIFIC OBJECTIVES IN SCHOOL AND WORK PLAN FOR THE NEXT 3 YEARS

SESSION 32: PLANNING FOR THE FUTURE

Putting It Together

- Do you think Luke has a realistic goal for his future? Why or why not? How has Luke made himself more effective?
- What about Lexi? Is she likely to have a future in acting? Has she found her real work?
- What can you do to help yourself maintain the changes you have made?
- What are your goals for the future?
- How has this program helped you to develop a healthy identity?

Using the Program Guides and Tools for Change

Rate your ability to plan healthy and pleasant activities that you will regularly enjoy.

0	1	2	3	4	5	6	7	8	9	10
Low					Medium					High

Show your understanding of what kind of work will be most satisfying for you.

0	1	2	3	4	5	6	7	8	9	10
Low					Medium					High

Indicate your degree of commitment to follow through with your 3-year plan for school and work

0	1	2	3	4	5	6	7	8	9	10
Low					Medium					High

- With your counselor, update and review all aspects of your SP, Plan for Change (PFC), and Master Skills List (MSL).
- Remember that your PFC is always a work in progress. As you continue on your journey through life, you will always be on your **Pathway to Self-Discovery and Change.**

Congratulations! You Have Done a Great Job! Good Luck for Your Future!

LUKE'S STORY

Every day is a struggle. Some days I just want to give up and get drunk or stoned, but other days everything seems all right and that I can make it at least another day.

I was in a detention treatment center for about 9 months after getting into some serious problems with the law. In the center, I spent a lot of time working with group therapy to change my thoughts, feelings, and actions. To some extent, I've learned that I'm the one in control of what I do.

After my completion in the program, my probation officer, counselor, and I decided it was best that I didn't go back to my family—or at least what technically is referred to as my family. Mainly it's just my drunk father, crazy mother, and a little brother that should be in a foster home. Since I'm 16, I was able to emancipate myself away from my family, and now I'm out on my own.

At first there was a sense of freedom, of control. I'm in a place of my own, I'm back in school with only a year before I graduate, and I have a job that gives me enough money to pay my bills and have extra to start building a life. But that freedom was quickly replaced by, I dunno, an empty space—a sense that I've lost something that is important to me, an important part of me.

I don't really talk with my old friends all that much. Most of them are still stoners, and that is a major part of what they do all the time. They aren't at school much, so that's not much of a risk. I do have a couple of friends that I still talk to, but we only see each other at school because they have parents who don't like them to be out on school nights, and I work most weekends. Besides, most of the people at school don't understand what I've been through and how I've changed.

Sometimes I find myself becoming bored and depressed. When I'm not at school or work, I sit in this apartment staring at the television. What I really want to do is write. I want to write about what I've been through, what everyone goes through. I want to write stories that, if they don't solve problems, at least shed light on a little bit of life. But when I get home from my job, get my homework done, and get everything ready for the next day, I'm so tired and frustrated that it's hard for me to pick up a pen and write.

The other day I was at my job, cleaning tables and getting my section ready, when a guy from my class came in. I always thought that he might have gone through some of the same problems I did but never had a chance to get to know him. He asked me to go have coffee. My shift was over early, so I agreed to spend some time talking with him.

As we walked through the park drinking coffee, he began talking about how hard it is right now staying sober and on the right side of the law, about how he can't talk to any of his friends anymore, and how he feels so depressed after getting home from his job every night. A door opened up for me. Suddenly I wasn't alone, and I think he knew that as well.

We stood and stared at the geese in the lake for a while. Then he asked me if I liked to hike. I said I haven't really had much experience outside the city, that my parents never went anywhere. He asked me to go hiking with him on my next day off, which happened to be the next Saturday. I struggled, because I knew Saturday would give me a chance to get ahead on my homework or maybe pick up a shift, when he began talking about how sometimes it's nice just to get away from everything for a while. So I agreed. He told me to bring my writing. I was confused, but I figured what the hell.

That Saturday we went into the mountains and took a small hike. It was more like a walk beyond the road since we are both smokers and city boys, but we got away from the traffic and sat down on a rock looking toward the surrounding mountains. He took out his guitar, which he brought with him, and I just sat there taking deep breaths and relaxing. For the first time in weeks, I felt the urge to write. We didn't need to do anything. We didn't even need to talk. And I was content.

So now we make a point of spending at least one day a week together. Sometimes we go see a band, which I thought would be difficult being sober, but it's easier with another straight person. Sometimes we go to a poetry reading, or we go hiking, or sometimes we just sit in the park and meet people. He's convinced me to join a book club, and I've begun to meet more people who like to read and write. They've convinced me to submit some of my writings that I did while in the detention center, and one of my writings even got accepted, with some serious editing of course.

I've started the application process to go to a school for writing, and I don't watch television much anymore. I spend that time writing. It's still really hard though. Every day is still a struggle between what I want to do and what I have to do to get there. The void is still there, and I still miss some of my friends and the times we used to have, but the emptiness is getting smaller. I just keep writing and thinking about how much better I feel now than I did then.

LEXI'S STORY

It's hard getting by. There are days when I think I'll give up . . . get drunk or stoned. Then other days, everything is all right and I know I can make it another day.

I was in a lockdown treatment center for 9 months after some pretty serious problems with the law. But at treatment I had therapy and really worked to change how I thought, felt, and acted. I learned that when it really comes down to it I'm in control of what I think and do.

My counselor and probation officer and I talked a lot about what I'd do when I finished treatment. We decided it was best if I didn't go back to my family—or at least what the court recognized as my family. Basically that's my drunk dad, psycho mom, and my little sister, who should probably be in a foster home. Since I'm almost 17, I was approved to get a place of my own.

In the beginning, I thought it was great to have a place and the freedom it gave me. The place isn't much, but I'm working to pay the bills myself and I'm back in school—set to graduate at the end of next year. I have a little extra cash to start building a life, too. But it wasn't long until I kind of started to feel like something was missing—like an important part of me was lost.

My old friends from school and I don't talk much anymore. Most of them still use, and it's pretty much all they do. I have a couple of friends to talk to, but their parents don't like them to go out on weeknights, and I work all the time on weekends. But it's okay, because most kids at school are hard to talk to 'cause they don't understand what I've gone through and how I'm different now.

It's easy for me to get lonely. When I'm not working or at school, all I do is sit in my apartment or go for a walk and listen to music. In my dreams, I'd like to be an actress. I'd like to play roles of people with lives different than mine. I used to dream up different scenes and act them out in my room at treatment. I guess I could do that now, but when school's out I go right to work and then I have to do my homework when I get home from the restaurant. Most of the time I'm too tired to think anything up, much less act it out.

A couple of days ago I ran into a girl from my treatment group at work. She started talking about how she was having a hard time staying clean and out of trouble and about how she couldn't talk with any of her old friends. She said she even feels depressed at the end of the day when she's alone. Right then I realized that I wasn't alone, and I think she felt the same way.

We sat and watched people walking by for a long time, and then she asked me if I was going to church. It was something we talked about in group to find sober support, but I didn't have much time between work and school. She asked if I wanted to go to a youth group meeting on my next day off, which happened to be Sunday. I had to think about it for a minute because having Sunday off would give me a chance to get ahead on schoolwork or pick up an overtime shift. She started talking about how it's nice to meet people who are sober and to have fun just hanging out and playing games. I didn't want to let her down, so I agreed to go.

That Sunday we went to her youth group, which met at the community center. When we got there, the other kids were in the gym shooting baskets. She introduced me to a couple of the kids she knew, and we shot around with them until a lady who was in charge said it was time to play a group game. I wasn't too excited at first, but she said we were going to tell everyone our name and act out something we liked to do in our free time. I couldn't think of anything at first, especially since I don't have much free time, but then I remembered what I did in my room to pass the time at treatment. So I said my name and acted like I was on stage in a play. The other kids were supposed to guess what we liked doing, and everyone took a long time guessing what I liked. They just sat there and listened as I acted out a scene from my imagination. Finally I stopped because they were just staring at me and I felt weird. But then they all clapped, like I really was an actress. The leader said that I did a great job and so did a bunch of the kids. I felt good pretending to be someone else for a minute or two. It made me forget that I didn't know the kids and I had other things I needed to do. I felt so happy.

Since that first day, my friend and I have made it a point to go to youth group together. My boss even agreed to give me Sundays off just so I could go. I'm getting used to the other kids, and we've even been doing some skits. Most of them are just a way to have fun, but one night a guy who works at the community center came in when I was doing my part. He watched until the skit was over and then talked to some of us about getting into community theater. He convinced me to go to an upcoming show right there at the center. I did and it was good. There were all kinds of people in the show, and I got the feeling that I could do it, too.

So I'm signed up to be in the next show. And the director says that I have real talent. She says that if I get through the production and decide to do more, she'll spend some time helping me prepare individually. Maybe she'd even write me a recommendation for the theater program at the local college—once I graduate high school, of course.

It's still hard to stay focused on my dream, and I have to keep reminding myself that I won't achieve it if I'm using. I still miss some of my old friends and the old times, but I'm not as lonely as I used to be. I just keep practicing my lines and thinking about how much better I feel now than I did then.

In Commemoration of International Youth Day

In a world in which different peoples and traditions are coming into closer, more frequent contact than ever before, it is crucial that young people learn how to listen intently, empathize with others, acknowledge divergent opinions, and be able to resolve conflicts. Few endeavors are more important than nurturing these skills, and educating young people about human rights, for in them we not only see the next generation of leaders, but also crucial stakeholders of today. Let us also recognize that older generations themselves stand to learn a great deal from the experiences and examples of young people as they come of age in a world of accelerating interconnectedness.

. . . Let us acknowledge and celebrate what youth can do to build a safer, more just world. Let us strengthen our efforts to include young people in policies, programmes and decision-making processes that benefit their futures and ours.

—Mr. Ban Ki-moon, Secretary General of the United Nations (UN)

PROGRAM GUIDE 1

Telling My Story: Narrative of Strengths and Problems to Work On

LIST OF STRENGTHS AND PROBLEMS TO WORK ON

List Problems that you need to work on for each of the focus areas.

A. Alcohol and Other Drug Assessment

1. ______________________________

2. ______________________________

3. ______________________________

4. ______________________________

B. Family, Parents, and Living Environment

1. ______________________________

2. ______________________________

3. ______________________________

4. ______________________________

C. Emotional and Psychological Issues

1. ______________________________

2. ______________________________

3. ______________________________

4. ______________________________

D. School Achievement and Adjustment

1. ______________________________

2. ______________________________

3. ______________________________

4. ______________________________

E. Relationship With Peers

1. ______________________________

2. ______________________________

3. ______________________________

4. ______________________________

F. Harm-Directing Thoughts and Criminal Conduct

1. ______________________________

2. ______________________________

3. ______________________________

4. ______________________________

G. Thinking and Feeling Patterns

1. ______________________________

2. ______________________________

3. ______________________________

4. ______________________________

H. Community and Living Problems

1. ______________________________

2. ______________________________

3. ______________________________

4. ______________________________

I. Physical and Health Issues

1. ______________________________

2. ______________________________

3. ______________________________

4. ______________________________

J. My Strengths and Strong Points

1. ______________________________

2. ______________________________

3. ______________________________

4. ______________________________

5. ______________________________

6. ______________________________

7. ______________________________

8. ______________________________

9. ______________________________

10. ______________________________

PROGRAM GUIDE 2

Master Skills List

Put the date you started working on the skill, and rate your mastery level. Update your level of mastery after each chapter. Put a new date under *Level of Skill Mastery* when your skill level improves. Make *Good* to *Very Good* your goal for each skill.

	Description of Skills	Start Date	Example of Skill Use	Level of Skill Mastery			
				Poor	Fair	Good	Very Good
MENTAL	1. Using a cognitive behavioral map						
	2. Using mental restructuring						
	3. Using relaxation skills						
	4. Changing alcohol and other drug (AOD) use patterns						
	5. Preventing AOD problems						
	6. Managing urges/cravings						
	7. Changing negative thinking						
	8. Changing thinking errors						
	9. Managing stress/anxiety						
	10. Managing depression						
RELATIONSHIP	11. Using anger management skills						
	12. Reading nonverbal cues						
	13. Using active sharing skills						
	14. Using active listening skills						
	15. Starting a conversation						
	16. Giving compliments/praise						
	17. Receiving compliments						
	18. Using problem-solving skills						
	19. Using assertiveness skills						
	20. Using close relations skills						
	21. Managing high-risk (HR) exposures						
SOCIETY	22. Using refusal skills						
	23. Preventing relapse						
	24. Using lifestyle balance skills						
	25. Preventing recidivism						
	26. Using prosocial skills						
	27. Strengthening moral character						
	28. Using empathy skills						
	29. Using conflict resolution skills						
	30. Using negotiation skills						

PROGRAM GUIDE 3

Self-Portrait

SELF-PORTRAIT

1. Alcohol and Other Drug Assessment

Drug Choice

Area of Assessment		**Low**				**Moderate**				**High**	
Alcohol Involement	0	1	2	3	4	5	6	7	8	9	10
Marijuana Involvement	0	1	2	3	4	5	6	7	8	9	10
Cocaine Involvement	0	1	2	3	4	5	6	7	8	9	10
Amphetamine Involvement	0	1	2	3	4	5	6	7	8	9	10
Other Drug Involvement	0	1	2	3	4	5	6	7	8	9	10
Poly Drug User	0	1	2	3	4	5	6	7	8	9	10

Style

Area of Assessment		**Low**				**Moderate**				**High**	
With Friends or at Parties	0	1	2	3	4	5	6	7	8	9	10
Sustained and Continuous	0	1	2	3	4	5	6	7	8	9	10
Compulsive and Obsessive	0	1	2	3	4	5	6	7	8	9	10

Benefits

Area of Assessment		**Low**				**Moderate**				**High**	
Cope with Social Discomfort	0	1	2	3	4	5	6	7	8	9	10
Cope with Emotional Discomfort	0	1	2	3	4	5	6	7	8	9	10
Cope with Relationships	0	1	2	3	4	5	6	7	8	9	10
Cope with Physical Distress	0	1	2	3	4	5	6	7	8	9	10

Results

Area of Assessment		**Low**				**Moderate**				**High**	
Behavioral Loss Of Control	0	1	2	3	4	5	6	7	8	9	10
Emotional Disruption	0	1	2	3	4	5	6	7	8	9	10
Physical Disruption	0	1	2	3	4	5	6	7	8	9	10
Social Irresponsibility	0	1	2	3	4	5	6	7	8	9	10
Overall Disruption	0	1	2	3	4	5	6	7	8	9	10

Ready

Area of Assessment		**Low**				**Moderate**				**High**	
Alcohol and Other Drug (AOD) Problem Awareness	0	1	2	3	4	5	6	7	8	9	10
Treatment Receptiveness	0	1	2	3	4	5	6	7	8	9	10
Motivation to Change	0	1	2	3	4	5	6	7	8	9	10

2. Family, Parents, and Living Environment

Family

Area of Assessment		**Low**				**Moderate**				**High**	
Degree of Family Disruption	0	1	2	3	4	5	6	7	8	9	10
Lack of Family Closeness	0	1	2	3	4	5	6	7	8	9	10
Lack of Family Support	0	1	2	3	4	5	6	7	8	9	10
Parents Have Problems	0	1	2	3	4	5	6	7	8	9	10

3. Emotional and Psychological Issues

Emotional

Area of Assessment		**Low**				**Moderate**				**High**	
Anxiety and Fears	0	1	2	3	4	5	6	7	8	9	10
Depression	0	1	2	3	4	5	6	7	8	9	10
Impulsive Acting	0	1	2	3	4	5	6	7	8	9	10
Angry Feelings and Acting	0	1	2	3	4	5	6	7	8	9	10
Concern About Self-Harm	0	1	2	3	4	5	6	7	8	9	10

4. School Achievement and Adjustment

School

Area of Assessment		**Low**				**Moderate**				**High**	
Conduct Problems	0	1	2	3	4	5	6	7	8	9	10
Poor and Failing Grades	0	1	2	3	4	5	6	7	8	9	10
Negative School Attitude	0	1	2	3	4	5	6	7	8	9	10
Skip Classes/Dropped Out	0	1	2	3	4	5	6	7	8	9	10

Peers

5. Relationship With Peers

Area of Assessment	Low				Moderate				High		
Negative Peers	0	1	2	3	4	5	6	7	8	9	10
No Close Friends	0	1	2	3	4	5	6	7	8	9	10
Criminal Associates	0	1	2	3	4	5	6	7	8	9	10
Drug Associates	0	1	2	3	4	5	6	7	8	9	10

Harm-Directing Thoughts & Criminal Conduct

6. Harm-Directing Thoughts and Criminal Conduct

Area of Assessment	Low				Moderate				High		
Property Offenses	0	1	2	3	4	5	6	7	8	9	10
Person Offenses	0	1	2	3	4	5	6	7	8	9	10
Violent Crimes and Conduct	0	1	2	3	4	5	6	7	8	9	10
Sex Offender Conduct	0	1	2	3	4	5	6	7	8	9	10
Alcohol and Other Drug (AOD) Impaired Driving	0	1	2	3	4	5	6	7	8	9	10
Antisocial Peers and Models	0	1	2	3	4	5	6	7	8	9	10
Impulsive Thinking/Acting	0	1	2	3	4	5	6	7	8	9	10
Cops Are Out to Get Me	0	1	2	3	4	5	6	7	8	9	10
Planning Crimes	0	1	2	3	4	5	6	7	8	9	10
Blame Others for Problems	0	1	2	3	4	5	6	7	8	9	10
Take Victim Stance	0	1	2	3	4	5	6	7	8	9	10
Lying and Not Telling Truth	0	1	2	3	4	5	6	7	8	9	10
Angry/Aggressive Attitude	0	1	2	3	4	5	6	7	8	9	10
Rebellious/Anti-Authority	0	1	2	3	4	5	6	7	8	9	10
Seeking Out a Victim	0	1	2	3	4	5	6	7	8	9	10
Want Revenge or to Get Back	0	1	2	3	4	5	6	7	8	9	10
They Deserve It	0	1	2	3	4	5	6	7	8	9	10
Lack of Empathy for Others	0	1	2	3	4	5	6	7	8	9	10
Reckless Thinking	0	1	2	3	4	5	6	7	8	9	10

Thinking & Feeling Patterns

7. Thinking and Feeling Patterns

Area of Assessment	Low				Moderate				High		
Put People Down	0	1	2	3	4	5	6	7	8	9	10
Narrow-Restricted Thinking	0	1	2	3	4	5	6	7	8	9	10
Personalizing Responses	0	1	2	3	4	5	6	7	8	9	10
Seeing Things My Way	0	1	2	3	4	5	6	7	8	9	10
Self-Defeating Thinking	0	1	2	3	4	5	6	7	8	9	10
Can't Trust Others	0	1	2	3	4	5	6	7	8	9	10
Self-Centered Thinking	0	1	2	3	4	5	6	7	8	9	10
Don't Need Anyone's Help	0	1	2	3	4	5	6	7	8	9	10
Feel Better Than Others	0	1	2	3	4	5	6	7	8	9	10
Feel Screwed Over	0	1	2	3	4	5	6	7	8	9	10
Mountains Out of Molehills	0	1	2	3	4	5	6	7	8	9	10
Think in Black and White Terms	0	1	2	3	4	5	6	7	8	9	10

Other

8. Other Areas

Area of Assessment	Low			Moderate				High			
Health/Physical Problems	0	1	2	3	4	5	6	7	8	9	10
Job and Employment Problems	0	1	2	3	4	5	6	7	8	9	10
Gangs in My Neighborhood	0	1	2	3	4	5	6	7	8	9	10

Readiness

9. Motivation and Readiness for Treatment

Area of Assessment		Low			Moderate				High		
Awareness of Alcohol and Other Drug (AOD)/ Criminal Conduct (CC)	0	1	2	3	4	5	6	7	8	9	10
Acknowledgement of Need for Help	0	1	2	3	4	5	6	7	8	9	10
Willingness to Accept Help	0	1	2	3	4	5	6	7	8	9	10
Other's Perception of Need	0	1	2	3	4	5	6	7	8	9	10
Has Taken Action to Change	0	1	2	3	4	5	6	7	8	9	10

Stage

10. Stage of Change

Area of Assessment		Low			Moderate				High		
Challenge to Change	0	1	2	3	4	5	6	7	8	9	10
Using Tools for Change	0	1	2	3	4	5	6	7	8	9	10
Calling Your Own Shots	0	1	2	3	4	5	6	7	8	9	10

Strengths & Resiliency

11. Strengths and Resiliency

Area of Assessment		Low			Moderate				High		
Relationship With Parents	0	1	2	3	4	5	6	7	8	9	10
Relationship With Family	0	1	2	3	4	5	6	7	8	9	10
Emotional and Mental Health	0	1	2	3	4	5	6	7	8	9	10
Positive Self-Thoughts	0	1	2	3	4	5	6	7	8	9	10
Control Of Anger	0	1	2	3	4	5	6	7	8	9	10
Have Successful Friends	0	1	2	3	4	5	6	7	8	9	10
School Adjustment	0	1	2	3	4	5	6	7	8	9	10
Follow Rules/Regulations	0	1	2	3	4	5	6	7	8	9	10
Obey Laws of the Community	0	1	2	3	4	5	6	7	8	9	10
Respect Rights of Others	0	1	2	3	4	5	6	7	8	9	10
Physical/Medical Health	0	1	2	3	4	5	6	7	8	9	10
Able to Not Use Alcohol	0	1	2	3	4	5	6	7	8	9	10
Able to Not Use Other Drugs	0	1	2	3	4	5	6	7	8	9	10

PROGRAM GUIDE 4

Plan for Change

...N FOR CHANGE

PROBLEM AREA AND DESCRIPTION	CHANGES NEEDED IN THOUGHT AND ACTION	TOOLS FOR CHANGE	DATE WORKED ON
1. Alcohol and Other Drug Assessment			
2. Family, Parents, and Living Environment			
3. Emotional and Psychological Issues			
4. School Achievement and Adjustment			
5. Relationship With Peers			
6. Harm-Directing Thoughts and Criminal Conduct			

PLAN FOR CHANGE

PROBLEM AREA AND DESCRIPTION	CHANGES NEEDED IN THOUGHT AND ACTION	TOOLS FOR CHANGE	DATE WORKED ON
7. Thinking and Feeling Patterns			
8. Other Areas			
9. Motivation and Readiness for Treatment			
10. Stage of Change			
11. Strengths and Resiliency			

PROGRAM GUIDE 5

Stages of Change

ALCOHOL AND OTHER DRUGS (AOD)

Rate yourself on each stage of change.

CHALLENGE TO CHANGE

KEY ELEMENTS IN STAGE	LOW			MODERATE					HIGH
Given thought to changing	0	1	2	3	4	5	6	7	8
Want information about myself	0	1	2	3	4	5	6	7	8
Level of self-awareness	0	1	2	3	4	5	6	7	8
Commitment to more treatment	0	1	2	3	4	5	6	7	8

USING TOOLS FOR CHANGE

KEY ELEMENTS IN STAGE	LOW			MODERATE					HIGH
Pledge to change	0	1	2	3	4	5	6	7	8
Open to self-disclosure	0	1	2	3	4	5	6	7	8
Efforts to recognize attitudes	0	1	2	3	4	5	6	7	8
Efforts to recognize harm-directing thoughts	0	1	2	3	4	5	6	7	8
Use relapse prevention skills	0	1	2	3	4	5	6	7	8
Mindful of alcohol and other drug [AOD] thought for long period	0	1	2	3	4	5	6	7	8
Corrected relapse thinking	0	1	2	3	4	5	6	7	8
Learned skills to avoid alcohol and other drug [AOD] thought	0	1	2	3	4	5	6	7	8

CALLING YOUR OWN SHOTS

KEY ELEMENTS IN STAGE	LOW			MODERATE					HIGH
In program because **I want to be**	0	1	2	3	4	5	6	7	8
No desire for alcohol and other drug [AOD] Involvement	0	1	2	3	4	5	6	7	8
Consistently mindful of harm-directing thoughts and values-based choices	0	1	2	3	4	5	6	7	8
Replace need for alcohol and other drug [AOD] use	0	1	2	3	4	5	6	7	8

CRIMINAL CONDUCT (CC)

Rate yourself on each stage of change.

CHALLENGE TO CHANGE

KEY ELEMENTS IN STAGE	LOW			MODERATE				HIGH
Given thought to changing	0	1	2	3	4	5	6	7	8
Want information about myself	0	1	2	3	4	5	6	7	8
Level of self-awareness	0	1	2	3	4	5	6	7	8
Commitment to more treatment	0	1	2	3	4	5	6	7	8

USING TOOLS FOR CHANGE

KEY ELEMENTS IN STAGE	LOW			MODERATE				HIGH
Pledge to change	0	1	2	3	4	5	6	7	8
Open to self-disclosure	0	1	2	3	4	5	6	7	8
Efforts to recognize attitudes	0	1	2	3	4	5	6	7	8
Efforts to recognize thoughts	0	1	2	3	4	5	6	7	8
Use recidivism prevention skills	0	1	2	3	4	5	6	7	8
Mindful of harm-directing thoughts for long period	0	1	2	3	4	5	6	7	8
Corrected criminal thinking	0	1	2	3	4	5	6	7	8
Learned skills to avoid criminal thinking	0	1	2	3	4	5	6	7	8

IN PROGRAM BECAUSE I WANT TO BE

KEY ELEMENTS IN STAGE	LOW			MODERATE				HIGH
In program because **I want to be**	0	1	2	3	4	5	6	7	8
No desire for criminal conduct	0	1	2	3	4	5	6	7	8
Consistently mindful of harm-directing thoughts and values-based choices	0	1	2	3	4	5	6	7	8
Replace need for criminal conduct	0	1	2	3	4	5	6	7	8

PROGRAM GUIDE 6

Thinking and Action Pattern Charting

You are asked to think back on your thinking and action patterns (TAPs) for the past week. In the first column, put the date of the session. Then, thinking back on the week, check yes or no for the questions in each column. In the last column, write down the skills you used to prevent alcohol and other drug (AOD) abuse or criminal conduct (CC).

DATE	Did you think about using alcohol or other drugs?		Did you think about committing a crime or doing other harmful actions?		Did you participate in any illegal or dangerous activity?		Name the skills you used to prevent harmful involvement in substance abuse or criminal conduct.
	NO	YES	NO	YES	NO	YES	